in **BLACK** and WHITE

"Son of man,
behold, the house of
Israel is saying, 'The
vision that he sees is
for many years from
now, and he
prophesies of times
far off.' Therefore
say to them, 'Thus
says the Lord God,
"None of My words
will be delayed any
longer. Whatever
word I speak will be
performed,"'
declares the Lord
God."

Ezekiel 12:27-28

Nicole DiCenzo

To The Coming King . . .

Unless otherwise noted, all scripture quotations are taken from the NASB. *New American Standard Bible* (Grand Rapids, Michigan: Zondervan, 1999).

Unless otherwise noted, all Greek/Hebrew word meanings and definitions are taken from Biblestudytools.com.

Scripture marked NIV comes from the *New International Version* (Grand Rapids, Michigan: Zondervan publishing House, 1995).

Scripture marked NCV comes from the *New Century Version* of Scripture. *Mom's Bible: God's Wisdom for Mothers* (Nashville, TN: Thomas Nelson, Inc., 2005).

Scripture marked JNTP comes from *The Complete Jewish Bible* (Clarksville, Maryland: Jewish New Testament Publications, Inc., 1998). This is an English version of scripture translated by David H. Stern.

Scripture marked NLT comes from *New Living Translation* (Carol Stream, Illinois: Tyndale House Publishers Inc., 2007).

Dragon Art done by Amanda Newman of Columbus, Georgia. Statue Art and Map done by Sherry Kitts of Hixson, Tennessee. Thank you both for everything you have done for this publication.

TABLE OF CONTENTS

From the Author:

In Acts 3:12, we meet a group of people that scripture calls "nobleminded."

> *Now these were more nobleminded than notes in Thessalonica, for they received the word with great **eagerness**, **examining** the Scriptures **daily** to see whether things were so.*
>
> *Acts 3:12, emphasis added*

People who are nobleminded will examine the scriptures daily and with eagerness. In the last days, there will be a spirit of deception (2 Thessalonians 2:11, Revelation 12:9). If we don't look into the Word and learn the real truth (John 14:6), we could fall prey to this deception (Matthew 24:11).

Jesus wants a relationship with you. He wants to meet with you. He wants you to seek Him (Matthew 7:7), not once a month, or once a week, but daily.

He is coming. That is the truth you will learn in the pages to come. And His return is our hope. This devotional is intended to put a fire in your heart and expand your mind to the awesomeness of our God. He is BIG. He is BOLD. And He SHINES.

One day we are going to lift our eyes to the heavens and see His light. Our world will never be the same. We will never be the same. And here is the kicker – our new life is going to rock.

So as you embark on this adventure keep in mind Jesus' own words . . .

*"Blessed are those who heed **THE REVELATION.**"*

Nic

DAY ONE
REVELATION 1:1-3
THE TIME IS NEAR

¹The Revelation of Jesus Christ, which God gave Him to show to His bond-servants, the things which must soon take place; and He sent and communicated it by His angel to His bond-servant John, ²who testified to the word of God and to the testimony of Jesus Christ, even to all that he saw. ³Blessed is he who reads and those who hear the words of the prophecy, and heed the things which are written in it; for the time is near.

Revelation 1:1-3

You know a book is exceptional when it begins with "the revelation of Jesus Christ." Consider for a moment this awe-inspiring introduction. Jesus, our Lord and Savior, the Lamb of God and the Lion of the tribe of Judah is about to tell us something previously unknown. Jesus is revealing, uncovering, and disclosing to us a truth that we could not possibly understand unless He Himself reveals it. You have undoubtedly heard Revelation is full of symbols, signs, and images we can't possibly comprehend. This is a false statement and the first verse of Revelation proves it. Jesus isn't trying to hide anything from us or it wouldn't be deemed revelation. The signs and symbols Jesus uses in Revelation are not intended to conceal, on the contrary, they are intended to uncover things He wants us to understand.

The Revelation of Jesus Christ is our Savior disclosing to us how, and in what manner, this age will end. The Revelation of Jesus Christ is about the return of the King. The Revelation of Jesus Christ is about our return to the King. The Revelation is Jesus Himself. This is profound. This is extraordinary. This is Revelation.

So let's open our eyes and dive right in, because the book of Revelation is a little more black and white than what many people think.

I wish I could sit down with you and discuss every verse in detail. Revelation is so rich in revelation (no pun intended) that volumes could be written about it. To know and understand Revelation, you have to know and understand the entire Word. There is so much treasure to uncover; you even find an occasional diamond. I just love God's Word!

However, I know our time is limited, so please forgive me if I do not touch on a verse you are curious about. Please feel free to e-mail me at nic@nicsrevelations.com with any questions you have. I may not be able to answer every e-mail, but I will sure try. I would love to hear from you, Christian soldier!

But for now, let's focus on a few phrases in the first three verses that might very well perk your interest:

Verse one says the vision must "soon take place."
Verse three says, "the time is near."

Does this mean the Revelation happened closer to John's day? Many scholars think so. They are called "preterists" because they point to the fall of Jerusalem in 70 AD and the later fall of Rome as fulfilling most of the prophecies. Another view called the "spiritual" view believes Revelation isn't literal, but a big spiritual allegory for events throughout history – a sort of rulebook for the bad and the good in the world. If you would like to study further about these views of Revelation, please pick up *Revelation: Four Views, A Parallel Commentary* by Steve Gregg.[1]

I would wager a guess that since you have this book in your hands you are probably of the "futurist" camp or those who believe the revelation John saw will unfold at some point in the future. Although a lot of biblical prophecy is both applicable to the past as well as the future, Revelation is mainly about end-time events. This is the view I hold and it will be the focus of the remainder of this book. So why does scripture say the vision must "soon take place" and the "time is near?"

In order to understand this, the reader must be aware of a scripture in Daniel:

He said, "Go your way, Daniel, for these words are
concealed and sealed up until the end time."
Daniel 12:9

So, the words discussed in Daniel could not be completely understood until the "time of the end." If you study the book of Daniel (I highly recommend Beth Moore's Daniel study[2]), it becomes plain some elements of Daniel are also in Revelation. In other words, some prophecies in Daniel are further clarified in Revelation. So Revelation, like Daniel, is very important for the "time of the end."

6

Both Daniel and Revelation deal with ushering in the Millennial Kingdom of Christ. The beast we will meet in Revelation 13 can only be explained by referring back to Daniel. Although we will not study Daniel in-depth, we will study parts of Daniel when we meet the beast of Revelation. Revelation, like Daniel, is for "the time of the end." So why do the first verses of Revelation say "must soon take place" and "the time is near?" I believe the meaning is two-fold.

First, Revelation is written to individual believers. It will become apparent as we study chapters two and three that Jesus is talking to each person throughout history urging them to prepare for His return. For each believer, the time is near. Life is fragile and short. Christ is urging each and every person to examine themselves because He is coming quickly. Once you are dead, there is no more time. "Repent!" Jesus urges, "The time is near!"

Secondly, the main body of Revelation, those chapters after chapter three, deal with the final generation of believers, the end time generation, the one for which the time would be near. Look at Jesus' own words regarding the timing of His return in Matthew 24:32-33.

> "Now learn the parable from the fig tree: when its branch has already become tender and puts forth its leaves, you know that summer is near; so, you too, when you see all these things, recognize that He is near, right at the door. Truly I say to you, this generation will not pass away until all these things take place."
>
> Matthew 24:32-34

What did Jesus mean by the "fig tree?" And what did He mean about "all these things?" In Jeremiah 24:5 and in Hosea 9:10 the fig tree is a metaphor for the people of Israel. So the fig tree (Israel) needs to put forth its leaves for the "end times" to begin. Has this happened? Yes! In 1948 Israel became a nation after being dispersed for almost two thousand years. Israel's rebirth is prophesied in Ezekiel 37 and clarified throughout scripture. This has come to pass in our lifetime. Israel is now "putting forth leaves." They are back in their nation and they are taking root.

It is interesting to note when Jesus entered Jerusalem a few days before His crucifixion He became hungry and saw a fig tree.

7

*He came to it and found nothing on it except leaves only;
and He said to it, "No longer shall there ever be any fruit
from you." And at once the fig tree withered.*

Matthew 21:19

I believe this was a representation of what would happen to
Israel because she did not recognize Jesus at His first coming. She
withered. Yet Jesus foretold of a future generation that would see
the fig tree bear, not figs, but leaves. Does this mean the Jews have
to come to faith for the end-times to begin? No, Jesus said they
would bear leaves, not fruit (Matthew 7:15-23).

Now, what about "all these things" referenced in the Matthew
24 scripture quoted previously? Right before this scripture, Jesus
described what would lead up to the end times in Matthew 24:1-14.
There would be false christs, there would be wars and rumors of
wars, there would be famines and earthquakes, and there would be
tribulation and the persecution of the saints.

Date setting is a "no-no" when it comes to end time events.
We aren't God and we shouldn't play gods by guessing about His
timing. But we do know this: Jesus says the generation who sees
"the fig tree produce leaves" and sees "all these things" (false
christs, wars, famines, persecution) would not pass away until the
end comes.

Jesus spoke to a future generation – our generation. That is
why Revelation is no longer in gray, but in black and white. We are
that generation.

What we need to remember is this: until 1948 the "end times"
could not begin. Why? Based on the prophecies of Daniel 9,
Ezekiel 37, and Revelation 12, the Jews have to be in their
homeland for the final events to begin that lead to Jesus' return.
The end time prophecies of Daniel and Revelation hinge on Israel
being a nation. Some of you doing this study have never lived
without the nation of Israel, but your parents may still remember the
day Israel was born. Israel's rebirth was a huge occurrence for
those who studied Biblical prophecy. This was, I daresay, the
event! I personally don't believe the generation born in 1948 will
completely pass away before Jesus' return. In Psalm 90:10 a
generation is defined as being either 70 or 80 years. We can't be
certain 1948 is the exact "start date" but it is perhaps a good
estimate as to how much longer we have without our Savior
returning as King.

Now, is Matthew 24 the only indication that we are living in the end times? I am glad you asked that question. Look at the following scripture:

> *But realize this, that in the last days difficult times will come. For men will be lovers of self, lovers of money, boastful, arrogant, revilers, disobedient to parents, ungrateful, unholy, unloving, irreconcilable, malicious gossips, without self-control, brutal, haters of good, treacherous, reckless, conceited, lovers of pleasure rather than lovers of God, holding to a form of godliness, although they have denied its power; avoid such men as these.*
>
> *2 Timothy 3:1-5*

That scripture always leaves me feeling a little uneasy. You need to make up your own mind whether or not we are in the last days, but to be clear, they can now start at any time because the nation of Israel is back in their homeland.

Let's end this day with the words of Revelation:

> *Blessed is he who reads and those who hear the words of the prophecy, and heed the things which are written in it."*
>
> *Revelation 1:3*

You have to heed to be blessed - not just read. Many have read Revelation and put it down, never to give it a second thought. But if you heed it, if you believe it enough to watch for the return of the King, you will be blessed. Why? Although we can't know the date, we can know something very important:

> *The Pharisees and Sadducees came up, and testing Jesus, they asked Him to show them a sign from heaven. But He replied to them, "When it is evening, you say, 'It will be fair weather, for the sky is red.' And in the morning, 'There will be a storm today, for the sky is red and threatening.' Do you know how to discern the appearance of the sky, but cannot discern the signs of the times?"*
>
> *Matthew 16:1-3*

9

We can know the signs of the times. In other words, we can know the season of His coming. And if we heed the book of Revelation, we will be prepared. The horseman will not surprise us, the famine will not surprise us, the beast will not surprise us, and the persecution will not surprise us. And God assures us, because we have heeded His Revelation we will be. . .

BLESSED.

Thought for the day:
If the time is near – how are you going to spend your time today? How are you going to act or react? How will you treat those around you? Will you look forward to your time with Jesus tomorrow? Or will you brush any time with Him aside? Hope to see you tomorrow.

1 Gregg, Steve. *Revelation: Four Views, A Parallel Commentary* (Nashville, Tennessee: Thomas Nelson, Inc., 1997). The Four Views in this book are the Historicist, Preterist, Spiritual, and Futurist.

2 Moore, Beth. DVD study *Daniel: Lives of Integrity, Words of Prophecy* (Nashville, Tennessee: LifeWay Press, 2006). This is by far one of the best Bible studies I have ever completed.

Day TWO
Revelation 1:4-8
He is Coming with the Clouds

⁴John to the seven churches that are in Asia: Grace to you and peace, from Him who is and who was and who is to come, and from the seven Spirits who are before His throne, ⁵and from Jesus Christ, the faithful witness, the firstborn of the dead, and the ruler of the kings of the earth. To Him who loves us and released us from our sins by His blood – ⁶and He made us to be a kingdom, priests to His God and Father – to Him be the glory and the dominion forever and ever. Amen. ⁷Behold, He is coming with the clouds, and every eye will see Him, even those who pierced Him; and all the tribes of the earth will mourn over Him. So it is to be. Amen. ⁸"I am the Alpha and the Omega," says the Lord God, "who is and who was and who is to come, the Almighty."

Revelation 1:4-8

John begins this section by addressing seven churches. Scholars say that seven in scripture symbolizes perfection, completion, wholeness, and entirety (take the seven days of creation as an example).[1] So although the letters in Revelation are addressed to seven actual churches that existed in John's day, they are also being addressed to the church universal – the church in its complete state – from John's day right up until the present time. Let me say that another way:

The letters to the churches are addressed to us.

My faithful friends, the letters are talking to us. Their condemnations and praises are ours. We can either learn from them or ignore them. More on this when we read the letters.

In verses four and five John introduces us to the Trinity. First He mentions God the Father, "From Him who was and who is and who is to come." This should remind us of Exodus 3:14 where God tells Moses His name is "I Am who I Am."[2]

Our God is eternal and ever present, as Psalm 90:2 says so beautifully:

Before the mountains were born or You gave birth to the earth and the world, even from everlasting to everlasting, You are God.

Psalm 90:2

In Exodus chapter three God *IS*, meaning He always has been and He always will be. The verse in Revelation mirrors this by literally stating He was and He is and He is to come. Glory!

Then John mentions the seven Spirits before the throne (Revelation 1:4), which represent the Holy Spirit. Again, because seven denotes completion, we see the all-seeing, all-knowing Spirit of God. Seven has been used to represent God's Spirit before.

*The **Spirit of the Lord** will rest on Him, the spirit of **wisdom** and **understanding**, the spirit of **counsel** and **strength**, the spirit of **knowledge** and the **fear** of the Lord.*
Isaiah 11:2, emphasis added

Although these seven attributes of God's Spirit are not an exhaustive list, they represent the Spirit's complete nature. Then Jesus is mentioned in Revelation 1:5: the faithful witness, the firstborn of the dead, and the ruler of the kings of the earth.

Our Lord is our faithful witness, the One who knows the wrongs committed against us. He reminds us that He has conquered death and will ultimately right those wrongs and rule over the kings of the earth. Let's look at these one at a time because all of these foreshadow what will take place at the return of the King.

He is our faithful witness . . .
And I saw heaven opened, and behold, a white horse, and He who sat on it is called Faithful and True, and in righteousness He judges and wages war.
Revelation 19:11

He is the firstborn of the dead . . .
But now Christ has been raised from the dead, the first fruits of those who are asleep. For since by a man came death, by a man also came the resurrection of the dead.
1 Corinthians 15:20-21

He is the ruler of the kings of the earth . . .
*And on His robe and on His thigh He has a name written,
"King of kings, and Lord of Lords."*

Revelation 19:16

In the first scripture Jesus is riding to the earth. This reminds us that never again will we be under tyranny, persecution, or oppression. For He is faithful and true. The second scripture tells us Christ is the first fruits of the dead and this should remind us that the resurrection of the dead will soon take place. Those asleep will be made alive! The third scripture clarifies that He is also ruler of the kings of the earth and He is coming to take possession of the earth as reigning King.

Take another look at Revelation 1:7: "Behold, He is coming with the clouds." I want you to write this verse in your mind because by the end of Revelation, this concept will become very special. But for now, let's take a look at a few other verses.

And after He had said these things, He was lifted up while they were looking on, and a cloud received Him out of their sight . . ."This Jesus, who has been taken up from you into heaven, will come in just the same way as you have watched Him go into heaven."

Acts 1:9, 11b

I kept looking in the night visions, and behold, with the clouds of heaven One like a Son of Man was coming, and He came up to the Ancient of Days and was presented before Him.

Daniel 7:13

Jesus said to him, "You have said it yourself; nevertheless I tell you, hereafter you will see the Son of Man sitting at the right hand of power, and coming on the clouds of heaven."

Matthew 26:64

Behold, He is coming with the clouds, faithful friends! Now look at this next verse:

The Lord is slow to anger and great in power, and the Lord will by no means leave the guilty unpunished. In

13

whirlwind and storm is His way, and clouds are the dust
beneath His feet.

Nahum 1:3

This is a second coming scripture. He is coming to judge the world – the guilty will not go unpunished. But when He comes, clouds are going to be the dust beneath His feet. Someone needs to shout, "Glory!" The clouds are the dust beneath His feet!

Let's go to the next treasure in Revelation. When He comes with the clouds, "every eye will see Him, even those who pierced Him (Revelation 1:7). Think about that for a minute. The people who pierced Him are dead, but they will see Him! This verse is saying that everyone will see the return of the King. That does not mean everyone will be resurrected at His return (some will not be resurrected until after the Millennial Kingdom – more on this in chapter 20), but it does mean everyone will see Him.

How, you might be wondering, if they are not resurrected? Remember the rich man and Lazarus in Luke 16:19-31? They were both dead, yet they were aware. No matter where the dead are, they will all see the Return of the King!

EVERYONE WILL SEE
THE RETURN OF THE KING!

Thought for the day:
Everyone will see the return of the King – even you. When He looks into your eyes will He see Himself (Romans 13:14)? Or will He see the enemy? What will you see in His eyes? A job well done? Or judgment? Find out what Christ will look like tomorrow.

1 Butler, Trent C. et al.,eds. *Holman Illustrated Bible Dictionary* (Nashville, Tennessee: Holman Bible Publishers, 2003), 1199-1200.

2 Moore, Beth. DVD Study *Here and Now ... There and Then: A lecture series on Revelation* (Houston, Texas: Living Proof Ministries, 2009), 7.

[9]I, John, your brother and fellow partaker in the tribulation and kingdom and perseverance which are in Jesus, was on the island called Patmos because of the word of God and the testimony of Jesus. [10]I was in the Spirit on the Lord's day, and I heard behind me a loud voice like the sound of a trumpet, [11]saying, "Write in a book what you see, and send it to the seven churches: to Ephesus and to Smyrna and to Pergamum and to Thyatira and to Sardis and to Philadelphia and to Laodicea." [12]Then I turned to see the voice that was speaking with me. And having turned I saw seven golden lampstands; [13]and in the middle of the lampstands I saw one like a son of man, clothed in a robe reaching to the feet, and girded across His chest with a golden sash. [14]His head and His hair were white like white wool, like snow; and His eyes were like a flame of fire. [15]His feet were like burnished bronze, when it has been made to glow in a furnace, and His voice was like the sound of many waters. [16]In His right hand He held seven stars, and out of His mouth came a sharp two-edged sword; and His face was like the sun shining in its strength. [17]When I saw Him, I fell at His feet like a dead man. And He placed His right hand on me, saying, "Do not be afraid; I am the first and the last, [18]and the living One; and I was dead, and behold, I am alive forevermore, and I have the keys of death and Hades. [19]Therefore write the things which you have seen, and the things which are, and the things which will take place after these things. [20]As for the mystery of the seven stars which you saw in My right hand, and the seven golden lampstands: the seven stars are the angels of the seven churches, and the seven lampstands are the seven churches."

Revelation 1:9-20

Now, we are pushing into the heart of Revelation – Jesus. Let's say that again – Jesus. Remember verse one of chapter one? Revelation is a revelation of Jesus Christ. Well, today, my faithful friends, you are going to see a vision of His glory. It just might take your breath away. But first we need to focus on John and his situation. In verse nine, John says he is "a fellow partaker in the tribulation." John is writing to some of the churches in Asia Minor (our present day Turkey), acknowledging the "tribulation" they were undergoing.

There are differing opinions regarding whether or not the church in its present form will live through the final years on earth described in the book of Revelation. One argument is that God won't allow His church to go through such a horrific time. John might disagree with this reasoning because in verse nine he basically says the early church went through tribulation and he was a "fellow partaker" in that tribulation. What makes us think the end time church will not endure such hardships? More on this as we continue our study.

How was John undergoing tribulation? Church tradition holds that the apostle John was exiled to the island of Patmos when he wrote Revelation.[1] Although the text does not explicitly state this (the word "exiled" does not appear in the original Greek text), there is a strong argument for this given the fact John indicated he was, in fact, undergoing tribulation.

If he was exiled, it comes as a slight shock to find the text stating he was in the "Spirit" on the Lord's Day. Think about the last time you were mad, frustrated, hurting, or isolated. Were you in the Spirit? Something to think about.

But even if John wasn't exiled (although it seems more likely he was), we can still learn a valuable lesson from the apostle. If he wasn't exiled, he was undergoing tribulation on the mainland, but he found himself on Patmos, or perhaps he sailed to Patmos for a little seclusion. Jesus also left the crowds to be with His Father:

But Jesus Himself would often slip away to the wilderness and pray.

Luke 5:16

We need to have time alone with God in order to better hear His voice.

In Revelation 1:10 John hears a voice like a trumpet and in verse 15 Jesus' voice is described like "many waters." Let's see if this is consistent with scripture (you know it will be).

So it came about on the third day, when it was morning, that there were thunder and lightning flashes and a thick cloud upon the mountain and a very loud trumpet sound, so that all the people who were in the camp trembled . . .

16

When the sound of the trumpet grew louder and louder,
Moses spoke and God answered him with thunder.

Exodus 19:16, 19

I also heard the sound of their wings like the sound of
abundant waters as they went, like the voice of the
Almighty, a sound of tumult like the sound of an army
camp; whenever they stood still, they dropped their wings.

Ezekiel 1:24

Imagine a trumpet blast so loud and powerful that it shakes you
to your very core. Visualize standing beside a raging waterfall and
being unable to hear anything else around you. That is the voice of
our Lord. He speaks and it is done (Genesis 1). His words are
power and His voice is unmatched in authority.

This awesome voice commands John to write what he sees and
hears to seven churches in Asia Minor. When John turns to the
voice he sees a vision of Jesus Christ. Before we study how Jesus
appears in Revelation, let's remind ourselves of how He appeared at
His first advent.

And she gave birth to her firstborn son; and she wrapped
Him in cloths, and laid Him in a manger, because there
was no room for them in the inn.

Luke 2:7

What do you think it was like to give birth in a stable? We
tend to romanticize Jesus' birth, but it was no cakewalk. Mary gave
birth on a dirty floor, the stable probably smelled like dung, and she
may have been a mere teenager. Do you think she was scared?
How would you feel in this circumstance? Now let's look at
another scripture.

For He grew up before Him like a tender shoot, and like a
root out of parched ground; He has no stately form or
majesty that we should look upon Him, nor appearance
that we should be attracted to Him. He was despised and
forsaken of men, a man of sorrows and acquainted with
grief; and like one from whom men hide their face He was
despised, and we did not esteem Him . . . But He was
pierced through for our transgressions, He was crushed

17

for our iniquities; the chastening for our well-being fell
upon Him, and by His scourging we are healed.

Isaiah 53:2-3,5

This is a prophecy about our Savior. His form had no majesty. He was acquainted with sorrow and grief. He was despised and rejected. He was pierced and crushed. I don't have to remind you of what He did. He took the nails – really big railroad-rail-sized spiked nails – for us. My faithful friends, He could have called down the angels to save Him (Matthew 26:53), yet He did not. He came in love and humility (Zechariah 9:9).

Now, back to Revelation and Jesus' second advent. John announced in Revelation 1:1 the revelation of Jesus Christ – and then He sees Jesus Christ – in His glory. What is the Revelation? It is Jesus in His *GLORY*.

Let's look at the robe reaching to His feet, and the golden sash around His chest (Revelation 1:13). Why is He wearing this?

He shall put on the holy linen tunic, and the linen
undergarments shall be next to his body, and he shall be
girded with the linen sash. . . (these are holy garments).

Leviticus 16:4a

These are the garments of the High Priest. Jesus is our High Priest (Hebrews 5:1-10). The High Priest was the one man who could enter the inner sanctuary of the Jewish Temple, the Holy of Holies, and make atonement for God's people. Jesus did so once and for all when His body was broken and His blood was shed on the cross nearly two thousand years ago.

His eyes are like a flame of fire. This speaks of judgment. Seems a little frightening, doesn't it? But there is nothing for us to be frightened of if we are His children. The Revelation is about the return of the King, and His return will be to judge mankind. Let's look at scripture.

Nothing in all creation is hidden from God's sight.
Everything is uncovered and laid bare before the eyes of
him to whom we must give account.

Hebrews 4:13 NIV

For God will bring every act to judgment, everything which is hidden, whether it is good or evil.

Ecclesiastes 12:14

"Therefore wait for Me," declares the Lord, "For the day when I rise up as a witness. Indeed, My decision is to gather nations, to assemble kingdoms, to pour out on them My indignation, all My burning anger; for all the earth will be devoured by the fire of My zeal."

Zephaniah 3:8

But by His word the present heavens and earth are being reserved for fire, kept for the day of judgment and destruction of ungodly men . . . But the day of the Lord will come like a thief, in which the heavens will pass away with a roar and the elements will be destroyed with intense heat, and the earth and its works will be burned up.

2 Peter 3:7, 10

Why are Jesus' eyes like a flame of fire? Because the fire of His jealousy is coming and the earth will be consumed (Zephaniah 3:8). He sees everything and everything will be judged. Before you start to worry about the earth's destruction, look at this scripture:

But who can endure the day of His coming? And who can stand when He appears? For He is like a refiner's fire and a fullers' soap.

Malachi 3:2

Fire destroys, but it also purifies. A refiner's fire takes something and makes it shine. Even amid the destruction, God will purify and make the world beautiful. Yes, fire is coming, but for the believer it will be a cleaning fire. Glory!

Jesus' hair is white like snow. What? Doesn't match our image of the Savior does it? What could Jesus' white hair mean? White in scripture represents holiness and righteousness.

It was given to her to clothe herself in fine linen, bright and clean; for the fine linen is the righteous acts of the saints.

Revelation 19:8

Jesus hair is white to convey a point – His righteousness reaches to the beginning of time. He is the ancient of days. His righteousness and holiness have not changed one iota. He is also the pure white sacrifice. He is the unblemished Lamb of God. Only by His sacrifice are we declared righteous. Only by His sacrifice are our robes washed clean.

Next let's look at Jesus' feet. They are like burnished bronze. Immediately we think heavy, and so we should, because when He passes judgment on the unrepentant the punishment will be heavy. And it will be forever. Yet, the bronze should also remind us of the bronze altar of the temple where the animals were slain in judgment for the people's sins. There, at that altar – and ultimately the cross – judgment was transformed into mercy and forgiveness. Although the altar should be where we die for our sins, we have a Savior that takes our place. Although bronze is heavy for the unbeliever, for the believer it should remind us of the altar and ultimately forgiveness.

And Moses made a bronze serpent and set it on the standard; and it came about, that if a serpent bit any man, when he looked to the bronze serpent, he lived.

Numbers 21:9

The bronze snake was set up in order to halt an infestation of snakes that had broken out in the camp. If you looked (believed) on the bronze symbol (Jesus, see John 3:14-15) then you lived. If you did not, you died. Let me tell you something faithful friends, if the "standard" the bronze snake was set up on wasn't a cross, I would be shocked.

We are running out of time, so let's move on. John saw a "double edged sword" coming out of Jesus' mouth. Again, seems a little frightening doesn't it? But no, this isn't a literal sword. It would be quite hard for John to see an invisible object coming out of Jesus' mouth, but a sword – got it! Let me prove it to you.

20

For the word of God is living and active and sharper than any two-edged sword, and piercing as far as the division of soul and spirit, of both joints and marrow, and able to judge the thoughts and intentions of the heart.

Hebrews 4:12

In the beginning was the Word, and the Word was with God, and the Word was God . . . And the Word became flesh, and dwelt among us, and we saw His glory, glory as of the only begotten from the Father, full of grace and truth.

John 1:1, 14

The Word is a two-edged sword and the Word is Jesus Himself. Now look at this scripture.

Listen to Me, O islands, and pay attention, you peoples from afar. The Lord called Me from the womb; from the body of My mother He named Me. He has made My mouth like a sharp sword.

Isaiah 49:1-2a

Can you believe that? Jesus' mouth is like a sharp sword, ready to judge the world when He returns. How will He judge the world? What standard will He use? God's Word – the sword! The Word is powerful, and we know that Jesus is the embodiment of the Word (John 1:1). John saw a sword coming out of Jesus' mouth in Revelation chapter one, but that sword is actually the Word spilling out of Jesus' mouth and it is able to pierce the heart and shatter it even more quickly than the sword. Once a sinner is judged by the Word, there is no doubt of their guilt.

Just to be clear. Jesus is the Word. The next time someone tells you that they don't "understand" the Bible so they don't read it, or they think it is "outdated," you need to tell them to think again. If they are letting their Bible sit dusty on their shelves, they are shelving Jesus. Ouch.

I just love God's Word! And if you love God's Word, guess who you love? You guessed it – Jesus. Okay, final thought for today: His face was like the sun.

It came about when Moses was coming down from Mount Sinai (and the two tablets of the testimony were in Moses'

21

hand as he was coming down from the mountain), that
Moses did not know that the skin of his face shone
because of his speaking with Him.

Exodus 34:29

Can you imagine? Just speaking with the Lord of lords caused Moses to reflect His brilliance. If the reflection was enough to terrify the Israelites, how much more the actuality of seeing God face to face? God is so pure He shines. There is no comparison. And what are we to be? The light of the world (Matthew 5:14). Why? We are to reflect God's glory just like Moses (2 Corinthians 3:18). Now look at these two scriptures.

Who alone possesses immortality and dwells in
unapproachable light, whom no man has seen or can see.
To Him be honor and eternal dominion! Amen.

1 Timothy 6:16

His splendor covers the heavens, and the earth is full of
His praise. His radiance is like the sunlight; He has rays
flashing from His hand.

Habakkuk 3:3b-4a

Oh, faithful friends, our Jesus is resplendent. Yes, that is a word. Resplendent! Let me say that another way. Jesus *SHINES.* He is light. And He is coming.

Amen and Amen, come quickly Lord Jesus.

Thought for the day:
   Jesus' light is coming and His Word (the sword) will judge.
How does His church hold up? How do you? Is there something
you want to change about your life? How you act? What you
say? How you treat those you love? Make the decision today to
change. Our next lessons are on the churches, but those churches
are you. Find out what Jesus says about one church tomorrow.

1 *English Standard Version Study Bible* (Wheaton, Illinois: Crossway, 2008), 2464.

Day Four
Revelation 1:12-13, 16, 20
The churches

[12]Then I turned to see the voice that was speaking with me. And having turned I saw seven golden lampstands; [13]and in the middle of the lampstands I saw one like a son of man, clothed in a robe reaching to the feet, and girded across His chest with a golden sash . . . [16]In His right hand He held seven stars, and out of His mouth came a sharp two-edged sword; and His face was like the sun shining in its strength . . .[20]"As for the mystery of the seven stars which you saw in My right hand, and the seven golden lampstands: the seven stars are the angels of the seven churches, and the seven lampstands are the seven churches."

Revelation 1:12-13, 16, 20

Here begins the letters to the churches. The first thing we need to understand is that these churches were actual physical churches that existed in John's day (in modern day Turkey). The warnings and commendations Jesus dictates were actual warnings and commendations to these churches. However because there were seven (perfection and entirety), Jesus' words are also directed to the church throughout the ages. The warnings and commendations in these letters are as applicable to us now as they were back then.

As individuals we can learn from these letters and adjust our lives accordingly. At some point in our Christian walk we can appear more like "Ephesus" and in later years, hopefully, we will appear more like "Philadelphia." So not only does the church benefit from reading these letters, but individual believers can also take away moral lessons that will bring us closer to Christ.

Some scholars maintain these churches not only represent the church universal, but also each church represents a different age in church history. For instance, the environment described in the first letter to Ephesus quite possibly describes the beginning church age – the apostolic church, or the church right after Jesus' ascension; the second letter would describe the next stage, or the church almost a hundred years after the time of Christ, known as the persecuted church, and so on until we come to the final letter addressed to Laodicea which would describe the environment of the final church age.[1]

However, if you look at a map of Turkey, the letters were dictated in the order in which a messenger would deliver them.

There may be no other significance to the letters' arrangement besides ease of transport. Although God could have planned the letters to correspond to ages, we do not need to get bogged down trying to pinpoint a church to an age, for if we do we may fail to grasp how relevant each letter is to us today, both as a church and an individual. So the following discussion will focus on what each letter says about Christ, and also about the environment of the church described.

Before we delve into the letters in chapter two, we need to evaluate a few more things from chapter one that deal with the churches. In Revelation 1:12-16 John sees Jesus walking among seven golden lampstands while He is holding seven stars. In verse 20 the stars are identified as "the angels of the seven churches" and the seven lampstands "are the seven churches."

In the Old Testament God commanded the Israelites to make a lampstand with seven lights. The lampstand was fashioned for the Holy Place of the tabernacle and gave light to the priests who entered (Exodus 25:37). Remember, the number seven in scripture means perfection, wholeness, or entirety. For the Jewish people, their light was one, emanating from one lampstand, symbolic of the Jewish people being a "light to the nations" (Isaiah 49:6). In Revelation, however, we see seven individual lampstands. This is symbolic of the Jewish nation's lampstand now reaching the entire world. Jesus emerged from Jewish roots, the Savior of not only the Jewish nation, but of all mankind. Now instead of one nation being God's light, He has the church that His chosen nation influenced and her light has spread to every nation on earth. These lights are bearing God's light and witnessing to the darkness.

The true light of the world is Jesus (Isaiah 2:5, John 1:9) but just as Moses' face shone when speaking to God, we should reflect His glory in our own lives. We are His light because we are bringing Him. Now look at this scripture:

> *For my eyes have seen Your salvation, which You have prepared in the presence of all peoples. A light of REVELATION to the Gentiles and the glory of Your people Israel.*
>
> *Luke 2:30-32 (emphasis added)*

Wow! Jesus is our light and He is our *REVELATION*. Someone needs to shout, "Glory!" We have looked at the lampstands, but there is another element we are missing.

24

Jesus defines the seven stars in His hand as the "seven angels of the seven churches." There are two ways of looking at this. In Daniel 10:12-14 an angel is speaking with Daniel and identifies another angel who is opposing him as a "prince." Then, a third angel is introduced – Michael – who comes to the first angel's aid. Who is Michael?

> *Now at that time Michael, the great prince who stands guard over the sons of your people, will arise.*
> *Daniel 12:1a*

Michael is the angel who protects Israel. Yes, there are angels assigned to kingdoms – both good and bad. There is a spiritual war waging over our heads that would make our brains explode if we knew the details. Never forget you are in a war, faithful friends. You are in a war.

So, the stars in Jesus' hands could literally be angels over the churches just like there are angels over kingdoms. Alternatively, the stars in Jesus' hand could be earthy ministers or heads of the church. Quite possibly, it could mean both. In scripture stars are used to represent both angels (Job 38:7) and faithful servants of God (Daniel 12:3). If we understand the letters are addressed to seven types of churches throughout the ages there will be many "heads" of the church (in human terms). But an angel is descriptive of something that lives on (like the church) even after certain "leaders" or "heads" die. Think of the stars in Jesus' hand as representing church leadership throughout the ages, both in angelic and human terms.

What we need to realize is that Jesus is addressing not only every church, but also every individual believer and examining how each is reflecting His glory. Some are shining brilliantly while other lights have gone out. Jesus wants every person to heed His revelation, to understand how each one appears in the heavenlies, and what they should be doing differently to positively impact the world around them.

Revelation 1:17 says, "When I saw Him, I fell at His feet like a dead man. And He placed His right hand on me, saying. 'Do not be afraid; I am the first and the last.'"

When John sees Jesus, he collapses! I do believe each and every one of us would do the same. As scripture says, "every knee will bow" (Isaiah 45:23). When confronted with the holy, with the perfect, with the all-powerful Savior we love, we will understand our inadequacy. But notice what comes next, Jesus reaches out to John and tells him, "Do not be afraid."

This is amazing. The Lord of the universe loves us so much He reaches out to us, calls us His children, and wants to be with us for eternity. When we fell in Genesis chapter three, God didn't give up on us, but sent His one and only Son to suffer and die for our sake. Why? So we could live with Him forever. The human mind cannot grasp the wonder of this. It is incomprehensible. That is grace; that is love; that is God.

Jesus identifies Himself as the first and the last, the living One that was dead, having the keys of death in His hands. Again, this is the Ancient of Days, the Savior of mankind, and the redeemer of the earth. He then commands John to write what he is now seeing (the vision of Jesus), the things which are (the present reality of the churches in chapters two and three) and what will take place after these things (the end time events and the return of the King).

Before we end our lesson, I want you to look ahead to part of Revelation 2:1.

The One who . . . walks among the seven golden lampstands.

Revelation 2:1

Notice Jesus is walking among the lampstands. We just learned that the lampstands represent the churches, so Jesus walking among them is symbolic of Jesus being present with His church.

"For where two or three have gathered together in My name, I am there in their midst"

Matthew 18:20

There is probably a second meaning, however, to Jesus walking among the lampstands. If the lampstands represent the church, they also represent the bride of Christ. John the Baptist refers to the church being the bride when he says:

"I am not the Christ, but I have been sent ahead of Him. He who has the bride is the bridegroom; but the friend of the bridegroom, who stands and hears him, rejoices greatly because of the bridegroom's voice."

John 3:28b-29a

26

Ephesians 5:22-33 compares a spousal relationship to the relationship Christ has with His church. Revelation 19:7 says, "Let us rejoice and be glad and give the glory to Him, for the marriage of the Lamb has come and His bride has made herself ready." Ready? Ready for what? For Christ's return!

Why is Christ walking among the lampstands? He is looking to see if the bride is ready. Jesus wants to "present to Himself the church in all her glory, having no spot or wrinkle or any such thing; but that she would be holy and blameless" (Ephesians 5:27b). My faithful friends, Jesus is excited, as we should be, about the reunion! He is walking – I daresay pacing – among the lampstands, examining His bride, wondering when she will get her act together.

This is a nice way to begin our study on the churches, and I daresay this is the reason our Lord directed John to specifically identify Jesus as "the One who walks among the seven golden lampstands." In these letters Jesus will admonish and acclaim, He will plead and beg her to repent of her sins, and He will praise and commend her for lighting the dark corners of the earth. He wants us ready because He wants to return to claim His bride, the church.

Now, my faithful friends, buckle your seatbelts and be prepared to be examined by the One who has "eyes like a flame of fire." We can do nothing under the sun without our Lord's awareness. Our Lord knows our faith, and our deeds. How will we stand up?

Thought for the day:
Jesus is anxious for the reunion. He wants His bride to be excited about His return. Our days here are numbered. Our time there is forever. Do we live for forever? Or do we live for today?

1 Lahaye, Tim. *Revelation Unveiled* (Grand Rapids, Michigan: Zondervan Publishing House, 1999), 35-36. This is a great commentary chapter by chapter of Revelation. Tim Lahaye is of the pre-tribulation rapture view and this book is a must have for further research on this position.

DAY FIVE
REVELATION 2:1-7
THE MESSAGE TO EPHESUS

[1]"To the angel of the church in Ephesus write: The One who holds the seven stars in His right hand, the One who walks among the seven golden lampstands, says this: [2]'I know your deeds and your toil and perseverance, and that you cannot tolerate evil men, and you put to the test those who call themselves apostles, and they are not, and you found them to be false; [3]and you have perseverance and have endured for My name's sake, and have not grown weary. [4]But I have this against you, that you have left your first love. [5]Therefore remember from where you have fallen, and repent and do the deeds you did at first; or else I am coming to you and will remove your lampstand out of its place – unless you repent. [6]Yet this you do have, that you hate the deeds of the Nicolaitans, which I also hate. [7]He who has an ear, let him hear what the Spirit says to the churches. To him who overcomes, I will grant to eat of the tree of life which is in the Paradise of God.'"

Revelation 2:1-7

The letters to the churches are not for the faint of heart. They cut and penetrate to the marrow. "Nothing in all creation is hidden from God's sight. Everything is uncovered and laid bare before the eyes of him to whom we must give account" (Hebrews 4:13 NIV). In chapter one, Jesus' eyes appear like flames of fire. We see the reason for His fire in the first letter. The church at Ephesus had left its first love – Jesus, the bridegroom. What had happened to this church?

First we learn Ephesus put to the test those who called themselves apostles but were false. This church was good at identifying false doctrine and they did not tolerate it. If you were teaching a "Jesus" other than the one to whom they had declared allegiance they would usher you to the nearest door. Take a look at this scripture:

Beloved, do not believe every spirit, but test the spirits to see whether they are from God, because many false prophets have gone out into the world. By this you know the Spirit of God: every spirit that confesses that Jesus Christ has come in the flesh is from God; and every spirit that does not confess Jesus is not from God; this is the spirit of the antichrist, of which you have heard that it is coming, and now it is already in the world. You are from God, little children, and have overcome them; because greater is He who is in you than he who is in the world.

1 John 4:1-3

Notice this scripture mentions "antichrist." But in these verses John says there are "many." Yes, there are. A few years back, Beth Moore said something that struck a cord in me.[1] She said, "Satan does not know when the end time will come. He has to raise up antichrists in every generation." Wow. Yes, according to 1 John, that is the truth. I believe many of us could name multiple people in history that fit this description nicely.

The church in Ephesus recognized what John was warning about in 1 John 4:1-3. They had tested the spirits and found some to be false. They knew those speaking of Christ and they knew the ones who were imposters.

What can we learn about Ephesus to help us on our walk with our Lord? We can test the spirits emphatically. As John said, the spirit of the antichrist is already in the world; we need to learn to recognize it. What is the spirit of the antichrist? In scripture the antichrist is said to be lying and deceptive (Daniel 9:27, 2 John 1:7), boastful and arrogant (Daniel 7:20, Revelation 13:6), against the Most High in both action and word (Daniel 7:25, Revelation 13:5), and he will oppose the saints (Revelation 13:7). We are looking for a spirit of deceit and trickery, of arrogance and pride, or anything that opposes Israel and the saints of the Most High God. This can be an entire society or an individual. Be on the alert.

I truly believe the tolerance the world now speaks of is part of this deceptive spirit. In today's culture tolerance has taken on an entirely different meaning than the definition of the word.[2] Look at the definition of tolerance.

Tolerance: the capacity for or the practice of recognizing and respecting the beliefs or practices of others.[3]

Today, however, we not only have to recognize and respect, we also have to agree to be considered "tolerant." Many of us find ourselves nodding to a false statement in order to keep the peace. That may be deemed acceptable if you are talking about mom's leftover fruitcake at Christmas, but if you are talking about Jesus, there can be no compromise. He is God's son, the Savior of the world, and the Lion of the tribe of Judah. If anyone says otherwise we need to stand our ground. In today's culture, this is dangerous. To say Jesus is the only way offends multitudes. If the final Antichrist does appear, will we stand firm in Christ even if a gun is placed next to our children's heads? There can be no compromise with this truth. Ephesus did not compromise with this truth. We need to absorb this lesson and determine to live it.

Where have you allowed the new "tolerance" to affect your own life? Where has the church allowed this "tolerance" to affect their worship?

Let's get back to Ephesus. If this church could discern false prophets so perfectly, how could they have left their first love? Scripture is clear that Ephesus endured for Jesus' name. So, if they were persevering how in the world could they have left Him? To answer this question I believe we have to look at the author of Revelation's first letter.

> *But whoever keeps His word, in him the love of God has truly been perfected. By this we know that we are in Him.*
> *1 John 2:5*

> *For this is the love of God, that we keep His commandments; and His commandments are not burdensome.*
> *1 John 5:3*

His love is perfected when we keep His Word, when we obey His commandments. This should not be a burden, but a joy. My faithful friends, I believe Ephesus knew of Jesus, did things for Jesus, but had either drifted away from the Word or had become so legalistic in their interpretation that they lost sight of Him. If you drift away from the truth of the Word, then you drift away from Jesus, your first love, because Jesus is the Word! Ephesus didn't really care about the truth of the scriptures. I daresay they were using clever stories in their sermons and not the Word of God. Let me prove it to you.

> *As I urged you upon my departure for Macedonia, remain on at Ephesus so that you may instruct certain men not to teach strange doctrines, nor to pay attention to myths and endless genealogies, which give rise to mere speculation*

rather than furthering the administration of God which is by faith. But the goal of our instruction is love from a pure heart and a good conscience and a sincere faith. For some men, straying from these things, have turned aside to fruitless discussion, wanting to be teachers of the Law, even though they do not understand either what they are saying or the matters about which they make confident assertions.

1 Timothy 1:3-7

The Ephesians were concerned about stories – myths – and not the truth of the Word. They were concerned about the law and not emphasizing grace.

How alike are we to the church of Ephesus? Do we want to hear the Word or do we attend church to hear a clever story in the sermon? Do we hang on the truth of scripture or do we go to church to be entertained? Do we let the Word penetrate our heart and change our lives or do we let it "go in one ear and out the other?" How is the church you attend, or the church today as a whole, like Ephesus? Do you think most churches are preaching the Word? Do you think the new "tolerance" we have let enter our society is watering down the Word? When was the last time you were convicted in church? When was the last time you heard a preacher preach an "unpopular" sermon?

Before we leave this section, I want you to look again at Jesus' words to Ephesus.

"But I have this against you, that you have left your first love."

Revelation 2:4

Let's broaden the search in our own lives. Where in your life have you left your first love? Do you allow entertainment or possessions to control your time or do you prioritize your day by the Word? Do you look forward to your favorite television show more than you enjoy opening the Word of God? What controls your thoughts: the Word, or things and possessions? Is there anything between you and Jesus? Is there anything between you and the Word?

These are hard questions that we all need to address. We all "stumble in many ways" (James 3:2). Let's think about and

31

evaluate our lives. May we bring glory to Jesus in all that we do.

Despite her failing love, Jesus praised this church for hating the deeds of the Nicolaitans. The Nicolaitans wanted to set up a hierarchy in the church. The Greek word "niko" means "conquer" and "laos" means "laity."[4] If a hierarchy is established, it takes the focus off Christ as the true head of the church. This in turn causes the masses to ignore the Holy Spirit and look to humans as holding solutions to their problems. How many in the church today look to a beloved Bible study teacher, a favored preacher, a popular deacon, or the pope as the "final word from the Lord" and not to the Lord Himself? How many of us look to a scholarly friend or a TV evangelist as having all the answers to spiritual issues but fail to examine the scriptures for ourselves? Jesus hated this doctrine and condemned it in His first letter to Ephesus.

Christ calls this church to repent or else He would remove her lampstand from its place. The church would fail and her light would extinguish if they did not realize their love was growing cold and the Word was lacking in their lives. If you are just going through the motions, pretty soon your reason for going in the first place will die and your light will fade.

As Christ's return draws near, are we going through the motions, or are we looking up? Are we expectant or have we grown complacent? Jesus is walking among the lampstands asking for the one who "has an ear, let him hear what the Spirit says to the churches." If we overcome, like Jesus says, and hold fast to our first love, He will grant us access to the "tree of life, which is in the Paradise of God." This speaks of eternity (Revelation 22:2) and unbroken fellowship with our Savior (Revelation 21:3).

Thought for the day:
Have you left the truth of the Word behind like Ephesus? Do you get Jesus second hand, or do you read the scriptures to verify and understand? Is today's tolerance weakening the faith of your family, your country, your church, or yourself? Persecution tends to shed light on whether or not you are truly with Him, or if you are following Him for other reasons. We meet a persecuted church

tomorrow. If this were Ephesus, what would happen to some of her members? Find out more tomorrow.

1 Moore, Beth. *Here and Now*. I have paraphrased this based on my memory of this study. This is not a word-for-word quote from Beth Moore.

2 McDowell, Josh and Hostetler, Bob. *The New Tolerance: How a Cultural Movement Threatens to Destroy You, Your Faith, and Your Children* (Tyndale House Publishers, Inc., 1998).

3 *The American Heritage College Dictionary, 3rd Edition* (Boston, Massachusetts: Houghton Mifflin Company, 1993).

4 Lahaye, Tim. *Revelation Unveiled* (Grand Rapids, Michigan: Zondervan Publishing House, 1999), 47.

⁸"And to the angel of the church in Smyrna write: The first and the last, who was dead, and has come to life, says this: ⁹'I know your tribulation and your poverty (but you are rich), and the blasphemy by those who say they are Jews and are not, but are a synagogue of Satan. ¹⁰Do not fear what you are about to suffer. Behold, the devil is about to cast some of you into prison, so that you will be tested, and you will have tribulation for ten days. Be faithful until death, and I will give you the crown of life. ¹¹He who has an ear, let him hear what the Spirit says to the churches. He who overcomes will not be hurt by the second death."

Revelation 2:8-11

Smyrna was a church without any warnings. Jesus knew she was enduring tribulation (afflictions) and had no material wealth, yet He calls her rich. We need to rejoice in the realization that despite what state we are in materially, we are rich in Christ. Focus on the One and not on the wealth we acquire in this life.

This church was enduring tribulation and blasphemy by "those who say they are Jews and are not, but are a synagogue of Satan." Not all Jews accepted Jesus as their Messiah, hence they "are not." To say it another way, if you are apart from God you are a "synagogue of Satan." This is harsh, but this is truth. What did Jesus say in Mathew 12?

"He who is not with Me is against Me; and he who does not gather with Me scatters."

Matthew 12:30

Jews were persecuting those who had seen the light not realizing the light belonged to them as well if they would only believe!

It is interesting to note Jesus identifies himself as "the first and the last, who was dead, and has come to life." Jesus wants this church to understand He too went through tribulation and paid the ultimate sacrifice with His death, yet the devil couldn't keep Him in the grave. He is alive. Jesus is telling Smyrna, who is under intense persecution, that even if some of her members are killed, they are

34

alive because of His sacrifice. As it says in Philippians 1:21, "to live is Christ and to die is gain." If you are "absent from the body" you are "at home with the Lord" (2 Corinthians 5:8b). For the believer, death is life!

Jesus says, "Behold the devil is about to cast some of you into prison, so that you will be tested, and you will have tribulation for ten days." Note, Satan is the one who was about to cast some of Smyrna's saints into prison; however, God knew about it. Why didn't He stop it? The same reason He doesn't stop tribulation in our own lives. Jesus even said, "In this world you have tribulation, but take courage; I have overcome the world" (John 16:33). Let me say this another way: God sometimes uses the enemy's persecutions to test our faith. Satan wants to tear you down, but God wants you to shine for Him.

In this you greatly rejoice, even though now for a little while, if necessary, you have been distressed by various trials, so that the proof of your faith, being more precious than gold which is perishable, even though tested by fire, may be found to result in praise and glory and honor at the revelation of Jesus Christ.

1 Peter 1:6-7

Although Satan will attempt to destroy us with everything he has, God will use that for good:

And we know that God causes all things to work together for good to those who love God, to those who are called according to His purpose.

Romans 8:28

When persecutions come, and come they will, God will be glorified and our faith will be perfected.

Although Jesus says the saints in Smyrna will undergo tribulation, God will give them a crown if they are found faithful and they will be unhurt by the second death. According to James 1:12 the crown of life is given to those who remain faithful under persecution, perhaps even persecution leading to death. Remember what Jesus said to Smyrna "be faithful until death, and I will give you the crown of life." If you remain faithful under persecution you will not be hurt by the second death. What is the second death?

Then death and Hades were thrown into the lake of fire.
This is the second death, the lake of fire.

Revelation 20:14

The first death is the death of our mortal bodies. The second death is eternal death, the death of the rebellious and unbelievers.

We can apply what Jesus said to Smyrna to our own lives. Most of us aren't living in places of persecution, but if we are the final generation Jesus talked about in Matthew 24, we could undergo persecution during the reign of the Antichrist. Once the Antichrist and his governmental system rises, scripture is clear – Satan will wage war with not only Israel, but also with the rest of the elect (Revelation 12:17).

Are you willing to stand up for the sake of Christ? Are you willing to suffer for His name? Are you willing to die for your Lord? The people in the church of Smyrna were prepared to die for the sake of Christ. May we remain as faithful as Smyrna under the most challenging circumstances.

Thought for the day:
The letters to the churches are painful at times. We wrestle with what we would do if faced with persecution or death. We try to envision our decision and waver. What would we do? But know this: Jesus is the life (John 14:6). When we die, we live, not a day, or a week, or a year, but forever. There is really no decision that needs to be made. The choice is obvious. Death forever or life forever? We will find out in a few days those walking without Him are dead even when they are alive. For a believer, we are alive even when faced with death. Pain for a moment, or pain for eternity? Choose Life. True Life. Choose Him.

[12]"And to the angel of the church in Pergamum write: The One who has the sharp two-edged sword says this: [13]'I know where you dwell, where Satan's throne is; and you hold fast My name, and did not deny My faith even in the days of Antipas, My witness, My faithful one, who was killed among you, where Satan dwells. [14]But I have a few things against you, because you have there some who hold the teaching of Balaam, who kept teaching Balak to put a stumbling block before the sons of Israel, to eat things sacrificed to idols and to commit acts of immorality. [15]So you also have some who in the same way hold the teaching of the Nicolaitans. [16]Therefore repent; or else I am coming to you quickly, and I will make war against them with the sword of My mouth. [17]He who has an ear, let him hear what the Spirit says to the churches. To him who overcomes, to him I will give some of the hidden manna, and I will give him a white stone, and a new name written on the stone which no one knows but he who receives it.'"

Revelation 2:12-17

The Pergamum church was praised because she held fast to Christ despite intense persecution that led to the death of one of Pergamum's saints, Antipas. It is interesting to note Jesus called Pergamum the place where Satan's throne dwells. This is important when we remember these letters are addressed to today's church as well as the churches of the past. Does Satan's throne still remain there? Will this in some form or fashion be where the Antichrist raises his ugly head? Every letter addressed went to modern day Turkey. We have already mentioned the letters made almost a circle. Could God be "circling" the area to watch? Turkey is now a follower of Islam. If you study Islam carefully it is Christianity's polar opposite. This will be important as we move further into our study.

Some in Pergamum's congregation held to the teaching of Balaam. Balaam was a prophet who directed the king of Moab to seduce the Israelites to intermarry with the Moabites in order to dilute their worship to God (Numbers 25:1-3, 31:16). The Bible is clear, once you intermarry with paganism it is only a matter of time before you find yourself compromising with the world. Read James 4:4 and let it penetrate your heart.

> *You adulteresses, do you not know that friendship with the world is hostility toward God? Therefore whoever wishes to be a friend of the world makes himself an enemy of God.*
>
> *James 4:4*

When you leave the church walls, do you compromise with the world around you? Are you complacent when some form of worldliness touches you or your household? Do the shows you watch on television mirror the world or God? The books you read? The music you listen to? Is your attitude godly? What about your dress? Your speech? Your possessions? Where has the world's influence taken hold of your life? Have you become a friend of the world?

We have all allowed the pagan culture, in some way, to touch our lives. Look at this scripture.

> *If the godly give in to the wicked, it's like polluting a fountain or muddying a spring.*
>
> *Proverbs 25:26 NLT*

How polluted have we become as individuals? As churches? As nations?

The people of Pergamum had begun to dabble with the pagan system by eating things sacrificed to idols and committing acts of immorality. Some of us tell ourselves we can do things that are ungodly and not be compromised within. This is a lie from the father of lies (John 8:44). There can be no compromise with the world if we want to walk God's path for our lives.

Others in Pergamum were falling prey to the Nicolaitans, wanting to establish a hierarchy that would take true authority away from Christ. Christ is our intercessor. "Christ Jesus is He who died, yes, rather who was raised, who is at the right hand of God, who also intercedes for us" (Romans 8:34b). You do not need a pastor, a minister, or a priest to approach the throne of the Almighty. All you need is faith in His Son (Hebrews 4:14-16). Jesus died for this truth. We need to praise our Father for this truth. This is God's mercy and grace being extended to the sinner because of the Son.

Jesus calls this church to repent or He will "make war" against her with the sword of His mouth. Again, this is not a literal sword, but the Word of God. Isaiah 11:4 says, "And He will strike the earth with the rod of His mouth, and with the breath of His lips He will slay the wicked." All Jesus has to do is speak and it is done. "Repent or else," He says. If you compromise His truth with paganism, you will be like muddy water. The bride will no longer be pure. The "sword of His mouth" is also referred to in conjunction with the second coming of Christ in Revelation 19:15.

From His mouth comes a sharp sword, so that with it He may strike down the nations, and He will rule them with a rod of iron . . .

Revelation 19:15

This should alert us to the fact that each letter is as relevant to churches and individuals today as it was back in John's day. If you do not repent, the sword will pierce you. You have to overcome and remain true to Christ despite the world's influence (Revelation 2:17). You can be in the church building, but apart from Christ. Let's pray we hold fast to the truth and flee from the muddy waters.

Christ then promises if they stand firm in Him He will give them hidden manna and a white stone with a "new name written on the stone which no one knows but he who receives it." Manna is reminiscent of the Exodus, where God sustained His people with "bread from heaven" (Exodus 16, John 6:31). The overcomer will enter God's kingdom and never again be hungry, but will be sustained by Him who will never leave us (Revelation 7:16).

The white stone stands for acquittal. In Jesus' day a judge would hand an accused criminal a white stone to declare their innocence.[1] Jesus will give those who overcome a white stone with a new name on it. Can you imagine Jesus giving you a new name only known to you and Him? When He whispers your name on the winds of heaven, you will hear. Most of us have had a pet name bestowed on us by someone who loves us. It made us feel special, valued, and cherished. So will our new name in heaven. It will be a name only you know. It will be your true name. Hallelujah!

Thought for the day:

If Jesus handed you a white stone with your name on it today, what do you think it would be? How do you shine for Christ? Do you shine at all? If you don't like the name that came into your head, what would you want it to be? How can you change your life in order to become what you want to become for Christ?

1 Gregg, Steve. *Revelation: Four Views, A Parallel Commentary* (Nashville, Tennessee: Thomas Nelson, Inc., 1997). The Four Views in this book are the Historicist, Preterist, Spiritual, and Futurist, p69-70.

[18]"And to the angel of the church in Thyatira write: The Son of God, who has eyes like a flame of fire, and His feet are like burnished bronze, says this: [19]'I know your deeds, and your love and faith and service and perseverance, and that your deeds of late are greater than at first. [20]But I have this against you, that you tolerate the woman Jezebel, who calls herself prophetess, and she teaches and leads My bond-servants astray so that they commit acts of immorality and eat things sacrificed to idols. [21]I gave her time to repent, and she does not want to repent of her immorality. [22]Behold, I will throw her on a bed of sickness, and those who commit adultery with her into great tribulation, unless they repent of her deeds. [23]And I will kill her children with pestilence, and all the churches will know that I am He who searches the minds and hearts; and I will give to each one of you according to your deeds. [24]But I say to you, the rest who are in Thyatira, who do not hold this teaching, who have not known the deep things of Satan, as they call them – I place no other burden on you. [25]Nevertheless what you have, hold fast until I come. [26]He who overcomes, and he who keeps My deeds until the end, to him I will give authority over the nations; [27]and he shall rule them with a rod of iron, as the vessels of the potter are broken to pieces, as I also have received authority from My Father; [28]and I will give him the morning star. [29]He who has an ear, let him hear what the Spirit says to the churches.'"

Revelation 2:18-29

The church at Thyatira was doing great things for the Lord. Their love, faith, service and perseverance were something He praised, yet they were tolerating a false prophetess in their midst. Scripture identifies this lady as "Jezebel." This pseudonym was intended to lead us back to the original Jezebel in scripture. The Jezebel of the past should give us a better understanding of the Jezebel of Thyatira. To proclaim the false prophetess a Jezebel was Jesus' way of directing this church to realize how sinful their tolerance had become. Let's pause to read when we first meet the original Jezebel in scripture.

It came about, as though it has been a trivial thing for him to walk in the sins of Jeroboam the son of Nebat, that he married Jezebel the daughter of Ethbaal king of the Sidonians, and went to serve Baal and worshiped him. So he erected an altar for Baal in the house of Baal which he built in Samaria. Ahab also made the Asherah. Thus Ahab did more to provoke the Lord God of Israel than all the kinds of Israel who were before him.

1 Kings 16:31-33

Jezebel was the woman who caused the nation of Israel to worship Baal, driving the promised nation into deep sin.[1] Her name became associated with wickedness and idolatry. Jesus was saying to the church of Thyatira, "Danger, danger, you are decaying from within!" Christ deems himself, "He who searches the minds and hearts" and as the "Son of God, who has eyes like a flame of fire." He sees and He will judge (bronze feet). He saw their sin, no matter their good deeds, and calls them to repent.

Thyatira appeared to be on fire for the Lord, but she was allowing someone inside to corrupt her from within. Unlike Pergamum that left the church walls and "befriended" the world, Thyatira was allowing the world to come into the church building! Instead of putting this "Jezebel" out of the church, they were letting her remain.

How alike are we to the church of Thyatira today? How many times do we turn a blind eye to relationships in the church that could influence the body of Christ to stray from the "narrow path" (Matthew 7:13)? There is little church discipline anymore, only tolerance, lest we offend.

The apostle Paul wrote to the Corinthian church about a similar issue. The Corinthians were allowing someone in their midst who was corrupting the church from within. In 1 Corinthians 5 Paul admonished the Corinthian church because they allowed a member of the church to have "his father's wife." Listen to Paul's words:

Do you not know that a little leaven leavens the whole lump of dough?

1 Corinthians 5:6b

Paul admonishes the church for not putting the man out immediately. Paul warned the Corinthian church if they tolerated one sin, others would creep in, affecting the entire church. If you compromise in one area, you are weakened and vulnerable. Many would stand up and shout, "But that would be judging others! A church can't do that!" Wrong.

Paul would approve of us confronting a fellow believer over sin. Listen to Paul's words:

> *For what have I to do with judging outsiders? Do you not judge those who are within the church? But those who are outside, God judges. Remove the wicked man from among yourselves.*
>
> *1 Corinthians 5:12-13*

Church discipline is important. It holds us in check and keeps us accountable. If someone is put out of the church, hopefully, he will repent. Hold the believer to account. Unbelievers, those outside of the church, are different. An unbeliever will be blind to the truth (to their own sin) without Jesus (1 Corinthians 2:14). Love the unbeliever in such a manner that you show them Jesus, then and only then can the Holy Spirit convict them of their sin. Don't judge the unbeliever, Paul says, leave that to God.

Paul is adamant: if you see a fellow believer going down the wrong path you have an obligation to try to steer them back to safe ground. Let's be clear, this doesn't mean you can judge a believer behind his back or even in your heart. Before you confront the person, make sure you do so out of love and not selfish ambition or pride. Let's look at a few more verses.

> *Do not speak against one another, brethren. He who speaks against a brother or judges his brother, speaks against the law and judges the law; but if you judge the law, you are not a doer of the law but a judge of it.*
>
> *James 4:11*

> *My brethren, if any among you strays from the truth and one turns him back, let him know that he who turns a sinner from the error of his way will save his soul from death and will cover a multitude of sins.*
>
> *James 5:19-20*

We should not speak against a fellow believer, *unless they are straying from the truth.* So, you might be thinking, what is the truth? I am glad you asked. Pilate asked the same thing of Jesus before His crucifixion.

Therefore Pilate said to Him, "So You are a king?" Jesus answered, "You say correctly that I am a king. For this I have been born, and for this I have come into the world, to testify to the truth. Everyone who is of the truth hears my voice." Pilate said to Him, "What is the truth?"

John 18:37-38

I love that scripture, because Pilate had the truth right before him.

We have mentioned this before, but let's refresh our memory. According to John 14:6, Jesus is the truth; according to John 17:17, the Word is the truth; and according to John 1:14, Jesus is the Word.

If a fellow believer strays from the Word of truth, we humbly need to approach them. If not, we need to keep our big traps shut. To judge a brother because he is doing something you find unsatisfying isn't the right reason to approach him. If he hasn't strayed from the truth we need to muzzle our mouth (Psalm 39:1) and keep our hearts from a judgmental attitude. We only need to approach a brother when he clearly strays from the truth (Jesus), like the man in the Corinthian church or Thyatira's Jezebel.

Jesus says He will throw Jezebel and those with her into great tribulation unless they repent. He goes on to say He will kill her children with pestilence. This is harsh language from our Lord and it is language right out of the apocalypse. The final years on earth are a time of unprecedented persecution and pestilence. Again, Jesus is telling us this church exists today and if she does not repent she will go through those years of unprecedented sorrow. If you are tolerating a Jezebel among you and are allowing her to lead you astray, you are not for Christ. Remember, friendship with the world is hostility toward God (James 4:4). The rest in Thyatira who did not hold to the "deep things of Satan" He places no other burden on.

What are the deep things of Satan? I believe the Word sums up the "deep things of Satan" quite nicely in Isaiah 5:20.

Woe to those who call evil good, and good evil; who substitute darkness for light and light for darkness; who substitute bitter for sweet and sweet for bitter!

Isaiah 5:20

This describes Thyatira and some of our churches today. When evil becomes good and good becomes evil, we have a problem. And isn't that what many are doing now? Jesus says, "Repent and stand for My light!" Do not call evil good and do not call my truth evil. Woe to those who do!

Jesus promises the overcomer authority over the nations. Again, this is language dealing with the second coming of Christ. The overcomer will help Christ rule in the Millennial Kingdom (Revelation 19:15, Daniel 7:22,27). Jesus also tells them they will be given the morning star. What is the morning star? Let's look at scripture.

> *"I, Jesus, have sent My angel to testify to you these things for the churches. I am the root and the descendant of David, the bright morning star."*
>
> *Revelation 22:16*

You might be thinking, "Is Jesus actually saying He is giving them Himself?" In all honesty, believers should already have Jesus, right? Yes, I do believe there is something more going on here.

> *So we have the prophetic word made more sure, to which you do well to pay attention as to a lamp shining in a dark place, until the day dawns and the morning star arises in your hearts.*
>
> *2 Peter 1:19*

This scripture is saying we need to follow the prophetic word because it is a light in a dark place. We are currently in the dark place and the prophecies are our light because they speak of Jesus. Take a look at 2 Peter 1:19 in the New Century Version:

> *This makes us more sure about the message the prophets gave. It is good for you to follow closely what they said as you would follow a light shining in a dark place, until the day begins and the morning star rises in your hearts."*
>
> *2 Peter 1:19 (NCV)*

If we are now in the dark, when will the day begin?

You see, faithful friends, that classic Sunday school answer of "Jesus" is actually fairly accurate! Isaiah 9:2 is a passage that is quoted all the time about Jesus' first coming, and that is not incorrect, but it also refers to His second coming.

The people who walk in darkness will see a great light; those who live in a dark land, the light will shine on them . . . For a child will be born to us, a son will be given to us; and the government will rest on His shoulders; and His name will be called Wonderful Counselor, Mighty God, Eternal Father, Prince of Peace. There will be no end to the increase of His government or of peace, on the throne of David and over his kingdom, to establish it and to uphold it with justice and righteousness from then on and forevermore.

Isaiah 9:2, 6-7

So, the "great light" is Jesus' presence on earth! At His first coming, the people were walking in darkness, and they saw a "great light" – Jesus. Once Jesus left, we were again in darkness (although we have the light of prophecies). The "great light" will appear again at the return of the King.

Let me say that another way: the day will begin again when the "great light" returns and the Millennial Kingdom of Christ is established.

We are living with the prophecies (light) that speak of Jesus' return (day). So then, what is the morning star in our hearts in 2 Peter 1:19? Yes, it is Jesus like Revelation 22:16 says, but its rising probably refers to the hope of His return!

Now, back to Revelation. When Jesus says, "I will give him the morning star," is that the hope of His coming? Let's dig deeper. We know the morning star is a herald of the breaking day. As in, the morning star (Jesus) will herald the day (or Jesus' return).

Now let's look at one more scripture.

Beloved, now we are children of God, and it has not appeared as yet what we will be. We know that when He appears, we will be like Him, because we will see Him just as He is.

1 John 3:2

When will we see Him as He is? When we are united with Him! For those of us who believe, we will see Him before He returns to the earth at the second coming. We will see Him at the rapture when we "meet the Lord in the air" (1 Thessalonians 4:17). Ah, faithful friends, we may have just uncovered a diamond! The rapture will occur before Jesus again walks the earth. Could Jesus be saying, Thyatira – if you overcome, I will give you Me (the morning star) in the rapture before I return in glory?

I will let you decide.

Thought for the day:

Scripture says, "Woe to those who call evil good, and good evil" (Isaiah 5:20). Really think about this as you walk through your day. Where has society done this? Those around you? You? When you see yourself calling something evil good, or good evil, change your thoughts. Make sure to inform your family and teach them to walk away from evil and cling to the good. We will learn about a church that can't tell the difference tomorrow.

1 Butler, Trent C. et al.,eds. *Holman Illustrated Bible Dictionary* (Nashville, Tennessee: Holman Bible Publishers, 2003), 921.

[1]"To the angel of the church in Sardis write: He who has the seven Spirits of God and the seven stars, says this: 'I know your deeds, that you have a name that you are alive, but you are dead. [2]Wake up, and strengthen the things that remain, which were about to die; for I have not found your deeds completed in the sight of My God. [3]So remember what you have received and heard; and keep it, and repent. Therefore if you do not wake up, I will come like a thief, and you will not know at what hour I will come to you. [4]But you have a few people in Sardis who have not soiled their garments; and they will walk with Me in white, for they are worthy. [5]He who overcomes will thus be clothed in white garments; and I will not erase his name from the book of life, and I will confess his name before My Father and before His angels. [6]He who has an ear, let him hear what the Spirit says to the churches.'"

Revelation 3:1-6

In this letter we are immediately introduced to the seven Spirits of God, or the all-seeing nature of God. Then follows a stern reminder to Sardis that Jesus can see not only their deeds, but also the condition of their hearts. Jesus' warning is clear, "You are dead!" Sardis needs to strengthen what little remains of their faith. Jesus pleads with this church to repent and to remember what she has heard. He warns her, "If you do not wake up, I will come like a thief, and you will not know at what hour I will come to you." This is second coming language.

But be sure of this, that if the head of the house had known at what time of the night the thief was coming, he would have been on the alert and would not have allowed his house to be broken into. For this reason you also must be ready; for the Son of Man is coming at an hour when you do not think He will.

Matthew 24:43-44

For you yourselves know full well that the day of the Lord will come just like a thief in the night.

1 Thessalonians 5:2

Many people use this scripture to emphatically prove we cannot possibly know the time or season when Christ will come. He will be like a thief, they say; there is no sign leading up to His return.

If we study scripture, however, this is a false doctrine.

We just looked at 1 Thessalonians 5:2 which indicates that the day of the Lord will come like a thief in the night, but many people fail to read the next two verses. Check out 1 Thessalonians 5:4:

But you, brethren, are not in darkness, that the day would overtake you like a thief.

1 Thessalonians 5:4

Let me paraphrase: Sardis you better wake up, or Jesus will come to you like a thief. But if you wake up, you will know the time of His coming, and you will be prepared.

As believers, the day should not overtake us like a thief. Now, if you have heard this "thief" doctrine your entire life and have never heard 1 Thessalonians 5:4, you might be fairly enraged right now. Rightfully so! Here is what we can learn from this:

You can't take one verse in isolation without looking at the entirety of scripture.

Yes, Jesus is coming like a thief – to those who are asleep! But as believers, we should not be surprised by His coming. Now, you must be thinking – then why the thief analogy?

The Jews called their High Priest a "thief in the night" and would instantly recognize Jesus' intention when He spoke of coming like a thief. The High Priest was known as a thief because sometimes in the dead of night he walked out of the temple with burning coals from the altar. If he found a guard sleeping, he would heap those hot coals on him, causing the guard to wake up, discard his clothing and run naked through the streets.[1] Take a close look at Revelation 16:15:

Behold, I am coming like a thief. Blessed is the one who stays awake and keeps his clothes, so that he will not walk about naked and men will not see his shame.

Revelation 16:15

If you did not know the Jewish tradition of calling the High Priest a "thief in the night" you would not understand that scripture. To whom is Jesus coming like a thief? To those who are asleep, not to those who are awake. The watchful church should recognize the signs of His coming, as Paul says in 1 Thessalonians. This is also emphasized with Jesus' own words in Revelation 16:15.

The second coming language in this discourse becomes clear when you realize God's wrath will fall on those in Sardis who are dead.

> *But the day of the Lord will come like a thief, in which the heavens will pass away with a roar and the elements will be destroyed with intense heat, and the earth and its works will be burned up.*
>
> *2 Peter 3:10*

At the second coming, our High Priest will heap burning coals on the earth. The warning to Sardis is clear. "If you do not wake up, I will come like a thief." God's wrath will fall, and you will be unprepared.

We don't know what caused this church to die, but we do know they had a reputation of being alive. Perhaps they are like many in the church today. They go to church for moral reasons or social factors. They say they believe but when push comes to shove, they know little of the truth. They may take their Bible to church, but they don't open it at home. The dead church attends worship services, but they don't feel any zeal for their Savior. They may have confessed their love once, but nothing in their lives really changed. They think they know the truth, but they have never truly met Him.

All the dead church is doing is going through the motions.

How alike are we to the church of Sardis? How many of us rely on the "once saved always saved" notion? If we have confessed Christ as a child, does that mean we achieve eternal salvation even if we never know the truth? If we walk through life "dead" in the faith, are we ever really saved?

Take a look at John 10:28:

> *And I give eternal life to them, and they will never perish; and no one will snatch them out of My hand.*
>
> *John 10:28*

50

This is the verse that people quote to support the theory that once you "say the sinner's prayer" you are "in" so to speak. Remember what we said about not looking at a verse in isolation? You need to back up one verse to John 10:27:

> My sheep hear My voice, and I know them, and they follow Me.
>
> *John 10:27*

The once-saved-always-saved notion is very dangerous. Once I heard of a lady who said her son would get to heaven even though he was a practicing Wiccan. Why did she say this? She said he had said the sinner's prayer as a child. This is a difficult discussion, and you need to make up your own mind, but let's look at a few other scriptures, shall we? First, we need to see if scripture gives any indication of what we can look for to see if someone is truly "with Him."

> *"Beware of the false prophets, who come to you in sheep's clothing, but inwardly are ravenous wolves. You will know them by their fruits. Grapes are not gathered from thorn bushes nor figs from thistles, are they? So every good tree bears good fruit, but the bad tree bears bad fruit. A good tree cannot produce bad fruit, nor can a bad tree produce good fruit. Every tree that does not bear good fruit is cut down and thrown into the fire. So then, you will know them by their fruits."*
>
> *Matthew 7:15-20*

> *What use is it, my brethren, if someone says he has faith but he has no works? Can that faith save him? If a brother or sister is without clothing and in need of daily food, and one of you says to them, "Go in peace, be warmed and be filled," and yet you do not give them what is necessary for their body, what use is that? Even so faith, if it has no works, is dead, being by itself. But someone may well say, "You have faith and I have works; show me your faith without the works, and I will show you my faith by my works." You believe that God is one. You do well; the demons also believe, and shudder. But are*

you willing to recognize, you foolish fellow, that faith
without works is useless?

James 2:14-20

To be sure, only faith saves us, but as James says, faith without deeds is dead – dead like Sardis. If you have true faith, you will want to do something with that faith. Faith should live for Jesus. It should strive to help. It should want to improve someone's life. It should desire for those around them to know the truth about Jesus. To be sure, each person's calling is different. Some are called to be stay-at-home moms. Others are called to be Billy Grahams. Whatever you are called to do, do it with all your might for Jesus. And then, my faithful friends, even if you do not know it, you will produce fruit. If you do not, take a look at Jesus words:

> *"The axe is already laid at the root of the trees; therefore every tree that does not bear good fruit is cut down and thrown into the fire."*

Matthew 3:10

So, what is the answer? What do we do? How can we be a tree that bears "good fruit?"

> *"I am the vine, you are the branches; he who abides in Me and I in him, he bears much fruit, for apart from Me you can do nothing. If anyone does not abide in Me, he is thrown away as a branch and dries up; and they gather them, and cast them into the fire and they are burned."*

John 15:5-6

We have to remain, or abide, in the vine – Jesus. And if we don't remain or abide in the vine we are thrown into the fire. This is second coming language, faithful friends. As scripture says, Jesus will keep a firm hold on us, but that doesn't mean we can't turn and walk away from Him.

How alike are we to Sardis? Do we put our faith into action? Do we study His Word or do we let it sit dusty on our shelves? Do we look forward to attending church or do we attend church out of duty? Do we profess Him or do we deny Him by our words and the way we live when we are outside of the church's walls? How many of us are dead inside, just going through another day?

52

I fear churches today are filled with those from Sardis. Let's pray for revival, my faithful friends. Jesus commends a few people in Sardis who had not gotten their garments soiled. Jesus says these saints would walk with Him for they are worthy. There is a point for us to understand here: we can be attending a church environment or be friends with a group of believers that could match one of the descriptions in Revelation, but that doesn't mean we have to look like them. We can remain faithful despite the environment surrounding us. Remember, Christian soldiers, we are in a war. Let's win the battle! Let's not become corrupt despite who or what surrounds us.

Jesus pleads with Sardis to overcome, telling her He can once again clothe her with white garments (righteousness). He also declares if they overcome He will not erase their name out of the book of life. What is the book of life?

Indeed, true companion, I ask you also to help these women who have shared my struggle in the cause of the gospel, together with Clement also and the rest of my fellow workers, whose names are in the book of life.
Philippians 4:3

The names of the saints are written in the book of life. To say it another way, those who have come to faith in Christ are written in the book of life. The confusion comes in when you look at scripture that defines the book of life in a slightly different way.

And nothing unclean, and no one who practices abomination and lying, shall ever come into it, but only those whose names are written in the Lamb's book of life.
Revelation 21:27

Some scholars believe there are two books of life: one book of life and another Lamb's book of life.[2] They maintain that when you are born you are written in the book of life and your name is blotted out if you do not come to faith in Christ. They also say that when you do come to faith, you are written in the Lamb's book of life. They profess once your name is written in the Lamb's book of life it can never be blotted out. Again, they point to John 10:27-28 because it says, "no one can snatch them out of my hand." However, as we have already discussed, it also says the sheep have to "follow" His voice. If the sheep do not follow – or stop following – are they His sheep? Let's look at Revelation 3:5 again:

> *He who overcomes will thus be clothed in white garments;*
> *and I will not erase his name from the book of life, and I*
> *will confess his name before My Father and before His*
> *angels.*
>
> *Revelation 3:5*

Here Jesus indicates those in Sardis can be blotted out of the book. He is talking to people in the church! This verse argues the point that those who once professed Christ can walk away from His truth and be blotted out. "If what you heard from the beginning abides in you, you also will abide in the Son and in the Father" (1 John 2:24b). If you once profess Christ and then turn away, are you ever really saved in the first place? There are arguments on both sides of this issue, but Jesus indicates in Revelation that names can be blotted out.

So are there two books or one book? Here is what I believe: there is only one way you can have life – Jesus. "I am the way, the truth, and the life" (John 14:6). The only way you are written in the book of life is when you are under a covenant relationship with Christ. When scripture calls the "book of life" the "Lamb's book of life" it is just clarifying the way to life!

Again, I will let you make up your mind whether or not there are two books of life or one book of life, but it seems to me if you once professed belief, like those in the Sardis church, and become dead (or stay dead), you can be blotted out.[3] As Jesus said:

> *"Many will say to Me on that day, 'Lord, Lord, did we not*
> *prophesy in Your name, and in Your name cast out*
> *demons, and in Your name perform many miracles?' and*
> *then I will declare to them, 'I never knew you; depart from*
> *Me, you who practice lawlessness.'"*
>
> *Matthew 7:22-23*

In eternity, we will be shocked at the faces we see and the faces we don't. Only God can judge the heart (1 Kings 8:39).

Let's not become like Sardis faithful friends. A dead believer is not a believer at all.

Thought for the day:
I find it interesting that zombies, or the walking dead, have become so popular theses days, because in actuality, the walking dead do exist. If you do not have Jesus, you do not have "the life" because He is the life (John 14:6). You are dead – dead like Sardis. There are many walking dead in the world today. There are many in the church. You know some of them. What are you going to do about it?

1 Blitz, Mark. A DVD study entitled *Feasts of the Lord*. (El Shaddai Ministries, 2008), 20. See also www.elshaddaiministries.us

2 Lahaye, Tim. *Revelation Unveiled* (Grand Rapids, Michigan: Zondervan Publishing House, 1999), 352. This is a great commentary chapter by chapter of Revelation. Tim Lahaye is of the pre-tribulation rapture view and this book is a must have for further research on this position.

3 For other scriptures on the book of life see Ex 32:32, Deut 29:19-21, Ps 69:28, 139:16, Daniel 12:1-2, Phil 4:3, Rev 3:5, 13:8, 17:8, 20:12, 20:15, 21:27, 22:19.

[7]"And to the angel of the church in Philadelphia write: He who is holy, who is true, who has the key of David, who opens and no one will shut, and who shuts and no one opens, says this: [8]'I know your deeds. Behold, I have put before you an open door which no one can shut, because you have a little power, and have kept My word, and have not denied My name. [9]Behold, I will cause those of the synagogue of Satan, who say that they are Jews and are not, but lie – I will make them come and bow down at your feet, and make them know that I have loved you. [10]Because you have kept the word of My perseverance, I also will keep you from the hour of testing, that hour which is about to come upon the whole world, to test those who dwell on the earth. [11]I am coming quickly; hold fast what you have, so that no one will take your crown. [12]He who overcomes, I will make him a pillar in the temple of My God, and he will not go out from it anymore; and I will write on him the name of My God, and the name of the city of My God, the new Jerusalem, which comes down out of heaven from My God, and My new name. [13]He who has an ear, let him hear what the Spirit says to the churches."

Revelation 3:7-13

There is no warning given to the church of Philadelphia, but unlike Smyrna (the other faithful church Jesus warned would go through testing) there is no tribulation associated with this unblemished church. This is a good reminder for us. Both Smyrna and Philadelphia were a faithful witness to the truth, yet one was undergoing intense persecution and the other was not. Do not despair if you are enduring hardships; one of the signs of a faithful church is tribulation. You do not have to be undergoing tribulation to be deemed faithful, like Philadelphia, but tribulation can be a result of faithfulness. Take heart and know that tribulation in general is not any indicator of our Lord's disapproval; our perseverance in Christ at times of great difficulty is extraordinarily pleasing to our Lord.

Jesus identifies Himself as the one who is holy, true and has the key of David. What is the key of David? This key stands in stark contrast to the "keys of death and of Hades" Jesus holds in

Revelation 1:18. Based on this, the obvious interpretation is David's key is the key to life, the city of God, and more broadly heaven itself.

However, when Jesus says to Philadelphia, "I have put before you an open door which no one can shut," it doesn't sound like Jesus is referring to a passageway to the city of God. It just doesn't fit the context of the scripture. The church is still grounded on earth and the rapture has yet to occur. It appears the "open door' is there to immediately benefit the church on earth. Some scholars believe the "open door" symbolizes missionary opportunities based on other scriptures such as Colossians 4:3:

> *Praying at the same time for us as well, that God will open up to us a door for the word, so that we may speak forth the mystery of Christ, for which I have also been imprisoned.*
>
> *Colossians 4:3*

Is Jesus telling the church of little strength that many missionary opportunities will be available to her? Again, this doesn't exactly fit the context.

There seems to be something more going on here. The key in Jesus' hand is assumed to be used to open the door Jesus is describing. Jerusalem and the Jewish nation as a whole have brought to light the truth, as had David, a man after God's own heart (1 Samuel 13:14, Acts 13:22). It was David who wrote many of the Psalms and proclaimed many of the truths about God. Jesus says He is holding the key of David. Could the open door Jesus has set before this church be understanding the truth of His Word? I believe it is. It is unlocking the mysteries; it is revelation!

But is this theory consistent with scripture? Let's take a look at Jesus' own words:

> *"Woe to you lawyers! For you have taken away the key of knowledge; you yourselves did not enter, and you hindered those who were entering."*
>
> *Luke 11:52*

The key of knowledge could unlock the door of understanding. When Jesus opens the door for a church or an individual to understand the scriptures no one can shut it again. He tells Philadelphia He knows she has a "little strength" but the open door before them, the Word of the Lord and hope in that Word, would give them the strength they need to overcome. Ultimately, our hope in His Word is the city of God. When we unlock the scriptures and go through the door open to us in those scriptures, we begin to see clearly God's plan, our future and hope – spending an eternity with Jesus in the city of God. I do love God's Word. May He open it to us as He promises to Philadelphia.

Jesus also knows those who professed to be Jews were wearing Philadelphia out, nipping at her heals if you will. We might even go so far as to say although this church wasn't undergoing physical persecution, she was enduring verbal persecution from the Jews. She was tired and worn, but she was not denying her Savior.

In the end, these unbelieving Jews will bow at Philadelphia's feet as Jesus the King of kings and Lord of lords professes His love for her. Can you imagine the day? This is the final reckoning, the final triumph of Jesus over Satan. I am getting chills just thinking about it. Someone needs to shout, "Hallelujah!"

How alike are we to Philadelphia? Those of us who are running the race marked out for us (Hebrews 12:1-2), who are trying our best to follow our Lord's call, are worn out! We are trying our best to let our light shine, yet the world around us is beating us down at every turn. Jesus says, "I have put before you an open door." Jesus encourages His bride to look in His Word, see the truth, and understand that He will return to claim her. "Hold fast to this! Hold fast to Me!" He says.

"Do not let your heart be troubled; believe in God, believe also in Me. In My Father's house are many dwelling places; if it were not so, I would have told you; for I go to prepare a place for you. If I go and prepare a place for you, I will come again and receive you to Myself, that where I am, there you may be also."

John 14:1-3

Philadelphia had also kept "the word of My perseverance." This phrase is a difficult one. What does it mean? The Greek word for perseverance is "upomone." It means, "A man who is not swerved from his deliberate purpose and his loyalty to faith and piety by even the greatest trials and sufferings; a patient, steadfast waiting for; a patient enduring." No matter what had happened to this church, no matter what individual believers had suffered, she was enduring in the truth. We could ask, "Patient enduring for what?" For the return of Christ! For the sound of the bridegroom's voice calling His bride home. The ultimate truth of scripture is the return of the King. He will call us home and until then we have to keep His perseverance. We need to focus, just like Jesus, on the end of the road, no matter what lies in our path, even if it is a cross.

We know the end is coming and we know there will be a time when He will call us home. Glory Hallelujah! May we be like Philadelphia, sweet Lord Jesus! "As the deer pants for the water brooks, so my soul pants for You, O God" (Psalms 42:1).

Because Philadelphia kept His perseverance, Jesus says He will keep her from the hour of testing that is to come over the whole earth. Remember, these letters are talking to the church throughout the ages, and most especially the church of the final generation. The hour of testing is the end time persecution of the saints.

When the Lamb broke the fifth seal, I saw underneath the altar the souls of those who had been slain because of the word of God, and because of the testimony which they had maintained.

Revelation 6:9

There will be a mass persecution of Christians in the end times. Even now, believers around the world are being killed for their faith. In America this has not yet occurred, but in other cultures it is commonplace.

If we carry that "open door" visual still further we can see why Jesus puts before Philadelphia this door. If the scriptures are "open" they are understood and the end time church of Philadelphia will recognize what is about to come on the face of the earth. Because of her perseverance, the open door will provide a clear path for this church to be protected from the persecution to come. She will know what is coming and she will be prepared.

He says to her, "I am coming quickly" to give her encouragement because of her little strength. The end time church of Philadelphia will be worn out, but she will know that her Savior will soon come. Hallelujah!

Jesus tells her to hold fast to what she has, so that no one can take her crown. He will make her a pillar in the temple of God and on her He will write the name of the city of God and Jesus' new name. In the tabernacle, there were pillars holding up the linen cloth that shrouded the courtyards and the Holy Place. There was only one way in (Jesus) and the pillars represented churches and individuals that held up God's truth.

> *I write so that you will know how one ought to conduct himself in the household of God, which is the church of the living God, the pillar and support of the truth.*
>
> *1 Timothy 3:15b*

If the Philadelphia church overcame, they would become pillars in the New Jerusalem (Revelation 3:12). Jesus would even write on her the name of God's city and Jesus' new name.

Thought for the day:
The key to the door of knowledge is available to the church. Jesus is holding out His hand, trying to give it to those who want it. If you are holding this book, you have the key to Revelation. The question is: Will you continue to turn the pages to unlock your understanding? Tomorrow we meet a church completely unlike Philadelphia. Jesus wants to "spit them out of His mouth." Part of the reason? They stopped seeking Him. They stopped turning the page.

[14]"To the angel of the church in Laodicea write: The Amen, the faithful and true Witness, the Beginning of the creation of God, says this: [15]'I know your deeds, that you are neither cold nor hot; I wish that you were cold or hot. [16]So because you are lukewarm, and neither hot nor cold, I will spit you out of My mouth. [17]Because you say, 'I am rich, and have become wealthy, and have need of nothing,' and you do not know that you are wretched and miserable and poor and blind and naked, [18]I advise you to buy from Me gold refined by fire so that you may become rich, and white garments so that you may clothe yourself, and that the shame of your nakedness will not be revealed; and eye salve to anoint your eyes so that you may see. [19]Those whom I love, I reprove and discipline; therefore be zealous and repent. [20]Behold, I stand at the door and knock; if anyone hears My voice and opens the door, I will come in to him and will dine with him, and he with Me. [21]He who overcomes, I will grant to him to sit down with Me on My throne, as I also overcame and sat down with My Father on His throne. [22]He who has an ear, let him hear what the Spirit says to the churches.'"

Revelation 3:14-22

There is not one good thing to say about Laodicea. There are not even a few faithful witnesses to commend like those in the dead church of Sardis. Everyone at Laodicea had become lukewarm. Jesus declares himself the "faithful and true Witness, the Beginning of the creation of God." He is telling Laodicea He is omniscient and He sees her state. He declares her neither hot nor cold. He goes so far as to say, "I will spit you out of My mouth." Why? What had this church done?

There are two ways of interpreting the "hot and cold" quality of this church. First we need to examine something that many people do not know about the ancient city of Laodicea: it had a spring with lukewarm water. There was a place not far from Laodicea with hot springs, the kind you would want to tentatively sink into to sooth your aching muscles and relieve tired joints. Another place nearby had a refreshing cold spring – the kind you would look forward to after a long day of travel to quench your thirst. In Laodicea these two sources of water became mixed and resulted in something not so fabulous. Laodicea's water was lukewarm.[1]

Have you ever drunk a glass of lukewarm water? Hot water is good for tea and coffee, cold water is refreshing, but lukewarm? It is horrific. If you think you are drinking something hot or cold and taste something lukewarm, you spit it out! Jesus is saying how can you, who once knew Me so well, become so disinterested? Jesus could be saying to this church: Be cold and refreshing, be passionate and hot for my truth, but don't be apathetic! The people who lived in Laodicea would have understood this. They knew about the hot springs and the cold springs. They also knew that their water was not so great. They would have instantly gotten the visual.

I do believe there is a deeper meaning we need to explore. Would Jesus say to us, "I would rather you be really good (cool and refreshing), or really good (on fire for me), not in-between?" That, in essence, was what He was saying if His only intention was to declare "hot" and "cold" both "good." I believe the more the people of Laodicea pondered Jesus' words, the more they would have understood them to have a deeper spiritual meaning.

The majority of church-goers have interpreted "cold" to be apart from God, "hot" to be with God, and "lukewarm" to be indifferent or apathetic toward God. I think that is almost correct, with a slightly different twist. We are talking here to the churches, and we have really already seen a cold church, have we not?

Sardis was dead. The dead aren't hot. They aren't even lukewarm. They are cold.

Why are they cold? As we explored in the message to Sardis, they never got the truth (Jesus). They may have confessed faith, but they never truly had it. They are going through the motions, never really understanding their motions are missing the mark. These are the people who will be shocked when Jesus says, "Depart from me, I never knew you" (Matthew 7:23).

If "cold" in this context is "dead," what is hot? These are the believers who know Christ. They get the truth, are on fire for the truth, and are proclaiming the truth (Jesus).

So what is lukewarm? To be lukewarm, you must first be hot. The lukewarm believer was once on fire for the Lord, and then grows cold, knowing the truth, but not caring at all for the truth. Just like the spring in Laodicea, the lukewarm believer has become diluted.

It is bothersome, is it not? Would God really rather us be cold, never truly knowing Him, than to drift so far away when we were once so close? If this is truth, we need scripture. We need to look at the reason behind this truth. We need to understand the heart of God. Look at this next verse. Let it cut your soul.

Some people cannot be brought back again to a changed life. They were once in God's light, and enjoyed heaven's gifts, and shared in the Holy Spirit. They found out how good God's word is, and they received the powers of his new world. But they fell away from Christ. It is impossible to bring them back to a changed life again, because they are nailing the Son of God to a cross again and are shaming him in front of others.

Hebrews 6:4-6 NCV

If this is the deeper meaning behind the "hot" and "cold" reference, now we know why – hope. There is little hope of reconciliation to God if we once walk in the light and then reject it like it was nothing to us. But the dead believer, or the unbeliever, who has never experienced the truth, has a much better chance of accepting it. It is not that God would rather us never know Him, it is the fact that God knows if we know Him and reject Him, there is little chance of our return. Read Hebrews 6:4-6 again.

In other words, they believed in Christ, and then they turned away. They have seen God's light, yet they don't care about it. This has to be why Jesus was so angry with Laodicea. This is not a church member who is unaware of Christ's truth or His love – that is a cold believer. This is a church member who knows her Savior, was at one time on fire for her Savior, and then became uncaring about the same Savior! The lukewarm "believer" does not care! Look at Peter's words:

For if, after they have escaped the defilements of the world by the knowledge of the Lord and Savior Jesus Christ, they are again entangled in them and are overcome, the last state has become worse for them than the first. For it would be better for them not to have known the way of righteousness, than having known it, to turn away from the holy commandment handed on to them. It has happened to them according to the true

63

proverb, "A dog returns to its own vomit," and, "A sow, after washing, returns to wallowing in the mire."

2 Peter 2:20-22

Laodicea says to herself, "I am rich and have need of nothing." Laodicea's material wealth had dulled her fire for the Lord so much she was worthless. She didn't look to Jesus anymore; she relied on herself. She knew the truth but didn't care about that truth. She was happy the way she was. Jesus calls her "wretched and miserable and poor and blind and naked." Those are harsh words from our Lord. Laodicea was poor and miserable despite her wealth, blind to the truth, and without clothes!

As I have said previously, many scholars believe that the different churches are representative of different points in history. If you hold to this theory, Laodicea would be the last church of the age, or the church of our generation.

Ouch.

But is this not true? In America, the poorest among us are among the richest in the world. Have we become lukewarm, depending on our wealth and not our King? Have we allowed the culture surrounding us to compromise our fire and turn it lukewarm? If we were once on fire we need to examine ourselves to see where we now stand. A lukewarm fire is no fire at all. It is worthless.

Jesus counsels the church to buy gold refined in the fire, white garments, and eye salve. Let's take a look at these one at a time.

So that the proof of your faith, being more precious than gold which is perishable, even though tested by fire, may be found to result in praise and glory and honor at the revelation of Jesus Christ.

1 Peter 1:7

Let us rejoice and be glad and give the glory to Him, for the marriage of the Lamb has come and His bride has made herself ready. It was given to her to clothe herself in fine linen, bright and clean; for the fine linen is the righteous acts of the saints.

Revelation 19:7-8

On that day the deaf will hear words of a book, and out of their gloom and darkness the eyes of the blind will see.

Isaiah 29:18

"Find your faith, cloth yourself with righteousness, and see Me for who *I AM*," Jesus is saying to Laodicea. Then He says, "Those whom I love, I reprove and discipline; therefore be zealous and repent." Despite her pathetic state, Jesus still loves her. How many times do we believe we have failed and feel like God doesn't love us? This is not truth; it is a lie from the enemy (John 8:44). Has this ever happened to you? Listen to scripture.

The Lord appeared to him from afar, saying "I have loved you with an everlasting love; therefore I have drawn you with lovingkindness.

Jeremiah 31:3

God loves us despite the stains saturating us. Remember, it was to the stained He came the first time. He died for sinners, not for saints.

In the letter to Laodicea we see another reference to a door. Jesus stands at the door and knocks. This time, the door has to be opened by the church. Unlike Philadelphia where Jesus had already opened the door, in Laodicea Jesus is standing behind the door.

I was asleep but my heart was awake. A voice! My beloved was knocking: "Open to me, my sister, my darling, my dove, my perfect one! For my head is drenched with dew, my locks with the damp of the night."

Song of Songs 5:2

Just like in the Song of Songs, Jesus is knocking at the door, knowing the church was once awake, and urging her to reopen the door to fellowship. Also, Jesus is the Word (John 1:1). Laodicea cannot understand the Word because she has closed the door – leaving the One who can save her and give her insight on the other side. If the door represents understanding the scriptures, Laodicea is in the dark. She will not understand the signs of His coming. He will come to her like a thief.

Jesus pleads with Laodicea to overcome and tells her if she is faithful, she will sit down with Him on His throne. This is referring to the millennial reign of Christ (Revelation 20:4).

How do you think our society and our churches have become lukewarm? Has your love grown cold in any way? Is there any aspect of your life that could be rejuvenated with the fire of God? The answer to that question is very important. Here is why:

> *At that time many will fall away and will betray one another and hate one another. Many false prophets will arise and will mislead many. Because lawlessness in increased, most people's love will grow cold.*
>
> *Matthew 24:10-12*

In the last days, many people's fire will go out. This is a terrifying prophecy. Only those who were once with Christ can fall away. Laodicea had already fallen away. May we never close the door to our hearts. May we always focus on the return of our bridegroom. Jesus wants His bride to be ready, clothed in white, refined, and looking up. He wants her pacing in her bedroom, looking outside for any sign of His return. The dead church will be asleep; the lukewarm church may hear the bridegroom's call. but when she wakes up it will be too late. She will try her best to put on her bridal gown, but she will be unable. She is naked and her clothes are no longer in sight.

Only the pacing bride, with eyes wide open, will be able to run into the streets, lift up her hands and shout, "My bridegroom! I have been watching and waiting and finally you have come!"

Amen and Amen. Come quickly, Lord Jesus!

Thought for the day:
Tomorrow we enter the throne room of God. If we had to enter today, would God find that we rely on Him, or like Laodicea, do we rely on our wealth and possessions to secure us? When you bow before a holy God, nothing will matter except you and Him. All other things will pass away.

1 Vander Laan, Ray. *Faith Lessons on the Early Church: Conquering the Gates of Hell*, Volume 5 (Colorado Springs, Colorado: Focus on the Family, 1999). Faith Lessons is a 7 Volume DVD study that is exceptional.

"To him who overcomes, I will grant to eat of the tree of life
which is in the Paradise of God . . . He who overcomes will not
be hurt by the second death . . . To him who overcomes, to him I
will give some of the hidden manna, and I will give him a white
stone, and a new name written on the stone which no one knows
but he who receives it . . . He who overcomes, and he who keeps
My deeds until the end, to him I will give authority over the
nations; and he shall rule them with a rod of iron, as the vessels
of the potter are broken to pieces, as I also have received
authority from My Father; and I will give him the morning star
. . . He who overcomes will thus be clothed in white garments;
and I will not erase his name from the book of life, and I will
confess his name before My Father and before His angels . . . He
who overcomes, I will make him a pillar in the temple of My
God, and he will not go out from it anymore; and I will write on
him the name of My God, and the name of the city of My God,
the new Jerusalem, which comes down out of heaven from My
God, and My new name . . . He who overcomes, I will grant to
him to sit down with Me on My throne, as I also overcame and
sat down with My Father on His throne . . ."
Revelation 2:7, 11, 17, 26-28, 3:5, 12, 21

We have come through the churches, and they were probably
fairly painful for some of us. But here is where we need to stop and
pause and look at one more thing in the letters. Notice in all of the
seven letters, even to the faithful witnesses in Smyrna and
Philadelphia, Jesus urges those reading to "overcome." Let me say
that again. In every single letter Jesus urges believers to overcome.
The question is, overcome what?

> *"These things I have spoken to you, so that in Me you may
> have peace. In the world you have tribulation, but take
> courage; I have overcome the world."*
> *John 16:33*

Here again, in Jesus own words, He tells us we will have
tribulation (see Revelation 1:9) and He also tells us what we need to
overcome – the world. We have to live with a victorious faith. We

have to overcome complacency (Ephesus), tribulation (Smyrna), idolatry (Pergamum), false teaching (Thyatira), dead faith (Sardis), weariness (Philadelphia), and lukewarmness (Laodicea). Now let's look at another verse in Revelation:

> *He who overcomes will inherit these things, and I will be his God and he will be My son.*
>
> *Revelation 21:7*

Overcomers inherit God's kingdom. Those who sleep do not. So the question is, how do we overcome the world? I mean, that is a tall task. Are we strong enough for that? No, we are not. Let me say that again. We aren't strong enough. Now look at 1 John 5:4:

> *"For whoever is born of God overcomes the world; and this is the victory that has overcome the world – our faith."*
>
> *1 John 5:4*

This is the good news. Jesus overcame. All we have to do is have faith in Him and remain in Him (John 15:5). That is it. That is what Ephesus, Pergamum, Thyatira, Sardis, and Laodicea did not do. They drifted away from Him. They let others lead them astray. They allowed the world to lead them astray. So the question is, how do we remain in Him?

Remember the sower with the seed (Matthew 13:18-23)? Let's take a look at a portion of that passage.

> *The one on whom seed was sown on the rocky places, this is the man who hears the word and immediately receives it with joy; yet he has no firm root in himself, but is only temporary, and when affliction or persecution arises because of the word, immediately he falls away.*
>
> *Matthew 13:20-21*

This is important, especially in the last days. This scripture paints a picture of someone who receives the Word with joy, seeing Jesus for who He is, but then when persecution comes, they fall away. This shallow believer is not Smyrna, for Smyrna did not turn from Jesus when persecution arose. This believer falls away – like Laodicea. The key to understanding what happened to this person is in Ephesians 3:17.

So that Christ may dwell in your hearts through faith; and that you, being rooted and grounded in love.

Ephesians 3:17

There are those who receive the Word with joy, but then troubles come and they fall away because they have no root. Let me translate: they fall away because they have no love. They do not love Him. They may obey for a time, they may follow for a time, but ultimately, when the rubber meets the road, they do not love Him. They may believe, but they do not love, and without love you have no root, and without a root you will not stay planted. You will fall away. The secret to following Him? Love Him. I don't know about you, but I find that extremely doable. He is a fairly lovable Savior.

Now think about this, if you love someone, what do you do? You spend time with them. If you are in a relationship with someone, you want to see them, be with them, and enjoy their company.

God isn't a physical presence in our lives, so how do we spend time with him? Good question.

"If you continue in My word, then you are truly disciples of mine."

John 8:31b

One way to remain in Him is to remain in the Word (Jesus). If you remain in the Word, you will not be fooled by false teachers because you will know His truth. You will not be led away by the world if you know His promises. You will shun lukewarmness because you see His light. You will cry out to dead believers because you understand His hope.

If you read my letter at the beginning of this devotional, you might remember a very important verse:

Now these were more nobleminded than those in Thessalonica, for they received the word with great eagerness, examining the Scriptures daily to see whether things were so.

Acts 17:11

People who are nobleminded will examine the scriptures daily and with eagerness.

What else can we do to build the relationship?

With all prayer and petition pray at all times in the Spirit,
and with this in view, be on the alert with all perseverance
and petition for all the saints.

Ephesians 6:18

The above verse says "pray at all times." Now this doesn't mean getting down on your knees twenty-four hours a day, but what it does mean is to be in constant communication. Sometimes we feel our prayers need to be complicated. Our prayers can simply be a silent, "Help me, Lord." Or a "Wow, thank you God." When you get up in the morning and see a beautiful sunrise, what Ephesians 6:18 is telling you to do is just take a moment and tell God how amazing you think He is. This creates a communication – a relationship – with the God of the universe.

That is what is truly miraculous. God, the creator of all things, wants a relationship with you. He wants to spend time with you. He wants you to walk with Him – daily.

Let's go back to the Garden of Eden for a minute.

They heard the sound of the Lord God walking in the
garden in the cool of the day . . .

Genesis 3:8a

God walked in Eden. He came to meet Adam and Eve "in the cool of the day." Try to wrap your minds around that. God wants to walk with you – not once a month, or once a week, but daily. During this study, we will see that God hasn't given up on His perfect plan of Eden. In fact, He wants this earth to return to Eden.

Indeed, the Lord will comfort Zion; He will comfort all
her waste places. And her wilderness He will make like
Eden, and her desert like the garden of the Lord; joy and
gladness will be found in her, thanksgiving and sound of a
melody.

Isaiah 51:3

Let's learn from the letters to the churches. Remain in Him by strengthening your relationship with Him. Study His Word and talk to Him. He wants to meet with you daily.

"He who has an ear let him hear what the Spirit says to the churches!"

The bride does not want to be surprised by His coming and find out she isn't wearing bridal attire at all.

Thought for the day:

What can you do today that can strengthen your relationship with the God of the universe? He wants a relationship with you more than anything else you can do for Him. If you fail to establish a relationship, are you truly with Him? Or like the man in the parable, have you no root? Tomorrow we start learning about the rapture. If you have no root, when the trumpet sounds, you will be left behind.

[1]After these things I looked, and behold, a door standing open in heaven, and the first voice which I had heard, like the sound of a trumpet speaking with me, said, "Come up here, and I will show you what must take place after these things."

Revelation 4:1

Hold onto your seats, faithful friends, we are now entering the throne room of God. The voice that John first heard now calls him to heaven. Can you imagine being called to heaven for a vision of revelation from our Lord? The thought is overwhelming. The voice tells John "I will show you what must take place after these things." After what things? After the present reality of the churches John saw in chapters two and three. This begins the revelation of the future or the "things that will take place after these things" (Revelation 1:19). The events that will be unlocked in the following chapters are foreshadowed throughout scripture, from Genesis through Jude. These are the end time events that will usher in the millennial reign of our Lord and Savior Jesus Christ.

Most scholars believe the opening of chapter four ushers in the beginning of the final years on earth before the return of the King. We know from Daniel that there will be a period of seven years at the end of history that will usher in the Millennial Kingdom of Christ. If you have studied end time events, you have probably heard of something called "the tribulation." When people use those words they are referring to these final seven years. The study of Daniel is far too complicated to get into here. If you want to study more about Daniel's prophecies, pick up the Daniel study by Beth Moore. You won't be disappointed.[1]

As we move forward, you will see how the future seven-year time frame carved out in Daniel matches the time frame we are about to study in Revelation. But for now, I do want you to see Daniel 9:27. This is the verse in Daniel that specifically talks about the final seven-year period.

> *He will confirm a covenant with many for one 'seven.' In the middle of the 'seven' he will put an end to sacrifice and offering. And on a wing of the temple he will set up*

an abomination that causes desolation, until the end that is decreed is poured out on him.

Daniel 9:27 NIV

The "he" in this scripture is the Antichrist. Because Israel is the subject of this section of scripture the "many" refers to the nation of Israel. In other words, the Antichrist will confirm a covenant with the nation of Israel for seven years. In the middle of that seven-year period, he will break the covenant and put up an abomination in the Jewish temple. Hence, from this scripture we learn a variety of things:

- The Antichrist will make a treaty with Israel for a seven-year period.
- In the middle of the seven-year period he will break the treaty. Then he will try to make Israel desolate. In other words, he will bring war.
- In the middle of the seven-year period, he will set up an abomination in the Jewish temple. From Matthew 24:15-16 we learn that this is the sign for Israel to flee: "Therefore when you see the abomination of desolation which was spoken of through Daniel the prophet, standing in the holy place (let the reader understand), then those who are in Judea must flee to the mountains."
- Because he sets up the abomination in the Jewish Temple, the Jewish Temple must be rebuilt before the mid-point of the final seven-year period.
- The end (God's wrath) will be poured out on him. God will have the victory!

Please do not get too overwhelmed with this right now. We will study all of this in detail as we move further in the study. For now it is important to understand that the remaining chapters of Revelation are written to clarify what will transpire during those final seven years.

On the following page, you will see a basic chart we will work from in the days to come. We will expand on this chart throughout the study to show where we are on the final seven-year timeline. Because Revelation is descriptive of those years, our Savior's words about the end times will become increasingly more understandable the closer we get to the starting point of the final seven-year period.

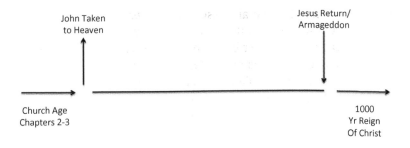

I know the question at the forefront of everyone's mind – when do we get our ticket out of here? No one wants to be here during those final seven years, and most of us have been taught that we won't be.

The word "rapture" doesn't appear in scripture; what we do see is the phrase "caught up" (1 Thessalonians 4:17). The Greek word "harpazo," which we translate "caught up," means to seize, carry off by force, to snatch out or away. We get the word rapture from the Latin word "rapturo" which is a translation of the Greek "harpazo."

Many scholars believe the rapture is right here in Revelation 4:1. This theory, called the pre-tribulation rapture position, has become well known because of some prominent people who hold to this view. Some very popular books and movies have been written based on this theory. Why is this theory called the pre-tribulation position? Those holding to this view have named the final seven years on earth "the tribulation" and because they believe the church will be raptured before the final seven years, it has been named the pre-tribulation theory.

I put "the tribulation" in quotes because I do not hold to this view. I believe the seven years will, without a doubt, hold some horrifically bad times, but not all of them should be categorized as "tribulation." We will study this when we study Revelation chapter six. For our purposes today, we need to get a good understanding of the pre-tribulation rapture position because the majority of Christians have accepted this theory, partially because it is the only one they have ever been taught.

As we move further into Revelation we will see three distinct series of "judgments" that fall upon the earth – the seals in chapter six, the trumpets in chapters eight and nine, and the bowls in chapter sixteen. Because of their severity those holding to the pre-tribulation view believe we will be raptured before the final seven-year period. They believe all these "judgments" are "the wrath of God." We will look at this theory in more detail on the next page. For now realize this: Pre-Tribulation proponents believe the seals, the trumpets, and the bowls are all God's wrath. Now let's look at some things the pre-tribulationists point out that they believe substantiates their theory.

Pre-Tribulation Rapture Theory Point One
We Aren't Destined for Wrath

Let's look at some verses.

Much more then, having now been justified by His blood, we shall be saved from the wrath of God through Him.
Romans 5:9

And to wait for His Son from heaven, whom He raised from the dead, that is Jesus, who rescues us from the wrath to come.
1 Thessalonians 1:10

For God has not destined us for wrath, but for obtaining salvation through our Lord Jesus Christ.
1 Thessalonians 5:9

These scriptures assure us we will be rescued or saved from God's wrath! There is no reason to think we are still here when God's wrath falls.

Pre-Tribulation Rapture Theory Point Two
The Open Door Indicates The Rapture

Pre-tribulation proponents believe John represents the church as a whole and when he is called to heaven at the beginning of chapter four, this represents the rapture. Look at Revelation 4:1 again.

Behold, a door standing open in heaven, and the first voice which I had heard . . . said, "Come up here, and I will show you what must take place after these things."
Revelation 4:1

75

In other words, John is the "church" and he is "raptured" to heaven before the opening of the seals. The only other time heaven is seen "open" is in Revelation 19 when Jesus returns with His saints. "And I saw heaven opened, and behold, a white horse, and He who sat on it is called Faithful and True, and in righteousness He judges and wages war" (Revelation 19:11). Hence, a door in heaven opens for the rapture at the beginning of chapter four, then heaven opens when Jesus returns.

Pre-Tribulation Rapture Theory Point Three
Israel is the Stated Purpose of End Time Events

Pre-tribulation proponents also reason Israel is the stated purpose of the final seven-year period according to Daniel chapter nine, hence the church should not be here when those final years begin. Let's look at this.

> *In the first year of his reign, I, Daniel, observed in the books the number of the years which was revealed as the word of the Lord to Jeremiah the prophet for the completion of the desolations of Jerusalem, namely, seventy years.*
>
> *Daniel 9:2*

An angel comes and answers Daniel's prayer in Daniel 9:24. The angel specifies "your people" (the Israelites) and the "holy city" (Jerusalem). Pre-tribulation proponents also point to the fact that after chapter three, the word "church" does not appear in any other chapter of Revelation. Hence, they say, the church is not present after chapter four where John is ushered into heaven. The focus then, of the end times, is solely on Israel.

Pre-Tribulation Rapture Theory Point Four
God Wouldn't let the Church Go Through Such Horrific Times

Another pre-tribulation argument for placing the rapture before the breaking of the seals is that God will not allow the church to go through such a horrific time. The "tribulation" is full of war, terror, famine, pestilence, and death. Pre-tribulation theorists hold that the church would not be persecuted so severely.

76

Pre-Tribulation Rapture Theory Point Five
The Day and the Hour No One Knows

Other pre-tribulation arguments stem from the "imminent coming" of Jesus. They claim there is nothing we can watch for that would lead us to conclude His return is near. They point to the fact that the early church was expecting Jesus' return at any moment. Let's look at some scriptures.

But of that day and hour no one knows, not even the angels of heaven, nor the Son, but the Father alone.

Matthew 24:36

Therefore be patient, brethren, until the coming of the Lord. The farmer waits for the precious produce of the soil, being patient about it, until it gets the early and late rains. You too be patient; strengthen your hearts, for the coming of the Lord is near.

James 5:7-8

Pre-tribulationists claim that the rapture has to come before the final seven years or we would "know" that He was about to return.

Are there any problems with the pre-tribulation rapture theory as we know it so far? No, not really. At face value, this theory looks very good. It actually gives you "warm fuzzies" does it not?[2] This theory says we are rescued before the rise of the Antichrist. We are rescued before any catastrophic event predicted from the foundation of the world ever takes place. If that doesn't give you a smile, I don't know what will. We will look at the counterarguments tomorrow.

Thought for the day:
Many believe the pre-tribulation rapture position. That means they believe they will be raptured to heaven before the Antichrist rises up. What if the pre-tribulation rapture position is wrong? Will anyone recognize the Antichrist for who he is? Or will they accept him as "good" if they haven't been raptured? If the pre-tribulation rapture position is wrong, will you be prepared emotionally for what is to come on the face of the earth? Find out about another rapture position tomorrow, one that says we are here for the Antichrist's persecution.

1 Moore, Beth. DVD study *Daniel: Lives of Integrity, Words of Prophecy* (Nashville, Tennessee: LifeWay Press, 2006). This is by far one of the best Bible studies I have ever completed.

2 A phrase coined by one of my bible study students, Chris Register. "Nic, the pre-trib view gives me warm-fuzzies, but it is looking more and more like pre-wrath is right!" This is a shout out to Chris!

¹After these things I looked, and behold, a door standing open in heaven, and the first voice which I had heard, like the sound of a trumpet speaking with me, said, "Come up here, and I will show you what must take place after these things."

Revelation 4:1

Now let's look at another theory in depth, shall we? This theory is called the pre-wrath theory. It was made popular by Robert Van Kampen.¹ Let's go through the pre-tribulation points one by one and compare the theories.

We Aren't Destined for Wrath - AGREED

The pre-wrath theory does not disagree that we are not destined for God's wrath; they emphatically agree. Where the two theories differ is at what point in the event timeline they place God's wrath. Are the seals, trumpets, and bowls all God's wrath? In other words, are all the "bad things" happening in Revelation descriptive of God's wrath? Those holding the pre-wrath view don't think so. They believe that the seals in Revelation chapter six are describing the rise of the Antichrist and Satan's end time governmental system. Pre-wrath proponents believe the wrath of God does not fall until the end of chapter six, when the wrath of God is first announced (Revelation 6:16). Hence the rapture does not have to take place before the seven years start, only before the trumpet judgments of Revelation chapters eight and nine begin. The pre-wrath theory says the church is here for the opening of the seals in chapter six.

The Door – Rapture or Understanding?

Pre-tribulation proponents say that John represents the church when he is called to heaven in Revelation 4:1. Pre-wrath would say: "But John is one man, not a great multitude. Wouldn't the raptured church appear a huge crowd before the throne? Can Jesus actually mean the entire church is being ushered to heaven through a door and represented by one man?" Let's look back at a verse we have already studied in Revelation.

> *"I know your deeds. Behold, I have put before you an open door which no one can shut, because you have a little power, and have kept My word, and have not denied My name."*
>
> *Revelation 3:8*

We said that this door probably represents an understanding of God's Word. If we take this theory from chapter three and apply it here, the open door in heaven could mean the "door" is really "the door of understanding." Do you remember the first five words of the book of Revelation?

> *The Revelation of Jesus Christ . . .*
>
> *Revelation 1:1*

The book of Revelation is a revelation! It is understanding! The "door" in Revelation 4:1 could very well mean that Jesus is giving John an understanding of the vision he is seeing. The door (understanding) is open and John is taken up to witness a revelation of our Lord.

Israel is the Stated Purpose of End Time Events – AGREED

We are now in what Jesus calls the times of the Gentiles (Luke 21:24). Think about it like this: chapters two and three of Revelation are the times of the Gentiles. Yes, the churches existed almost two thousand years ago, but types of these churches still exist today. The environments the letters are describing are the "times of the Gentiles."

> *For I do not want you, brethren, to be uninformed of this mystery – so that you will not be wise in your own estimation – that a partial hardening has happened to Israel until the fullness of the Gentiles has come in."*
>
> *Romans 11:25*

Although we are living in the "times of the Gentiles" that in no way excludes Israel from being around! Israel is still here despite

80

the fact God's current focus is on the Gentile nations. Even if Israel is the stated purpose of the final seven years, it in no way mutually excludes the church from being present during that time.

It is true the word "church" is not used after chapter three of Revelation but does this mean the church isn't around? We need to understand that many in the churches of chapters two and three are failing our Savior. They are not walking the talk. In other words, there are many in the church that are not the church. After chapter three of Revelation the words "elect" and "saint" are used over and over again. Let's look at a few scriptures.

He who has an ear, let him hear what the Spirit says to the churches.

Revelation 3:6

If anyone has an ear, let him hear. If anyone is destined for captivity, to captivity he goes; if anyone kills with the sword, with the sword he must be killed. Here is the perseverance and the faith of the saints.

Revelation 13:9-10

"He who has an ear, let him hear what the Spirit says to the churches," was in each and every letter in chapters two and three. It is also found in Revelation 13. Could the church still be here then? It seems the same message is given.

God's People Have Lived in Horrific Times Before

Another pre-tribulation argument for placing the rapture before the breaking of the seals is that God will not allow the church to go through such horrific times. If we look back in history, Christians were treated horribly. Even John, the writer of Revelation, said he was undergoing tribulation (Revelation 1:9). Let's read Hebrews 11:36-38:

And others experienced mockings and scourgings, yes, also chains and imprisonment. They were stoned, they were sawn in two, they were tempted, they were put to death with the sword; they went about in sheepskins, in goatskins, being destitute, afflicted, ill-treated (men of

81

whom the world was not worthy), wandering in deserts
and mountains and caves and holes in the ground
Hebrews 11:36-38

To say the church can't endure hard times insults those that are undergoing tribulation in the church today. And horrible persecution is occurring in many nations across the world.

Will We Not Know The Timing of Jesus' Return?

Does scripture teach the "imminent coming" of Jesus as the pre-tribulation theory suggests? They point to Matthew 24:36, but Jesus goes on to say the day of His coming will be just like the days of Noah. Noah knew the rain was coming. It was the unbelievers around Him who did not.

> *"But of that day and hour no one knows, not even the*
> *angels of heaven, nor the Son, but the Father alone. For*
> *the coming of the Son of Man will be just like the days of*
> *Noah. For as in those days before the flood they were*
> *eating and drinking, marrying and giving in marriage,*
> *until the day that Noah entered the ark. And they did not*
> *understand until the flood came and took them all away;*
> *so will the coming of the Son of Man be."*
> *Matthew 24:36-39*

Notice, Jesus says, "they did not understand." They – meaning those outside of the ark!

We "will not know the day and the hour" has been preached in churches for centuries. But is the context of this scripture represented accurately? Take a look at another verse that might contradict that theory:

> *But you, brethren, are not in darkness, that the day would*
> *overtake you like a thief; for you are all sons of light and*
> *sons of day. We are not of night nor of darkness; so then*
> *let us not sleep as others do, but let us be alert and sober.*
> *1 Thessalonians 5:4-6*

Wait a minute. Are we going to be surprised or are we going to be "alert" for His coming? We have to remember, "the sum of

Your word is truth" (Psalm 119:160a). Could it be that some will be surprised at His coming and others will be alert as we discussed in the letter to Sardis? Could it be that if we are sleeping we will be surprised, and if we are awake we will be prepared? I believe so. Even Jesus says, "be on the alert." Do not be asleep, because the coming of our Lord will be like a thief for those who are asleep. However, if we are "sons of light" the day of His return won't overtake us like a thief.

We also need to remember the Bible is very Jewish centric. The Bible came to us from the Jewish nation and Jesus himself was born a Jew. Jewish tradition and customs are woven throughout the Word and as a non-Jewish reader, although the context of the scripture is understood, the underlying idiosyncrasies can be missed. As I discussed earlier, the Jews called their High Priest a "thief in the night" and would instantly recognize Jesus' intention when He spoke of coming like a thief. If you need to refresh your memory on our discussion, please refer back to day nine. Let's look again at Jesus' words to the church of Sardis.

"So remember what you have received and heard; and keep it, and repent. Therefore if you do not wake up, I will come like a thief, and you will not know at what hour I will come to you."

Revelation 3:3

But if they are awake, will they be surprised by His coming? You decide.

We will continue to discuss the pre-wrath view because, according to this theory, the rapture has yet to be depicted in the book of Revelation. We will wrap up the pre-tribulation rapture theory here because this theory states the rapture happens here, at that beginning of chapter four, when the door in heaven is opened and John is taken up.

As we bring to a close the pre-tribulation rapture position, realize the majority of church attendees place the rapture of the church in chapter four. If this theory is correct, well and good. If this theory is faulty, many people won't be prepared for the intense persecution that is about to come upon the world. Jesus warns that many will "fall away from the faith" (Matthew 24:10). Those who haven't prepared their hearts and minds for what is to come, and grounded their faith more securely, will be ill-equipped to fight for their faith. I want you to make up your own mind when the rapture will take place based on our continued discussion. If I haven't convinced you by the end of this study that the rapture is not in chapter four, I will not be offended. I want you to search the scriptures yourself and make up your own mind. God does too.

May God give you revelation!

Let's summarize the pre-tribulation rapture view in a final graph.

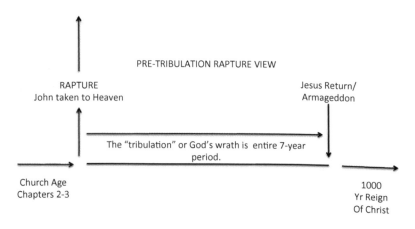

Thought for the day:

Tomorrow you will see God on His throne. You will witness His power and see His majesty. If you had to meet Him today, would you be ready? If you had to give an account of your life, what would you say?

1 Van Kampen, Robert. *The Rapture Question Answered* (Grand Rapids, MI: Fleming H. Revell, 1997).

DAY FIFTEEN
REVELATION 4:1-4
THE THRONE ROOM

¹After these things I looked, and behold, a door standing open in heaven, and the first voice which I had heard, like the sound of a trumpet speaking with me, said, "Come up here, and I will show you what must take place after these things." ²Immediately I was in the Spirit; and behold, a throne was standing in heaven, and One sitting on the throne. ³And He who was sitting was like a jasper stone and a sardius in appearance; and there was a rainbow around the throne, like an emerald in appearance. ⁴Around the throne were twenty-four thrones; and upon the thrones I saw twenty-four elders sitting, clothed in white garments, and golden crowns on their heads.

Revelation 4:1-4

The first verses of chapter 4 tell us John was "in the Spirit." We do not know if John's transport to Heaven was a physical transformation, a spiritual transport, or a spiritual vision (2 Corinthians 12:1-5). I tend to think it was the latter, a spiritual vision, but that is something that we may not know until Jesus explains it to us in His kingdom. There are other examples in Scripture of prophets who had visions of Our Lord. Daniel's book is full of visions and dreams. Ezekiel saw the valley of dry bones coming back to life (Ezekiel 37). Scripture is consistent with revelation through visions. In any case, whether physically or spiritually, John saw the throne room of God.

Notice God Himself is not described, only the aura emitting from the throne is explained. Why do you think that is? Let's examine a few scriptures.

But He said, "You cannot see My face, for no man can see Me and live."

Exodus 33:20

"Not that anyone has seen the Farther, except the One who is from God; He has seen the Father."

John 6:46

No one can see the Father and live. Why is this?

Who alone possesses immortality and dwells in unapproachable light, whom no man has seen or can see. To Him be honor and eternal dominion! Amen.

1 Timothy 6:16

In Revelation John sees God the Father's aura as blazing colors, like a jasper and sardius (or carnelian) stone. Jasper is a variety of colors. It can be clear, red, yellow, brown and green. Sardis is orange red to brownish red. If you look deeper into Revelation the glory of God is described as being like "crystal clear jasper" (Revelation 21:11). In chapter four, the colors emitting from the Father are probably red (sardius) and white (jasper). This would make sense given the fact that we are purified through Jesus' blood and sanctified by His pure water. Only by the water and the blood can we enter the throne room of God.

This is the One who came by water and blood, Jesus Christ; not with the water only, but with the water and with the blood. It is the Spirit who testifies, because the Spirit is the truth.

1 John 5:6

Therefore, brethren, since we have confidence to enter the holy place by the blood of Jesus, by a new and living way which He inaugurated for us through the veil, that is, His flesh, and since we have a great priest over the house of God, let us draw near with a sincere heart in full assurance of faith, having our hearts sprinkled clean from an evil conscience and our bodies washed with pure water.

Hebrews 10:19-22

My faithful friends, I cannot say this enough. We cannot enter the throne room of God without being washed in His blood and His water (the Word, see Ephesians 5:26). In Old Testament times the first and the last stone worn on the High Priest's breastplate were a ruby and a jasper (Exodus 28). Again we see both colors, red and white, in anticipation of Jesus and His water and blood sacrifice (John 19:34). The Father radiates these colors to remind both John and us that only through His Son can we approach the throne of grace.

An emerald rainbow surrounds the throne. The Greek word for "around" is "kuklothen" which means an entire circle, not a half circle like we associate with a rainbow. God gave Noah the rainbow as a covenant never to destroy the earth again with water (Genesis 9:11-17). The rainbow represented life and deliverance to Noah. As we approach God's throne, by the water and the blood, we have life eternal – not the half circle of an earthly rainbow, but a full circle – eternal life. Because of the water and the blood, we are rescued from God's wrath, just like Noah. The rainbow represents that rescue and reminds us of God's promises. At times I wonder if we now only see half of the rainbow. In eternity will the rainbow be a circle? I wonder!

Next we are introduced to twenty-four elders who are clothed in white garments and have golden crowns on their heads. Many scholars believe these elders represent the twelve tribes of Israel and the twelve apostles of the Lamb. If their assessment is accurate, the elder's presence would be representative of all Old Testament and New Testament saints. However, let me point out that John is one of the disciples and he is seeing the vision. Although it is possible he may not have seen the elders in any detail, John himself should be one of the twenty-four. I find it curious he does not specify twelve of those elders as apostles if, in fact, that is what they are.

Another popular theory is that the elders represent the twenty-four divisions of the priesthood that David established in 1 Chronicles 24. This is also plausible given the fact that the priests are those who offered the sacrifices for the people. Again, this would represent the redeemed as a whole because of the ultimate sacrifice of Jesus.

There is a third theory, however, which I find intriguing, but I want you to see it with your own eyes. Some of you may have never seen this verse. It might just be the coolest thing you have ever read.

The tombs were opened, and many bodies of the saints who had fallen asleep were raised; and coming out of the tombs after His resurrection they entered the holy city and appeared to many.

Matthew 27:52

After Jesus was raised to life, bodies of saints were also raised to life. How many? Scripture doesn't say. But what is curious about the elders in Revelation is that they are already crowned and robed. If you move deeper into Revelation you see souls handed robes (Revelation 6:11), but they aren't asked to put them on. The elders in chapter four are already wearing white garments and we know from Revelation 19:8-14 that white linen stands for the righteous acts of the saints. The crowns on their heads aren't kingly crowns (diadems) but victor's crowns (stephanos), for those who have just run a race.

Do you not know that those who run in a race all run, but only one receives the prize? Run in such a way that you may win.

1 Corinthians 9:24

The elders seen in Revelation chapter four have already run and received their prize. Could these twenty-four be twenty-four selected saints God chose to raise from the dead and enter glory after Jesus' resurrection? If you think about it, where else would those raised go? They wouldn't reenter their tombs would they? Isn't that just like God? He can't wait for His saints to be with Him!

Now I do want to pause here and consider the pre-tribulation position on the twenty-four elders, because I want you to have all the information possible so that you can make your own decision regarding the timing of the rapture. Most of those holding to the pre-tribulation view believe in one of the theories I quoted above, although I cannot say this is the majority with any certainty. Other pre-tribulation proponents believe the twenty-four elders represent the raptured church. For clarification sake, in my view, I think this is unlikely given the fact these elders are already in heaven when John arrives. Can they represent the church at the rapture if John himself represents the rapture?

You decide.

Thought for the day:
Tomorrow you will meet creatures who day and night do not cease to say "Holy, Holy, Holy," to the One sitting on the throne. Day and night, over and over – continuously. How often do you pause in your day to speak to God? How often do you tell Him how amazing He is? Hourly? Daily? Weekly? Yearly?

⁵Out from the throne come flashes of lightning and sounds and peals of thunder. And there were seven lamps of fire burning before the throne, which are the seven Spirits of God; ⁶and before the throne there was something like a sea of glass, like crystal; and in the center and around the throne, four living creatures full of eyes in front and behind. ⁷The first creature was like a lion, and the second creature like a calf, and the third creature had a face like that of a man, and the fourth creature was like a flying eagle. ⁸And the four living creatures, each one of them having six wings, are full of eyes around and within; and day and night they do not cease to say, "Holy, Holy, Holy is the Lord God, the Almighty, who was and who is and who is to come." ⁹And when the living creatures give glory and honor and thanks to Him who sits on the throne, to Him who lives forever and ever, ¹⁰the twenty-four elders will fall down before Him who sits on the throne, and will worship Him who lives forever and ever, and will cast their crowns before the throne, saying, ¹¹"Worthy are You, our Lord and our God, to receive glory and honor and power; for You created all things, and because of Your will they existed, and were created."

Revelation 4:5-11

We are still in the throne room of God. What an awesome scene so far! Let's read more.

First we see "flashes of lightning and sounds and peals of thunder" coming out of the throne. Think about this for a minute. The lightning and thunder weren't in the sky; they were coming out of the throne. The picture of this is awe-inspiring. This is the majesty of God, yet despite God's all-consuming power, we are allowed to approach Him because of Jesus' sacrifice (Hebrews 4:16).

Lightning and thunder in scripture represent God's power:

The sound of Your thunder was in the whirlwind; the lightnings lit up the world; the earth trembled and shook.
Psalm 77:18

Lightning and thunder also represent God's judgment:

Then the Lord will appear over them, and His arrow will
go forth like lightning; and the Lord God will blow the
trumpet, and will march in the storm winds of the south.
Zechariah 9:14

Revelation is about God's awesome display of power and the
coming judgment of the earth. You see this represented by the
thunder and lightning emitting from His throne. God is angry at the
unrepentant (Romans 2:5) and He will judge the nations according
to the way they treated His people Israel (Joel 3:2).

In chapter one, we saw God's Spirit announced as "the seven
Spirits who are before His throne" (Revelation 1:4). In chapter four
we see John describe the Spirit in more detail: as seven lamps of
fire. Other versions of scripture translate the Greek word "lampas"
in this verse to be torches. Personally I envision God's Spirit to be
flames of fire before the throne, similar to what the disciples
witnessed on Pentecost (Acts 2:3). Fire represents God's holiness,
His cleansing nature, His protection, and His vengeance. Let's look
at some scripture.

Behold, the name of the Lord comes from a remote place;
burning in His anger and dense is His smoke; His lips are
filled with indignation and His tongue is like a consuming
fire.
Isaiah 30:27

And to the eyes of the sons of Israel the appearance of the
glory of the Lord was like a consuming fire on the
mountain top.
Exodus 24:17

God's consuming fire will be released on the unrepentant
sinner during the end times. We are reminded of this as we see the
Spirit in the form of seven lamps of fire. Isaiah 33:14 says:

Sinners in Zion are terrified; trembling has seized the
godless, "Who among us can live with the consuming
fire? Who among us can live with continual burning?"
Isaiah 33:14

We, as the redeemed of the Lord, can approach our God
because when God sees us, He sees Christ, the sinless Son of God

(Romans 5:1). We are spared His fiery wrath, but woe to those who are unrepentant!

We are next introduced to the sea of glass, described as being like crystal. What is this sea of glass? Scripture does not say; however, we do know that when God's throne moves, the sea of glass moves with it.

I want you to see this for yourself. In Ezekiel, you are introduced to some creatures in chapter one that are identified as cherubim in Ezekiel 10:1. Now look at a few descriptions of them:

Within it there were figures resembling four living beings. And this was their appearance: they had human form.
Ezekiel 1:5

Now over the heads of the living beings there was something like an expanse, like the awesome gleam of crystal, spread out over their heads . . . Now above the expanse that was over their heads there was something resembling a throne, like lapis lazuli in appearance; and on that which resembled a throne, high up, was a figure with the appearance of a man. Then I noticed from the appearance of His loins and upward something like glowing metal that looked like fire all around within it, and from the appearance of His loins and downward I saw something like fire; and there was a radiance around Him. As the appearance of the rainbow in the clouds on a rainy day, so was the appearance of the surrounding radiance. Such was the appearance of the likeness of the glory of the Lord.
Ezekiel 1:22, 26-28a

The sea of glass was over the cherubim's heads! When God needs to move, He remains seated on His throne, and creatures called the cherubim hold up the sea of glass with God's throne on top of it. Can you imagine? Someone needs to shout, "Glory!"

The cherubim in Ezekiel look very similar to the creatures introduced to us in Revelation. However, the cherubim have four wings (Ezekiel 1:6); the creatures in Revelation have six. The six-winged creatures in Revelation do not cease to say, "Holy, Holy, Holy is the Lord God, the Almighty, who was and who is and who is to come." We know from Isaiah chapter six these creatures are the seraphim.

The seraphim do not hold up God's throne: they surround God's throne (Revelation 4:6). The faces of the four seraphim differ from the cherubim as well. One has a face of a lion, the other the face of a calf, the third has a face of a man, and the fourth has the face of an eagle. We see the cherubim described in Ezekiel having the same faces, yet each one has all four.

As for the form of their faces, each had the face of a man; all four had the face of a lion on the right and the face of a bull on the left, and all four had the face of an eagle . . . and each went straight forward; wherever the spirit was about to go, they would go, without turning as they went.
Ezekiel 1:10,12

Because the cherubim have four faces they do not need to turn to see where they are going. When God's Spirit says, "north" they move without turning. If He says, "back" they move without turning. They are the throne carriers, and when the throne needs to move there is no hesitation. The seraphim, on the other hand, are around God's throne continuously praising God. They have no need of four faces, but one, focusing on the One sitting before them.

The four unique faces of both the seraphim and the cherubim remind us that the Lord is King over all creation. He rules mankind and all the creatures of the earth. Four in scripture also denotes the four corners of the earth.

And He will send forth His angels with a great trumpet and they will gather together His elect from the four winds, from one end of the sky to the other.
Matthew 24:31

The faces of the cherubim and seraphim are representative of creation as a whole and the totality of the earth. This is also evident in that the seraphim's bodies are filled with "eyes in front and behind." Again, this is the all-seeing nature of God enveloping His entire creation.

Why didn't John describe the cherubim as well? I believe it is because he was before the throne on top of the sea of glass, unlike Ezekiel who was looking up from below the sea of glass. If John could look down through the sea, he would probably notice the cherubim as described in Ezekiel. Whoever said God's Word is boring really needs to read Revelation.

Before we leave the cherubim and seraphim I would like to make an observation that has opened my eyes. Ezekiel 1:13 describes the cherubim as having something like burning coals, or stones of fire, darting back and forth between them.

In the midst of the living beings there was something that looked like burning coals of fire, like torches darting back and forth among the living beings. The fire was bright, and lightning was flashing from the fire.

Ezekiel 1:13

Ezekiel later describes Satan from God's point of view.

You had the seal of perfection, full of wisdom and perfect in beauty. You were in Eden, the garden of God; every precious stone was your covering . . . You were the anointed cherub who covers, and I placed you there. You were on the holy mountain of God; you walked in the midst of the stones of fire.

Ezekiel 28:12b-13a, 14

Satan is depicted as a cherub who walked amidst the "stones of fire." Satan, then, could have been one of the cherubim that held up God's throne, or an angel who was allowed to enter the burning coals of fire darting back and forth between the cherubim such as the one depicted in Ezekiel 10:2. And what did God say was Satan's fall? Satan's heart was filled with pride (Ezekiel 28:17). If he was one of the cherubim, you can just picture him below God's throne, looking up, and wanting to be on the throne. Just think for a minute about the betrayal: Satan was either allowed to carry God's throne or to walk among the fiery stones. He was trusted and loved, but pride filled his spirit and he fell. He wanted to be on the throne and not under the throne. May we always remember our place before the throne of God.

The final scene in this chapter depicts the twenty-four elders falling on their knees in worship and casting their crowns at His feet saying, "Worthy are You, our Lord and our God, to receive glory and honor and power; for you created all things, and because of Your will they existed and were created." We exist only because God willed us into existence. Here again, we see all of creation represented, just like the faces of the seraphim. We are forever indebted to our Creator not only because He made us, but also because He loves us. And when our Lord calls us home, our first response should be praise.

There is one other observation I should make. Notice that everything in heaven is described in relation to its position around God's throne. Everything in the universe exists because God spoke it into existence.

For He spoke, and it was done; He commanded, and it stood fast.

Psalm 33:9

We need to define our own lives by our position around God's throne. We are part of His creation and our entire being exists to worship our Creator.[1]

Think about where you are in relation to God's throne based on our Savior's words to the churches. Where do you need to adjust? Where does your pride need to adjust?

Thought for the day:
Satan wanted to be on the throne – not below the throne. He wanted control of His life without the One who created Him. Have you surrendered control of you life? In every area of your life? Or are you still fighting for the throne?

1 Moore, Beth. DVD Study *Here and Now ... There and Then: A lecture series on Revelation* (Houston, Texas: Living Proof Ministries, 2009), 24.

[1]Then I saw in the right hand of Him who was seated on the throne a scroll written within and on the back, sealed with seven seals. [2]And I saw a strong angel proclaiming with a loud voice, "Who is worthy to open the scroll and break its seals?" [3]And no one in heaven or on earth or under the earth was able to open the scroll or to look into it, [4]and I began to weep loudly because no one was found worthy to open the scroll or to look into it. [5]And one of the elders said to me, "Weep no more; behold, the Lion of the tribe of Judah, the Root of David, has conquered, so that He can open the scroll and its seven seals." [6]And between the throne and the four living creatures and among the elders I saw a Lamb standing, as though it had been slain, with seven horns and with seven eyes, which are the seven spirits of God sent out into all the earth. [7]And He went and took the scroll from the right hand of Him who was seated on the throne. [8]And when He had taken the scroll, the four living creatures and the twenty-four elders fell down before the Lamb, each holding a harp, and golden bowls full of incense, which are the prayers of the saints. [9]And they sang a new song, saying, "Worthy are you to take the scroll and to open its seals, for you were slain, and by your blood you ransomed people for God from every tribe and language and people and nation, [10]and you have made them a kingdom and priests to our God, and they shall reign on the earth." [11]Then I looked, and I heard around the throne and the living creatures and the elders the voice of many angels, numbering myriads of myriads and thousands of thousands, [12]saying with a loud voice, "Worthy is the Lamb who was slain, to receive power and wealth and wisdom and might and honor and glory and blessing!" [13]And I heard every creature in heaven and on earth and under the earth and in the sea, and all that is in them, saying, "To Him who sits on the throne and to the Lamb be blessing and honor and glory and might forever and ever!" [14]And the four living creatures said, "Amen!" and the elders fell down and worshiped.

Revelation 5:1-14 ESV

God the Father is holding a scroll in His right hand. Let us remember who is supposed to be at the Father's right hand.

So then, when the Lord Jesus had spoken to them, He was received up into heaven and sat down at the right hand of God.

Mark 16:19

This scroll is intended for the One at the Father's right hand. It is written on the inside and on the back and sealed with seven seals.

An angel proclaims in a loud voice, "Who is worthy to open the scroll and to break its seals?" There is a search made in heaven and on earth for someone to open the scroll, but no one is found.

Notice in verse four it says no one was found "worthy to open the scroll. Then John begins to weep. This tells us this scroll is important. So what is this scroll? In Hal Lindsey's *There's a New World Coming*, he says:

Sealing a scroll was a common and important practice in Biblical times. The wills of both Emperor Vespasian and Caesar Augustus, for example, were secured with seven seals . . . When a Jewish family was required to forfeit its land and possessions through some distress, the property could not be permanently taken from them. Their losses were listed in a scroll and sealed seven times, then the conditions necessary to purchase back the land and possessions were written on the outside of the scroll. When a qualified redeemer could be found to meet the requirements of reclamation, the one to whom the property had been forfeited was obligated to return the possessions to the original owner.[1]

In ancient times, a will was sealed with seven seals. Of course, you draft a will when you are still alive. Only upon your death can the will be opened and the seals broken. Also, when a Jewish family had to sell their land to pay a debt, they would write their losses on a scroll and seal it with seven seals. The conditions to purchase back the land were written on the outside of the scroll. The land could be bought back when all the conditions on the outside of the scroll were met. So, for a scroll of antiquity to be opened, there needed to be a meeting of conditions, and/or a death of a person. Keep this in mind as we continue our study.

One of the elders tells John to stop weeping because "the Lion of the Tribe of Judah . . . has overcome" (some versions say conquered) so as to open the scroll. Remember in the letters to the churches, Jesus tells each and every church to "overcome." What we need to realize is that Jesus overcame, and it is announced in Revelation 5:5. Jesus is telling His followers in the letters to the churches to do the same. And in John 16:33 it tells us what we need to overcome – the world.

So the Lion is announced as overcoming the world, but instead of the Lion, John sees a Lamb – standing as if slain. First let's look at the Lion reference. Let's look at Genesis 49:9-10. This is one of the oldest prophesies about the Messiah.

Judah is a lion's whelp; from the prey, my son, you have gone up. He crouches, he lies down as a lion, and as a lion, who dares rouse him up? The scepter shall not depart from Judah, nor the ruler's staff from between his feet.

Genesis 49:9-10a

The scepter will not depart from Judah. Jesus was a descendent of Judah, and the fulfillment of this prophecy is found in Revelation. Jesus is about to lay claim to the earth, declaring His rightful position of authority. A lion is also a symbol of royalty and majesty. Jesus in chapter one was all of that, and much more. The lion is also king of the beasts, just as Jesus will be King over all the earth. Yet despite that, Jesus is seen as a Lamb because only by becoming the Lamb did Jesus "overcome." Jesus became the "lamb" of sacrifice, giving His life so that we could have life eternal with Him.

He was oppressed and He was afflicted, yet He did not open His mouth; like a lamb that is led to slaughter, and like a sheep that is silent before its shearers, so He did not open His mouth.

Isaiah 53:7

If we carry our ancient scroll theory to this passage, we know exactly why Jesus is announced as the Lion and seen as the Lamb. He is announced as a lion because of what He is about to do – reclaim the earth! But He is seen as a lamb because the Lamb is the only one worthy. Why? For He was slain! The scroll (or will) can only be opened upon the death of an individual, and Christ, because of His death, is able to take the scroll from the Father. This is even announced by the four living creatures and the elders when they say

97

in verse nine, "Worthy are you to take the book and to break its seals; *for You were slain.*" Jesus is worthy because of His sacrifice, and because of that sacrifice, a death has happened and the seals on the scroll can be broken.

So a death has happened. But what about the "meeting of conditions" in regard to purchasing back forfeited land? Remember, we just learned that in ancient Jewish culture, if any family lost their land, they put their losses in a scroll and sealed it seven times with conditions that had to be met before they could reclaim it. In Revelation, what land would Jesus be buying back?

I kept looking in the night visions, and behold, with the clouds of heaven one like a Son of Man was coming, and He came up to the Ancient of Days and was presented before Him. And to Him was given dominion, glory and a kingdom, that all the peoples, nations and men of every language might serve Him. His dominion is an everlasting dominion which will not pass away; and His kingdom is one which will not be destroyed.
Daniel 7:13-14

The Son of Man is presented with a kingdom and all peoples and nations are serving Him there. In Revelation 5:10 it names this kingdom: the earth.

The land is a kingdom and that kingdom is earth. The earth and its inhabitants are now under the grip of Satan whom Jesus calls the "ruler of this world" in John 12:31. In Revelation chapter five Jesus is about to take back the land and those redeemed by His blood. He is about to break the seals because through His death He is "worthy" to do so, and once those seals are opened (the conditions are met) the earth can be returned to its rightful owner.

When the seals are opened and the scroll is unrolled, Jesus can begin to lay claim to the earth. How will He do that? Well, first He has to destroy His enemies, and then He has to purify the land. How will He do this? His wrath! The wrath of God is defined in scripture as being the "day of the Lord." It is a time when God's wrath rains down on the earth in order to wipe out His enemies. Both rapture theories we are looking at in this study, the pre-tribulation and the pre-wrath theory, say we are not here for God's wrath. 1 Thessalonians 5:9 says we aren't "destined for wrath." So, when you see the "day of the Lord" in scripture, we are rescued before that time. Jesus will rescue us from the day of the Lord (wrath of God).

But by His word the present heavens and earth are being reserved for fire, kept for the day of judgment and destruction of ungodly men.

2 Peter 3:7

Jesus has to cleanse the earth of evil before He rules in the Millennial Kingdom. Fire is necessary, because fire not only destroys, it also purifies.

But who can endure the day of His coming? And who can stand when He appears? For He is like a refiner's fire and like fullers' soap.

Malachi 3:2

A refiner's fire takes something and makes it shine. Even amid the destruction, God will purify and make the world beautiful.

Once the conditions on the outside of the scroll are met, Jesus can start His work of reclamation. Let's look at the scroll another way: before Jesus can reclaim the earth, the prophecies spoken of since the creation of the world (the seals) have to be fulfilled. Think of these as the conditions to buy back the land. These stipulations on the outside of the scroll – the prophecies – lead to the day of the Lord. Jesus breaks the seals (the prophecies) as they are happening on the earth and once all the seals are open (all the prophecies have come to pass), He can unroll the scroll. Once He unrolls the scroll, God's wrath falls in order to cleanse the earth of sin and plead with mankind to repent and turn to His Son. Once everyone on earth has made their choice, Jesus returns and lays claim to His kingdom.

Who said the Bible wasn't exciting? I need to shout, "Hallelujah!"

The scroll was written on both sides. It seems from this passage, "written inside and on the back," the scroll in Revelation is replete with written instruction. Once Jesus opens the seals and unrolls the scroll, those words will come to pass. Those words are God's wrath. This should convey to us God has a lot to say about how the world has treated His saints and His nation of Israel. God says in Romans 12:19, "Vengeance is mine, I will repay." In the day of God's wrath, He will repay, you can be assured of that.

The Lord will go forth like a warrior, He will arouse His
zeal like a man of war. He will utter a shout, yes, He will
raise a war cry. He will prevail against His enemies.

Isaiah 42:13

God is a God of justice and He will have the final word. If you think the wicked are getting away with a lot now, just wait. Like they say, "it's not over 'til it's over." Centuries ago God's wrath rained down on Sodom and Gomorrah; imagine that same wrath raining down on the totality of the earth. Believe me, you don't want to be here when that happens.

On a final note, notice the praise happening in the throne room of God. Not only does John witness the four living creatures (who never stop singing) and the twenty-four elders (who worship constantly) but he also sees thousands upon thousands of angels around the throne, singing a song of the Lamb. This is an uncountable number of angels. Can you imagine this for a moment with me? Think of being in the throne room of God and looking out over a sea of majestic angels, unable to even fathom the number of them. Think of the sound of their voices as they praise their Creator. This is quite a picture. Why are they singing? They have found the One who is worthy! The Lion has come forth and because He is also the Lamb, He is able to take the scroll. Again, here we see the angels emphasizing Jesus' worth to "receive power and riches and wisdom and might and honor and glory and blessing." Then, all creation announces the dominion of God. Dominion over what? Over the earth! The four beings keep saying "Amen" and the elders fall down and worship. Once the Lamb is handed the scroll, all creation erupts into praise.

For we know that the whole creation groans and suffers
the pains of childbirth together until now.

Romans 8:22

All creation suffers because of the curse and looks forward to the day the curse will end and the Savior of the world will take His rightful throne.

We have just been over the pre-wrath version of chapters four and five. Again, the seals are not the wrath of God, but once the scroll is opened, the wrath of God is unleashed. The seals on the scroll are the prophecies that must come to pass before the day of the Lord can begin.

Remember, in the pre-tribulation rapture theory the church disappears in chapter four. In the pre-wrath theory, the rapture has yet to occur.

Until tomorrow, we all need to say, "Amen and Amen. Come quickly, Lord Jesus!"

Thought for the day:
The opening of the scroll has been prophesied throughout scripture. It is the first step before the King can return. Can you imagine the anticipation in heaven? It should be the same anticipation we feel about the King's return. Do we look forward to it like we should? Do we long for the day? Or just complacently believe we will be ushered to heaven before it all begins? Seal One opens tomorrow.

1 Lindsey, Hal. *There's a New World Coming* (Eugene, Oregon: Harvest House Publishers, 1984), p74-75.

SEAL ONE – FALSE CHRIST

¹Then I saw when the Lamb broke one of the seven seals, and I heard one of the four living creatures saying as with a voice of thunder, "Come." ²I looked, and behold, a white horse, and he who sat on it had a bow; and a crown was given to him, and he went out conquering and to conquer.

Revelation 6:1-2

There are a variety of opinions about who this horseman is, but I have yet to really understand why. The identity of this rider seems to be clearly revealed, but I will give you all the opinions that I have researched.

First, the rider could be Jesus. Why would some say this? Jesus returns on a white horse:

And I saw heaven opened, and behold, a white horse, and He who sat on it is called Faithful and True, and in righteousness He judges and wages war.

Revelation 19:11

Second, the rider could represent the gospel being proclaimed in all the earth. Jesus does say, "this gospel of the kingdom shall be preached in the whole world" before the end will come.[1] Yet, neither of these fit the context of seal number one. Jesus does not return until Revelation 19, and to say this is the gospel because of the white horse isn't convincing. Would the gospel be described as "conquering?" Yes, the gospel must be preached to all nations before the end will come. Is there any other place in Revelation this could happen?

And I saw another angel flying in midheaven, having an eternal gospel to preach to those who live on the earth, and to every nation and tribe and tongue and people.

Revelation 14:6

So the gospel will be preached, but in chapter fourteen it is represented by an angel, not a horseman. If that is the case, why does this rider have a white horse?

Let's go back to our prophecy in Daniel, where we derive our seven-year timeline. We know there is a man, the Antichrist, who will make a seven-year peace treaty with Israel (Daniel 9:27). Obviously, he will have to be a world leader in order to do so. He will deceive the Jews for the first half of the last seven years, then he will "break" the treaty at the midpoint.

Let no one in any way deceive you, for it will not come unless the apostasy comes first, and the man of lawlessness is revealed, the son of destruction, who opposes and exalts himself above every so-called god or object of worship, so that he takes his seat in the temple of God, displaying himself as being God.

2 Thessalonians 2:3-4

Why a white horse? It seems fairly clear to me that this horseman will be the embodiment of Jesus' first warning when He told His disciples about the signs leading up to the end times.

"See to it that no one misleads you. For many will come in My name, saying, 'I am the Christ,' and will mislead many."

Matthew 24:4-5

This horseman is the spirit and end time fulfillment of Jesus' warning. This is the ultimate false Christ. Scripture warns us that although many will come, there will be one final ruler who will rise up and control the final empire we will see in Revelation 13. This horseman represents that man, the Antichrist, or the man of lawlessness of 2 Thessalonians. Because the Antichrist is riding a white horse as Jesus does in Revelation 19, this indicates he will be a false savior to many and will lure multitudes away from the true King of kings.

The Antichrist will be Satan's minion on earth who will ultimately profess deity and try to take the glory away from Christ. Jesus warns us there will be those who claim to be Him, and the Antichrist is the ultimate fulfillment of our Savior's warning. He will appear to be the answer to people's hopes, not only religiously, but also politically (we will study this more in Revelation 13 and

17). Satan disguises himself as an angel of light (2 Corinthians 11:14), and he will do so yet again with the Antichrist. The Antichrist will be the bearer of false peace. We know this because he has a bow, but no arrows, meaning he takes over peacefully (makes a treaty). Although he takes over peacefully, he has the capacity for war (the bow). He is successful because he is given a crown.

So when does this happen on our timeline? According to Daniel, it is the signing of the peace treaty that ushers in the final seven years on earth before Jesus' return. We have already learned this peace is false, and that in the middle of the final seven years, the Antichrist will break his treaty with the nation of Israel. Satan desires complete control of the world and he has yet to accomplish it. He tried with the tower of Babel (Genesis 11). He has tried with many regional empires, and finally World War I and II. This will be his last and greatest attempt to control mankind. But yet again, our nemesis will fail.

If we put this on our graph, we would place the first seal opening at the beginning of the final seven years. The treaty is actually the starting point of that period.

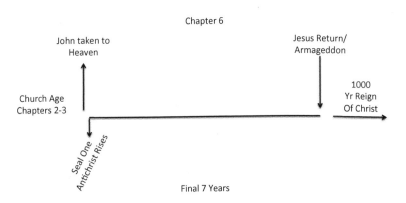

Scripture has a lot to say about the antichrist. The word antichrist refers to any who oppose Christ. The title of antichrist is found in 1 and 2 John. Let's look at these scriptures.

Children, it is the last hour; and just as you heard that antichrist is coming, even now many antichrists have appeared; from this we know that it is the last hour
1 John 2:18

Who is the liar but the one who denies that Jesus is the Christ? This is the antichrist, the one who denies the Father and the Son.

1 John 2:22

For many deceivers have gone out into the world, those who do not acknowledge Jesus Christ as coming in the flesh. This is the deceiver and the antichrist.

2 John 1:7

We know there are many antichrists as the scriptures above indicate, but we also know from scripture that there will be a final antichrist, the leader of the end time governmental system. This man will oppose everything Christ stands for and will turn the world upside down. He will convince the masses that evil is good and good is evil. "Woe to those who call evil good, and good evil" (Isaiah 5:20a). We already see the spirit of this happening. We call the killing of innocents pro-choice. We call sexual promiscuity on television entertainment. Religious extremism is flourishing and we fear we will be called "intolerant" if we hold others to account. What are we doing? Where are our moral values? Like the church of Thyatira, we are decaying from within.

The Antichrist will profess goodness but will be wicked. He will rise to power through deception (Daniel 8:25), promising peace, and the masses will believe him – so will the nation of Israel. In due time, the world will discover his true intentions – the destruction of the Jewish race and the annihilation of Israel. He will also hate the saints.

He will speak out against the Most High and wear down the saints of the Highest One, and he will intend to make alterations in times and in law.

Daniel 7:25a

In other words, he will blaspheme God, hurt His people, and will try to make changes in governmental systems around the world.

Looking forward to Revelation 13, we discover that the Antichrist's empire will rise out of the sea. Many scholars believe this means the Antichrist will arise during turbulent times (like the tossing of the sea). Others say this means that this empire will come from the Gentile nations because in scripture "sea" can represent the Gentile world.

> *Then thou shalt see, and flow together, and thine heart shall fear, and be enlarged; because the abundance of the sea shall be converted unto thee, the forces of the Gentiles shall come unto thee.*
>
> *Isaiah 60:5 KJV*

Quite possibly, the beast's emergence from the sea is both from a Gentile world power and in the midst of turbulent times. What will ultimately happen to the Antichrist?

> *And through his shrewdness he will cause deceit to succeed by his influence; and he will magnify himself in his heart. And he will destroy many while they are at ease. He will even oppose the Prince of princes, but he will be broken without human agency.*
>
> *Daniel 8:25*

Although the Antichrist will raise his ugly head, the King of kings and Lord of lords will ultimately destroy him. Jesus will win the victory. What we need to realize at this point in our study is that the final seven years will begin when a peace treaty is signed with the nation of Israel. The man signing that treaty will be the Antichrist.

We hear talks of peace treaties and discussions of world peace every day. The Middle East is consistently the focus of the nightly news. Remember what prophecy says:

> *It will come about in that day that I will make Jerusalem a heavy stone for all the peoples; all who lift it will be severely injured. And all the nations of the earth will be gathered against it.*
>
> *Zechariah 12:3*

The world's current focus is on the Middle East, the tiny nation of Israel, and the Israeli-Palestinian conflict. Let us be on the alert.

Remember, according to the pre-tribulation theory the seals are God's wrath, hence they believe we will not be here when the Antichrist signs the peace treaty with Israel. The pre-wrath theory believes that the seals are the precursors to God's wrath – they are the prophecies that have to be fulfilled. God's wrath only starts when the scroll is unrolled. So according to pre-wrath we will see the Antichrist sign the treaty with Israel.

Before we wrap up today's lesson, we need to look at the word "come" when it is uttered by the four living creatures. There are two ways you can look at this command. First, the living creatures could be calling the horseman himself, commanding he come. This would seem to indicate that God himself is commanding the horseman. This would favor pre-tribulation's interpretation of the seals being God's wrath. If you arrive at this conclusion and understand God has not destined us for wrath (1 Thessalonians 5:9), you would obviously conclude we aren't here for the seals. However, if you look at seal number five, you notice it discusses martyrs. God neither kills His saints, nor orders they be killed. The thought is ludicrous. So what is going on here?

The living creature could be calling to John, commanding he come and witness the horseman who is riding across the earth. Some translations (KJV) and one early manuscript (according to the NASB) actually translate this command as "Come and see." Come and see seems to indicate the creature is talking to John, commanding the disciple to come witness the condition on earth that would warrant the breaking of the seals.

Here is another way to look at this: nothing is done under the sun without God's approval. Although the killing of God's saints is not His wrath, He could stop it. Nothing takes Him by surprise, not even the persecution and death of His saints.

Who is there who speaks and it comes to pass, unless the Lord has commanded it? Is it not from the mouth of the Most High that both good and ill go forth?

Lamentations 3:37-38

This scripture isn't saying God commands evil to happen to His saints, but the story of Job proves that sometimes He allows it.

The Lord said to Satan, "Have you considered My servant Job? For there is no one like him on the earth, a blameless and upright man, fearing God and turning away from evil."

Job 1:8

Satan replies that Job is only faithful because God has blessed him. Satan then taunts God, "But put forth Your hand now and touch all that he has; he will surely curse You to Your face" (Job 1:11). God replies, "Behold, all that he has is in your power, only do not put forth your hand on him" (Job 1:12b). Satan then leaves and devastates Job, his family, and everything he owns.

If you recall, in Revelation 2:10 Jesus warned Smyrna that the devil was about to throw some of them into prison. He also told Smyrna why this was going to happen: *so that you will be tested.*

God doesn't bring evil to His saints, but He allows evil to happen to bring glory to His name and to reward us for our faithfulness. "Blessed is a man who perseveres under trial; for once he has been approved, he will receive the crown of life which the Lord has promised to those who love Him" (James 1:12). We also need to remember, even though terrible things do happen, God will work them for His glory and our good.

> *And we know that God causes all things to work together for good to those who love God, to those who are called according to His purpose.*
>
> *Romans 8:28*

So what are the four horseman of Revelation 6:1-8 if we are looking at them from a pre-wrath perspective? Although they are not God's wrath, they are His will. In Daniel 9:24, one of the reasons the final seven years has to occur is "to seal up vision and prophecy." The rise of the Antichrist and the final end time events have been prophesied throughout scripture. For Jesus to return, those prophecies have to be fulfilled and one of those prophecies is the persecution of God's saints. God will not cause the final system to emerge, Satan will, but God will allow it. He will say, "Come," and Jesus will break the seal, confirming the horseman's arrival. Once the seals are broken and all prophecy leading up to His return has been fulfilled, the scroll can be unrolled and His wrath can fall. He will lay claim to the earth as soon as His prophecies (the seals) are fulfilled.

Pre-wrath says the church will not be raptured at the beginning of the seven-year period because the seals are not yet God's wrath – they are the rise of the Antichrist and his government. The wrath of God will only fall when the scroll is unrolled.

Thought for the day:
The Antichrist's rise will bring a type of peace, but that peace will be false. Do you think you will recognize him when he comes? Even if the world is telling you he is "good?" Even if he speaks "peace?" Even if the masses believe him? Will you stand up to warn those around you, even if it will ultimately bring persecution? More on this tomorrow.

1 Moore, Beth. DVD Study *Here and Now ... There and Then: A lecture series on Revelation* (Houston, Texas: Living Proof Ministries, 2009), p32.

Day NINETEEN
REVELATION 6:3-6
SEALS TWO AND THREE

SEAL TWO - TERROR

³When He broke the second seal, I heard the second living creature saying, "Come." ⁴And another, a red horse, went out; and to him who sat on it, it was granted to take peace from the earth, and that men would slay one another; and a great sword was given to him.

Revelation 6:3-4

Jesus says in Matthew 24:6-7a, "You will be hearing of wars and rumors of wars. See that you are not frightened, for those things must take place, but that is not yet the end. For nation will rise against nation, and kingdom against kingdom." Jesus' words foreshadow the rider on the red horse. This rider will cause world-wide social unrest and conflict. The rider on the red horse appears after the Antichrist has made a peace treaty with Israel. This seems to indicate the rise of the Antichrist will spur the second rider into action, bringing terror to the rest of the world. If we think about this horseman in relation to the first, his appearance might become clear. If Israel signs a peace treaty, whom will that peace treaty be with? With whom, my faithful friends, is Israel constantly at war? You guessed it –the Middle Eastern powers surrounding them.

The Antichrist, then, will be a player in the Middle East. He will promise both Israel, and the rest of the world, peace – and the world will believe him. When that peace treaty is signed, do you think everyone in the Islamic world will be content? No! Terrorists will rise around the world, protesting the peace. It would even be very logical to assume the followers of Islam might even know their leader will ultimately go back on his word and break the very peace treaty he signed – the very deception scripture warns us about. Did you know that if a Muslim nation signs a treaty with a non-Muslim nation the Muslim leadership doesn't believe that treaty is binding? Why? The treaty is signed by an infidel. Muslims see the infidel, or those who do not believe in Islam, as lower class citizens. They believe a treaty is time to regroup and prepare for war. The following quote is by Walid Shoebat in *God's War on Terror*:

To this very day, Muslims do not view peace treaties in the same way that most people understand a "peace-treaty." To the Muslim mind, treaties are not binding agreements, but rather opportunities to grow stronger or buy time or to appear peaceful while preparing for war. But make no mistake, making peace treaties with the infidels simply for the sake of peace is never the ultimate goal. The only goal of Islam is victory over the whole world. Concepts such as honor, ethics, or obligations are afforded only a secondary importance against the supreme importance that is given to establishing the supremacy and domination of Islam throughout the whole world.[1]

Now the first two horsemen come into sharp focus. The Antichrist will be leading the nations who hate Israel. He will promise peace and Israel will believe him. Then, after the peace treaty is signed and the world believes peace has finally been achieved, the terrorists' swords will rise across the land. The Antichrist will secretly support such efforts because his ultimate aim is the destruction of Israel and dominion of the world.

SEAL THREE - FAMINE

[5]When He broke the third seal, I heard the third living creature saying, "Come." I looked, and behold, a black horse; and he who sat on it had a pair of scales in his hand. [6]And I heard something like a voice in the center of the four living creatures saying, "A quart of wheat for a denarius, and three quarts of barley for a denarius; and do not damage the oil and the wine.

Revelation 6:5-6

Jesus says, "And in various places there will be famines and earthquakes. But all these things are merely the beginning of the birth pangs" (Matthew 24:7b-8). Jesus' words here correlate to the rider on the black horse. This rider will bring famine because the rider on the red horse has caused worldwide upheaval. Where unrest occurs, food supplies run short. This in turn creates more chaos as desperate people struggle to stay alive. The rider on the black horse has a "pair of scales in his hand," representing the rising cost of food in a dwindling food supply. I believe this means the government will start rationing food to keep the masses from rioting.

A voice from the center of the four living creatures says, "A quart of wheat for a denarius, and three quarts of barley for a denarius." In biblical times, a denarius represented one person's wages for a day.[2] Let's put this into perspective. You will work an entire day and only be able to purchase four cups of wheat, which will make approximately two loaves of bread. If you are feeding a family, you might have just enough to make it through the day. People will be able to eat, but there will be no surplus, and if you have a large family, there may be a shortage. This will cause increased unease and fear in increasingly dangerous times.

Some scholars believe the call not to damage the oil and the wine indicates the rich will not be affected by the famine, only the middle to lower classes. This could be, but I think we need to dig deeper. Let's relook at Daniel 9:27.

He will confirm a covenant with many for one 'seven.' In the middle of the 'seven' he will put an end to sacrifice and offering."

Daniel 9:27a NIV

After the Antichrist makes a treaty or a "covenant" with Israel for seven years, he will deceive them and "put an end to sacrifice and offering" at the middle of the final seven-year period. In other words, the Antichrist will stop the Jewish sacrificial system. If he stops the sacrificial system at the middle of the seven years, obviously, the Jewish temple will have to be rebuilt sometime before that. As of today, the temple remains a dream in the minds of the Jewish people. I firmly believe when the Antichrist signs the treaty with Israel, the treaty will allow the Israelites to rebuild their sacred temple. I do not believe the Jewish people would sign a treaty without the rebuilding of their temple as a stipulation of peace. The Jews have already formed The Temple Institute (www.templeinstitute.org), which is an organization committed to rebuilding the temple. They have recreated the breastplate of the High Priest, the bronze altar, the candlesticks and many other things God commanded they build for the tabernacle in the Exodus (Exodus 25-40). The Jews are ready for construction. If they received a green light from the international community their temple could be rebuilt in a very short period of time.

So, between the time the peace treaty is signed at the beginning of the final seven years and the mid-point of the final seven years when the Antichrist stops sacrifice and grain offering, the Jewish people will once again have a fully functioning temple.

We know from scripture oil and wine were very important to the sacrificial process.

> *Now this is what you shall offer on the altar: two one year old lambs each day, continuously. The one lamb you shall offer in the morning and the other lamb you shall offer at twilight; and there shall be one-tenth of an ephah of fine flour mixed with one-fourth of a hin of beaten oil, and one-fourth of a hin of wine for a drink offering with one lamb.*
>
> *Exodus 29:38-40*

The Jewish people offered two lambs each and every day. Although the Jewish people do not believe in Christ, they have been predicting His death through the daily sacrifice for thousands of years. With each sacrificial lamb, a fourth of a hin of oil mixed with fine flour and a fourth of a hin of wine were poured out over the lamb. This would represent to us Jesus' body (bread) and His blood (wine) being broken and poured out for us (Luke 22:19-20).

Why do the creatures in Revelation chapter six cry out a command not to hurt the oil and the wine? I believe God is telling us the famine will not stop the daily sacrifices in the temple. Many people say you cannot know the timing of Revelation. To some degree, they are right, but God is a very specific God. He has told us the signs of His return in Matthew 24, and let us not forget the Revelation is "the revelation of Jesus Christ." Revelation means revealing. God is telling us exactly when things will happen. This seal proves it. This is before the midpoint, when the oil and the wine are still being poured out on the temple altar. The Antichrist has yet to take "his seat in the temple of God, displaying himself as being God" (2 Thessalonians 2:4b). Let's add this to our timeline.

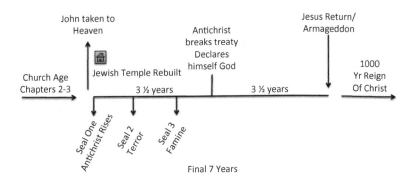

Final 7 Years

Note, in the above timeline, there are a few things we can know with relative certainty: the beginning of the seven years will be the signing of the peace treaty; the midpoint is when the Antichrist sets himself up as god in the temple of God and stops the sacrificial system. Seal two and three could move closer to the beginning or closer to the midpoint; we cannot know for sure when they will start. But the above timeline is a very good model for what will occur.

Thought for the day:

After you have read this study, you should recognize the Antichrist when he rises. Once you see that happen, you know terror and famine are coming. Do you think you could do something to help your family prepare? Something to think about. Tomorrow you will see the tribulation start. Hang tight.

1 Shoebat, Walid, written with Joel Richardson. *God's War on Terror* (Top Executive Media, 2008). Also check out Joel Richardson's *Antichrist Islam's Awaited Messiah* published in 2006. Both are well worth the read.

2 *Holman Illustrated Bible Dictionary* published in 2003 by Holman Bible Publishers in Nashville, Tennessee, p412.

SEAL FOUR - DEATH

⁷When the Lamb broke the fourth seal, I heard the voice of the fourth living creature saying, "Come." ⁸I looked, and behold, an ashen horse; and he who sat on it had the name Death; and Hades was following with him. Authority was given to them over a fourth of the earth, to kill with sword and with famine and with pestilence and by the wild beasts of the earth.

Revelation 6:7-8

The opening of this seal is a direct result of the opening of the previous seals. The Antichrist has risen up, promising false peace but causing the rider of the second horse to rear his ugly head. Terror enters the world by the sword. When the sword rides, famine follows close behind, and then comes death. This seal is death due to the sword (the second seal), famine (the third seal) and disease (the aftermath of the second and third seals).

Remember, according to the pre-wrath theory this is not yet God's wrath. The seals are the rise of the Antichrist that culminates into the persecution of God's saints. Although these are horrifically bad times, God's wrath has yet to fall.

We are told this rider has power over a fourth of the earth. During the fourth seal, one quarter of the world's population will die due to famine, sword, and disease. Think about this for a minute. There are approximately seven billion people in the world today. If a fourth of them perish during this seal it means over 1.75 billion people die. The famine is severe and the disease following the famine is catastrophic.

We are also told that there is another way the people of the earth are killed: "by the wild beasts of the earth." Is this actually saying lions and tigers are going to come to the cities and kill? Let's look at scripture.

For thus says the Lord God, "How much more when I send My four severe judgments against Jerusalem: sword, famine, wild beasts and plague to cut off man and beast from it!

Ezekiel 14:21

There are four judgments God mentions in the above scripture. These are the same four judgments we see in Revelation: sword, famine, plague, and wild beasts. Yes, if there is a shortage of food, the beasts of the forests will be hungry too. They will fight for food just as much as we will. And don't forget, we also have smaller wild beasts that can do a great deal of harm. Insects can devastate our bodies with sickness and disease. Yes, the beasts Revelation speaks of could very well be actual wild beasts. But I think there is more to it than that. Let's dig deeper.

The Greek word translated "wild beasts" is "qhrivon." It is used thirty-eight times in the King James Version of the New Testament. Thirty-four of those times, it is translated "beast" not "wild beast." In three of the other four passages where it is translated "wild beast" the passage obviously meant animals, such as when Jesus was tempted in the wilderness among the "wild beasts" (Mark 1:13) and when Peter receives his vision to "kill and eat" (Acts 10:12 and 11:6). But the last "qhrivon" that is translated "wild beast" occurs here, in the fourth seal of Revelation. But this passage could have been translated "to kill with sword and with famine and with pestilence and by the beasts of the earth." Of the thirty-eight times the word "qhrivon" is used in the King James Version of the New Testament, thirty of those times are in Revelation, and each time, other than chapter six, "qhrivon" is translated "beasts."[3] Let me say that another way: every other time the word "qhrivon" is used in Revelation, it is always translated "beast" and it always refers to personas that persecute the saints!

As we continue reading Revelation, we will find there are three beasts introduced and discussed in detail: Satan (the dragon), the Antichrist (the beast from the sea), and the false prophet (the beast out of the earth). Why would verse eight of chapter six be translated "wild beasts" instead of "beasts" if in every other passage in Revelation it is translated differently? In this seal, God is telling us something profound: this is when the Antichrist's persecution begins and the mark of the beast is introduced.

Although we haven't read about "the mark of the beast" yet in our study, it is described in Revelation 13.

And he causes all, the small and the great, and the rich and the poor, and the free men and the slaves, to be given a mark on their right hand or on their forehead, and he provides that no one will be able to buy or to sell, except the one who has the mark, either the name of the beast or the number of his name."

In the fourth seal, a quarter of the earth's population is killed, and one way they are killed is by the "beasts." The beasts of Revelation 12 and 13 institute what is deemed "the mark of the beast" in order to terrorize the world. This mark will be anti-Christ and anti-God. Without this mark you will be unable to buy and sell. Jesus is telling us this seal will start at the midpoint of the last seven years. Why? Because that is when the Antichrist takes his seat in the temple of God and declares to the entire world he is god (Daniel 9:27, 2 Thessalonians 2:4). This is when his persecution begins – when he breaks the treaty with Israel. This is what Jesus warns us about in Matthew 24:9: "Then they will deliver you to tribulation, and will kill you and you will be hated by all nations because of My name." Seal number four is when the mark of the beast will be forced upon the world and "the tribulation" will begin. Remember when I said the entire seven-year period is not "the tribulation?" This is what I meant: nowhere in the Bible does "tribulation" specifically describe the final seven years. Let's look at scripture.

And Jesus answered and said to them, "See to it that no one misleads you. For many will come in My name, saying 'I am the Christ,' and will mislead many [SEAL ONE]. You will be hearing of wars and rumors of wars. See that you are not frightened, for those things must take place, but that is not yet the end. For nation will rise against nation, and kingdom against kingdom [SEAL TWO], and in various places there will be famines and earthquakes [SEAL THREE]. But all these things are merely the beginning of birth pangs. Then they will deliver you to tribulation [SEAL FOUR], and will kill you, and you will be hated by all nations because of My name.

Matthew 24:4-9, explanation added

First comes false christs (seal one), then war and national unrest (seal two) and then famines (seal three), and then the culmination of all (seal four) and then, ultimately, they will begin to kill you (we will see this in seal five).

The tribulation (affliction) begins at the fourth seal, when the mark of the beast is introduced and the peace treaty is broken. The mask of the Antichrist is now off and his true intentions will be made known – dominion of the world and the destruction of Israel.

This seal begins the persecution of God's saints. If you do not take the mark of the beast, you will be unable to buy or sell, so you will be unable to buy food that will already be in short supply because of seal number three (famine); you will be unable to receive medical care if you contract a disease because of seal number four (pestilence); and the Antichrist's sword (the beasts sword) will begin to hunt you down if you do not take the mark. Now let's pause here for a moment. Who are those that will not take the mark? Christians and Jews: Those who worship the one true God. Let me say that another way: a quarter of the earth will die during this seal because of the sword (seal two), the famine (seal three), disease (seal four), and persecution (mark of the beast)! The saints are now officially undergoing tribulation.

How many of us have ever gone a day without the food we need to survive? If that supply is taken away, how many will take the mark? Is our faith genuine under tribulation (Smyrna) or will we crumble to the pagan society (Thyatira) desperate to feed our families? Will we stand firm in our faith (Philadelphia) despite our little strength, or will we turn from the faith and become lukewarm by taking the mark and rationalizing it as survival (Laodicea)?

Many Christians fear they will take the mark by accident. You will not. The mark will be anti-Christ and anti-God. If you take it, you will be denying the Father and the Son (1 John 2:22). You will be glorifying Satan and denying Christ (Revelation 13:4). This mark will not be a credit card number unless that number has a blasphemous name associated with it. This mark will be blatantly denying the King of kings and Lord of lords.

The persecution has begun. The Antichrist has declared himself God. The ramifications are seen in the next seal. Let's look at this on our timeline.

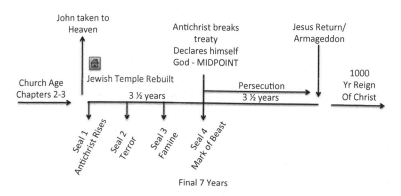

Final 7 Years

Some pre-wrath books I have read do not show a timeline. Others place the fourth seal before the mid-point and do not necessarily pinpoint when the mark of the beast is introduced. I feel the mark of the beast and the fourth seal have to occur when the Antichrist is revealed at the midpoint (2 Thessalonians 2:3-4).[4] But please, search scripture and come to your own conclusions about when the seals take place.

Thought for the day:
The mark of the beast will one day become a reality. You will be unable to buy or sell if you do not accept it. Don't rationalize this mark away. No one who takes the mark will enter heaven. Tomorrow we will take it one step further. If food is in short supply, and the population of the earth is after it, soon those who do not take the mark will be expendable. Don't you agree? Who wants those who won't be "tolerant" of the mark to try to take the food that everyone else wants?

3 Check out Robert Van Kampen's *The Rapture Question Answered (*Grand Rapids, MI: Fleming H. Revell, 1997), p.149.

4 Nigro, H.L. *Before God's Wrath, The Bible's Answer to the Timing of the Rapture* (Milesburg, PA: Strong Tower Publishing, 2004), 218. This author did a very extensive job of expounding on the pre-wrath timing of the rapture as first explained by Robert Van Kampen. She places the fourth seal before the midpoint.

Salerno, Donald A, Jr. *Revelation Unsealed* (College Station, TX: Virtualbookworm.com Publishing Inc., 2004), 96-107. This author places the mark of the beast somewhere during the fourth seal at the midpoint.

SEAL FIVE - MARTYRS

⁹**When the Lamb broke the fifth seal, I saw underneath the altar the souls of those who had been slain because of the word of God, and because of the testimony which they had maintained; ¹⁰and they cried out with a loud voice, saying, "How long, O Lord, holy and true, will You refrain from judging and avenging our blood on those who dwell on the earth?" ¹¹And there was given to each of them a white robe; and they were told that they should rest for a little while longer, until the number of their fellow servants and their brethren who were to be killed even as they had been, would be completed also.**

Revelation 6:9-11

Today we are in for a wild ride, so fasten your seatbelts. God has a lot to show us today. In Matthew 24:9 notice Jesus says "you" will be enduring tribulation. This is a very important distinction. During Jesus' teaching known as the Olivet Discourse seen in Matthew 24, Luke 21, and Mark 13, Jesus is speaking to His disciples about the end times, and our Savior tells them "you" will be delivered to tribulation.

The opening of the fifth seal ushers in Jesus' warning:

For then there will be a great tribulation, such as has not occurred since the beginning of the world until now, nor ever will. Unless those days had been cut short, no life would have been saved; but for the sake of the elect those days will be cut short.

Matthew 24:21-22

The persecution of the saints began with the fourth seal and rises to a crescendo in seal number five. The saints are being martyred for their faith because they refuse to take the mark of the beast. If you are discovered, you are killed: this is what Jesus refers to as "the great tribulation" in Matthew 24:21. They are crying out, "How long, O Lord, holy and true, will You refrain from judging and avenging our blood on those who dwell on the earth?" How will God avenge these saints? His wrath! As of yet it has not been

120

poured out, and the saints are begging God to hurry up. Always remember, our prayers are like incense before the throne of grace (Revelation 5:8). God always hears us, and He will have the final word.

So again, "the tribulation" according to the pre-wrath theory is really not the entire seven-year period. The first half of the final seven years is the rise of the Antichrist and his false religion. The tribulation of the saints starts at the midpoint of the final seven years and rises to all out martyrdom in seal number five. After the rapture of the church (coming soon) those remaining on earth who turn to Christ will still endure tribulation because of the continued persecution of the Antichrist. In essence, you can say the entire second half of the final seven years is "the tribulation."

After the souls of the martyrs cry out to God, they are handed white robes, but told to rest until more martyrs are ushered into heaven. The Greek word used for rest is "anapauo" and it means "to keep quiet, of calm and patient expectation." Patient expectation of what? The rapture and the wrath of God, which will unite the saints and unleash the righteous anger of the judge of the universe. God knows exactly how many martyrs there will be before He will rescue us from the hand of the Antichrist. As Jesus says in Matthew 24, there will be a time when He will "cut short" the tribulation. That, my faithful friends, will be the great escape, the rapture, and the day we meet the King!

The first five seals correspond perfectly to Jesus' own words in Matthew 24:4-10. Jesus says first comes false christs (seal one), then comes the sword (seal two), then comes famine (seal three) and then comes tribulation (seal four), and then they will kill you (seal 5).[1] Note, that the last time "tribulation" is mentioned in the book of Revelation is in 7:14, right after the sixth seal is opened. This will become important as we study the next seal.

In summary, the seal judgments as we have studied them do not appear to be the wrath of God, but the rise of the Antichrist and his governmental system that will fulfill all prophecy and cause God's anger to ignite to such levels that the destruction of the ungodly will be paramount. In fact, the martyrs in seal five actually cry out to God, asking Him how long He will wait to avenge their blood (with His wrath). Let's look at seal number five on our timeline before we study seal six.

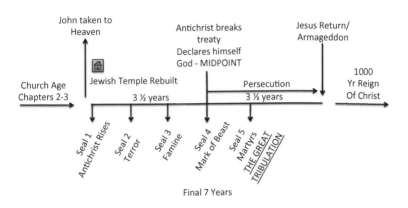

Final 7 Years

SEAL SIX – SUN DARK AND MOON TO BLOOD

[12]I looked when He broke the sixth seal, and there was a great earthquake; and the sun became black as sackcloth made of hair, and the whole moon became like blood; [13]and the stars of the sky fell to the earth, as a fig tree casts its unripe figs when shaken by a great wind. [14]The sky was split apart like a scroll when it is rolled up, and every mountain and island were moved out of their places. [15]Then the kings of the earth and the great men and the commanders and the rich and the strong and every slave and free man hid themselves in the caves and among the rocks of the mountains; [16]and they said to the mountains and to the rocks, "Fall on us and hide us from the presence of Him who sits on the throne, and from the wrath of the Lamb; [17]for the great day of their wrath has come, and who is able to stand?"

Revelation 6:12-17

Hear Jesus' own words, "For then there will be a great tribulation, such as has not occurred since the beginning of the world until now, nor ever will. Unless those days had been cut short, no life would have been saved; but for the sake of the elect those days will be cut short" (Matthew 24:21-22). When Jesus is talking to His disciples in the Olivet Discourse, He tells them:

And just as it happened in the days of Noah, so it will be also in the days of the Son of Man: they were eating, they were drinking, they were marrying, they were being given in marriage, until the day that Noah entered the ark, and the flood came and destroyed them all. It was the same as happened in the days of Lot: they were eating, they were drinking, they were buying, they were selling, they were planting, they were building; but on the day that Lot went out from Sodom it rained fire and brimstone from heaven and destroyed them all. It will be just the same on the day that the Son of Man is revealed . . . I tell you, on that night there will be two in one bed; one will be taken and the other will be left. There will be two women grinding at the same place; one will be taken and the other will be left."

Luke 17:26-30, 34-36

In the day the Son of Man is revealed one will be taken and the other left. This is referring to what believers call the rapture and what Jesus calls "cutting short" the tribulation. Remember, the tribulation is the persecution of God's saints beginning in the fourth seal and continuing into the "great tribulation" of the fifth seal. Now the six seal will cut short that time of tribulation as Jesus says in Matthew 24. In the above scripture the wrath of God has yet to fall because everything is going on "normally." Jesus said the days of the rapture would be just like the days of Noah and the days of Lot. If you look at Noah (Genesis 7:11-13) and Lot (Genesis 19:15, 23-24), both were saved from the wrath of God the same day God's wrath fell. Noah entered the ark the same day the floodwaters started. Lot was taken out of Sodom the same day fire and brimstone rained down and destroyed the city. Jesus is telling us the rapture will be no exception. We will be taken out of the world on the same day the wrath of God pours down on the wicked.[2] Let's see if this is clarified in scripture.

Brothers, we do not want you to be ignorant about those who fall asleep, or to grieve like the rest of men, who have no hope. We believe that Jesus died and rose again and so we believe that God will bring with Jesus those who have fallen asleep in him. According to the Lord's own word, we tell you that we who are still alive, who are left till the coming of the Lord, will certainly not precede those who have fallen asleep. For the Lord himself will come down from heaven, with a loud command, with the voice of the archangel and with the trumpet call of God, and the dead in Christ will rise first. After that, we who are still alive and are left will be caught up together with them in the clouds to meet the Lord in the air [RAPTURE]. And so we will be with the Lord forever. Therefore encourage each other with these words. Now, brothers, about times and dates we do not need to write to you [TIMES AND DATES OF THE RAPTURE], for you know very well that the day of the Lord [SAME DAY!] will come like a thief in the night. While people are saying, "Peace and safety," destruction will come on them suddenly, as labor pains on a pregnant woman, and they will not escape. But you, brothers, are not in darkness so that this day should surprise you like a thief. You are all sons of the light and sons of the day. We do not belong to the night or to the darkness. So then, let us not be like others, who are asleep, but let us be alert and self-controlled.

1 Thessalonians 4:13-5:6 NIV, explanation added

This passage starts off by telling us about the rapture and then equates the rapture to the day of the Lord. What is the day of the Lord? I am glad you asked. That, my faithful friends, is the wrath of God. As soon as we are raptured, the wrath of God starts to fall, just like in the days of Noah and the days of Lot. Is there another scripture we could look at that would link the wrath of God, or the day of the Lord, past the fifth seal? Yes, there is.

I will display wonders in the sky and on the earth, blood, fire and columns of smoke. The sun will be turned into darkness and the moon into blood before the great and awesome day of the Lord comes. And it will come about that whoever calls on the name of the Lord will be delivered.

Joel 2:30-32a

In the letter to the Thessalonians, Paul indicates the rapture and the day of the Lord are the same day. This matches Jesus' words that the time of the Son of Man will be just like the days of Noah and Lot. Joel then clarifies when the rapture takes place by saying "the sun will be turned into darkness and the moon into blood *before* the great and awesome day of the Lord comes." So, before the day of the Lord (God's wrath), the sun will be turned into darkness and the moon will turn into blood, and at that time, whoever calls on the name of the Lord will be delivered (the rapture – the same day as the wrath falls).

Do we see where this is happening in Revelation? Yes, in Revelation 6:12 where the sun turns black and the moon turns to blood. Look at the Joel scripture again. The same thing is happening here. Joel is talking about the sixth seal.

After the sign in the sun and the moon, we "escape" as it says in Joel. So the rapture occurs sometime after the sixth seal, before the seventh seal is opened.

Let's say that another way. After the persecution of the fifth seal (the great tribulation), Jesus will cut the time short by giving His elect a sign in the sun and moon and stars (the sixth seal), and before the wrath of God starts to fall (the seventh seal). If you aren't convinced yet, let's look at another verse.

Now we request you, brethren, with regard to the coming of our Lord Jesus Christ and our gathering together to Him [THE RAPTURE], that you not be quickly shaken from your composure or be disturbed either by a spirit or a message or a letter as if from us, to the effect that the day of the Lord [WRATH OF GOD] has already come [SAME DAY]. Let no one in any way deceive you, for it will not come unless the apostasy comes first, and the man of lawlessness [ANTICHRIST] is revealed, the son of destruction, who opposes and exalts himself above every so-called god or object of worship, so that he takes his seat in the temple of God, displaying himself as being God.

2 Thessalonians 2:1-4, explanation added[3]

Again, we see the rapture being equated to the day of the Lord, and here we have something else to watch for – the rise of the Antichrist – the seals! When does the apostasy come? When people have to choose a side at the midpoint of the final seven years, during the fourth seal and the mark of the beast. At that time there will be a falling away. If you can't buy food without the mark, many will take it. There will be a mass exodus from the church.

"Then they will deliver you to tribulation [SEAL FOUR], and will kill you [SEAL FIVE], and you will be hated by all nations because of My name. At that time many will fall away and will betray one another and hate one another."

Matthew 24:9-10, explanation added

The opening of the sixth seal begins the signs in the stars. Not only does the sun turn black and the moon to blood, but there is also a great earthquake. "The sky was split apart like a scroll when it is rolled up, and every mountain and island were moved out of their places." This is a massive earthquake. In 2011 an earthquake and tsunami hit Japan, decimating the country. Experts say Japan shifted approximately thirteen meters and the earth's axis shifted six and a half inches, causing the earth to rotate faster, shortening the day by millionths of a second.[4] This is shocking. An earthquake can cause not only islands to shift, but also the earth itself.

Look at the following scriptures to see what exactly will happen to the earth at the pouring out of God's wrath.

Therefore I will make the heavens tremble, and the earth will be shaken from its place at the fury of the Lord of hosts in the day of His burning anger.

Isaiah 13:13

Behold, the Lord lays the earth waste, devastates it, distorts its surface and scatters its inhabitants.

Isaiah 24:1

The earth is broken asunder, the earth is split through, the earth is shaken violently. The earth reels to and fro like a drunkard and it totters like a shack, for its transgression is heavy upon it, and it will fall, never to rise again. So it will happen in that day, that the Lord will punish the host of heaven on high, and the kings of the earth on earth. They will be gathered together like prisoners in the dungeon, and will be confined in prison; and after many days they will be punished.

Isaiah 24:19-22

These scriptures are speaking of the day of the Lord. The earth will be shaken like a drunkard. Seal six says there will be a massive earthquake and every island and mountain will be moved from their places. This isn't symbolic; this is truth. Just as the earthquake moved Japan and the entire earth, so will this earthquake, but even more so. What we are in now are the birth pangs. When the wrath of God is about to fall, there will be no mistaking it.

"The stars from the sky fell to the earth as a fig tree casts its unripe figs when shaken by a great wind." Revelation goes on to say that the sky is rolled up like a scroll. This could actually be literal stars falling from the sky, or because the earth is shaking so violently, it shifts the earth's axis and causes the stars to look like they are falling. We see this also in Isaiah:

And all the host of heaven will wear away, and the sky will be rolled up like a scroll; and their hosts will also wither away as a leaf withers from the vine, or as one withers from the fig tree. For My sword is satiated in heaven, behold it shall descend for judgment upon Edom and upon the people whom I have devoted to destruction.
Isaiah 34:4-5

I find it interesting that the fig tree is used as the illustration both in Revelation chapter six and in Isaiah 34. Both scriptures also discuss the sky rolling up like a scroll. Remember, most scholars believe the fig tree represents Israel. According to Daniel chapter nine, the end times are for the nation of Israel to come to repentance and see Jesus as their Messiah (see also Romans 11:26-27). In these verses the fig tree casts its unripe figs to the ground and its leaves wither. We know from scripture that most in Israel will not come to repentance until the final moments leading to Jesus' return.

"Behold, your house is left to you desolate; and I say to you, you will not see Me until the time comes when you say, 'Blessed is He who comes in the name of the Lord.'"
Luke 13:35

The fig tree isn't exempt from God's wrath. The chosen nation will cast some unripe figs to the ground (unbelievers) when God's wrath is about to fall. In fact, we know exactly how many in Israel will be saved.

"It will come about in all the land," declares the Lord, "that two parts in it will be cut off and perish; but the

third will be left in it. And I will bring the third part through the fire, refine them as silver is refined, and test them as gold is tested. They will call on My name, and I will answer them; I will say, 'They are My people,' and they will say, 'The Lord is my God.'"

Zechariah 13:8-9

Israel will come to faith! Glory! Look again at Revelation 6:16:

And they said to the mountains and to the rocks, "Fall on us and hide us from the presence of Him who sits on the throne, and from the wrath of the Lamb."

Revelation 6:16

The sixth seal announces the wrath of God quite clearly. We already learned the wrath of God is the day of the Lord and the day of the Lord is also the rapture (as in the days of Noah and Lot). This is the first time in the book of Revelation the word "wrath" is used, but it is not the last. It appears over ten more times in the book of Revelation.

The followers of the pre-wrath theory place the rapture after the sixth seal, right when the wrath of God is announced.[5] "For God has not destined us for wrath, but for obtaining salvation through our Lord Jesus Christ" (1 Thessalonians 5:9). We are rescued before the opening of the seventh seal, or the wrath of God.

Let's look at this on our timeline. Seals one through five are depicted below the timeline because they are events transpiring on earth. Seal six is depicted above the timeline because at this point the saints are raptured to heaven. This is the final prophecy that has to be fulfilled before the scroll can be unrolled and the wrath of God can begin.

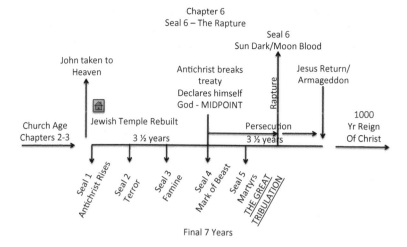

Thought for the day:

The sun goes dark, the moon turns to blood, people are hiding in caves, mountains are moving, the earth is shaking, and people are disappearing. But do you think anyone will really notice the missing faithful if there is fire falling from the sky? More on the fire in a few days. Keep pressing on.

1 Nigro, H.L. *Before God's Wrath, The Bible's Answer to the Timing of the Rapture* (Milesburg, PA: Strong Tower Publishing, 2004), 139. This author did a very extensive job of expounding on the pre-wrath timing of the rapture as first explained by Robert Van Kampen. She places the fourth seal before the midpoint.

2 Kampen, Robert Van. *The Rapture Question Answered* (Grand Rapids, MI: Fleming H. Revell, 1997), 58-64.

3 Kampen, Robert Van, 119-127

4 BBC News, 14 March 2011, *How the Quake has Moved Japan*, by Paul Rincon.

5 Kampen, Robert Van, 151-162.

Day TWENTY-TWO
REVELATION 7:1-8
SEALING THE BOND SERVANTS

¹After this I saw four angels standing at the four corners of the earth, holding back the four winds of the earth, so that no wind would blow on the earth or on the sea or on any tree. ²And I saw another angel ascending from the rising of the sun, having the seal of the living God; and he cried out with a loud voice to the four angels to whom it was granted to harm the earth and the sea, ³saying, "Do not harm the earth or the sea or the trees until we have sealed the bond-servants of our God on their foreheads." ⁴And I heard the number of those who were sealed, one hundred and forty-four thousand sealed from every tribe of the sons of Israel: ⁵from the tribe of Judah, twelve thousand were sealed, from the tribe of Reuben twelve thousand, from the tribe of Gad twelve thousand, ⁶from the tribe of Asher twelve thousand, from the tribe of Naphtali twelve thousand, from the tribe of Manasseh twelve thousand, ⁷from the tribe of Simeon twelve thousand, from the tribe of Levi twelve thousand, from the tribe of Issachar twelve thousand, ⁸from the tribe of Zebulun twelve thousand, from the tribe of Joseph twelve thousand, from the tribe of Benjamin, twelve thousand were sealed.

Revelation 7:1-8

John sees angels standing at the four corners of the earth, holding back the four winds. What are the winds and why are the angels holding them back? In scripture, the four winds have been used to refer to the entire world or the four corners of the earth.

> *"And He will send forth His angels with a great trumpet and they will gather together His elect from the four winds, from one end of the sky to the other."*
> *Matthew 24:31*

In Jesus' own words, the four winds are "from one end of the sky to the other." So this is the totality of the earth. These angels are holding back the winds from the entire globe.

The four winds are also associated with something that is very important to our study.

"I will bring upon Elam the four winds from the four ends of heaven, and will scatter them to all these winds; and there will be no nation to which the outcasts of Elam will not go. So I will shatter Elam before their enemies and before those who seek their lives; and I will bring calamity upon them, even my fierce anger," declares the Lord.

Jeremiah 49:36-37, (Elam is modern day Iran[1])

Does God sound a little angry? Yes! The four winds are being used to describe His wrath. Remember, Gods wrath is announced at the end of the sixth seal (Revelation 6:16). Right after God's wrath is announced in chapter six, we see the winds in chapter seven being "held back." Let me say that another way: God's wrath is announced at the end of chapter six; here we see the winds, or God's wrath, being held back until the angels "have sealed the bond-servants of our God on their foreheads." The wrath of God, announced in chapter six, is only delayed long enough for the bond-servants of God to be sealed.

In scripture we see that we, too, have a seal.

Now He who establishes us with you in Christ and anointed us is God, who also sealed us and gave us the Spirit in our hearts as a pledge.

2 Corinthians 1:21-22

We are sealed when we come to faith in Christ.[2] Scripture is telling us these 144,000 have just come to faith in Jesus.

Suddenly, we have 144,000 Jewish believers come to faith in the true Messiah, Jesus Christ. We know these are Jewish believers because they are identified as "sons of Israel" and scripture goes on to say that 12,000 from each tribe are sealed with the seal of the living God.

The twelve sons of Jacob (or Israel) were Reuben, Simeon, Levi, Judah, Issachar, Zebulun, Gad, Asher, Dan, Naphtali, Joseph, and Benjamin. However, the twelve tribes of Israel are different than the above list. The priestly tribe of Levi wasn't given an inheritance of land the other tribes received because their focus was the temple of God.

Therefore, Levi does not have a portion or inheritance with his brothers; the Lord is his inheritance.

Deuteronomy 10:9

Instead, the Levites were allotted cities within the twelve divisions of the land (Joshua 21:41). In Old Testament times, the firstborn son received a double portion of the father's inheritance. Reuben, the firstborn of Jacob lost that inheritance when he slept with his father's concubine (Genesis 35:22, 1 Chronicles 5:1). Joseph then, Jacob's favorite son, received the double portion through his two sons whom Jacob claimed as his own.

"Now your two sons, who were born to you in the land of Egypt before I came to you in Egypt, are mine; Ephraim and Manasseh shall be mine, as Reuben and Simeon are"

Genesis 48:5

So, the twelve tribes became: Ephraim and Manasseh (Joseph's sons), Reuben, Simeon, Judah, Issachar, Zebulun, Gad, Asher, Dan, Naphtali, and Benjamin. Levi was not included in this count because they would forever be the priestly tribe, without a land portion.

Look at the twelve tribes who were sealed in Revelation. Based on the above list, with Ephraim and Manasseh substituting for Joseph, and Levi not included, what do you find odd?

Levi is included in the list and Dan is not there at all. Note also in Revelation seven, although Manasseh (Joseph's firstborn) is named in the sealing of the twelve tribes, Ephraim (Joseph's second son) is not. The angel in Revelation seven seals Joseph and Manasseh, not Ephraim and Manasseh. Although Ephraim and Manasseh both came through Joseph and both are technically of the tribe of Joseph, it is curious that Manasseh and Joseph are specified and not Manasseh and Ephraim.

We could reason since the Levitical tribe is no longer needed as temple priests (because of Jesus' sacrifice) they are mentioned as one of the twelve, but then why is Dan suspiciously absent? Some scholars believe Dan may be involved in the end time rebellion against God. Some even go so far to say that the Antichrist comes from the tribe of Dan. Let's dig deeper.

Dan shall judge his people, as one of the tribes of Israel,
Dan shall be a serpent in the way, a horned snake in the
path that bites the horse's heels, so that his rider falls
backwards.

Genesis 49:16-17

Dan is associated with a snake. Does this sound like any other entity in scripture? If you said, Satan, you are right. In Genesis 3:1 we first meet Satan as a serpent. Now let's look at a very interesting story. We find it in Judges 18.

In those days there was no king of Israel; and in those
days the tribe of the Danites was seeking an inheritance
for themselves to live in, for until that day an inheritance
had not been allotted to them as a possession among the
tribes of Israel . . . They passed from there to the hill
country of Ephraim and came to the house of Micah . . .
When these went into Micah's house and took the graven
image, the ephod and household idols and the molten
image, the priest said to them, "What are you doing?" . . .
The sons of Dan set up for themselves the graven image;
and Johnathan, the son of Gershom, the son of Manasseh,
he and his sons were priests to the tribe of the Danites
until the day of the captivity of the land.

Judges 18:1, 13, 18, 30

The tribe of Dan took a graven image and worshiped it instead of traveling to worship the Lord. And they took the image from the tribe of Ephraim. If you read further in scripture, after Solomon's death, his son acted foolishly and ten of the twelve tribes of Israel separated. The southern two tribes became "Judah" and the northern ten tribes became "Israel." Israel is sometimes referred to as Ephraim in scripture.

The Lord will bring on you, on your people, and on your
father's house such days as have never come since the day
that Ephraim separated from Judah.

Isaiah 7:17a

In this passage, "Ephraim" refers to Israel. Why did God sometimes call Israel "Ephraim?" If you look in 1 Kings, you see Jeroboam, the first king of the northern country of Israel was from

133

Ephraim (1 Kings 11:26). He didn't want his people to worship the Lord in Jerusalem (where they were supposed to worship) in fear they would turn back to the king of Judah.

So the king consulted, and made two golden calves, and he said to then, "It is too much for you to go up to Jerusalem; behold your gods, O Israel, that brought you up from the land of Egypt." He set one in Bethel, and the other he put in Dan.

1 Kings 12:28-29

King Jeroboam set up two golden calves. Where did he set these images up? One was in Bethel (a city on the border of Ephraim and Judah) and became the center of worship for the northern kingdom, and the other one was in Dan. The tribes of Ephraim and Dan became the symbols of idolatry in the northern kingdom. Why did God not include their names? I think we have just stumbled upon the answer. The tribe of Dan became a serpent, setting up and worshiping idols, and so did Ephraim.

As of yet, I haven't found scripture that would lead me to believe the Antichrist is a Jew; however, it could be reasonable to conclude the tribe of Dan or Ephraim will be involved in the peace treaty with the Antichrist. Someone in Israel has to sign it, so will this leader be from one of the tribes missing in Revelation chapter seven? Only time will tell.

What we do need to focus on is the fact that these one hundred and forty-four thousand Jews suddenly believe. Pre-tribulation proponents would tell you that their conversion in chapter seven is due to the rapture of the church in chapter four, but that doesn't fit the timing.

Right after the wrath is announced in chapter six, the four winds are halted in chapter seven, and right after the bond servants of God are sealed we see a great multitude in heaven.

When does the rapture occur?

You decide.

Thought for the day:
The winds are held back long enough to seal the bond-servants of God. God does not want His wrath to fall until everyone who will come to faith has come to faith (2 Peter 3:9). He will hold back the winds. Think of the winds as things that want to rob you of true life. He will hold back the winds in your life today, so that you can do what He has planned for your life.*

1 Deluxe Then and Now Bible Maps (Torrance, California: Rose Publishing, 2008).

2 Moore, Beth. DVD Study *Here and Now ... There and Then: A lecture series on Revelation* (Houston, Texas: Living Proof Ministries, 2009), 40.

⁹After these things I looked, and behold, a great multitude which no one could count, from every nation and all tribes and peoples and tongues, standing before the throne and before the Lamb, clothed in white robes, and palm branches were in their hands; ¹⁰and they cry out with a loud voice, saying, "Salvation to our God who sits on the throne, and to the Lamb." ¹¹And all the angels were standing around the throne and around the elders and the four living creatures; and they fell on their faces before the throne and worshiped God, ¹²saying, "Amen, blessing and glory and wisdom and thanksgiving and honor and power and might, be to our God forever and ever. Amen." ¹³Then one of the elders answered, saying to me, "These who are clothed in the white robes, who are they, and where have they come from?" ¹⁴I said to him, "My lord, you know." And he said to me, "These are the ones who come out of the great tribulation, and they have washed their robes and made them white in the blood of the Lamb. ¹⁵For this reason, they are before the throne of God; and they serve Him day and night in His temple; and He who sits on the throne will spread His tabernacle over them. ¹⁶They will hunger no longer, nor thirst anymore; nor will the sun beat down on them, nor any heat; ¹⁷for the Lamb in the center of the throne will be their shepherd, and will guide them to springs of the water of life; and God will wipe every tear from their eyes."

Revelation 7:9-17

Suddenly, we see a great multitude in heaven from every nation, tribe, people and tongue. They are clothed in white and are praising the Lord and the Lamb. Everyone else we met in chapter four are also present: the angels, the elders, and the four living creatures.

Now we have a reason the one hundred and forty-four thousand have converted to faith in Jesus – the rapture of the church. This fits both the timing of Jesus' words in Matthew 24 and the rapture passages in Thessalonians (review day twenty-one). The big question is: Are the 144,000 Jews part of the raptured saints or are they left behind? This is a good question. Most scholars believe they are left behind and become powerful witnesses to Jesus in the final days on earth. This seems most likely seeing that the wrath of God is announced before they are sealed. Yet, I don't want to be too ridged in my interpretation. These saints may have realized the truth just in time. Keep this in mind as we continue our study.

Let's look at our time line. I have added the 144,000 converts right where the rapture occurs according to pre-wrath.

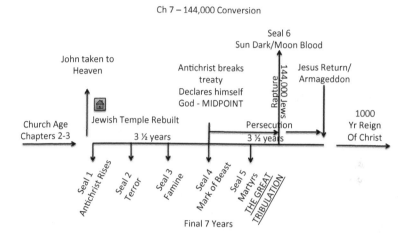

Ch 7 – 144,000 Conversion

Why does Revelation record the 144,000 conversions before we see the multitude in heaven? Well, in chapter six, John is witnessing things happening on earth. Revelation continues with the "earth" scene after the sixth seal and then moves to a "heaven" scene, which continues into chapter eight. So we are finishing the scene on earth before we move to heaven. Also, we need to remember, when John wrote Revelation, it was a continuous letter. Years later, chapters were added so we would be better able to find a passage. If you read the end of chapter six with chapter seven, it is all happening during the sixth seal. Man put chapter breaks in scripture, not God.

The tribulation of God's saints has just been "cut short" (Matthew 24:22) with the sign of the sixth seal (Joel 2:30-32). The saints are seen in chapter seven with their bodies, unlike seal five when we only see their souls. Those in chapter seven are wearing white robes and waving palm branches, unlike the souls in seal number five who are merely handed robes. In chapter four, where pre-tribulation places the rapture, you have John and twenty-four elders. Here we have what we would expect to find after the rapture – a great multitude!

The palm branch was specifically mentioned in Leviticus 23 to make temporary shelters or booths for the Jewish festival of the Feast of Tabernacles. God told them:

> *"All the native-born in Israel shall live in booths, so that your generations may know that I had the sons of Israel live in booths when I brought them out from the land of Egypt. I am the Lord your God."*
>
> *Leviticus 23:42-43*

The Jewish people celebrate this feast as a sign of their escape from Egypt. Here, the saints have been rescued from the wrath of God, and they are celebrating with palm branches, the same branches used to celebrate Israel's escape from Egypt. The escape in Revelation 7 is indeed an escape, a great escape. As the wrath of God falls, we will be ushered into heaven.

The great multitude is defined by an elder as "the ones who come out of the great tribulation, and they have washed their robes and made them white in the blood of the Lamb." They have come out of the great tribulation (seal five). This matches Jesus' own words about the tribulation:

> *"Unless those days had been cut short, no life would have been saved; but for the sake of the elect those days will be cut short."*
>
> *Matthew 24:22*

Seal number six (sign in the stars) has cut short the time of seal number five (the martyrs) with the rapture of the church (the great multitude in heaven). Glory!

These people will serve God day and night – forever and ever. The Lamb will spread His "tabernacle" over them. If you study a Jewish wedding, when the Jewish groom takes his bride back to his father's house they sit under a tent, or tabernacle, called a "hupah" to symbolize their life together. This is what Jesus is doing here. We have now gone to the "Father's house" and we are under His "tabernacle." Let's look at Isaiah 4:5 and see what will be over our heads in this place.

138

Adonai [God] will create over the whole site of Mount Tziyon [ZION] and over those who assemble there a smoking cloud by day and a shining, flaming fire by night; for the Glory will be over everything like a hupah.
                                      Isaiah 4:5 JNTP, explanation added

God's glory will be our hupah, symbolizing our union for eternity with the bridegroom!

Revelation also speaks of protection and provision, "They will hunger no longer, nor thirst anymore; nor will the sun beat down on them, nor any heat." This is the provision of the bridegroom for His bride. The Jewish people would recognize the cloud by day and fire by night in Isaiah 4:5 as the constant protection and provision of God. In the Exodus, He manifested Himself visibly with fire and a cloud, keeping them safe as they traveled through the wilderness. He provided water from the rock and manna from Heaven. Isaiah 4:6 says, "There will be a shelter to give shade from the heat by day, and refuge and protection from the storm and the rain." God will be our protection. We can apply this to our own lives today. God is here with us as we wander in this wilderness waiting for the Promised Land. Revelation seven is the moment of arrival in that Promised Land.

The Lamb is seen in the center of the throne, or the center of our worship and homage, and He is the shepherd that will guide us to the springs of the water of life.

"But whoever drinks of the water that I will give him shall never thirst; but the water that I will give him will become in him a well of water springing up to eternal life."
                                      John 4:14

Revelation chapter seven is showing us eternal life! Jesus will guide us to those springs and we will drink from them.

Then he showed me a river of the water of life, clear as crystal, coming from the throne of God and of the Lamb.
                                      Revelation 22:1

We will drink in eternity – have faith in that! – both physically, and spiritually. We will never go thirsty again. Amen!

It says God will wipe every tear from our eyes. He will take away the sorrows of this life and replace them with joy. That does not mean we will forget this life; it means the pain of this life will be like the pain of childbirth. Yes, we remember, but no, we won't remember the pain. The joy of the child takes away the painful memory of the birthing process once the child is out of the womb. Once we are with our Savior, the pain we have experienced here will be a distant memory, one that will no longer affect us. Glory!

Some people worry that we won't remember our lives in eternity. I don't believe we will forget anything, only that we won't dwell on anything. Once we are there, the pain of this life will be washed away.

And after you suffer for a short time, God, who gives all grace, will make everything right. He will make you strong and support you and keep you from falling. He called you to share in his glory in Christ, a glory that will continue forever.

1 Peter 5:10 NCV

The prior pain will not be brought to mind (Isaiah 65:17). Scripture implies this when it discusses certain things that will be with us in eternity: the names of the twelve tribes of Israel will be on the gates of the New Jerusalem (Revelation 21:12); the names of the twelve apostles of the Lamb will be written on the New Jerusalem's foundation (Revelation 21:14). Why would they be written there if history was no longer with us? Do you remember the following scripture?

Six days later Jesus took with Him Peter and James and John his brother, and led them up on a high mountain by themselves. And He was transfigured before them; and His face shone like the sun, and His garments became as white as light. And behold, Moses and Elijah appeared to them, talking with Him. Peter said to Jesus, "Lord, it is good for us to be here; if You wish, I will make three tabernacles here, one for You, and one for Moses, and one for Elijah."

Matthew 17:1-4

But they didn't know Moses or Elijah. How did they recognize them? My faithful friends, this scripture might be telling us that we will even recognize people we have never met! Never again will we be unknown. We will remember and we will praise God for our escape for eternity.

What a humdinger of a week! We have just been over the pre-wrath version of the rapture. I believe it is clarified in scripture time and again, but you need to make up your own mind. May God give you revelation.

There are a few things I want to point out before we conclude. Look back at the chart in this session. Understand that you can move seal number five and six closer to the midpoint or closer to Jesus' return, just as seal number two and three can move closer to the beginning or the midpoint. As we move onward into Revelation, I will give you my opinion of when exactly the rapture will take place, but for now, understand we still won't know the day and the hour.

Let me point out something else that may be of interest. There have been many books written about the pre-tribulation rapture. Most of them have multitudes disappearing, causing catastrophic upheaval in the world. These books propose multiple theories as to why billions of people have disappeared in a second. There is a huge outcry in the world, an awakening of those left behind. This makes for a great movie, but it will not be the case if you hold to the pre-wrath view of the rapture.

When the rapture happens, there may not be many believers left. First, beginning with the fourth seal, a quarter of the earth will be wiped out, many of which will be followers of Jesus. Secondly, other Christians will fall away from the faith when they see the persecution (Matthew 24:10). Thirdly, the fifth seal shows us there will be multitudes that will be martyred for their faith. When the rapture occurs after the opening of the sixth seal, there may not be many faithful remaining.

We do not know with certainty when the faithful will be taken during the sixth seal, but Jesus did indicate that things would be going on "normally" in Matthew 24:40-41 when the rapture occurs. There have always been dictators who want to control the world, war, famines, and pestilence. And yes, there has always been persecution of the faithful. So when Jesus says, things would be going on "normally" the seals would be considered normal. However, the massive earthquake described in chapter six where "every mountain and island were moved out of their places" and the "sky was split apart like a scroll" doesn't sound too "normal" to me.

One clue about when the rapture might happen is found in Exodus 19:16-19 when God appeared to Israel in fire and smoke.

*So it came about on the third day, when it was morning,
that there were thunder and lightning flashes and a thick
cloud upon the mountain and a very loud trumpet sound,
so that all the people who were in the camp trembled.
And Moses brought the people out of the camp to meet
God, and they stood at the foot of the mountain. Now
Mount Sinai was all in smoke because the Lord descended
upon it in fire; and its smoke ascended like the smoke of a
furnace, and the whole mountain quaked violently. When
the sound of the trumpet grew louder and louder, Moses
spoke and God answered him with thunder.*

Exodus 19:16-19

As God's presence was made known, the sound of the trumpet
grew louder and the mountain quaked. When will we rise up? At
the sound of the "trumpet of God" (1 Thessalonians 4:16). And
what happens when the trumpet of God is manifest – the mountains
quake.

If the rapture occurs right before or at the exact moment of the
massive earthquake described in seal six, the missing faithful may
very well go unnoticed. Multitudes will be buried in moments.
Rising seas will bring catastrophe. There will be many who will be
unaccounted for; the faithful few will be among the "casualties."
Will anyone suspect? Perhaps, but many others will fail to notice
who is missing. Even if they do, the wrath of God will be falling
down on the same day. I think they might be dodging fire, not
worried about the missing faithful. Doesn't make for a good movie.
But it makes for an exciting exit!

Thought for the day:
*Tomorrow we will see Jesus break the seventh seal. When
the seventh seal breaks, the scroll can be unrolled. The scroll
unleashes the wrath of God. Imagine being in heaven and seeing
the Lamb break that last seal. How would you feel? Who do you
know and love that might still be left on earth? Is there anything
you can do about that?*

[1]When the Lamb broke the seventh seal, there was silence in heaven for about half an hour. [2]And I saw the seven angels who stand before God, and seven trumpets were given to them. [3]Another angel came and stood at the altar, holding a golden censer; and much incense was given to him, so that he might add it to the prayers of all the saints on the golden altar which was before the throne. [4]And the smoke of the incense, with the prayers of the saints, went up before God out of the angel's hand. [5]Then the angel took the censer and filled it with the fire of the altar, and threw it to the earth; and there followed peals of thunder and sounds and flashes of lightning and an earthquake. [6]And the seven angels who had the seven trumpets prepared themselves to sound them.

Revelation 8:1-6

When the last seal is opened, the scroll can be unrolled. What happens when the scroll is unrolled? Let's look at scripture.

Then I lifted up my eyes again and looked, and behold, there was a flying scroll. And he said to me, "What do you see?" And I answered, "I see a flying scroll; its length is twenty cubits and its width ten cubits." Then he said to me, "This is the curse that is going forth over the face of the whole land; surely everyone who steals will be purged away according to the writing on one side, and everyone who swears will be purged away according to the writing on the other side."

Zechariah 5:1-3

This is a big scroll "going forth" over the whole land and it is God's curse.

Then I looked, and behold, a hand was extended to me; and lo, a scroll was in it. When He spread it out before me, it was written on the front and back, and written on it were lamentations, mourning and woe.

Ezekiel 2:9-10

Here is another scroll written on two sides, just like the scroll of Revelation, and it is filled with woe. We can relate both of these scrolls to the one in Revelation. If you remember, the scroll represents the title deed to the earth. Once the scroll is unrolled, Jesus can begin to reclaim the earth. In other words, once the scroll is unrolled, God's wrath – the curse, the woes – can begin. Once Jesus breaks that seventh seal, the scroll is unrolled and the day of the Lord begins.

The breaking of the seventh seal ushers in the trumpets, or the writing on the scroll. When this happens, there is silence in heaven (Revelation 8:1).

This will be such a catastrophic time for the earth that heaven falls to silence. Heaven is never without the sound of praise. Let's look back to Revelation chapter four:

And the four living creatures, each one of them having six wings, are full of eyes around and within; and day and night they do not cease to say, "Holy, Holy, Holy is the Lord God, the Almighty, who was and who is and who is to come." And when the living creatures give glory and honor and thanks to Him who sits on the throne, to Him who lives forever and ever, the twenty-four elders will fall down before Him who sits on the throne, and will worship Him who lives forever and ever, and will cast their crowns before the throne, saying, "Worthy are You, our Lord and our God, to receive glory and honor and power; for You created all things, and because of Your will they existed, and were created."

Revelation 4:8-11

Contrast that scripture with the scene in Revelation 8:1. For heaven to go silent is mind-boggling. Remember, sometime between the sixth and seventh seal the church is raptured. We see this represented in chapter seven where John witnesses the great multitudes praising God and saying, "'Salvation to our God, who sits on the throne, and to the Lamb,' and the angels, elders, and four living creatures respond, 'Amen, blessing and glory and wisdom and thanksgiving and honor and power and might, be to our God forever and ever. Amen.'" This is a vast celebration. Now heaven grows silent when the seven trumpets are handed to the seven angels. The wrath of God is about to begin and His judgment is sobering.

144

An eighth angel is seen, holding a golden censer, and incense was given to him so that he might add it to the saints' prayers. It is interesting to note that the incense in the Holy Place was only lit from the coals from the altar (Leviticus 16:12-13). The coals from the altar represent Jesus' suffering and sacrifice. In chapter five we saw that incense also represents the prayers of the saints (Revelation 5:8). Only with our belief in His sacrifice are our prayers a fragrant offering to God.

In this chapter we see more incense being added to those prayers. I believe God is adding His own sentiment to the saints' prayers and His response to the suffering of His Son. His response is more than the saints have prayed for, and it is righteous rage for the rejection of His Son. These prayers go up to God, away from the angel. This is descriptive of God replaying every prayer ever uttered by the saints. "The eyes of the Lord are toward the righteous and His ears are open to their cry" (Psalm 34:15). He thinks about their pain and struggles, their sorrow and tears. In Revelation God wants us to understand He has not forgotten one prayer uttered by His children. No tear has gone unnoticed (Psalm 56:8). No prayer will be left unanswered. Even if your prayers and pain are not righted in this lifetime, they will be righted in the end. Every prayer ever uttered is precious to God. Why is the response to our prayers sometimes delayed?

> *"For the sake of My name I delay My wrath, and for My praise I restrain it for you, in order not to cut you off."*
>
> *Isaiah 48:9*

God, the creator of the universe, does not want any to perish; He wants His children with Him. But there will be an end. There will be a response. And that response is fire.

> *Then the angel took the censer and filled it with the fire of the altar, and threw it to the earth; and there followed peals of thunder and sounds and flashes of lightning and an earthquake.*
>
> *Revelation 8:5*

This occurs right before the seven trumpets sound. Fire, thunder, and lightning are all representative of a fiery judgment; God's wrath and Jesus' second coming are replete with fire. It should be noted that many question the validity of the rapture because, they reason, Jesus can't come to earth twice, or there would be two second comings. Scripture doesn't teach two second comings of our Savior. It teaches our going and His coming. Scripture associated with the rapture uses the word "parousia" that English versions translate "coming," but "parousia" is not a verb – it is a noun. That means Jesus isn't descending or coming at the rapture as many have come to believe. He is there, He is present, but He isn't descending to the earth. We go to Him. He does not come to us. I like to think our Savior arises and steps down from His throne, and shouts "Come!" We hear a trumpet blast and the sound of the archangel, and we rise up (1 Thessalonians 4:17). Look at the following verses.

Men will go into caves of the rocks and into holes of the ground before the terror of the Lord and the splendor of His majesty, when He ARISES to make the earth tremble.
Isaiah 2:19, emphasis added

And when do we see men going into caves? After the sixth seal, where we have just placed the rapture. Jesus arises here; He does not descend.

"Because of the devastation of the afflicted, because of the groaning of the needy, now I will ARISE," says the Lord; "I will set him in the safety for which he longs."
Psalm 12:5, emphasis added

He will set them in safety when He arises and calls them home. At the rapture, Jesus will arise and meet us in the clouds, in the heavens, but He in no way descends to the earth.

The second coming verses in scripture have the Greek word "erchomai" and that, faithful friends, is a descent. "Erchomai" is associated with fire and wrath, and just like "parousia," it too signifies Jesus arising. This time when Jesus arises, He is coming for judgment, and He is angry. Please, my faithful friends, be present in the "parousia," not the "erchomai."[1]

Throughout scripture, we see references to God's hand being stretched out (see Isaiah 9). I'll tell you why His hand is stretched out; He is judging the earth while still sitting on His throne. When you see God arising, we better sit up and take notice – something major is about to transpire. The only other passage in scripture

146

where we see the Lord standing before His throne is when Stephen, the first martyr, is ushered into heaven (Acts 7:56). I believe this could mean Jesus will again arise when His faithful are raptured. In scripture, Jesus also arises in another way – with fire.

Let God ARISE, let His enemies be scattered, and let those who hate Him flee before Him. As smoke is driven away, so drive them away; as wax melts before the fire, so let the wicked perish before God.

Psalm 68:1-2, emphasis added

"Now I will ARISE," says the Lord, "Now I will be exalted, now I will be lifted up. You have conceived chaff, you will give birth to stubble; my breath will consume you like a fire, the peoples will be burned to lime, like cut thorns which are burned in the fire."

Isaiah 33:10-12, emphasis added

This time, when Jesus arises, God's enemies are chaff, burned to lime, and melting away like wax before the fire. This is the second coming. We will study this more in chapter nineteen. For now, realize when you see fire, it is God's wrath. And when the angel throws down fire to the earth from the censer, it is after the prayers drift up to God. This is God's response to those souls under the altar in Revelation 6:10: "How long, O Lord, holy and true, will You refrain from judging and avenging our blood on those who dwell on the earth?" God has just raptured His saints – those under the altar have received their new bodies (1 Corinthians 15:51-53). Now, God is responding to not only the martyrs' prayers, but also to every other prayer ever uttered by His saints.

The fire the angel throws to earth is symbolic of God's wrath beginning. We are told in scripture the destruction of the earth and God's wrath will be full of fire.

But the day of the Lord will come like a thief, in which the heavens will pass away with a roar and the elements will be destroyed with intense heat, and the earth and its works will be burned up.

2 Peter 3:10

There follows peals of thunder and flashes of lightning. We learned in chapter four that thunder and lightning are also associated with God's wrath (Exodus 9:23).

At the end of chapter six, the wrath of God was announced. In chapter seven the wrath of God was held back until 144,000 Jewish faithful were sealed. Now, the wrath of God is beginning, right after the great multitude appears in heaven. It is announced with thunder, lightning, and fire. The wrath of God is about to begin because of the way the world has treated His saints and the nation of Israel (seal four and five). Although God wants everyone to come to repentance, there will be a day of judgment (2 Peter 3:9-10). Let's look at this on our timeline.

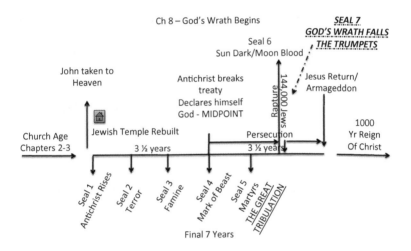

Before we enter the trumpet judgments, we need to look at why God's wrath is represented by "trumpets." Trumpets were blown for many reasons in scripture.

> "*Make yourself two trumpets of silver, of hammered work you shall make them; and you shell use them for summoning the congregation and for having the camps set out.*"
>
> *Numbers 10:2*

> "*When you go to war in your land against the adversary who attacks you, then you shall sound an alarm with the*

trumpets, that you may be remembered before the Lord your God, and be saved from your enemies."

Numbers 10:9

Blow a trumpet in Zion, and sound an alarm on My holy mountain! Let all the inhabitants of the land tremble, for the day of the Lord is coming; surely it is near.

Joel 2:1

Trumpets were blown to call the assembly together. Sometimes that call indicated it was time for the camps to break up and move in the Exodus. Trumpets were also used as a call to war or as a cry for repentance, especially in Israel. The trumpets in Revelation can be seen as all of these things in one: God is calling the people of the earth to assemble and journey to the valley of decision (Joel 3:2,14); the trumpets of Revelation are a call to war, which will ultimately be unleashed at the battle of Armageddon; they are a call for those remaining on earth to come to repentance, especially the nation of Israel; they are a warning that the day of the Lord is at hand.

Before we look at the trumpet judgments of God, we need to pause here and think about why they have to happen at all. God could rain down fire from heaven and wipe out everyone on earth. Why then, do those on earth have to go through the trumpet judgments? Why does the earth have to feel God's wrath for any length of time?

Remember, even though the rapture of the church happened after seal six, 144,000 Jews have come to faith in the Messiah. There will be people coming to faith after the rapture. The gospel will still be heard. People will still be turning to Christ. In fact, this is the main reason why the earth is under God's wrath. He wants those remaining to repent. It is actually one of the reasons in scripture that trumpets sound. Sometimes the only way God can get our attention is to turn up the heat! God wants no one to perish (2 Peter 3:9).

Keep this in mind as we study the seven trumpets. God is shaking the earth – shaking those remaining on earth – pleading with them to see Him for who He is!

Those in heaven grow silent. Those remaining on earth have one more chance to repent. Can you imagine the gravity of this? This is God's final warning before He calls checkmate.

149

"Then the seven angels who had the seven trumpets prepared themselves to sound them" (Revelation 8:6).

Thought for the day:
The silence in heaven should help you understand the gravity of the judgments of God. What would you be feeling if you were looking down on the earth when the angels begin to sound their trumpets? Would there be someone you would be praying for? Why don't you pause and pray for them now. Remember, your prayers are like incense to God. Tomorrow, the first trumpet sounds.

1 Van Kampen, Robert. *The Rapture Question Answered* (Grand Rapids, MI: Fleming H. Revell, 1997), 93-108.

Before we get into the specifics of the trumpets, I need to mention that some scholars say these judgments are symbolic and we should not take them at face value. Metaphors are used many times in scripture. For example, trees can refer to kings or nations: "Behold, Assyria was a cedar in Lebanon with beautiful branches and forest shade" (Ezekiel 31:3a). Grass can refer to the masses: "The grass withers, the flower fades, when the breath of the Lord blows upon it; surely the people are grass" (Isaiah 40:7). Many times scripture defines what it is referring to within the next few verses, such as the ones just quoted. The cedar in Ezekiel is clearly talking about Assyria; the grass in Isaiah is obviously referring to the masses. However, in Revelation there is no distinction defined. It says earth, trees, grass, and seas. There could be a double meaning in this passage. Revelation could be referring to both kings and masses, as well as earth and trees and grass, but there is no reason to assume the earth and trees and grass are not intended. Look at this next scripture.

Behold, the Lord lays the earth waste, devastates it, distorts its surface and scatters its inhabitants . . . The earth will be completely laid waste and completely despoiled, for the Lord has spoken this word. The earth mourns and withers, the world fades and withers, the exalted of the people of the earth fade away.

Isaiah 24:1, 3-4

This chapter of Isaiah is referring to the day of the Lord. Isaiah is talking about the earth under God's wrath, and because the earth is judged, the people of the earth are affected.

When studying the plagues of Egypt, no one questions their meaning. Why should we think differently about the judgments in Revelation unless scripture indicates otherwise?

Because the Isaiah passage quoted above is quite frightening to people who love God's creation, I need to reiterate something. When scripture speaks of earth's "destruction" it does not mean the earth is completely destroyed. God's fire will be a fire of wrath, but it will also be a cleansing fire (Malachi 3:2). Scripture also says, "A generation goes and a generation comes, but the earth remains forever" (Ecclesiastes 1:4). The earth will remain forever. The destruction scripture speaks of is cleansing the earth of evil and regenerating it to what it was supposed to be before the fall. The fire cleanses the earth of wickedness, corruption, crime, and sin. Destruction becomes purification, and Eden rises from the ashes.

Indeed, the Lord will comfort Zion; He will comfort all her waste places. And her wilderness He will make like Eden, and her desert like the garden of the Lord; joy and gladness will be found in her, thanksgiving and sound of a melody.

Isaiah 51:3

Oh, let us look forward to that day!

TRUMPET ONE – HAIL AND FIRE

⁷The first sounded, and there came hail and fire, mixed with blood, and they were thrown to the earth; and a third of the earth was burned up, and a third of the trees were burned up, and all the green grass was burned up.

Revelation 8:7

Have we seen any literal judgments in scripture similar to the first trumpet? Yes, we have.

Then the Lord rained on Sodom and Gomorrah brimstone and fire from the Lord out of heaven. . . and he looked down toward Sodom and Gomorrah, and toward all the land of the valley, and he saw, and behold, the smoke of the land ascended like the smoke of a furnace.

Genesis 19:24, 28

We do not question the destruction of Sodom and Gomorrah. We should not question the first trumpet judgment of Revelation. In Genesis, God destroyed two cities in a heartbeat. During the first trumpet judgment God will rain down hail and fire from heaven that will cause catastrophic burning (2 Peter 5:10). Look at this next verse that is talking about God's wrath.

152

Therefore, a curse devours the earth, and those who live in it are held guilty. Therefore, the inhabitants of the earth are burned, and few men are left.

Isaiah 24:6

Remember, in Zechariah 5:3 the scroll going forth over the whole land was a curse. In Isaiah, a curse devours the earth and few men are left due to a burning. The curse is the opening of the scroll and the destruction of the land. The first phase of this is the first trumpet. Fire comes down and devours some of the earth. Now look at another similar judgment:

Moses stretched out his staff toward the sky, and the Lord sent thunder and hail, and fire ran down to the earth. And the Lord rained hail on the land of Egypt . . . The hail struck all that was in the field through all the land of Egypt, both man and beast; the hail also struck every plant of the field and shattered every tree of the field.

Exodus 9:23, 25

In Egypt we see a catastrophic fire during a hailstorm. In the first trumpet judgment, the same thing occurs, but it is over a third of the earth. The fire will be so severe and hot all the grass will die, and a third of the trees will be destroyed. When God talks, people need to listen. But they will not. They will explain away this judgment just like they did in Egypt. People will rationalize scientifically why the hail and fire are falling: a meteor shower, a solar flare, anything to be gods in their own minds.

Notice in verse seven it says, "fire mixed with blood." Is this real blood? God can do anything, so we can't discount it; however, it may mean that what falls from the sky looks like blood. I believe God worded this trumpet this way in order to remind us why God is raining down fire in the first place. The blood of the martyrs and their cry in seal number five is foremost on God's mind. The first trumpet judgment will cause blood to be poured out on the world. The fire and the hail will kill many so blood will be part of this judgment. Let's look at some more scripture:

For the waters of Nimrim are desolate. Surely the grass is withered, the tender grass died out, there is no green thing.

Isaiah 15:6

And say to the forest of the Negev, "Hear the word of the Lord: thus says the Lord God, 'Behold, I am about to kindle a fire in you, and it will consume every green tree in you, as well as every dry tree; the blazing flame will not be quenched and the whole surface from south to north will be burned by it.'"

Ezekiel 20:47

"Alas for the day! For the day of the Lord is near, and it will come as destruction from the Almighty. Has not food been cut off before our eyes [SEAL 3], gladness and joy from the house of our God? . . . To You, O Lord, I cry; for fire has devoured the pastures of the wilderness and the flame has burned up all the trees of the field."

Joel 1:15,19, explanation added

The Nimrim is ten miles south of the Dead Sea, in ancient Moab (modern day Jordan), one of Israel's neighboring nations and an enemy. The Nimrim will be judged by God at the time of the end for how they treated Israel, both then and now. The Negev is southern Israel, and it too will be judged and called to repentance. Remember, God wants the nation of Israel to repent. Israel's repentance is one of the main reasons the final seven-years are carved out (Daniel 9:24). Jesus is about to return to the earth and God wants His nation to recognize her coming King. The epicenter of the destruction will be the Middle East, although the wrath of God will affect the entire world.

Ezekiel 20 speaks about the re-gathering of Israel in the same breath as it speaks of purging the evil from among them before Jesus returns:

"As I live," declares the Lord God, "surely with a mighty hand and with an outstretched arm and with wrath poured out, I shall be king over you. I will bring you out from the peoples and gather you from the lands where you are scattered, with a mighty hand and with an outstretched arm and with wrath poured out; and I will bring you into the wilderness of the peoples, and there I will enter into judgment with you face to face. As I entered into judgment with your fathers in the wilderness of the land of Egypt, so I will enter into judgment with you," declares the Lord God. "I will make you pass under the rod, and I

154

*will bring you into the bond of the covenant; and I will
purge from you the rebels and those who transgress
against Me; I will bring them out of the land where they
sojourn, but they will not enter the land of Israel. Thus
you will know that I am the Lord."*

Ezekiel 20:33-38

God will gather them, God will judge them, and God will
purge the rebels from among them, but a remnant will remain and
turn to the Lord (Isaiah 10:20). Israel is not exempt from God's
wrath. Sometimes the only way God can wake us up is to shake us
from our comforts. He wants Israel to return to Him and believe in
His Son so they will be with Him for eternity.

In the Joel passage quoted previously, Joel even announces the
day of the Lord, warning the nation of Israel to repent.

Now, look at the following verse.

*Behold, the Lord has a strong and mighty agent; as a
storm of hail, a tempest of destruction, like a storm of
mighty overflowing waters, He has cast it down to the
earth with His hand. The proud crown of the drunkards
of Ephraim is trodden under foot. And the fading flower
of its glorious beauty, which is at the head of the fertile
valley, will be like the first-ripe fig prior to summer,
which one sees, and as soon as it is in his hand, he
swallows it. In that day the Lord of hosts will become a
beautiful crown and a glorious diadem to the remnant of
His people.*

Isaiah 28:2-5

Isaiah is foretelling the first trumpet. The Lord has an agent of
hail and He casts it down to the earth (He is still in heaven). It is
affecting Ephraim (or northern Israel). And in that day, the Lord
will become a glorious crown to the remnant of His people.
Currently, He is still in heaven. If we look in Revelation 19, He is
crowned when He returns to the earth. The saints of God will
witness Christ being crowned King in the heavenlies, while the
trumpet judgments are purging the world of evil.

[8]The second angel sounded, and something like a great mountain burning with fire was thrown into the sea; and a third of the sea became blood, [9]and a third of the creatures which were in the sea and had life, died; and a third of the ships were destroyed.

Revelation 8:8-9

We have seen waters become blood in the past with the same catastrophic results.

So Moses and Aaron did even as the Lord had commanded. And he lifted up the staff and struck the water that was in the Nile, in the sight of Pharaoh and in the sight of his servants, and all the water that was in the Nile was turned to blood. The fish that were in the Nile died, and the Nile became foul, so that the Egyptians could not drink water from the Nile. And the blood was through all the land of Egypt.

Exodus 7:20-21

Sounds like our second trumpet, does it not? The phenomenon of a red tide has recently come to my attention. A red tide is a natural occurring phenomenon that causes stretches of ocean to appear red. It is caused by an over population of algae. This alga produces a toxin that can shut down the central nervous system of fish. The fish can't breathe, so they die and are washed onto shore. Some scientists believe high temperatures and lack of rainfall causes a red tide. No one knows for sure why a red tide occurs, but it isn't uncommon.

We know from scripture the world will be destroyed by fire (2 Peter 3:10). Trumpet number one has already heated up the globe; if a meteor entered the earth's atmosphere and struck the sea (trumpet number two), it would cause the waters to overheat. This in turn could cause a red tide, fish to die, water to become unusable (see trumpet number three). The first trumpet could also cause smoke and debris to rise in the skies, which in turn could cause the luminaries to be darkened (see trumpet number four). We don't know for sure that a red tide will result from the sounding of the second trumpet, but men will discount it as science, not God. Those who want to disbelieve will continue to do so. Do we see any other scripture pointing to this trumpet?

For the waters of Dimon are full of blood; surely I will bring added woes upon Dimon, a lion upon the fugitives of Moab and upon the remnant of the land.

Isaiah 15:9

Again, this is in the chapter of Isaiah we have already looked at in trumpet number one. In Isaiah 15:6 we see the grass withering (trumpet number one). Three verses later we see the waters in Moab or Dimon (modern day Jordan) turning to blood (trumpet number two). These are end time predictions for the lands near Israel.

Thought for the day:
If you are not in the rapture, you will be under the judgment of fire. No one will be concerned about the few missing faithful. They will be running for their lives. How do you think the population of the earth will explain these phenomenon? Do you think many will give the credit to God? And if they do, will they see Him as a vengeful God, or as a just one? More trumpets sound tomorrow.

157

Day Twenty-Six
Revelation 8:10-13
Trumpets Three and Four

THE THIRD TRUMPET - WORMWOOD

¹⁰**The third angel sounded, and a great star fell from heaven, burning like a torch, and it fell on a third of the rivers and on the springs of waters.** ¹¹**The name of the star is called Wormwood; and a third of the waters became wormwood, and many men died from the waters, because they were made bitter.**

Revelation 8:10-11

Moses warned the Israelites about "wormwood."

"Now not with you alone am I making this covenant and this oath, but both with those who stand here with us today in the presence of the Lord our God and with those who are not with us here today . . . so that there will not be among you a man or woman, or family or tribe, whose heart turns away today from the Lord our God, to go and serve the gods of those nations; that there will not be among you a root bearing poisonous fruit and wormwood."

Deuteronomy 29:14-15, 18

In the Bible, wormwood is associated with bitterness and poison. (Jeremiah 9:15, Lamentations 3:15,19, Deuteronomy 29:18, Proverbs 5:4). God also uses wormwood to represent both the actions of the people and the judgment He will deliver because of those actions.

Therefore thus says the Lord of hosts concerning the prophets, "Behold, I am going to feed them wormwood and make them drink poisonous water, for from the prophets of Jerusalem pollution has gone forth into all the land."

Jeremiah 23:15

Seek the Lord that you may live, or He will break forth like a fire, O house of Joseph, and it will consume with

158

none to quench it for Bethel, for those who turn justice
into wormwood and cast righteousness down to the earth.

Amos 5:6-7

In Amos, God's wrath is about to break forth because the people have turned justice into bitterness (wormwood) and turned away from righteousness.

Remember, spoken prophecy of the past will ultimately be fulfilled at the time of the end (Daniel 9:24). A star falls from heaven, burning, and it falls on the rivers and springs of water. The name of the star is Wormwood. It will turn the water bitter, and multitudes will die because of the poisoned water. This is a literal judgment on what has and what will occur prior to this judgment. People have deemed themselves prophets and have uttered falsehood, they have sinned, turned away from righteousness and polluted justice. God will now literally give them poisoned water to drink.

I tend to believe that trumpets one through four may perhaps be the same event (a raining down of meteors on the earth) but that event happens very quickly and causes multiple things to occur. Whether or not this is a series of different events, or whether they are all caused by one phenomenon that happens very quickly, they will be cataclysmic.

THE FOURTH TRUMPET – STARS STRUCK

[12]The fourth angel sounded, and a third of the sun and a third of the moon and a third of the stars were struck, so that a third of them would be darkened and the day would not shine for a third of it, and the night in the same way.

Revelation 8:12-13

At the sound of the fourth trumpet, hail and fire have already fallen, burning a third of the earth; something like a great mountain has been hurled into the sea, causing a third of the sea to become red and kill a third of the animals in the sea; and a third of the waters have become bitter, killing multitudes. The famine that started in seal three is now devastating. Although a fourth of the earth was killed in the fourth seal, now untold multitudes of people have been added to that number.

Remember, this is exactly what God said would happen: "Therefore, a curse devours the earth, and those who live in it are held guilty. Therefore, the inhabitants of the earth are burned, and few men are left" (Isaiah 24:6).

In the fourth trumpet, God's judgments are affecting the luminaries.

> *"It will come about in that day,"* declares the Lord God, *"That I will make the sun go down at noon and make the earth dark in broad daylight."*
>
> *Amos 8:9*

It will probably have scientific basis and it will cause many people to discount what is occurring as a natural, albeit significant, event. There are two observations I would like to make at this point.

Scripture says the day of the Lord is the same day as the rapture (1 Thessalonians 4:13-5:4, 2 Thessalonians 2:1-8). As I have said previously, many books have been written about how the rapture will cause the people of the earth to ponder what has happened. Where did all the people go? How and why did they disappear? But the rapture happens the same day as hail and fire raining down on the earth, trees being decimated, and grass burning up. Not many on the earth are going to care about what just happened; they will be concerned with staying alive. When God's wrath is raining down, you aren't going to be concerned about much else. Imagine the people in Sodom and Gomorrah. They weren't worried about where Lot and his family had gone. Imagine the people at the time of the flood. They weren't asking any questions. They were running for their lives. So it will be in the day of the Lord. These are cosmic events that will affect billions. It will be terrifying, crushing, and quick (like the days of Noah and Lot).

Many scholars have attempted to attribute these judgments to nuclear war. They detail descriptions of weapons of mass destruction burning a third of the earth, killing sea life, poisoning water, and blotting out the sun. The weapons we now have could do all of those things, however, the impact of nuclear war pales in comparison to the impact of the heavens being shaken from their place. God's wrath is falling down. The earth is reeling like a drunkard. This isn't nuclear war; it is God's all-consuming wrath. Look at the following scriptures that describe the day of the Lord.

Behold, the Lord lays the earth waste, devastates it, distorts is surface and scatters it inhabitants.

Isaiah 24:1

Therefore I will make the heavens tremble, and the earth will be shaken from its place at the fury of the Lord of hosts in the day of His burning anger.

Isaiah 13:13

The earth is broken asunder, the earth is split through, the earth is shaken violently. The earth reels to and fro like a drunkard and it totters like a shack, for its transgression is heavy upon it, and it will fall, never to rise again. So it will happen in that day, that the Lord will punish the host of heaven on high, and the kings of the earth on earth. They will be gathered together like prisoners in the dungeon, and will be confined in prison; and after many days they will be punished.

Isaiah 24:19-22

In 2011 an earthquake shook the world and moved the earth almost six inches. Imagine, when the humdinger of earthquakes hits (seal six). Imagine hail and fire hurling down on the earth (trumpet one). This isn't nuclear war. This is cosmic. This is the wrath of God. May we all be in heaven when this occurs.

THE THREE WOES ANNOUNCED

[13]**Then I looked, and I heard an eagle flying in midheaven, saying with a loud voice, "Woe, woe, woe to those who dwell on the earth, because of the remaining blasts of the trumpet of the three angels who are about to sound!"**

An eagle announces the three woes, which are the blasts of the next three trumpets. So, what trumpets are these? These are the final plagues that will strike the world: the fifth, sixth, and seventh trumpet judgments.

If you remember back in Revelation 8:1-2, when the Lamb broke the seventh seal, there was silence in heaven. Part of the reason for this silence is the fact that angels are being handed the trumpets – they will bring the first of God's wrath

The breaking of the seventh seal was not a "judgment" in itself, but it served to usher in the trumpet judgments. As I have said before, when the seventh seal was broken, the scroll could be unrolled. At he breaking of the seventh seal, the scroll is unrolled and the trumpet judgments are released. So, just like the seventh seal, the seventh trumpet is not a judgment in itself but ushers in the bowl judgments. In other words:

Seventh Seal = Trumpet Judgments
Seventh Trumpet = Bowl Judgments

So, the fifth trumpet, the sixth trumpet, and the bowl judgments (the seventh trumpet) are the three woes. An eagle makes this announcement as it flies in mid-heaven. This is an eagle flying where it normally does, above the earth, announcing the catastrophic events that are to follow. Look at the following scriptures to see what an eagle can represent.

Their horses are swifter than leopards and keener than wolves in the evening. Their horsemen come galloping, their horsemen come from afar; they fly like an eagle swooping down to devour.

Habakkuk 1:8

Like an eagle that stirs up its nest, that hovers over its young, He spread His wings and caught them, He carried them on His pinions. The Lord alone guided him, and there was no foreign god with him.

Deuteronomy 32:11-12

In Habakkuk, the eagle represents swiftness and strength. So the woes will come swiftly and with power. In Deuteronomy the eagle represents God's mercy and protection. I have read reports where people claim to have witnessed eagles swooping down to carry their young on their backs for a brief repose when the baby eagle is learning to fly. Although I do not know if this is true, it is a good picture of what God does for us. He carries us on His wings and protects us when we are under attack from the enemy or wading through difficult times (Psalm 68:19-20). This is the second reason the eagle is seen announcing the woes: although the woes will be swift, there is still mercy. Those remaining on the earth are called to repent and turn to the Lord. They can still mount up on eagle's wings and cling to God's protection and grace.

At night my soul longs for You, indeed, my spirit within me seeks You diligently; for when the earth experiences Your judgments the inhabitants of the world learn righteousness.

Isaiah 26:9

In the midst of His wrath, there will be those who realize who God is and what is happening. They will trust in the Savior and be cleansed from their sin. They will mount up on wings like eagles (Isaiah 40:31). Hallelujah!

There is one more scripture I would like to point out and it has to do with the second coming of Christ.

The earth has quaked at the noise of their downfall. There is an outcry! The noise of it has been heard at the Red Sea. Behold, He will mount up and swoop like an eagle and spread out His wings against Bozrah; and the hearts of the mighty men of Edom in that day will be like the heart of a woman in labor.

Jeremiah 49:21-22

This scripture is describing Christ swooping in like an eagle. This is the third reason the eagle is mentioned: it is anticipating the return of the King! In summary, the eagle itself is symbolic for the swiftness of the next judgments, the mercy God still extends, and the soon to be return of the King.

Amen and amen, come quickly, Lord Jesus.

Thought for the day:
One of the reasons an eagle is seen in the sky is to tell us that God's mercy is still being extended. Despite the severity of the judgments, God is still wooing His children. He wants every soul to turn to Him and be washed clean by His Son. In a few days, we will see that at some point mercy will be cut off. Why do you think that would be?

THE FIFTH TRUMPET – THE FIRST WOE

[1]Then the fifth angel sounded, and I saw a star from heaven which had fallen to the earth; and the key of the bottomless pit was given to him. [2]He opened the bottomless pit, and smoke went up out of the pit, like the smoke of a great furnace; and the sun and the air were darkened by the smoke of the pit. [3]Then out of the smoke came locusts upon the earth, and power was given them, as the scorpions of the earth have power. [4]They were told not to hurt the grass of the earth, nor any green thing, nor any tree, but only the men who do not have the seal of God on their foreheads. [5]And they were not permitted to kill anyone, but to torment for five months; and their torment was like the torment of a scorpion when it stings a man. [6]And in those days men will seek death and will not find it; they will long to die, and death flees from them. [7]The appearance of the locusts was like horses prepared for battle; and on their heads appeared to be crowns like gold, and their faces were like the faces of men. [8]They had hair like the hair of women, and their teeth were like the teeth of lions. [9]They had breastplates like breastplates of iron; and the sound of their wings was like the sound of chariots, of many horses rushing to battle. [10]They have tails like scorpions, and stings; and in their tails is their power to hurt men for five months. [11]They have as king over them, the angel of the abyss; his name in Hebrew is Abaddon, and in the Greek he has the name Apollyon. [12]The first woe is past; behold, two woes are still coming after these things.

Revelation 9:1-12

With the blowing of the fifth trumpet, the first woe begins. An eagle has just announced, "Woe, woe, woe to those who dwell on the earth, because of the remaining blasts of the trumpet of the three angels who are about to sound" (Revelation 8:13). Things are progressively getting worse. The fourth seal announced the killing of a quarter of the earth's population. The third trumpet announced the death of many because of the bitter water. Here we see the first woe, heralded by the fifth trumpet, and it will be worse than anything that has come before.

Before this woe, the things falling to the earth were due to cosmic happenings. Here we see something different. A "star" is seen, but that star is referred to as a "him." This tells us what follows will need to be taken symbolically. This is a trumpet Jesus couldn't show John unless He used images so John could better understand what was taking place. This is common in scripture and is best illustrated in the book of Daniel. In Daniel chapter seven beasts are seen rising from the sea. These beasts correspond perfectly to the "kingdoms" referred to in Daniel chapter two; however it is very hard, in fact impossible, for a human to visualize an entire political system rising to power. A beast, however, representing that kingdom can be understood with ease. Keep this in mind as we study the fifth trumpet.

John says the star "had fallen to the earth." This is past tense in the Greek. Meaning, this star is already on the earth. It had fallen some time ago. John doesn't see it fall here.

We have already seen that a "star" in scripture can represent an angel such as in Job 38:7 and also a head of a church like in Revelation 1:20. Let's look at the identity of this star.

And He said to them, "I was watching Satan fall from heaven like lightning."

Luke 10:18

How you have fallen from heaven, O star of the morning, son of the dawn! You have been cut down to the earth, you who have weakened the nations!

Isaiah 14:12

And the great dragon was thrown down, the serpent of old who is called the devil and Satan, who deceives the whole world; he was thrown down to the earth, and his angels were thrown down with him.

Revelation 12:9

Look again at Revelation 9:1.

Then the fifth angel sounded, and I saw a star from heaven which had fallen to the earth; and the key of the bottomless pit was given to him.

Revelation 9:1

When was Satan thrown down? Some scholars think he was thrown down at Jesus' crucifixion and has no more power to accuse us.

When He (Jesus) had disarmed the rulers and authorities, He made a public display of them, having triumphed over them through Him.
Colossians 2:15, explanation added

Others believe there will be a final war in heaven and Satan will be thrown down during the midpoint of the final seven-year period when the Antichrist declares himself to be god (we will discuss this timing more in chapter 12). In either case, by trumpet number five, Satan is down, and he is angry (Revelation 12:12).

The key to the bottomless pit, or the shaft of the abyss, is given to Satan. This key stands in contrast to the key of David we saw in Revelation 3:7. We learned that the key of David not only symbolized access to the city of God, but also represented understanding the scriptures. Now, we see Satan gaining the key to the bottomless pit. He opens the pit and smoke comes out, like a great furnace, and darkens the light of day.

What is darkening the day? What is coming up out of the abyss? Let us not forget, if the "key of David" in Revelation chapter three means understanding the scriptures, the key to the bottomless pit will be clouding the minds of man to God's truth. The smoke is darkening the day, or the light of the gospel. The smoke is symbolic of a spiritual darkness that will deceive mankind. This smoke will blind those unwilling to repent to the truth of Jesus' return.

For this reason God will send upon them a deluding influence so that they will believe what is false, in order that they all may be judged who did not believe the truth, but took pleasure in wickedness.
2 Thessalonians 2:11-12

It seems that trumpet number five could be that delusion.

The "key of David" also literally means access to the New Jerusalem, or God's city. Satan obtaining the key to the abyss refers to undeniable access to the abyss. Some scholars believe this gives Satan command of those angels God has locked in the abyss.

And I remind you of the angels who did not stay within the limits of authority God gave them but left the place where they belonged. God has kept them securely chained in prisons of darkness, waiting for the great day of judgment. And don't forget Sodom and Gomorrah and their neighboring towns, which were filled with immorality and every kind of sexual perversion. Those cities were destroyed by fire and serve as a warning of the eternal fire of God's judgment.

Jude 6-7 NLT

I find it extremely interesting Jude mentions Sodom and Gomorrah right after he reminds the reader about the angels reserved for "judgment" because smoke and fire also went up from those doomed cities like a furnace (Genesis 19:28), the same language used in Revelation 9:2. Could this also be trumpet number five? Could Satan release fallen angels from the abyss to help be a deluding influence? Some scholars think so.

This seems outlandish to most of us. Demons released on earth? Could this be what scripture is saying? Scripture does say locusts come up out of the abyss. They are described like horses prepared for battle, with gold crowns and faces of men. They have woman's hair and teeth like lions. They are wearing iron breastplates and sound like rushing chariots. Their tails are like scorpions and they do not kill, but torment men for five months. We know these are not literal locusts because they are commanded not to hurt the grass or any green thing. Are these demon tormentors? Again, some scholars think so. Some believe they will be visible, others maintain they will be invisible. But is this what scripture is saying? Let's dig deeper.

In scripture, a locust invasion can be symbolic of an invading army.

For they would come up with their livestock and their tents, they would come in like locusts for number, both they and their camels were innumerable; and they came into the land to devastate it.

Judges 6:5

Just as a locust invasion strips everything in its path, so does an invading army. I believe scripture is telling us that the armies already under Satan and his minion, the Antichrist, will be

167

influenced by the spiritual darkness that Satan and the leader of his false religious system will release in trumpet number five.

The locusts are Satan's army, the Antichrist's army. Their minds are being clouded to God's truth by Satan himself. Does this also mean the demons from the abyss are unleashed as well? Perhaps, but in either case, the important thing to realize is that the army is being deluded by Satan's darkness and the Antichrist's leadership. If this darkness involves demons, it will be even more demonic. If you think an army could be cruel before, wait until you see this one. It will be pure deception and pure evil, and it will devour everything in its path. The smoke surrounding them is deceptive, swaying many to join their ranks, deceiving people to stray from the true God.

How is this God's wrath? Just like what we saw in the seals, nothing is done without God's approval. God has said the Antichrist will rise; He told us nation would rise against nation; He proclaimed famine would be severe; and He told us the mark of the beast would be implemented. Nothing is done under the sun without God allowing it to happen. This trumpet is the same concept yet with a different twist. Only God has the key to the abyss. Many deem Satan king of hell and God king of heaven but that is not the case. Satan is no more king of hell than you are. God has the key to heaven, and He has the key to hell (Revelation 1:18). He is the One who allows entrance into heaven, and He is the One who ushers into hell. He is the King of kings and Lord of lords. He will now hand that key to Satan for the fifth trumpet.

I believe Joel gives us another description of this army.

What the gnawing locust has left, the swarming locust has eaten; and what the swarming locust has left, the creeping locust has eaten; and what the creeping locust has left, the stripping locust has eaten . . . For a nation has invaded my land, mighty and without number; its teeth are the teeth of a lion, and it has the fangs of a lioness. It has made my vine a waste and my fig tree splinters. It has stripped them bare and cast them away; their branches have become white. Wail like a virgin girded with sackcloth for the bridegroom of her youth. The grain offering and the drink offering are cut off from the house of the Lord . . .

Joel 1:4, 6-9

168

A nation has invaded God's land. It will possess and claim, it will strip and torment. Killing is not its aim, but dominion. They will torment the land for five months. In Joel it mentions the land being devastated. In Revelation the army is commanded not to harm the grass or any green thing. Why is this command included? And why don't we see this army obeying that command in Joel?

First, the scripture in Revelation is steering us away from "locusts" being actual locusts. I believe God is telling us, "Yes, I am using this term, but no, the invasion this vision is portraying has nothing to do with literal locusts and everything to do with an army."

Second, we have to remember where we are in the judgments. The first trumpet has burned the grass and a third of the trees. The second trumpet killed a third of the fish. The third brought about poisoned water. Famine is the name of the day. There are no more crops, a third of the trees are gone, there are no fish anywhere close, and the water has been poisoned. This army is commanded to not hurt those things needed for survival. The order not to harm the grass contrasts greatly with what this army is told to do – torment people! Like I have said previously, this is one evil army.

But when armies move, they devour, and that is on a normal day. This is no normal day. This army is famished. It is eating everything in its path because of the previous trumpet judgments. It is coming in to claim what land is left to grab. There is no thought to destroy the land; in fact they are moving so they can claim the land, but when armies march, they take the clearest path. It is a consequence of war. The land is destroyed. Note in Joel 1:8-9 it mentions the drink offering and the grain offering being cut off from the house of the Lord. During the third seal, there was a cry not to damage the oil and the wine. This indicates seal three came before the midpoint of the final seven years because the grain and drink offering are cut off at the midpoint (Daniel 9:27). Now we have no grain or drink offering in the house of the Lord. This proves this army rides after the midpoint.

He will also lift up a standard to the distant nation, and will whistle for it from the ends of the earth; and behold, it will come with speed swiftly. No one in it is weary or stumbles, none slumbers or sleeps; nor is the belt at its waist undone, nor its sandal strap broken. Its arrows are sharp and all its bows are bent; the hoofs of its horses seem like flint and its chariot wheels like a whirlwind. Its

*roaring is like a lioness, and it roars like young lions; it
growls as it seizes the prey and carries it off with no one
to deliver it. And it will growl over it in that day like the
roaring of the sea. If one looks to the land, behold, there
is darkness and distress; even the light is darkened by its
clouds.*

Isaiah 5:26-30

Here, we see the darkness mentioned, and this will be both
literal and spiritual. An invading army lifts dust to the heavens. So
will the armies of the Antichrist.

*You will go up, you will come like a storm; you will be
like a cloud covering the land, you and all your troops,
and many peoples with you.*

Ezekiel 38:9

This army is commanded to harm "only the men who do not
have the seal of God on their foreheads." We immediately think of
the seal God has placed on the 144,000 in chapter seven. The Greek
word used for "seal" is derived from another Greek word that means
"to fence." Most scholars believe that this means once you are
sealed by God, you are enclosed in a shield of protection and
sheltered from any of His wrath. A good example of God's
protection is found in Ezekiel.

*The Lord said to him, "Go through the midst of the city,
even through the midst of Jerusalem, and put a mark on
the foreheads of the men who sigh and grown over all the
abominations which are being committed in its midst."
But to the others He said in my hearing, "Go through the
city after him and strike; do not let your eye have pity and
do not spare. Utterly slay old men, young men, maidens,
little children and women, but do not touch any man on
whom is the mark; and you shall start from My
sanctuary." So they started with the elders who were
before the temple.*

Ezekiel 9:4-6

The ones who were marked by God in Ezekiel were spared. So
is the evil army of trumpet number five commanded not to hurt the

people of God? Perhaps, but there is another mark in Revelation that we have already mentioned.

And he causes all, the small and the great, and the rich and the poor, and the free men and the slaves, to be given a mark on their right hand or on their forehead.

Revelation 13:16

Christians refer to this mark as "the mark of the beast." We discussed this at length in chapter six, where seal four says "wild beasts" are one way people will die. We know from scripture there will be a time the Antichrist will force everyone to take a mark in order to declare allegiance to him (Revelation 13:16). Without the mark, you will be unable to buy or sell. The point is this: if you don't take the mark, you will die.

The question we need to ask ourselves is who is telling the "locusts" not to harm those with the seal of God? When you read chapter nine, it sounds like the "locusts" are receiving orders from "him" or the one opening the bottomless pit – Satan himself!

Let's remind ourselves what the Antichrist will do at the midpoint, where we placed the mark of the beast (seal four) in chapter six.

Who opposes and exalts himself above every so-called god or object of worship, so that he takes his seat in the temple of God, displaying himself as being God.

2 Thessalonians 2:4

If this is Satan's army he will tell the "locusts" to torment those who do not have his seal – the mark of the beast – but he will say it is a seal of God. He will protect those with his mark. What is happening here? We are at the very end of the trumpet judgments, only one more trumpet sounds (trumpet number six) before the bowls are unleashed (trumpet number seven).

Let's look back to Revelation 7:2 where God marked the 144,000 Jews.

And I saw another angel ascending from the rising of the sun, having the seal of the living God; and he cried out with a loud voice to the four angels to whom it was granted to harm the earth and the sea.

Revelation 7:2

The angel here had the seal of the *living* God. This could be the difference. Only with Jesus do you have life – because He is the way, the truth, and the life (John 14:6).

The army in chapter nine is commanded by the fallen star – Satan himself. Satan wouldn't command his army to hurt those who have taken the mark of the beast – his mark. So the locust army is tormenting those who have not yet made their choice! This is a trumpet judgment that will torment those remaining, forcing them to pick a side. You are either on the side of Satan or the side of God. Make your choice! God knows the time is short; Satan knows the time is short (Revelation 12:12). There are only two more blasts of the trumpets. Now is the time to choose. God has given the key of the abyss to Satan so that the world will come to a decision quickly. His Son is about to return.

What will this "locust" horde do? They will torment those remaining who do not have the mark of the Antichrist or the seal of God. It will be like a sting of a scorpion. I have never been bitten by a scorpion, but I hear it feels like fire through your veins. The locust army of trumpet number five will prolong the agony. Again, God is worried about the salvation of the earth.

"Do not fear those who kill the body but are unable to kill the soul; but rather fear Him who is able to destroy both soul and body in hell."
Matthew 10:28

Make a choice; pick a side; and do so quickly. Remember, one reason for God's wrath is so that those remaining will repent!

The king that rules over this army is the angel of the abyss, or the fallen star. His name is Abaddon in Hebrew and Apollyon in Greek. This means destroyer. Who is the destroyer?

"The thief comes only to steal and kill and destroy."
John 10:10a

The thief, Satan, is the destroyer. Satan will be a thief, coming to deceive and steal God's truth from the world. He wants our destruction and he will stop at nothing until he takes as many people as he can down with him. Evil will be the order of the day.

The fifth trumpet – Satan and the Antichrist's army – is the first woe.

Thought for the day:
We said the smoke from the pit is clouding the world to God's truth. Even though the deception in the last days will be unequaled, we have many things, traditions, laws, and cultural norms that hide God's truth. What are some of these? Have you fallen prey to any of them? Tomorrow is the second woe.

THE SIXTH TRUMPET – THE SECOND WOE

[13]Then the sixth angel sounded, and I heard a voice from the four horns of the golden altar which is before God, [14]one saying to the sixth angel who had the trumpet, "Release the four angels who are bound at the great river Euphrates." [15]And the four angels, who had been prepared for the hour and day and month and year, were released, so that they would kill a third of mankind. [16]The number of the armies of the horsemen was two hundred million; I heard the number of them. [17]And this is how I saw in the vision the horses and those who sat on them: the riders had breastplates the color of fire and of hyacinth and of brimstone; and the heads of the horses are like the heads of lions; and out of their mouths proceed fire and smoke and brimstone. [18]A third of mankind was killed by these three plagues, by the fire and the smoke and the brimstone which proceeded out of their mouths. [19]For the power of the horses is in their mouths and in their tails; for their tails are like serpents and have heads, and with them they do harm. [20]The rest of mankind, who were not killed by these plagues, did not repent of the works of their hands, so as not to worship demons, and the idols of gold and of silver and of brass and of stone and of wood, which can neither see nor hear nor walk; [21]and they did not repent of their murders nor of their sorceries nor of their immorality nor of their thefts.

Revelation 9:13-21

First we see the altar before God's throne. It is described as having four horns. At first glance, this sounds a little bizarre, but the altar in the tabernacle had four horns at the corners. Let's look at why the horns are specifically mentioned in Revelation.

One of David's sons, Adonijah, tried to take the throne before King David could anoint Solomon as his heir. Let's see what Adonijah did to beg for mercy.

And Adonijah was afraid of Solomon, and he arose, went and took hold of the horns of the altar. Now it was told Solomon, saying, "Behold, Adonijah is afraid of King

Solomon, for behold, he has taken hold of the horns of the altar, saying 'Let King Solomon swear to me today that he will not put his servant to death with the sword.'"

1 Kings 1:50-52

If you wanted to seek mercy you grabbed onto the horns. It was a place of refuge for a guilty man.[1] The significant thing to note is this: if the horns of the altar are seen in Revelation, this tells the reader mercy is still being extended to the world if people would repent and believe in Jesus. Why do the horns of the altar represent mercy? Because that is where the priest smeared the blood from the sacrifice, symbolizing forgiveness through the blood (Leviticus 4:30). Of course, the blood sacrifice ultimately represented Jesus' complete and pure offering to cleanse us of sin.

And according to the Law, one may almost say, all things are cleansed with blood, and without shedding of blood there is no forgiveness.

Hebrews 9:22

There will be a time when the horns of the altar will be cut off, and mercy will no longer be available.

"For on the day that I punish Israel's transgressions, I will also punish the altars of Bethel; the horns of the altar will be cut off and they will fall to the ground."

Amos 3:14

There will be a point where your decision is final and God's mercy will no longer be available.

At the opening of the sixth trumpet, the horns are available; God is pleading with the world to repent and turn to Him. Mercy is still extended! Grab the horns! Grab onto My Son! Grab onto forgiveness!

When the sixth angel sounds the four angels who are bound at the Euphrates River are released to kill a third of mankind. These are evil angels because scripture says they are "bound." Scripture doesn't say why they are bound, but we may be able to infer the reason. I believe the key is this: they are bound at the great river Euphrates.

The Euphrates River was the eastern boundary of the land God originally gave to Abraham:

175

On that day the Lord made a covenant with Abram, saying, "To your descendants I have given this land, from the river of Egypt as far as the great river, the river Euphrates."

Genesis 15:18

The area by the Euphrates became home to two of Israel's worst enemies, Assyria and Babylon. The Euphrates River was also one of the rivers God said flowed out of Eden.

Now a river flowed out of Eden to water the garden; and from there it divided and became four rivers . . . the fourth river is the Euphrates.

Genesis 2:10,14b

The city of Babylon, the symbol of evil in scripture, was also built on the Euphrates River.

You could say that the beginning of civilization started at the Euphrates River, the rise of the four world empires mentioned in Daniel that crushed Israel centered there, and the final end time system will originate from there (more on this as we continue our study).

We know from Daniel there are both evil and good angels assigned to kingdoms. In Daniel 10, an angel appears to give Daniel a message but exclaims:

"But the prince of the kingdom of Persia was withstanding me for twenty-one days; then behold, Michael, one of the chief princes, came to help me, for I had been left there with the kings of Persia."

Daniel 10:13

We know from scripture Michael is an archangel (Jude 1:9) and is identified in Daniel 12:1 as "the great prince who stands guard" over Israel. In other words, Michael is the angelic prince who protects Israel. He is also the angel who battles Satan in Revelation (12:7). Why? Because Israel is the target of Satan's persecution (Revelation 12:13).

So, when the angel speaking to Daniel says "princes" he means angels. He tells Daniel he was battling the prince of Persia. Persia was one of the world empires that took control of Israel. Could the bound angels of the sixth trumpet be the four angels who were over the four world empires identified in Daniel chapter two and seven (Babylon, Medo-Persia, Greece, and the Iron Kingdom)? Each of these empires conquered Israel, which is what Satan will want to do in the end times. This makes a lot of sense to me, especially since the four world empires (represented in Daniel chapter two) that took control of Israel all encompassed the area of the Euphrates. Please don't get bogged down with this now, we will study the empires more in Revelation 13.

These four angels are now released and they amass a large army two hundred million strong. In John's day, this was next to impossible, but now it is not so far fetched. This could be an army composed of every nation on earth, all marching toward Israel, the epicenter of the war. Most of us have heard the term "Armageddon" which indicates the final worldwide conflict between Satan and the Lamb. Let's look forward to Revelation 16:14:

> *For they are spirits of demons, performing signs, which go out to the kings of the whole world, to gather them together for the war of the great day of God, the Almighty.*
> *Revelation 16:14*

The spirits of demons will "go out to the kings of the whole world, to gather them together for the war of the great day of God, the Almighty." The fifth and sixth trumpets are the beginning of that preparation. It takes more than a day to move an army. For the nations of the world to be assembled before Jesus on the day of His return, they have to start marching sometime before that. Let's look at scripture.

> *And I saw heaven opened, and behold, a white horse, and He who sat on it is called Faithful and True, and in righteousness He judges and wages war . . . And I saw the beast and the kings of the earth and their armies assembled to make war against Him who sat on the horse and against His army.*
> *Revelation 19:11,19*

> *For behold, in those days and at that time, when I restore the fortunes of Judah and Jerusalem, I will gather all the nations and bring them down to the valley of Jehoshaphat.*

Then I will enter into judgment with them there on behalf of My people and My inheritance, Israel, whom they have scattered among the nations; and they have divided up My land.

Joel 3:1-2

"Therefore wait for Me," declares the Lord, "For the day when I rise up as a witness. Indeed, My decision is to gather nations, to assemble kingdoms, to pour out on them My indignation, all My burning anger; for all the earth will be devoured by the fire of My zeal."

Zephaniah 3:8

Jesus will gather all the nations to pour out on them His anger. Trumpet number five (the army of the Antichrist) and trumpet number six (the armies of the world) are the initial preparation for the final showdown. However, the army in the sixth trumpet will be the mother of all armies, and this army will be deceived by four fierce angels who have been bound for centuries.

John sees a description of the armies: "And this is how I saw in the vision the horses and those who sat on them; the riders had breastplates the color of fire and of hyacinth and of brimstone; and the heads of the horses are like the heads of lions; and out of their mouths proceed fire and smoke and brimstone. . . for the power of the horses is in their mouths and in their tails; for their tails are like serpents and have heads, and with them they do harm."

If we took someone from ancient history and showed them two modern armies engaging in battle, their description of it might be very similar to what John described. This is another World War among the nations.

John says what he sees kills a third of mankind. If we take the fourth seal, which kills a fourth of mankind and add it to the sixth trumpet, which kills a third of mankind, half of mankind is now obliterated. This doesn't take into account the great earthquake of seal number six, the hail and fire of trumpet number one, the mountain falling into the sea of trumpet number two, and the bitter water that killed "many" in trumpet number three. If I had to guess, not much more than a fourth of the earth's population may remain after the sixth trumpet judgment.

Why would God allow so many to be killed? Take another look at Revelation 9:20-21:

The rest of mankind . . . did not repent of their murders nor of their sorceries nor of their immorality nor of their thefts.

Revelation 9:20a, 21

And let me remind you what it says in Isaiah 24:6.

Therefore, a curse devours the earth, and those who live in it are held guilty. Therefore, the inhabitants of the earth are burned, and few men are left.

Isaiah 24:6

The trumpet judgments, the open scroll, are the curse, and few men are left.

Even though the horns from the altar are still available to grab (Revelation 9:13), mankind is not taking them. Mankind is breaking God's commandments and not caring about the ramifications. Here is the first warning in Revelation about non-repentance. Up until this point, you do not see John making this statement. Until the gathering of the world's armies in trumpet number six, there has been repentance and a turning back to God. Not so after this point. They are unwilling to repent. Those remaining on earth have made their choice. They have chosen either the seal of God or the mark of the beast. The next stop for these armies and the armies of the Antichrist is the battle of Armageddon.

The sixth trumpet judgment – the armies of the world – is the second woe. Yet, unlike the first woe, which was announced immediately after the description of the Antichrist's army (Revelation 9:12), the second woe is not announced until two chapters later. We will see why when we move into chapter 11. There is something else happening on earth that Jesus wants to show us, and that something will also be part of the second woe. But make no mistake

The Sixth Trumpet = Second Woe

Let's look at a more detailed timeline of the final three and one half years. This timeline adds in the two woes we have just discussed.

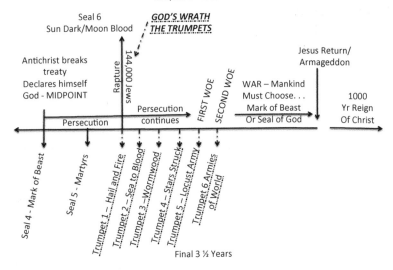

Final 3 ½ Years

Thought for the day:

The second woe kills a third of mankind, this is on top of a quarter of the earth perishing during the fourth seal. Really wrap your head around this. Half of the earth's population is gone – washed away by the wrath of God. Even though people are perishing, "mercy" is still being offered – that is until the end of the sixth trumpet – for then no one else repents. But before the horns of the altar are cut off, if someone repents, they have the "life," even if they perish during the wrath. It was like this in Noah's day. As the water rose, did some on earth turn to the Lord? And what about now? Today, when catastrophic things happen, do some turn to the Lord? Sometimes the only way to get our attention is to turn up the heat. Tomorrow John will prophesy again. Be ready for his words.

1 Butler, Trent C. et al.,eds. *Holman Illustrated Bible Dictionary* (Nashville, Tennessee: Holman Bible Publishers, 2003), 1199-1200.

DAY TWENTY-NINE
REVELATION 10:1-11
NO MORE DELAY

[1]I saw another strong angel coming down out of heaven, clothed with a cloud; and the rainbow was upon his head, and his face was like the sun, and his feet like pillars of fire; [2]and he had in his hand a little book which was open. He placed his right foot on the sea and his left on the land; [3]and he cried out with a loud voice, as when a lion roars; and when he had cried out, the seven peals of thunder uttered their voices. [4]When the seven peals of thunder had spoken, I was about to write; and I heard a voice from heaven saying, "Seal up the things which the seven peals of thunder have spoken and do not write them." [5]Then the angel whom I saw standing on the sea and on the land lifted up his right hand to heaven, [6]and swore by Him who lives forever and ever, who created heaven and the things in it, and the earth and the things in it, and the sea and the things in it, that there will be delay no longer, [7]but in the days of the voice of the seventh angel, when he is about to sound, then the mystery of God is finished, as He preached to His servants the prophets. [8]Then the voice which I heard from heaven, I heard again speaking with me, and saying, "Go, take the book which is open in the hand of the angel who stands on the sea and on the land." [9]So I went to the angel, telling him to give me the little book. And he said to me, "Take it and eat it; it will make your stomach bitter, but in your mouth it will be sweet as honey." [10]I took the little book out of the angel's hand and ate it, and in my mouth it was sweet as honey; and when I had eaten it, my stomach was made bitter. [11]And they said to me, "You must prophesy again concerning many peoples and nations and tongues and kings."

Revelation 10:1-11

An angel is seen coming down out of heaven clothed with a cloud. Many scholars claim this angel is Jesus Himself due to the similarities between the angel and Jesus' characteristics in chapter one. This angel is clothed with a cloud, reminiscent of Jesus' ascension: "And after He had said these things, He was lifted up while they were looking on, and a cloud received Him out of their sight" (Acts 1:9); and His ultimate return: "Behold, He is coming with the clouds, and every eye will see Him" (Revelation 1:7a). A

181

rainbow is upon his head, also reminding us of the rainbow seen around God the Father in Revelation 4:3. His face shines like the sun and he has feet like pillars of fire. Jesus had these attributes in Revelation 1:15-17.

Although it isn't a stretch to believe this angel is Jesus Himself, my gut tells me this isn't Jesus, but a mighty angel just like the text describes. John has already identified Jesus multiple times in Revelation; why does he not identify Jesus here if this is, in fact, Jesus? So if this isn't Christ, what do the angel's attributes mean? The same thing they would mean if this was Jesus. As we are to reflect His glory (2 Corinthians 3:18), so should the angels. He is reflecting God's glory (face like the sun), the coming eternal kingdom (rainbow), and the coming judgments of the earth (feet as pillars of fire). Taken as a whole, this angel is announcing the return of the King, the judgment He will bring, and the eternal nature of His reign.

The angel is clutching an open book, or a scroll, in his hand. This doesn't seem to be the same sealed scroll identified in chapter five and six. This scroll is described as being little; the sealed scroll was not. This is probably another book that will open up the visions we will now see in the next few chapters. The angel puts one foot on the sea and the other on the earth, declaring whatever he is about to say will affect the entire globe.

This angel cries out and it sounds like a lion's roar. Amos 3:8 says, "A lion has roared! Who will not fear? The Lord God has spoken! Who can but prophesy?" This is an announcement from the Almighty. Everyone on the earth will be affected by the angel's words. It is no accident scripture calls Jesus the Lamb of God and the Lion of the tribe of Judah. His first coming was in humility; His second coming will be in power. This angel is foreshadowing the cry of Jesus as He returns to lay claim to the earth.

The Lord roars from Zion and utters His voice from Jerusalem, and the heavens and the earth tremble. But the Lord is a refuge for His people and a stronghold to the sons of Israel.

Joel 3:16

He first came as the suffering servant; He will return as the King of kings!

The roar of this angel is also very significant for Israel.

They will walk after the Lord, He will roar like a lion;
indeed He will roar and His sons will come trembling
from the west. They will come trembling like birds from
Egypt and like doves from the land of Assyria; and I will
settle them in their houses, declares the Lord.

Hosea 11:10

The lion's roar initiates Israel's return to the Savior. As we move forward into Revelation, we will better understand why the roar is seen here. Six trumpets have sounded, only one trumpet remains. When the seventh trumpet sounds it opens up the bowl judgments, or the final judgments. During the bowl judgments Jesus will return, but before He returns, Israel has to come to faith (Luke 13:35). This is the roar that calls Israel to faith and ushers in Israel's repentance. The Jews who have not yet come to faith in Christ are now beginning to see Jesus for who He truly is to them – their Lord, their King, and their Messiah! More on this as we continue our study.

The roar introduces seven peals of thunder, yet God commands that the seven thunders be sealed. Although Revelation is a revealing, God is choosing to keep the seven thunders concealed. We shouldn't try to guess what these thunders will be because they are closed to us. They will come after the sixth trumpet, before the seventh trumpet (or the bowl judgments) rain down on earth.

Then the angel lifts his hand and swears by Him who lives forever and ever. The angel reminds us that God has created all things by placing his feet on the earth and the sea. Everything under the sea and on the earth belongs to God Almighty. There is nothing He cannot judge. "For everything comes from him and exists by his power and is intended for his glory. All glory to him forever! Amen" (Romans 11:36 NLT).

The angel announces that there will be no more delay. Some translations say "time" but the Greek word *chronos* can also be translated "delay." Obviously, the bowls have yet to fall and so "time" is not the correct translation; there will still be time after this event. So what does this angel mean when he says there will be no more delay? For this answer, let's go back Revelation 1:7:

Behold, He is coming with the clouds, and every eye will
see Him, even those who pierced Him; and all the tribes of
the earth will mourn over Him. So it is to be. Amen.

Revelation 1:7

183

There will be no more delay for the King to return! This fits the context of Revelation at this point. Again, six trumpets have been blown; when the seventh angel sounds his trumpet the bowls are poured out. With the bowl judgments, the King will return and all prophecy will be fulfilled. The bowls are the last and worst judgments for the earth. This will be the final purification of the land and the beginning of the millennial reign of Christ.

We know the fifth and sixth trumpets bring the armies of the Antichrist and the world. This does not come overnight – it takes time to amass an army of any size. I firmly believe the first four trumpet judgments will come almost back-to-back – in a very short period of time. Because of their severity, the armies of the world will want to control the oil-rich land of the Middle East. They will mobilize and march, bringing with them the two woes. There will probably be a significant period of time between the sounding of the sixth trumpet (armies) and the blast of the seventh (the bowl judgments). This actually makes sense given the fact that the seventh trumpet does not sound until the end of chapter eleven. This also makes sense given the fact that there are seven "thunders" that are hidden to us and will fall after the sixth trumpet. There must be time for the thunders to fall, and there must be time for the armies of the world to march to the Holy Land – ultimately for the final showdown at Armageddon. Let's look at this on our shortened (yet complicated) timeline.

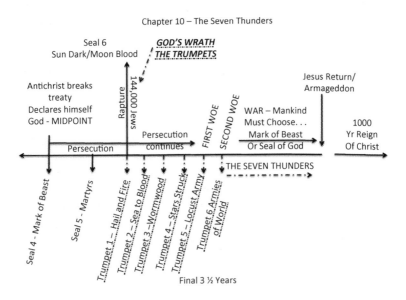

Chapter 10 – The Seven Thunders

Unlike the trumpet judgments, the bowl judgments will be without pause or delay. I would argue that the bowls can last no longer than four days because no one can survive four days without water (bowl number one). I will even argue they will occur in one twenty-four hour period. We will study this more in chapter 16. For now, the reader needs to understand the announcement of this angel is an anticipatory announcement for the final judgments that will be quick and deadly for the unrepentant. You can infer the "no more delay" statement really means, "The King is coming!"

We will see that this is, in fact, the case. When this angel makes his announcement I envision Jesus mounting His horse, lifting His nail scared hands to the mounted troops behind Him and shouting a battle cry.

The "no more delay" is clarified when the angel announces, "the mystery of God is finished." Again, this makes sense given the context. Like I said, when the seventh trumpet sounds, the bowls begin, Jesus returns, the world is judged, and His kingdom is established. But is Jesus' return the only "mystery of God?" There are seven mysteries referred to in the New Testament: the mystery of the rapture (1 Corinthians 15:51-52); the mystery of the gospel (Ephesians 6:19); the mystery of Christ in you (Colossians 1:27); the mystery of Christ (Colossians 2:2); the mystery of godliness (1 Timothy 3:16); the mystery of the Gentiles (Romans 11:25); the mystery of the bride of Christ (Ephesians 5:32).

Again, seven means perfection. Although these seven mysteries are probably not an exhaustive list, they represent knowledge that will be ours when Jesus returns. Many of these should be understood at the rapture (back in chapter six). However others may not be fully known until Jesus' second coming, especially the mystery of the bride of Christ. Why do I say this? At the beginning of Revelation chapter seven we saw four angels holding back the winds (God's wrath) so that one hundred and forty-four thousand Jews could be sealed (come to faith). And after the rapture, there is a chance for the rest of the world to repent. So, the entirety of the bride will not yet be united. When the seventh trumpet sounds and the bowls are poured out, the King of kings returns and the bride of Christ will be united. Then all the mysteries will be understood. "For the earth will be filled with the knowledge of the glory of the Lord, as the waters cover the sea" (Habakkuk 2:14).

The angel in chapter ten is announcing Jesus' imminent return. When the seventh angel sounds his trumpet, get ready – it is time for the return of the King!

On a side note, some scholars believe the bride of Christ is the church only, not Israel. I adamantly disagree with this reasoning. The Old Testament is full of verses that declare God the husband of Israel:

> *For your husband is your Maker, whose name is the Lord of hosts; and your Redeemer is the Holy One of Israel, who is called the God of all the earth.*
>
> *Isaiah 54:5*

We are the ones who are grafted into the vine (Romans 11:17-26). Yes, we are the bride of Christ, but so is Israel. We will be joined as one in the Millennium. Hallelujah! Look at this next Hosea passage, where God is speaking to Israel.

> *I will betroth you to Me forever; yes, I will betroth you to Me in righteousness and in justice, in lovingkindness and in compassion, and I will betroth you to Me in faithfulness. Then you will know the Lord.*
>
> *Hosea 2:19-20*

To reiterate, the Lord is the husband of Israel. We are the one's who are grafted into the vine (Romans 11:17-26).

After we see the angel holding the scroll, we see something very odd. John takes the book (scroll) and eats it! We have seen this before in scripture.

> *Then He said to me, "Son of man, eat what you find; eat this scroll, and go, speak to the house of Israel." So I opened my mouth, and He fed me this scroll. He said to me, "Son of man, feed your stomach and fill your body with this scroll which I am giving you." Then I ate it, and it was sweet as honey in my mouth.*
>
> *Ezekiel 3:1-3*

Ezekiel's scroll tasted like honey too. Let's see if we can figure out what these scrolls represent and why they taste like honey. In Psalm 81:10 God says, "Open your mouth wide, and I

186

will fill it with good things" (NLT). So God is filling our mouths –
but with what?

*How sweet are Your words to my taste! Yes, sweeter than
honey to my mouth!*

Psalm 119:103

Oh faithful friends, God's Word is sweet. Why is that? I can't
say this enough.

*And the Word became flesh, and dwelt among us, and we
saw His glory, glory as of the only begotten from the
Father, full of grace and truth.*

John 1:14

When you immerse yourself with God's Word (Jesus) you will
never be disappointed and the benefits will come back to you.

*And He said to them, "Be careful what you are hearing.
The measure of thought and study you give to the truth
you hear will be the measure of virtue and knowledge that
comes back to you – and more besides will be given to you
who hear."*

Mark 4:24 AMP

The more you hear, study, and "eat" God's Word, the more
virtue and knowledge will be given you. And I caution you, when
you immerse yourself with God there will never be enough time in
the day for Bible study. You won't be able to get enough!
Now, why, if God's Word is honey, did it taste bitter in John's
stomach? The answer is in the next verse. John is told to prophesy
again. When someone eats a scroll, like Ezekiel and John, it is a
commission by God to prophesy.

*Then He said to me, "Son of man, go to the house of
Israel and speak with My words to them."*

Ezekiel 3:4

John needs to go to the people of the earth and tell them again
what he saw and heard. The words he will speak will be sweet and
bitter to those who hear. God's coming kingdom is sweet for the
faithful, but bitter for the unrepentant. When the angel tells John to

prophesy again, this indicates to the reader that the coming chapters will be a flashback in time. They are clarifying things that are happening during the seal and trumpet judgments. God gave us an overview from chapter six through chapter nine. Now, He is getting specific about other things transpiring on the earth. Why? Because, there will be no more delay.

Jesus is mounting His horse.

Thought for the day:

God's words are sweeter than honey. If you are faithfully reading this devotional every day, you should feel like you are being fed, not only with something filling, but with something exceptional. Tomorrow we meet two people who use God's words with power. But the world will hate them. If you use God's words, sometimes the world will hate you. Rejoice in this fact. Jesus said they would (John 15:18).

Day Thirty
Revelation 11:1-14
The Two Witnesses

¹Then there was given me a measuring rod like a staff; and someone said, "Get up and measure the temple of God and the altar, and those who worship in it. ²Leave out the court which is outside the temple and do not measure it, for it has been given to the nations; and they will tread underfoot the holy city for forty-two months."

Revelation 11:1-2

In the first verse of Revelation 11, we have talk of a temple. A voice tells John to go measure the temple and the altar and those who worship in it. Although we do not see John doing this, the implication is clear: a Jewish temple is standing in Jerusalem. As we discussed in chapter six, the temple will be rebuilt before the midpoint of the final seven-year period. We know this because scripture says the Antichrist will set himself up there as god at the midpoint of the final seven years (2 Thessalonians 2:4). We do not know if the construction will occur before the seven years starts or after the peace treaty is signed, although it seems logical that the peace treaty will usher in temple construction. What we do know is that it will be built by the midpoint.

Revelation 11 says the courtyard of the temple will be trampled on for forty-two months, or three and one-half years. This fits with what we already know: the Antichrist will station himself in God's temple and declare himself to be God at the midpoint of the final seven years (Daniel 9:27, Matthew 24:15, 2 Thessalonians 2:3-4). At the beginning of the seven years, there will be a peace treaty and the temple will be rebuilt; at the midpoint, the Antichrist will desecrate the temple and the gentiles will trample the temple grounds for forty-two months.

Let's look at this on a simplified timeline.

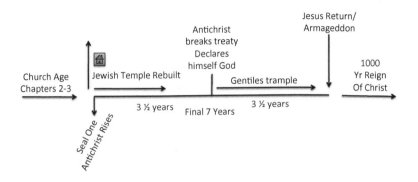

³"And I will grant authority to my two witnesses, and they will prophesy for twelve hundred and sixty days, clothed in sackcloth. ⁴These are the two olive trees and the two lampstands that stand before the Lord of the earth. ⁵And if anyone wants to harm them, fire flows out of their mouth and devours their enemies; so if anyone wants to harm them, he must be killed in this way. ⁶These have the power to shut up the sky, so that rain will not fall during the days of their prophesying; and they have power over the waters to turn them into blood, and to strike the earth with every plague, as often as they desire. ⁷When they have finished their testimony, the beast that comes up out of the abyss will make war with them, and overcome them and kill them. ⁸And their dead bodies will lie in the street of the great city which mystically is called Sodom and Egypt, where also their Lord was crucified. ⁹Those from the peoples and tribes and tongues and nations will look at their dead bodies for three and a half days, and will not permit their dead bodies to be laid in a tomb. ¹⁰And those who dwell on the earth will rejoice over them and celebrate; and they will send gifts to one another, because these two prophets tormented those who dwell on the earth. ¹¹But after the three and a half days, the breath of life from God came into them, and they stood on their feet; and great fear fell upon those who were watching them. ¹²And they heard a loud voice from heaven saying to them, "Come up here." Then they went up into heaven in the cloud, and their enemies watched them. ¹³And in that hour there was a great earthquake, and a tenth of the city fell; seven thousand people were killed in the earthquake, and

the rest were terrified and gave glory to the God of heaven. ¹⁴The second woe is past; behold, the third woe is coming quickly.

Revelation 11:3-14

Again we see the three and one half year time period depicted when it states that the two witnesses will prophesy for twelve hundred and sixty days (or forty-two months). The two witnesses will start prophesying near the midpoint of the final seven years. How do we know this? Because in verse 14 it announces the end of the second woe.

Their deaths are coordinated with the second woe, which is the sixth trumpet. If you recall, in chapter nine the first woe was announced at the end of the fifth trumpet but the second woe wasn't announced. We don't find the second woe announced until here, in chapter eleven. Remember, based on the angel's words "prophesy again" in chapter ten, chapter eleven is a flashback in time to clarify other things transpiring during the seal and trumpet judgments.

The end of the sixth trumpet is the death of the two witnesses, and the end of the sixth trumpet is right before the seventh trumpet sounds or the bowl judgments begin. We can be fairly certain that the witnesses will start their ministry near the midpoint of the final seven years because they prophesy three and a half years. This is also when the Antichrist begins His persecution. The two witnesses will work to turn the nations back to God.

Who are these two witnesses? Most scholars believe they will be Moses and Elijah. If you look at verse six it says they will have power to shut the sky so it doesn't rain, turn water into blood, and to strike the nations with every plague they desire. These attributes are descriptive of Moses and Elijah's ministries. Let's look at this a little more closely.

So Moses and Aaron did even as the Lord had commanded. And he lifted up the staff and struck the water that was in the Nile, in the sight of Pharaoh and in the sight of his servants, and all the water that was in the Nile was turned to blood. The fish that were in the Nile died, and the Nile became foul, so that the Egyptians could not drink water from the Nile. And the blood was through all the land of Egypt.

Exodus 7:20-21

If you recall in Revelation 8:8-9 the water turned to blood and creatures in the water died. Interesting, but hold that thought. Let's go even further.

Now the Lord said to Moses, "One more plague I will bring on Pharaoh and on Egypt; after that he will let you go from here. When he lets you go, he will surely drive you out from here completely."

Exodus 11:1

God called what he sent on the Egyptians a "plague" and the two witnesses in Revelation 11:6 will "strike the earth with every plague as often as they desire."

Moses was God's chosen instrument who inflicted on Egypt ten horrifying plagues (Exodus 7-11). You can see why some scholars think one of the two witnesses is Moses. Now let's look at Elijah.

Now Elijah the Tishbite, who was of the settlers of Gilead, said to Ahab, "As the Lord, the God of Israel lives, before whom I stand, surely there shall be neither dew nor rain these years, except by my word.

1 Kings 17:1

Elijah was a man with a nature like ours, and he prayed earnestly that it would not rain, and it did not rain on the earth for three years and six months.

James 5:17

Wow. That is the exact time frame it says the two witnesses will prophesy! Three years and six months! And let us not forget what scripture says the two witnesses will do, "These have the power to shut up the sky, so that rain will not fall during the days of their prophesying; and they have power over the waters to turn them into blood, and to strike the earth with every plague, as often as they desire."

Are we convinced yet? There is still another reason why scholars believe Moses and Elijah will be the two witnesses.

Six days later, Jesus took with Him Peter and James and John, and brought them up on a high mountain by themselves. And He was transfigured before them . . .

192

Elijah appeared to them along with Moses; and they were talking with Jesus.

Mark 9:2, 4

Moses and Elijah appeared with Jesus during His transfiguration!

I do believe there is sufficient evidence to expect Elijah as one of the two witnesses. First, it is prophesied in scripture. Take a look at Malachi 4:5.

Behold, I am going to send to you Elijah the prophet before the coming of the great and terrible day of the Lord.

Malachi 4:5

The disciples didn't understand the Messiah would come once as the suffering servant and a second time to conquer Israel's enemies. So when they questioned Jesus about this particular scripture, Jesus answered them by saying Elijah had already come, meaning John the Baptist, who heralded Jesus' ministry at His first coming (Mark 9:13). Although Jesus clarified this prophecy was partially fulfilled by John the Baptist, its true meaning is the final wrath of God, or day of the Lord as stated in Malachi. It says Elijah would come again. How is that possible?

As they were going along and talking, behold, there appeared a chariot of fire and horses of fire which separated the two of them. And Elijah went up by a whirlwind to heaven.

2 Kings 2:11

Elijah never died! God ushered him to heaven without the prophet tasting death. In Hebrews 9:27 it says, "And inasmuch as it is appointed for men to die once and after this comes judgment." Men should die once, but Elijah never did. This would allow him to be one of the two witnesses and fulfill the prophecy in Malachi.

Moses, however, died and was buried by God (Deuteronomy 34:5-6). If he returned from heaven, he would die twice (Revelation 11:7). Although most scholars I have read still believe the two witnesses will be Moses and Elijah, there is another Old Testament character we should look at. Did you know there was another man in scripture that didn't die? Let's meet him, shall we?

193

Jared lived one hundred and sixty-two years, and became the father of Enoch . . . Enoch lived sixty-five years, and became the father of Methuselah. Then Enoch walked with God three hundred years after he became the father of Methuselah, and he had other sons and daughters. So all the days of Enoch were three hundred and sixty-five years. Enoch walked with God; and he was not, for God took him.

Genesis 5:18, 21-24

Some of you may be wondering whether "and he was not, for God took him" really meant he did not die. Take a look at Hebrews 11:5:

By faith Enoch was taken up so that he would not see death; and he was not found because God took him up; for he obtained the witness that before his being taken up he was pleasing to God.

Hebrews 11:5

Here is another interesting tidbit. Enoch is listed as an ancestor of Jesus in Luke 3:37. He was of the line that birthed the Messiah. Isn't that interesting? Now look at this gem.

It was also about these men that Enoch, in the seventh generation from Adam, prophesied, saying "Behold, the Lord came with many thousands of His holy ones, to execute judgment upon all, and to convict all the ungodly of all their ungodly deeds which they have done in an ungodly way, and of all the harsh things which ungodly sinners have spoken against Him."

Jude 14-15

Enoch prophesied about the second coming of Christ seven generations from Adam! I find this fascinating. Both Enoch and Elijah did not taste death. Elijah was one of the greatest prophets who ever lived, and Enoch was a man who prophesied about the second coming long before Abraham walked the earth. More on the two witnesses tomorrow.

Thought for the day:
Can you imagine being taken up in a whirlwind to heaven? Can you imagine never dying? Don't think too hard. If you are a believer in the last days, you may get to do just that. If you are here when the trumpet sounds, you will never taste death. But remember, even if you die before the rapture, you are still alive. The moment your eyes close at death, they open in life, because Jesus is "the Life." Glory! You have forever, faithful friends, you have forever!

DAY THIRTY-ONE
REVELATION 11
FIRE COMES OUT OF THEIR MOUTHS

We left yesterday's lesson with a bit of a cliffhanger. Who are the two witnesses? Are they Moses and Elijah? Enoch and Elijah? Or someone else?

First, we need to understand one critical factor that I believe many scholars overlook. Who turned the water into blood? Moses? No, Moses was just God's chosen instrument, a prophet who announced what God was about to do. Same with Elijah. Yes, Elijah announced there would be no rain for three and a half years, but God is the one who closed up the heavens.

If God wants you to be one of the two witnesses, then so be it. He can do anything He pleases. We really don't have to look at similar characteristics in the text dealing with the plagues that occur. God can use anyone He chooses to do the miracles in the text.

But there is another clue in the text as to the identity of the two witnesses. So let's dig deeper. Revelation informs us the two witnesses are the two olive trees and the two lampstands that stand before the Lord of all the earth. Olive oil is representative of the Holy Spirit. When a king was chosen his head was anointed with oil (1 Samuel 16:12-13). When a prophet was commissioned he was anointed with oil (1 Kings 19:16). Priests and temple objects were also anointed with oil to serve in worship duties (Exodus 40:13, Leviticus 8:10). If someone was anointed with oil it was an outward sign of the Lord's favor. The final fulfillment of God's anointing came with the coming of the Holy Spirit in Acts 2:3-4.

The olive trees seen in Revelation stand for the Holy Spirit's anointing of the two witnesses. They will prophesy for twelve hundred and sixty days, and are anointed by God for the task. The olive tree also bears fruit and would also be representative of the two witnesses bearing fruit (converting people to Christ) for the three and one half years of their ministry.

The two witnesses are also represented by two lampstands. We know from chapter one that lampstands represent the church universal. The church bears light for all around it (Matthew 5:15). Scripture says the Antichrist will turn people away from each other (Mark 13:12-13); the two witnesses will try to turn them back. The two witnesses are anointed by God and they are God's light to the dark world that will surround Israel in the last days.

We can go deeper still. In Zechariah chapter four we see something similar: two olive trees lighting a lampstand. If you read the entire chapter you learn the two olive trees represent the "two anointed ones." In Zechariah chapter three and four, the two anointed ones are identified as the "governor" of Judah who was in the lineage of Christ and the "priest" of Judah who was of the priestly line of the Levites. So the two olive trees represent royalty and the priesthood. If we take this image back to Revelation and apply it to our mystery we might get a better idea of the identity of the two witnesses.

If you recall Enoch was an ancestor Jesus – he could represent the "royalty" line.

What about the priesthood? Moses was considered a priest (Psalm 99:6) and according to Jewish tradition, Elijah was of the priestly line as well. However, only one of these two people were "taken" by God without death. I find it extremely interesting two men never tasted death, and there are two witnesses in Revelation. God had to have a purpose for taking these men without seeing death. "And inasmuch as it is appointed for men to die once and after this comes judgment" (Hebrews 9:27).

If the two witnesses are Enoch and Elijah, you would see both the kingship of Jesus and the priesthood of Jesus represented. I am personally convinced that the two witnesses are Enoch and Elijah, but please, review the information and ask God for insight.

These prophets will prophesy during some of the seal and trumpet judgments. Just like Moses and Elijah were God's instruments to strike the world with plagues, these witnesses might very well be the ones heralding the trumpet judgments. Like I have said previously, although many scholars insist Moses is one of the two witnesses because of the plagues of Egypt, the reader needs to remember it was God, not Moses, bringing the plagues. We see the same thing occurring in Revelation. Do you remember how similar one of the plagues described in Revelation 11:6 was to the second trumpet judgment of Revelation 8:8? "The water will turn to blood unless you repent," the two witnesses will shout. As soon as their words are spoken the angel will sound the second trumpet, causing the water to turn to blood. I am convinced that the two witnesses will be God's warning to the unrepentant. "Turn, or else!"

Fire will come forth from their mouths if anyone tries to harm them. Is this literal fire? Perhaps, but there is another fire referred to in scripture that could quite possibly be the real interpretation.

Therefore, thus says the Lord, the God of hosts, "Because you have spoken this word, behold, I am making My words in your mouth fire and this people wood, and it will consume them."

Jeremiah 5:14

"Is not My word like fire?" declares the Lord, "and like a hammer which shatters a rock?"

Jeremiah 23:29

God's words are fire, and in the day of judgment He will be a consuming fire.

Behold, the name of the Lord comes from a remote place; burning is His anger and dense is His smoke; His lips are filled with indignation and His tongue is like a consuming fire.

Isaiah 30:27

The day of the Lord will bring the earth's destruction by fire (2 Peter 3:10) through the trumpets and the bowls. These witnesses will be on earth heralding the trumpets' destruction through their words, pleading with those remaining on earth to turn to God. "Repent," they will cry, "or else!" Their words, God's words, will become a fire of destruction through the trumpet judgments. The witnesses will be the harbinger of those judgments and their words will literally become fire to the souls of mankind.

Note the environment in the Holy Land is so bad the Lord refers to it as "Sodom and Egypt." Sodom was the city destroyed by fire in Genesis 19, and Egypt was where the plagues similar to those in Revelation were carried out. This is significant. This is saying the fire of God's judgments and the plagues will come to pass in the Holy Land. John further clarifies he is talking about the Holy Land and Jerusalem by recording "where also the Lord was crucified."

No enemy can touch the two witnesses for three and a half years. However, when they have finished their testimony, Satan (the beast from the abyss) and the Antichrist (the beast out of the sea – see chapter 13) will find a way to kill them. But note when Satan is allowed to kill them.

When they have finished their testimony, the beast that comes up out of the abyss will make war with them, and overcome them and kill them.

Revelation 11:7

God won't allow anything to touch us until our testimony is complete. Only He knows when that time is for each of us. No matter if we are in the prime of life, or hunched over from age, our death is under God's watchful eyes. No one can take the fire from our mouths until the moment God says our words are complete.[1]

When the two witnesses are killed, their bodies are allowed to lie in the streets for three and a half days. Those who dwell on the earth will rejoice and celebrate as they look on the mutilated bodies of the witnesses. They will even send gifts to each other because of their deaths. Sadly, we have cultures today that do this very thing. In radical Islamic nations, when enemies are killed, they are displayed in the streets and people rejoice over their torture. The citizens of these nations also pass out candies in celebration. These countries surround Israel. The witnesses will be in Israel. The nations surrounding her will hate the two witnesses, will degrade them, and will pass out candies in joy upon their deaths. How backwards our world has become!

It's not surprising the whole world will witness this event. Modern technology has made communication effortless and immediate. What happens across the world can be seen instantaneously by nations around the globe. Everyone remaining on earth will witness these prophets' deaths.

Yet, after three and a half days, when the celebrations are still continuing, there will be a miracle. The two witnesses will stand on their feet. Their mutilated bodies will become whole and they will rise in the air at the command of our Savior. Someone needs to shout, "Hallelujah!"

They will rise in a cloud. We learned in Revelation 10 the cloud represented Jesus' ascension and return. In the Exodus, God's visible presence manifested itself in a cloud (Exodus 40:34). The witnesses are rising with God's glory, just like Jesus did in His ascension, and just like Jesus will return in Revelation.

The same hour the witnesses are taken in the clouds there is an earthquake. A tenth of the city falls and seven thousand people are killed. Then scripture tells us when this will take place: "The second woe is past; behold, the third woe is coming quickly." In chapter eight we learned the final three trumpets were the three woes. The first woe corresponds to the locust invasion of trumpet number five, and the second woe corresponds to the army of two hundred million.

The two witnesses will be killed after the sixth trumpet sounds and right before the seventh trumpet (or the bowl judgments) begin. Why did God feel the need to place the witnesses in chapter 11 and not in chapter nine? Chapter nine is a summary of the trumpet judgments. If you recall, chapter 10 brought an angel telling John to "prophesy again." Hence, chapter 11 begins a "flashback" in time; it clarifies other things happening during the seal and trumpet judgments. Because the witnesses prophesy three and a half years, they are ushered into the scene during the seals, but their deaths are not until the end of the sixth trumpet – or the second woe.

From the time the two witnesses begin to prophesy until their deaths there will be one thousand two hundred and sixty days. They will remain in the streets for an additional three and one half days and then take to the sky. Then and only then will the third woe, the seventh trumpet, be unleashed. With the sounding of the seventh trumpet, the bowl judgments begin and they will be the final destruction of the surface of the earth. Remember, the bowl judgments will be very quick, in rapid succession, as we discussed in chapter nine. Let's look at this on our seven-year timeline, and also on our three and one-half year timeline.

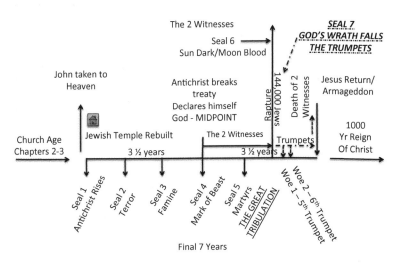

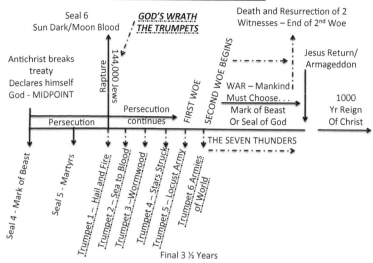

2 Witnesses – Shortened Timeline

Thought for the day:
Not only are God's words like honey, they are also like fire to those who are not with Him. They have the power to penetrate the heart and convict the sinner. How often do we use them to wake someone up? How many of them do we know? Have we read them all? Or have we ignored the Word? Find out what the Word's fire can do tomorrow.

1 Moore, Beth. DVD Study Here and Now … There and Then: A lecture series on Revelation (Houston, Texas: Living Proof Ministries, 2009).

DAY THIRTY-TWO
REVELATION 11
THE TWO WITNESSES AND THE RAPTURE

I just want to say, "You've come a long way baby!" Did you ever think you would get this far in Revelation and understand half of it? If some things are still a little fuzzy, please press on. Although the graph is saturated with information, it will be increasingly understandable. The more we read and learn, the more we will understand. So press on Christian soldier!

I want to pause here for a moment and focus on the two witnesses in regards to Jewish tradition. I firmly believe the two witnesses are important not only for their prophetic significance, but also their inherent symbolism. In Judaism, there are seven feasts. Three are in the spring, one shortly thereafter, and the final three are in the fall. Jesus fulfilled the first three during His first coming, when He suffered and died for the sins of mankind. The fourth was fulfilled at Pentecost when the Holy Spirit was poured out on the disciples. God's specific design for each feast is amazing.

I will give you just a small example of the detail God went to in fulfilling the first four feasts (Leviticus 23).

The first feast, the feast of Passover, was the day our Savior died for our sins. The Jews always killed two lambs every day.

"You shall say to them, 'This is the offering by fire which you shall offer to the Lord; two male lambs one year old without defect as a continual burnt offering every day. You shall offer the one lamb in the morning and the other lamb you shall offer at twilight.'"
Numbers 28:3-4

History shows the morning sacrifice was at nine, the exact time Jesus was hung on the cross (Mark 15:25). The evening sacrifice was at three in the afternoon, the exact time Jesus died on the cross (Matthew 27:45-51). Jesus became our "Passover Lamb." Just as the lamb's blood in the Exodus covered the people as the angel of death passed by, Jesus' blood covers us and saves us for life eternal. Glory!

The next feast is the "Feast of Unleavened Bread." On this feast, Jesus was buried, the sinless (unleavened) Son of God.

The third feast is the "Feast of First Fruits." It is on this day that our Savior was resurrected, the "first fruits" of the dead.

202

But now Christ has been raised from the dead, the first fruits of those who are asleep.

1 Corinthians 15:20

The fourth feast is the feast of Pentecost. Christians tend to believe this is solely a Christian holiday, yet the Jews have been celebrating Pentecost for thousands of years. Jewish tradition states Pentecost was the day Moses received the Ten Commandments from God. Jesus fulfilled the law of Moses in life (Matthew 5:17) and also satisfied the law with His death (1 Corinthians 15:56-57). Notice, when the disciples received the Spirit there was a huge crowd in Jerusalem. Why? God had told the Jewish people to celebrate the feast of Pentecost.

For more information on the feasts, please study *The Feasts of the Lord*, by Mark Biltz.[1] Although the detail of the first four feasts would be too much for us to study here, we will look at the remaining three feasts because they will be fulfilled with Jesus' second coming. We will study each of the three unfulfilled feasts when they come into play during our tour of Revelation.

The first annual fall feast (occurring in September or October on our calendar) is Rosh Hashanah. The significance of this feast for Jesus' second coming is evident due to its trumpet blasts and symbolic gates of heaven. Rosh Hashanah is also known as the Feasts of Trumpets and the Day of the Awakening Blast. This feast is different from the other feasts because it lasts for two days. Rosh Hashanah is also the only Jewish feast that starts on the first day of the month. Because the Jews use a lunar calendar, the month begins with the new moon, but the new moon is very hard to see. It can only be spotted in the daylight hours right next to the sun. Each Jewish month is either twenty-nine or thirty days long, because new moons come every 29.5 days. So in ancient times no one knew when the new moon would be sighted and another month declared. Because of the importance of Rosh Hashanah, the new moon had to be sighted by two witnesses. If you lived in Jesus' day you knew when the month was ending and another beginning, but you had no idea when two witnesses would confirm the new moon. Hence, no one knew when the Feast of Trumpets would start. If the moon wasn't sighted on the first day, the feast started on the next day. For this reason, the feast is always celebrated for two days. So, it is the only feast the Jews had to be alert and watch for. What did Jesus say?

"Therefore be on the alert, for you do not know which day your Lord is coming."

Matthew 24:42

Rosh Hashanah is also called the "last trump" for on these feast days the shofar is blown one hundred times and the last blast was known as the "last trump."

Behold, I tell you a mystery; we will not all sleep, but we will all be changed, in a moment, in the twinkling of an eye, at the last trumpet; for the trumpet will sound, and the dead will be raised imperishable, and we will be changed.

1 Corinthians 15:51-52

The Jews would recognize Paul's language here to be referring to the "last trump" or Rosh Hashanah.

Because the feast was two days long and had to be confirmed by two witnesses, it was also known as "the hidden day" and "the day and the hour no one knows." Does that sound familiar?

"But of that day and hour no one knows, not even the angels of heaven, nor the Son, but the Father alone."

Matthew 24:36

The Rapture will be on Rosh Hashanah. We still won't know the day or the hour because the feast lasts two days! And you know what else? There will be two prophets – two witnesses – in Jerusalem who will declare the new moon – the start of Rosh Hashanah. We meet these prophets in Revelation 11.

The two witnesses will prophesy for the last half of the final seven years. While they are prophesying, the rapture will occur. This means, they will announce the new moon; they will announce the rapture.

One final note, Rosh Hashanah is also known as the "opening of the gates of heaven" (Ezekiel 46:1).

Open the gates, that the righteous nation may enter, the one that remains faithful.

Isaiah 26:2

204

If you turn back to Revelation chapter four, you see an "open door." If you remember, this is where pre-tribulation proponents place the rapture. We have gone over the reasons why I believe it is not in chapter four, but in chapter seven, where we find a great multitude coming from the great tribulation, just before God's wrath falls. But the pre-tribulation rapture view is right in one respect: the door is open. It is Rosh Hashanah. Although the rapture doesn't occur here, the open door is telling us the feast of Rosh Hashanah is when the final seven-year period will begin! If you think about it, this makes sense. If the seven years ends in the fall, it has to start in the fall. It has to start at approximately the same place it ends. More on this as we continue our study.

To recap, John is ushered into heaven when the door is "opened," on Rosh Hashanah! This feast starts the final seven-year period.

If the Rosh Hashanah of chapter four will not be the rapture, which one will be? There will be seven total Feast of Trumpets in the final seven-year period. We know when the Antichrist sets himself up as god, which would logically correspond to the beginning of the persecution of God's saints at the midpoint (starting in the 4th seal). So the fifth and sixth seal will be after the midpoint. Therefore, we can say with relative certainty we will live through at least four Rosh Hashanahs before we are raptured on the fifth, six, or seventh feast celebration. I believe the sixth Rosh Hashanah is the most likely scenario based on the following scriptures:

When a man takes a new wife, he shall not go out with the army nor be charged with any duty; he shall be free at home one year and shall give happiness to his wife whom he has taken.

Deuteronomy 24:5

For the Lord has a day of vengeance, a year of recompense for the cause of Zion.

Isaiah 34:8

The first scripture above states the bridegroom cannot go to war for one year. At the rapture Jesus, the bridegroom, will be united with His raptured bride, the church. When Jesus returns to earth at His second coming, He will be going to war. That would place the rapture one year prior to the second coming.

The second scripture states that there will be a year of vengeance. Seeing that the bride of Christ is raptured on the same day the "day of the Lord" or the "vengeance" starts, that would place the rapture at the sixth Rosh Hashanah in the final seven years.

Also, the battle of Armageddon will have the armies of the world united at Jerusalem. The seventh Rosh Hashanah is insufficient time for the armies to unite to battle the King of kings. If the church is raptured at the beginning of the sixth year, there would be an ample amount of time for the trumpet and bowl judgments to fall on the earth and for the armies of the world to unite. Noah was on the boat for just over a year. So will the earth be under God's wrath for a year. Let's look at this on our time line.

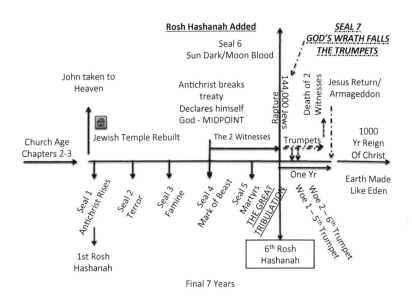

Final 7 Years

God is telling us exactly what will happen, my faithful friends. Exactly.

Thought for the day:

Just think, many in the church believe we will be raptured before the Antichrist is known, before the famine, and before the persecution. How do you think the majority of the church will react if they are here to see it all start? Will they even believe the Antichrist is the enemy if they are sure they will be taken out before he is known? Will the mark look evil or will it look like salvation? Will they recognize God's wrath, or will they still be ignorant when the seventh trumpet sounds? The seventh trumpet sounds tomorrow.

1 Blitz, Mark. A DVD study entitled *Feasts of the Lord*. See also Feasts of the Lord by Kevin Howard and Marvin Rosenthal (Nashville, Tennessee:Thomas Nelson, Inc., 1997).

[15]Then the seventh angel sounded; and there were loud voices in heaven, saying, "The kingdom of the world has become the kingdom of our Lord and of His Christ; and He will reign forever and ever." [16]And the twenty-four elders, who sit on their thrones before God, fell on their faces and worshiped God, [17]saying, "We give You thanks, O Lord God, the Almighty, who are and who were, because You have taken Your great power and have begun to reign. [18]And the nations were enraged, and Your wrath came, and the time came for the dead to be judged, and the time to reward Your bond-servants the prophets and the saints and those who fear Your name, the small and the great, and to destroy those who destroy the earth." [19]And the temple of God which is in heaven was opened; and the ark of His covenant appeared in His temple, and there were flashes of lightning and sounds and peals of thunder and an earthquake and a great hailstorm.

Revelation 11:15-19

At the blowing of the seventh trumpet, Christ's reign is foreseen. This makes absolute sense when you realize three things: first, the seventh trumpet opens the bowl judgments which are the final judgments of the earth; second, the bowl judgments will be quick; third, Jesus will return during the bowls. Let's look at these one at a time.

First, just like the seventh seal wasn't an "action" per say, but only instigated the blowing of the trumpets, the seventh trumpet blast will not be an "action" but will initiate the bowls. Some scholars like to place the rapture of the church with the seventh trumpet in Revelation because of this next scripture.

> *Behold, I tell you a mystery; we will not all sleep, but we will all be changed, in a moment, in the twinkling of an eye, at the last trumpet.*
>
> *1 Corinthians 15:51-52a*

However, Messianic Jews don't associate the "last trumpet" with the trumpets of Revelation; they associated the last trump with the feast of Rosh Hashanah, which we looked at yesterday. The last trumpet is a feast, not the final trumpet of Revelation. Here is another way to look at it: the "last trump" mentioned in Corinthians is a saving trumpet – corresponding to the "last trump" of Rosh Hashanah and the rescuing of the saints; the final trumpet in Revelation is a judgmental trumpet with the final plagues that will fall on mankind.

With the blowing of the seventh trumpet of Revelation, Jesus will lay claim to the earth. As I have said previously, Jesus will be mounting His white horse and calling to His troops to do the same when the final trumpet is blown.

Secondly, because of the severity of the bowl judgments, they will be quick. If the entire water supply on earth turns to blood, well, life cannot last more than four days (see Revelation 16:3-4). Although Isaiah 34:8 says there will be a "year of recompense" which will start with the trumpet judgments, there will also be a final "day of the lord." This will be a one-day period of time where Jesus will lay claim to the earth. Will this encompass the entirety of the bowls? We will study this as we move further into Revelation.

Finally, Jesus will return with the bowls and fight the Antichrist in the battle of Armageddon. We will look at this in chapter sixteen. Because of the brevity of the bowls, it is announced that Christ will reign forever and ever. It is an anticipatory announcement of the coming King!

Picture this, Jesus is mounting His horse as the saints shout, "The kingdom of the world has become the kingdom of our Lord and of His Christ; and He will reign forever and ever." As the saints are mounting their own horses, the twenty four elders fall down on their faces and say, "We give You thanks, O Lord God, the Almighty, who are and who were, because You have taken Your great power and have begun to reign." Jesus is about to lift His hands and usher His troops to earth. His reign is now imminent. The twenty-four elders continue, "And the nations were enraged, and Your wrath came." The elders are confirming the trumpet judgments were the wrath of God on the earth.

They continue to say, "The time came for the dead to be judged, and the time to reward Your bond-servants the prophets and the saints and those who fear Your name, the small and the great, and to destroy those who destroy the earth." If we understand what happens at the rapture we will better understand this praise. In Luke 14:14 Jesus tells His disciples, "For you will be repaid at the resurrection of the righteous." The resurrection of the righteous is the rapture that happens after the sixth seal. When scripture talks of the judgment seat of Christ, it is talking about the believer's judgment. (Note that unbelievers are not raised or judged until after the Millennium, as we will see in Chapter 20.)

This does not mean that believers will be judged according to our sins. "For as high as the heavens are above the earth, so great is the lovingkindness toward those who fear Him. As far as the east is from the west, so far has He removed our transgressions from us" (Psalm 103:11-12).

So what does this next verse mean?

For we must all appear before the judgment seat of Christ, so that each one may be recompensed for his deeds in the body, according to what he has done, whether good or bad.

2 Corinthians 5:10

If you look at the Greek word for "seat" it is "bema," and the bema seat was used by judges in the Olympic games. It was the place where the winners of the races were rewarded. We will not be judged by our sin, but rewarded based on what we have done for Christ (Romans 8:1).

Crowns will be given and rewards will be handed out when we are with Christ in heaven after the rapture.[1] The twenty-four elders are referring to the rewards already handed out in heaven and the ones that will ultimately be given to those faithful few remaining on earth. It is interesting to note that Rosh Hashanah, the feast on which the rapture will take place, is also known as the day when the books are opened, or the day when the bema "judgment" seat begins.

After the twenty-four elders finish their song, the temple of God in heaven is opened and the Ark of the Covenant is seen. Although the ark rested in the Holy of Holies, the innermost room of the temple, it is seen when the Holy Place is open, the first room of the temple. Why do I say this? Look at Revelation 15:5.

After these things I looked, and the temple of the tabernacle of testimony in heaven was opened.

Revelation 15:5

The "temple of the tabernacle of testimony," the temple housing the ark, the Holy of Holies, is not opened until chapter 15.

Let me remind you of something. The Holy of Holies was separated from the Holy Place by a veil.

And behold, the veil of the temple was torn in two from top to bottom; and the earth shook and the rocks were split.

Matthew 27:51

The tabernacle on earth mirrors the tabernacle in heaven (Hebrews 9:23-24). The veil was torn at Jesus' death. The way to God was no longer belief in the daily sacrifice that pointed the way to Christ, but belief in Christ Himself. The ark is seen here in the temple because the veil is no longer there! The Israelites have seen the truth and they are symbolically walking into the Holy Place. They see the ark, which is no longer shrouded by the veil. Now they need to make the final choice. Will they accept Jesus as their Messiah? Or, now that they see the truth, will turn and walk away?

Let's pause here to see the importance of the ark. First, the presence of God rested above the ark (Exodus 25:21-22). Second, the cover of the ark was known as the mercy seat, where God extended mercy to the nation of Israel. It was where the blood of the sacrifice was sprinkled, representing Christ's perfect sacrifice. The cherubim who were on the mercy seat looked down at the blood, reminding us that God looks at us through eyes of mercy because of the blood of His Son that covers us from sin and allows us to enter into His presence. We are allowed into the Holy of Holies, to the mercy seat of Christ, where we will be judged and rewarded, not judged and condemned. The mercy seat is Christ's bema seat where we will receive mercy on behalf of His blood and crowned according to His grace. One of the main reasons the final seven years takes place is for Israel to come to repentance and sit at His mercy seat (Hosea 3:5).

When the Ark of the Covenant is seen in God's temple, it is telling us the faithful in heaven have already met Christ at his "bema seat." Rewards have been handed out! It is also declaring Israel's salvation is now imminent. Christ will return during the bowls, but He will not return until all of Israel says, "Blessed is He who comes in the name of the Lord" (Luke 13:35b, see also Romans 11:26-27). Remember the lion's roar we discussed in chapter ten? The lion's roar initiated Israel's call to faith and the two witnesses' deaths correspond to the second woe back in chapter nine. You can say that the lion's roar in chapter ten is immediately followed by the sounding of the seventh trumpet and appearance of the ark, declaring mercy is being extended, and now, finally, Israel will start to believe. In other words, the lion's roar in chapter ten and the call of Israel to faith is what ushers in the sounding of the seventh trumpet – the return of the King! Only after the Jews come to faith will the Lion of the tribe of Judah descend to the earth and save His chosen nation. The ark seen in Revelation 11, at the sounding of the seventh trumpet, is a visual representation of the moment of realization of the Jewish people that Jesus can, in fact, be their Messiah.

Thunder, lightning, a hailstorm, and an earthquake also occur representing the final judgments of mankind. These judgments are seen in the seventh bowl as well. Let's compare these.

The Seventh Trumpet
And there were flashes of lightning and sounds and peals of thunder and an earthquake and a great hailstorm.
Revelation 11:19b

The Seventh Bowl
And there were flashes of lightning and sounds and peals of thunder; and there was a great earthquake, such as there had not been since man came to be upon the earth, so great an earthquake was it, and so mighty . . .and huge hailstones, about one hundred pounds each, came down from heaven upon men.
Revelation 16:18,21a

The beginning of each verse is the same. Where they differ is the description of the earthquake. I believe this is telling us the seventh trumpet and the seventh bowl will be on the same day. The bowl judgments will be so quick that they occur on the same day the seventh trumpet ushers them in, and Jesus will return during their fall and cleanse the earth of the unrepentant in one day.

The Ark of the Covenant is seen only once a year, on Yom Kippur. Again, the feast of Yom Kippur has yet to be fulfilled. Could the bowl judgments occur on Yom Kippur? This feast takes place ten days after Rosh Hashanah. Yom Kippur means "Day of Atonement." This was the one day each year the High Priest of the Jewish nation was allowed into the Holy of Holies where the ark sat. This was the day when the High priest sprinkled the mercy seat with blood, representing Jesus' sacrifice. Because God's presence was above the mercy seat, this is the day where the High Priest met

God "face to face." And when will the rest of the world see God face to face? At Jesus' second coming! The ark in chapter 11 represents the High Priest walking into the temple on Yom Kippur to atone for the nation once and for all – through belief. And this in turn ushers in the second coming of Christ.

The High Priest went into the Holy of Holies on Yom Kippur to make atonement for the nation of Israel as a whole.

"This shall be a permanent statute for you: in the seventh month, on the tenth day of the month, you shall humble your souls and not do any work, whether the native, or the alien who sojourns among you. . . now you shall have this as a permanent statute, to make atonement for the sons of Israel for all their sins once every year." And just as the Lord had commanded Moses, so he did.

Leviticus 16:29,34

So once a year, on Yom Kippur, the nation of Israel's sins were cleansed as a whole. They were forgiven! As we said before, there will be a day when the nation of Israel realizes Jesus is her Messiah.

I will pour out on the house of David and on the inhabitants of Jerusalem, the Spirit of grace and of supplication, so that they will look on Me whom they have pierced; and they will mourn for Him, as one mourns for an only son, and they will weep bitterly over Him like the bitter weeping over a firstborn.

Zechariah 12:10

This is the day Jesus will return, one year and ten days after the rapture. He will fulfill the second fall feast, Yom Kippur. Do we see this in scripture? Yes we do.

All Jews wear white on Yom Kippur, symbolizing their atonement from sin. This ritual does not exclude the High Priest, who is performing the bloody sacrifices. His white robes would be splattered with the blood of bulls and goats. Now, listen to this scripture:

Who is this who comes from Edom, with garments of glowing colors from Bozrah, this One who is majestic in His apparel, marching in the greatness of His strength? "It is I who speak in righteousness, mighty to save." Why is Your apparel red, and Your garments like the one who treads the wine press? *"I have trodden the wine trough alone, and from the peoples there was no man with Me. I also trod them in My anger and trampled them in My wrath; and their lifeblood is sprinkled on My garments, and I stained all My rainment. For the day of vengeance was in My heart, and My year of redemption has come."*

Isaiah 63:1-4

Jesus is walking on earth here, treading the wine press. He is executing His wrath on the earth on the day of vengeance. What is the day of vengeance? The second coming, when He fights the battle of Armageddon. This garment stained red would be instantly recognizable to the Jew. This is the Day of Atonement, the day when Israel's sins are wiped clean as a nation.

Yom Kippur is also known as the "closing of the book" or the day when judgment is over. It is also called the "great trump." We see this in scripture.

"And then the sign of the Son of Man will appear in the sky, and then all the tribes of the earth will mourn, and they will see the Son of Man coming on the clouds of the sky with power and great glory. And He will send forth His angels with a great trumpet and they will gather together His elect from the four winds, from one end of the sky to the other."

Matthew 24:30-31

The tribes of the earth see Jesus in the sky. This is Jesus at His second coming – in God's wrath – to judge mankind. And when he comes, a great trumpet will sound.

This is a second coming scripture, not a rapture passage, when people will disappear like a thief. This is when Jesus is coming in glory and every eye will see Him. Glory!

There may be a question in your mind right now that might go something like this: "But in Isaiah 34:8, scripture says there is a day of vengeance and a year of recompense. If we are raptured on the sixth Rosh Hashanah and Jesus doesn't return until the final Yom Kippur, there is a time span of one year and ten days. Ten days is not a long time, but is this consistent with scripture?"

This same thought bothered me for quite some time, and then one day, God put into my heart to turn back to Noah and Lot.

214

Remember, Jesus said the days of the Son of Man would be just like the days of Noah and the days of Lot (Luke 17:26, 28). Lot was recued the same day the wrath fell. This corresponds to Israel in the day of the Lord. They will be rescued in one day, the day the bowl judgments fall cleansing the earth of evil. But although Noah was rescued the same day the wrath of God started (just like we are recued on the same day the trumpet judgments begin to fall) he was protected on the ark for a lot longer. Let's see how long Noah was on the ark:

> *In the sixth hundredth year of Noah's life, in the second month, on the seventeenth day of the month, on the same day all the fountains of the great deep burst open, and the floodgates of the sky were opened.*
>
> *Genesis 7:11*

> *In the second month, on the twenty-seventh day of the month, the earth was dry. Then God spoke to Noah, saying, "Go out of the ark."*
>
> *Genesis 8:14-16a*

Noah was on the ark for one year and ten days! Just like the days of Noah, the faithful church will be ushered into heaven at the rapture and be protected for a year and ten days as Gods wrath comes down (the trumpets). Just like the days of Lot, there will be one final day when the final wrath of God pours down and the Jews are rescued (the bowls).

In Revelation 1:8, Jesus describes himself as "who is and who was and who is to come." Now look at Revelation 11:17.

> *"We give You thanks, O Lord God, the Almighty, who are and who were . . ."*
>
> *Revelation 11:17*

Glory! This means that there is no more delay. There is no longer an "is to come." The coming is *NOW*. It is happening. "The kingdom of the world has become the kingdom of our Lord and of His Christ; and He will reign forever and ever" (Revelation 11:15).

The ark is seen because the Jews are at the threshold of belief but they haven't yet made their commitment. We will see this commitment in chapter fifteen, but the reader needs to realize the time lapse between chapter eleven and chapter fifteen is seconds in real time. When the seventh trumpet is blown, the bowls begin to fall and the King returns. Although there is a pause for those reading Revelation between the sounding of the seventh trumpet and the pouring out of the bowls, there is no pause in real time.

Israel is at the cusp of belief. They have walked through "the Way" . . . Jesus has mounted His horse . . . they have seen "the Truth" . . . Jesus is raising His hands to ready His army . . . they have entered the Holy Place in the tabernacle . . . they look upon the ark . . . the veil is gone . . . their path is clear . . . they are about to enter the Holy of Holies . . . when they do, they will claim "the Life" and will say, "Blessed is He who comes in the name of the Lord!"

And Jesus returns to save them.

Thought for the day:
We will be with Him when He returns. Think about that for a minute. When Jesus returns on Yom Kippur, we will be right behind Him. When Israel comes to faith, we will be riding the skies behind our King to cleanse the earth. Just like Jesus involves His saints now, so will we be involved in His return. More on that in future lessons. For now, long for the day!

1 For more information on crowns see: 1 Corinthians 9:24-25, 1 Thessalonians 2:19-20, James 1:12, Revelation 2:8-11, 2 Timothy 4:8, and 1 Peter 5;1-4

[1]A great sign appeared in heaven: a women clothed with the sun, and the moon under her feet, and on her head a crown of twelve stars; [2]and she was with child; and she cried out, being in labor and in pain to give birth.

Revelation 12:1-2

The end of the previous chapter announced the reign of Christ with the sounding of the seventh trumpet. With the blast of the seventh trumpet, the bowls will be unleashed and the end will come swiftly. Before Jesus shows John the bowl judgments and their severity, He takes John back in time so that His faithful disciple understands the big picture. Although the bowl judgments will come immediately after the seventh trumpet, Jesus wants the reader of His revelation to understand why the last trumpet has to sound in the first place. We tend to look at the bowl judgments in Revelation and cringe at their severity, but there is a reason behind their gravity. The world has accepted a dragon and a beast. To emphasize the righteousness of the coming judgment, we go back to the beginning and work our way once again up to the sounding of the seventh trumpet in the next three chapters.

The first thing John sees is a woman. She is clothed with the sun with the moon under her feet and has on a crown of twelve stars. Some scholars insist this is Mary, the mother of Jesus, but in verse six it describes this woman running into the wilderness to be protected for a time and times and half a time. We know based on our study this refers to one year, plus two years, plus one half year, or three and a half years. This vision has nothing to do with Mary and everything to do with the nation of Israel. Mary isn't present during the end times; Israel is very present. When must Israel be protected? When the Antichrist declares himself God during the midpoint of the final seven years on earth before the return of the King. Chapter 12 shows us Israel's beginnings and takes us up to the time of Israel's persecution, beginning at the midpoint of the final seven-year period. Let's dig deeper.

Jacob (who was renamed Israel by God – Genesis 35:10) had twelve sons. One of those sons was Joseph who became the overseer of Egypt and ultimately rescued his family from a severe famine that swept the land. Before he went to Egypt he was known as "the dreamer" (Genesis 37:19). He had a dream his eleven brothers and his two parents would bow to him.

> *Now he had still another dream, and related it to his brothers, and said, "Lo, I have had still another dream; and behold, the sun and the moon and eleven stars were bowing down to me." He related it to his father and to his brothers; and his father rebuked him and said to him, "What is this dream that you have had? Shall I and your mother and your brothers actually come to bow ourselves down before you to the ground?"*
>
> *Genesis 37:9-10*

Joseph's brothers were the "stars" and his parents were "the sun and the moon." Well, Joseph's dream came true. His brothers, jealous of Joseph, sold him as a slave. God worked mightily in Joseph's life and after years he rose to be second in command of Egypt. What is important for our study is that the sons of Jacob were depicted as "stars" and the parents of those stars were depicted as "the sun and the moon." So, the nation of Israel was founded by the patriarchs (sun and moon) and is represented by the twelve tribes (twelve stars). This is exactly what we see depicted in Revelation.

The woman gives birth to a child: our Lord and Savior, Jesus. The nation of Israel was the chosen nation to bring forth the Messiah. The "labor pains" she undergoes are the persecutions she has endured throughout history, both before and after Jesus was born. Next we meet the reason for that persecution. There is an enemy who doesn't want Israel to exist; there is an enemy who didn't want the Messiah to come; there is an enemy who doesn't want the Messiah to return. Let's read the next few verses in Revelation.

³Then another sign appeared in heaven: and behold, a great red dragon having seven heads and ten horns, and on his heads were seven diadems. ⁴And his tail swept away a third of the stars of heaven and threw them to the earth. And the dragon stood before the woman who was about to give birth, so that when she gave birth he might devour her child.

Revelation 12:3-4

218

In these verses, we meet a dragon. If you look forward to verse nine, the dragon is identified for you.

And the great dragon was thrown down, the serpent of old who is called the devil and Satan, who deceives the whole world . . .

Revelation 12:9

John sees Satan taking a third of the stars from heaven and throwing them to the earth. In Revelation 1:20, stars are depicted as angels. From this scripture many scholars maintain, I believe correctly, when Satan fell he persuaded a third of the angels to follow him. This matches Revelation 12:7 where we see Satan fighting with an army of angels. Satan's original fall is described in Isaiah.

How you have fallen from heaven, O star of the morning, son of the dawn! You have been cut down to the earth, you who have weakened the nations! But you said in your heart, I will ascend to heaven; I will raise my throne above the stars of God, and I will sit on the mount of assembly in the recesses of the north. I will ascend above the heights of the clouds; I will make myself like the Most High.

Isaiah 14:12-14

Satan enters the scene, wanting to devour the woman's child. Jesus' birth wasn't peaceful; it involved Herod slaying every male child in Bethlehem under the age of two (Matthew 2:16). When Jesus grew up, Satan met Him in the wilderness, tempting Him to deny His Father (Matthew 4:1-11). Ultimately, Satan entered Judas and betrayed Jesus, causing our Savior to be killed (Luke 22:3,48). The dragon, like the rest of the Jews, was expecting a conquering king. Satan wanted Jesus dead, and at the cross he thought he had claimed the victory, but Jesus conquered death and promised life eternal to those who believe in Him. "O death, where is your victory? O death, where is your sting? The sting of death is sin, and the power of sin is the law; but thanks be to God, who gives us the victory through our Lord Jesus Christ" (1 Corinthians 15:55-57).

Satan is seen with seven heads, ten horns, and seven crowns on his heads. In Revelation 13 we will meet another beast who has very similar attributes, so we will study Satan's horns, heads, and crowns when we meet the second beast in the next chapter.

⁵And she gave birth to a son, a male child, who is to rule all the nations with a rod of iron; and her child was caught up to God and to His throne. ⁶Then the woman fled into the wilderness where she had a place prepared by God, so that there she would be nourished for one thousand two hundred and sixty days.

Revelation 12:5-6

The woman, Israel, gave birth to a male child and the child was caught up to heaven out of Satan's hand. This refers to the resurrection and ascension of Christ, where He took His rightful place at the right hand of God (Hebrews 12:2). As we continue our study in Revelation we will find He will ultimately rule the nations with a rod of iron.

From His mouth comes a sharp sword, so that with it He may strike down the nations, and He will rule them with a rod of iron.

Revelation 19:15a

We see this depicted here in verse five. Jesus will rule with a rod of iron. This is why the dragon is trying to destroy both the woman and the child. He doesn't want the world he thought he won to be taken from him.

We see the "rod of iron" foreshadowed in the Old Testament as well.

Then a shoot will spring from the stem of Jesse, and a branch from his roots will bear fruit . . . and He will strike the earth with the rod of His mouth, and with the breath of His lips He will slay the wicked.

Isaiah 11:1,4b

The "stem of Jesse" is the kingly line that descended from the linage of David, Israel's greatest king and ancestor of Jesus (Luke 3:23-38).

Once Jesus takes His rightful place, the story jumps forward to after the church age and refocuses on Israel at the time of the end. Israel is seen fleeing to the wilderness where there is a place

220

prepared for her by God. There she will be nourished for three and a half years. This would be at the midpoint of the final seven years, when the Antichrist is fully revealed and starts persecuting Israel and the church. The woman flees to the wilderness, or the desert. Although scripture doesn't say explicitly where the Jews will flee, we know she will be protected for the second half of the final seven-year period. Most scholars believe the wilderness John refers to is Petra, Jordan. It is a mountainous desert location about a hundred miles from Jerusalem and the Jews have fled there in the past. Petra is literally a city in sandstone cliffs. It has tunnels and shafts that could house many people and keep them safe from the outside world. The main access to Petra is a narrow gorge only two miles in length and at its maximum about thirty feet in width.[1]

Therefore when you see the abomination of desolation which was spoken of through Daniel the prophet, standing in the holy place (let the reader understand), then those who are in Judea must flee to the mountains.
Matthew 24:15-16

Here Jesus tells the Jews to flee to the mountains because of the abomination of desolation. The Antichrist will set up the abomination of desolation at the midpoint, and this corresponds nicely to Jesus' own words in Matthew 24 and the woman (or Israel) fleeing to the wilderness in Revelation 12. Another clue we find is in Daniel 11:41 when the prophet is talking about the Antichrist.

He will also enter the Beautiful Land, and many countries will fall; but these will be rescued out of his hand: Edom, Moab and the foremost of the sons of Ammon.
Daniel 11:41

Edom and Moab are modern day Jordan, where Petra is located. Daniel says that Jordan will not be captured by the Antichrist.

In scripture the place known to us as Petra was called Sela (Isaiah 42:11) which means cliff, crag, rock, or stronghold of Jehovah. Sela (or Petra) is literally a city in the cliffs. If Petra is the place the Jews will flee, it will also be a stronghold for those who worship God. This gets interesting when you realize that in the Psalms many times you find the word Selah written after a stanza of song. No one knows exactly what this means, but many suspect "Selah" means a pause, or an interlude in the song. The word Sela (the city) is actually translated as Selah in some translations of scripture. I find it very intriguing that most scholars believe the city of Sela (or Petra) is a place the Jews will flee. In other words, the city of Sela will rescue and protect the Jews for an interlude, or a pause (Selah). I believe God is telling us that Sela will give the Jews a place to flee, but it will only be a pause in their persecution. There will be a time the Antichrist will find them. At that time, they will recognize their Messiah. Then they will say, "Blessed is He who comes in the name of the Lord" (Matthew 21:9b)! And our Lord and Savior will come to their rescue. The Antichrist will be unable to touch them.

Could God be giving us a secret meaning to the word Selah in the Psalms? Could the Psalms "interlude" actually be referring to a city as well? Let's see what some of these Psalms have to say.

You are my hiding place; You preserve me from trouble; You surround me with songs of deliverance. Selah.

Psalm 32:7

You, O Lord God of hosts, the God of Israel, awake to punish all the nations; do not be gracious to any who are treacherous in iniquity. Selah . . . Destroy them in wrath, destroy them that they may be no more; that men may know that God rules in Jacob to the ends of the earth. Selah.

Psalm 59:5, 13

Let me dwell in Your tent forever; let me take refuge in the shelter of Your wings. Selah.

Psalm 61:4

Now turn ahead to Revelation 12:14.

But the two wings of the great eagle were given to the woman, so that she could fly into the wilderness to her place, where she was nourished for a time and times and half a time, from the presence of the serpent.

Revelation 12:14

Selah is associated with God being a hiding place and a deliverer. It is associated with destroying in wrath. It is associated with a refuge. The only other place "Selah" is used in scripture as it is used in the Psalms is in Habakkuk chapter three. Let's look at these scriptures closely.

> *God comes from Teman, and the Holy One from Mount Paran. Selah. His splendor covers the heavens, and the earth is full of His praise.*
>
> *Habakkuk 3:3*

This is talking about the second coming of Christ! Teman is a region south of Israel, near Petra. He will come from south of Judah, and He will rescue those in Sela!

> *Your bow was made bare, the rods of chastisement were sworn. Selah. You cleaved the earth with rivers.*
>
> *Habakkuk 3:9*

When will Jesus come with a rod? At the second coming (Revelation 19:15).

> *You went forth for the salvation of Your people, for the salvation of Your anointed. You struck the head of the house of the evil to lay him open from thigh to neck. Selah.*
>
> *Habakkuk 3:13*

When will He come forth for salvation? At the second coming! Who is the house of evil? The Antichrist! Someone needs to shout, "Glory!" Read Habakkuk chapter three. It is all about the second coming of Christ and it is the only other time in scripture the word "Selah" is used like it is in the Psalms. I guarantee you those who flee to Petra will be singing the Selah psalms of deliverance.

In nearly every "Selah" psalm, the pause is surrounded by second coming literature. Where are the Jews? In Selah, being protected by their rock, Daddy God, in the clefts of the rock, in Petra. And when they are delivered, God will be pouring out His wrath on all the nations. I just can't even stand it. God is so cool. He gives us hidden messages throughout scripture.

We see Jesus' rescue reiterated in Isaiah 63:1-2, a passage we have already looked at that identifies Jesus coming from Bozrah, in Edom, wearing red garments.

Who is this who comes from Edom, with garments of glowing colors from Bozrah, this One who is majestic in His apparel, marching in the greatness of His strength? "It is I who speak in righteousness, mighty to save." Why is Your apparel red, and Your garments like the one who treads in the wine press?

Isaiah 63:1-2

Is there any other reference to Bozrah and the second coming? Take a look at this scripture:

The sword of the Lord is filled with blood, it is sated with fat, with the blood of lambs and goats, with the fat of the kidneys of rams. For the Lord has a sacrifice in Bozrah and a great slaughter in the land of Edom . . . for the Lord has a day of vengeance, a year of recompense for the cause of Zion.

Isaiah 34:6, 8

Here we see Bozrah associated with the day of vengeance. The second coming! Bozrah was the capital of Edom and is just north of Petra. Jesus is coming from south of Israel, through the land of Teman (Edom, Habakkuk 3:3) to Bozrah and into Petra to rescue the Jews that were faithful to His command to flee. Someone needs to shout, "Hallelujah!"

Whew! I know that was a lot today. But Revelation is a marathon, not a sprint. May your day be blessed with psalms of deliverance. Selah.

Thought for the day:
Just as the dragon stands before the woman, so does the dragon stand before you. He wants to rob you of joy and steal your faith. Don't let him. Stand firm in the truth of the Word and use your sword (the Word). He will flee from it. Find out about the dragon's wrath tomorrow.

1 Hutchings, Dr. N. W. Petra In History and Prophecy (Oklahoma City, OK: Hearthstone Publishing, Ltd., 1991, 6-9.

⁷And there was war in heaven, Michael and his angels waging war with the dragon. The dragon and his angels waged war, ⁸and they were not strong enough, and there was no longer a place found for them in heaven. ⁹And the great dragon was thrown down, the serpent of old who is called the devil and Satan, who deceives the whole world; he was thrown down to the earth, and his angels were thrown down with him. ¹⁰Then I heard a loud voice in heaven, saying, "Now the salvation, and the power, and the kingdom of our God and the authority of His Christ have come, for the accuser of our brethren has been thrown down, he who accuses them before our God day and night. ¹¹And they overcame him because of the blood of the Lamb and because of the word of their testimony, and they did not love their life even when faced with death. ¹²For this reason, rejoice, O heavens and you who dwell in them. Woe to the earth and the sea, because the devil has come down to you, having great wrath, knowing that he has only a short time. ¹³And when the dragon saw that he was thrown down to the earth, he persecuted the woman who gave birth to the male child. ¹⁴But the two wings of the great eagle were given to the woman, so that she could fly into the wilderness to her place, where she was nourished for a time and times and half a time, from the presence of the serpent. ¹⁵And the serpent poured water like a river out of his mouth after the woman, so that he might cause her to be swept away with the flood. ¹⁶But the earth helped the woman, and the earth opened its mouth and drank up the river which the dragon poured out of his mouth. ¹⁷So the dragon was enraged with the woman, and went off to make war with the rest of her children, who keep the commandments of God and hold to the testimony of Jesus.

Revelation 12:7-17

In verse four we saw Satan throwing a third of the stars to the earth and persecuting the woman Israel who was about to give birth to the Messiah. This fight depicts Satan's initial rebellion and the angels who joined his revolt. In verse seven we see something different. We have already learned Michael is an archangel (Jude 1:9) and he is also the protector of Israel (Daniel 12:1). Michael and his angels and Satan and his angels fight. This is a fight we haven't seen before and it will happen during the final seven-year period. Because the woman was just seen fleeing to the wilderness, and Jesus warned His disciples to flee when they saw the abomination of desolation (Matthew 24:15-21), I believe this fight is at the midpoint, right when the Antichrist takes his seat in the temple of God and declares himself God (2 Thessalonians 2:4).

When Satan is thrown down, there is an announcement: "Now the salvation, and the power, and the kingdom of our God and the authority of His Christ have come, for the accuser of our brethren has been thrown down, he who accuses them before our God day and night. And they overcame him because of the blood of the Lamb and because of the word of their testimony, and they did not love their life even when faced with death. For this reason, rejoice, O heavens and you who dwell in them. Woe to the earth and the sea, because the devil has come down to you, having great wrath, knowing that he has only a short time" (12:10b-12)

This announcement is describing the persecution that began in seal number four (the mark of the beast) and continued through seal number five (the martyrs). Remember, chapter 12 is a flashback for John. He already saw the persecution occurring, but here it is reiterated so it sounds past tense. Satan has accused them, just like he did Job, and what happens? "They did not love their life even when faced with death." He accused, he persecuted, he killed, yet he did not win. The martyrs have held fast to their testimony. Satan can't turn them. They love their Savior, their Father, and they trust the Spirit inside them. They would rather die than take the mark of the beast.

There is another clue as to when Satan is thrown down. "And when the dragon saw that he was thrown down to the earth, he persecuted the woman who gave birth to the male child. But the two wings of the great eagle were given to the woman, so that she could fly into the wilderness to her place, where she was nourished for a time and times and half a time, from the presence of the serpent" (Revelation 12:13-14).

A time is one year, a times is two years, and a half a time is one half year. So, the woman, or Israel, is protected for the final three and one half years of the seven-year period. This corresponds nicely to the mid-point of the final seven years, when the Antichrist will put a stop to sacrifice and offering (Daniel 9:27) and set himself up in God's temple displaying himself as God (2 Thessalonians 2:3-4).

He is thrown down at the midpoint of the tribulation. His banishment from heaven probably initiates the mass martyrdom in seal number five and the all out persecution of the woman, or Israel.

We already know Satan is on the earth (1 Peter 5:8), but Job tells us he has access to heaven (Job 1:6). When Michael throws Satan out, he is no longer able to approach the throne. Why does God throw Satan out now? God wants Satan to feel every bit of His wrath. Satan will be confined to earth during this time and he will see his kingdom unraveling before his eyes. His fury will know no bounds.

If you recall in Revelation 9:1, at the beginning of the fifth trumpet, a "star" is seen on the earth with the key to the bottomless pit. We identified this star as Satan. This trumpet doesn't depict the "star" falling but it says it "had fallen." So at the fifth trumpet Satan is already down, and in chapter twelve we see his fall. Remember, trumpet five is after the midpoint and after the rapture. Satan will be desperate to retain control of the earth, but instead, he will experience every drop of God's wrath. Someone needs to shout, "Hallelujah!"

There is another reason why this expulsion is probably at the midpoint.

And you know what restrains him [ANTICHRIST] now, so that in his time he will be revealed. For the mystery of lawlessness is already at work; only he who now restrains will do so until he is taken out of the way.
2 Thessalonians 2:6-7, explanation added

Paul states this right after he declares the Antichrist will display himself as God.

Who is the restrainer? Who now restrains the Antichrist from appearing and persecuting the nation of Israel? Michael! Daniel defines the archangel Michael as the prince who stands guard over Israel (12:1). Daniel also says that there will be a time when Michael will arise. The Greek word for arise is "amad" and can also mean "stop moving or doing." Stop moving or doing what? Protecting Israel! And when does this happen? At the midpoint! Satan will be thrown out, furious and on a rampage, and this will in turn cause Satan to influence (some even say inhabit) the Antichrist to display himself as god in the temple. Satan wants the glory. He wants the nations to bow to him. The Antichrist will be his identity on earth. Satan will no longer have access to God's throne. He will demand the earth's worship.

Water like a river pours out of Satan's mouth in pursuit of Israel. He wants her destroyed and he will do anything to accomplish that goal. Is this an actual river or is it symbolic of something? One possibility is that it could be actual water, just like the text says. If this is the case, and Satan somehow is able to pursue the woman with a flood, the earth will swallow that water up. Remember Petra, where the woman flees, is a city in the cliffs. If she runs there and water pours in, she could be dashed to pieces if she is in the narrow gorge leading to the safety of the city.

In contrast, when scripture refers to "sea" or "water," it can refer to the Gentile nations. It could be that Satan unleashes a massive army of Gentile nations in order to destroy Israel. Does this match scripture?

During the fifth trumpet, the fallen "star" unleashes an army of locusts and we said in scripture locusts can represent an army (Judges 6:3-5). Then, in the sixth trumpet, there are more armies.

Right after John sees the fallen star in Revelation chapter nine, armies are unleashed on the world in the fifth and sixth trumpet. In Revelation 12 we see this depicted again, by Satan being thrown down to the earth and the "river" (or armies) coming out of his mouth. One of these armies is seen in Ezekiel.

After many days you will be summoned; in the latter years [END TIMES] you will come into the land that is restored from the sword [MIDPOINT OF FINAL SEVEN YEARS], whose inhabitants have been gathered from many nations to the mountains of Israel which had been a continual waste; but its people were brought out from the nations, and they are living securely, all of them. You will go up, you will come like a storm; you will be like a cloud covering the land, you and all your troops, and many peoples with you.

Ezekiel 38:8-9, explanation added

There will be a multitude of Gentile nations all riding toward Israel to destroy her. This is depicted in Ezekiel and again in Revelation 12 when the "river" flows from the dragon's mouth.

The Jews who take Jesus' warning to heart in Matthew 24:16-18 will flee to the mountains (Petra or Selah). Recall, to enter Petra you have to go through a narrow gorge for two miles. Because of the narrowness of the passage (about 30 feet at its widest point), any army approaching could be easily slaughtered. To top it off, if anyone is in the gorge when rains come, the gorge becomes a torrent of rushing water, often ten feet deep. Anyone caught there will be drowned or dashed to pieces against the jagged rocks of the cliffs to each side.[1] So yes, the earth as it now is in Petra could easily protect the woman from the "river" or approaching armies.

God may do something even more miraculous. There is an instance in scripture where the earth did something astonishing when someone sought to usurp Moses' authority.

Moses said, "By this you shall know that the Lord has sent me to do all these deeds; for this is not my doing. If these men die the death of all men or if they suffer the fate of all men, then the Lord has not sent me. But if the Lord brings about an entirely new thing and the ground opens its mouth and swallows them up with all that is theirs, and they descend alive into Sheol, then you will understand that these men have spurned the Lord." As he finished speaking all these words, the ground that was under them split open; and the earth opened its mouth and swallowed them up, and their households, and all the men who belonged to Korah with their possessions.

Numbers 16:28-33

Don't think the earth can't literally open up. Our God is amazing. He can do anything He pleases with this "river" rushing from the mouth of Satan.

The woman will ride from the dragon on wings of an eagle. Remember, as we learned in chapter eight, an eagle represents swiftness and strength (Habakkuk 1:8). God's hand and mighty arm are ushering the fleeing Jews out of Jerusalem with swiftness and strength. The eagle also represents God and His mercy and protection (Deuteronomy 32:11-12). Satan will not be able to touch this remnant. God will protect them from all harm. Let's look at the last scripture we referred to in chapter eight.

The earth has quaked at the noise of their downfall. There is an outcry! The noise of it has been heard at the Red Sea. Behold He will mount up and swoop like an eagle and spread out His wings against Bozrah; and the hearts of the mighty men of Edom in that day will be like the heart of a woman in labor.

Jeremiah 49:21-22

The eagle's wings at the midpoint foreshadow the real Savior at His second coming. Christ is going to swoop in like an eagle and rescue the Jews who put their trust in Him. And where is Petra? Near Bozrah, as we studied in yesterday's lesson. Someone needs to shout, "Hallelujah!"

When the dragon is unsuccessful in his attempt to destroy Israel, he turns his attention to making war with the rest of her offspring – Christianity (Revelation 12:17). Here is where the massive persecution, seal number five, begins.

Now, I want you to do something for me. Read the last verse in chapter twelve with the first verse of chapter thirteen:

So the dragon was enraged with the woman, and went off to make war with the rest of her children, who keep the commandments of God and hold to the testimony of Jesus. And the dragon stood on the sand of the seashore. Then I saw a beast coming up out of the sea, having ten horns and seven heads, and on his horns were ten diadems, and on his heads were blasphemous names.

Revelation 12:17-13:1

The first thing we need to recognize is that the dragon is standing on the seashore watching this second beast rise from the sea. This indicates to us that Satan is in control of this beast and he is bringing it to fruition. This scene takes place after Satan makes "war" with the rest of the woman's children – or Christians. God is trying to tell us that this beast is going to affect not only the Jews, but also the Christians of the world.

How much will the rest of the world be affected? We do not know, but I firmly believe everyone, no matter where you are, will be affected by the beast. The epicenter of the beast's rise to power will be the Middle East, as we will see in tomorrow's lesson, but the influence of this beast will stretch around the globe. Are any of us unaffected by what transpires in the Middle East?

No.

Scripture says the dragon gives the beast "his power and his throne and great authority" (Revelation 13:2). We have already learned "sea" in scripture can represent turbulent times (Psalm 46:1-

230

3) and the Gentile world (Isaiah 60:5). I daresay this beast is arising from both. This beast will arise when the world is in chaos and he will come from a Gentile system.

We will study the beast Satan is forming tomorrow. But before we do, I want you to look at one more scripture.

> *And the beast was seized . . . [and] thrown alive into the lake of fire which burns with brimstone.*
>
> *Revelation 19:20*

Jesus wins, my faithful friends. Jesus wins!

Thought for the day:
In the last days, the dragon will be enraged, because he knows his time is short. He will steal. He will kill. He will destroy. And he will deceive. If you do not know the truth (the Word) you could fall prey to that deception. Take notice. Prepare your faith. The dragon is coming for the world. The dragon is coming for you. He is preparing a system that will woo the world. More on this system tomorrow.

1 Hutchings, Dr. N. W. Petra In History and Prophecy (Oklahoma City, OK: Hearthstone Publishing, Ltd., 1991, 6-9.

[1]And the dragon stood on the sand of the seashore. Then I saw a beast coming up out of the sea, having ten horns and seven heads, and on his horns were ten diadems, and on his heads were blasphemous names. [2] And the beast which I saw was like a leopard, and his feet were like those of a bear, and his mouth like the mouth of a lion. And the dragon gave him his power and his throne and great authority.

Revelation 13:1-2

We see a beast coming out of the sea. Recall, the fourth seal announced there would be death from "the wild beasts of the earth." The same word used for "wild beast" in that seal is the same word used here for "beast." As we discussed in chapter four, the fourth seal could be referring to the two beasts described in this chapter, along with Satan, the dragon.

We can be sure the beast arising from the sea has a Gentile heritage because it is described as a leopard, with feet like a bear, and a mouth like a lion. Do you recall I commented at the beginning of our study that to understand Revelation you must understand Daniel? The beast in chapter 13 is a direct reference back to Daniel. Although we can't study Daniel in-depth, we can try to fit some pieces together to help us better understand the beast in Revelation 13.

In Daniel chapter two, King Nebuchadnezzar of Babylon dreams about a statue: its head is made of gold, its chest and arms of silver, its belly and thighs of bronze, it legs of iron, and its feet partly of iron and partly of clay.

"You, O king, were looking and behold, there was a single great statue; that statue, which was large and of extraordinary splendor, was standing in front of you, and its appearance was awesome. The head of that statue was made of fine gold, its breast and its arms of silver, its belly and its thighs of bronze, its legs of iron, its feet partly of iron and partly of clay. You continued looking until a stone was cut out without hands, and it struck the statue on its feet of iron and clay and crushed them. Then the iron, the clay, the bronze, the silver and the gold were

crushed all at the same time and became like chaff from the summer threshing floors; and the wind carried them away so that not a trace of them was found. But the stone that struck the statue became a great mountain and filled the whole earth. This was the dream; now we will tell its interpretation before the king. You, O king, are the king of kings, to whom the God of heaven has given the kingdom, the power, the strength and the glory; and wherever the sons of men dwell, or the beasts of the field, or the birds of the sky, He has given them into your hand and has caused you to rule over them all. You are the head of gold."

Daniel 2:31-38

If Nebuchadnezzar is the king of Babylon, the gold head represents the Babylonian Empire. The other kingdoms are not named in Daniel chapter two, but in chapter seven Daniel dreams about these same kingdoms. This time they are described as a lion (which correlates to the head of gold), a bear (which correlates to the silver), a leopard (which correlates to the bronze) and a "terrifying" beast (which correlates to the iron). Here again, the other three kingdoms are not named; however, we know from history what kingdoms did rule the Middle East and subdued Israel. But I want scripture to tell us the answer if possible. So let's move further into Daniel.

After all these visions Daniel is, shall I say, perplexed and somewhat terrified. Needless to say, I would be too. But in Daniel chapter eight God gives Daniel a detailed description of the next two kingdoms (the silver/bear and the bronze/leopard) that will arise after Babylon. This time they are depicted by a ram and a goat. Don't let all these images confuse you. We are still talking about the same kingdoms. Let's discover their identity:

"The ram which you saw with the two horns represents the kings of Media and Persia. The shaggy goat represents the kingdom of Greece."

Daniel 8:20-21

Babylon has already been named in Daniel 2:38 as the first kingdom in Nebuchadnezzar's dream statue. Daniel eight names two more kingdoms – Medo-Persia and Greece. History shows that Medo-Persia defeated Babylon in one night and took over the

Babylonian empire and their subject Israel in 539 BC,[1] Daniel actually saw this kingdom come to power in Daniel chapter five. Medo-Persia eventually let the Jews return to rebuild their temple (see Ezra and Nehemiah).

History then attests to the fact that Alexander the Great of the Grecian Empire took over Medo-Persia in 330BC. So now we have the identity of three of the four kingdoms. The fourth, at this time, is still a mystery. Let's look at what we have so far.

Babylon – Gold Head – Lion – 2:32, 37-38, 7:4

Medo-Persia – Silver Chest and Arms – Bear – 2:32-39, 7:5, 8:29

Greece – Bronze Belly and Thighs – Leopard – 2:32-39, 7:6, 8:21

Mystery Kingdom – Iron legs/feet iron and clay – Terrifying Beast
2:33-40, 7:7-8

Now, here is where it gets dicey. History shows us that two kingdoms arose and conquered Israel after Greece took power. The first was the Roman Empire. It conquered the land of Israel in 63 BC. The Roman Empire eventually split and became the Roman/Byzyntine Empire. However, after the split, another empire took over the Holy Land and the entire Middle East. We know this kingdom as the Turkish Ottoman Empire. It came and reigned in the Holy Land for over 1300 years. When the Turkish Ottoman Empire was dismantled after World War I, the Jews started returning to the Holy Land. So what is the identity of the fourth kingdom in Daniel? The Roman or the Turkish Ottoman? Turn with me to the description of this empire.

Then there will be a fourth kingdom as strong as iron; inasmuch as iron crushes and shatters all things, so, like iron that breaks in pieces, it will crush and break all these in pieces.

Daniel 2:40

Most scholars believe the fourth kingdom is the Roman Empire, so most end time theories have been based on a Roman Antichrist. Here is where I part with most scholars. Daniel says the iron kingdom will "crush and break all these in pieces" (Daniel 2:40b). We have to ask ourselves, crush and break all these *what*? All the other kingdoms listed! The fourth kingdom will rise up and take over all the territory of the other three kingdoms. Let me say that another way: the fourth kingdom encompasses all the other kingdom's territories.

I first read this other view in Walid Shoebat's *God's War on Terror*.[2] The Roman Empire was primarily a western empire. Although it conquered some of the Middle East, it never crushed and broke all the territory of the other three kingdoms. The Turkish Ottoman Empire, however, conquered all the territories of the previous empires. The Turkish Ottoman Empire was a Middle Eastern Empire, just like Babylon, Medo-Persia, and Greece. Rome in no way fits the equation. It was the one empire that originated in the west.

But can scripture clarify this interpretation? I mean, this is rather important don't you think? It is the fourth empire in Daniel that matches our beast in Revelation. If we aren't sure about the final kingdom, we will be unsure of where the Antichrist will emerge, and that is a rather important fact.

Rest assured, faithful friends, we have more scripture to look at, but we won't get through it all today. Hang with me. Revelation is coming. Let's find out the mystery kingdom's identity tomorrow.

Thought for the day:
Given today's environment, which area of influence do you think matches "the beast" of Revelation? Europe? Or the Middle East? No matter what opinion we have, we need clarification from God's Word. Think about this: is there a religion present in our day that would match the persecution we discussed in the fifth seal? Find out the beast's identity tomorrow.

1 NASB Study Bible. *New American Standard Bible* (Grand Rapids, Michigan: Zondervan, 1999).

2 Shoebat, Walid, written with Joel Richardson. *God's War on Terror* (Top Executive Media, 2008). Also check out Joel Richardson's *Antichrist Islam's Awaited Messiah* published in 2006 by Pleasant Word in Enumclaw, WA. Both are well worth the read.

² **And the beast which I saw was like a leopard, and his feet were like those of a bear, and his mouth like the mouth of a lion. And the dragon gave him his power and his throne and great authority.**

Revelation 13:2

We left yesterday with a little bit of a cliffhanger. Is the fourth kingdom of Daniel Rome? Or is it the Middle East? In the above scripture, the beast is described with the attributes of three animals: a leopard, a bear, and a lion. We already know the identities of these animals. Babylon is the lion, Medo-Persia is the bear, and Greece is the leopard (Daniel 7:1-8). In Revelation, we see these same depictions except they are in the opposite order: leopard, bear, and lion. This makes sense because we are looking backwards in history, and the leopard's influence on the current empire would be far greater than the lion's. Just as people influence other people, so nations influence other nations. When the bear conquered the lion, he drank some of the lion's ideology, took some of its gods and adapted some of its culture. This happened again when the leopard conquered the bear; it to took some of its gods, adapted some of its ideology, and drank some of its culture.

The beast depicted in Revelation has a little of all three, but predominately more of the leopard than the lion. In Daniel, the fourth kingdom, or as of now the "mystery kingdom," is not seen as a particular creature, but is described as "dreadful and terrifying and extremely strong" (Daniel 7:7). This beast is the same beast we see in Revelation. This is the fourth empire and it is "dreadful." Finally, because of the land the empires acquired, the region of their influence will be where this beast takes control. The beast of the sea's dominion will encompass the leopard, the bear, and the lion's territory. This, in essence, is the entire Middle East.

If you remember back in chapter nine, we saw four angels bound by the Euphrates. We said these angels represented the four kingdoms that had taken power in that area. These are the same kingdoms we are now discussing. The final system will, once again, encompass the area of the Euphrates. Rome touched the Euphrates on the western side, but never the eastern. Rome never encompassed the entire area around the Euphrates like the

Babylonian, Medo-Persian, Grecian and Turkish-Ottoman Empires. When the angels bound at the Euphrates are released their influence will abound. Each angel led a kingdom to conquer the world. These angels will stir up that influence again – this time over the entire globe. The earth will be filled with the desire for control. The world will come to battle Christ at Armageddon, but first, the global powers will battle each other for control of the Holy Land.

The dragon will give the beast its power. It specifically says the dragon will give "him" his power, and his throne. Although this beast is a political system that will arise, there is a man controlling it, and this man is known to us as the Antichrist.

In Revelation 13:2 it says that the dragon will give his power and throne to the beast. If you recall in Revelation chapter two, in the message of Pergamum, Jesus says, "I know where you dwell, where Satan's throne is" (2:13a). Satan has his throne where Pergamum sat. We mentioned the fact that all the churches discussed were in the region we now know as Turkey. The letters were almost in a semi-circular pattern. It is almost as if God is "circling" the spot that we need to keep our eye on. There were more than seven churches in John's day, but Jesus picked those seven for a reason. It is almost as if God is saying, "X marks the spot." Watch the Middle East; watch Turkey; watch for a leader to emerge. Every kingdom we just discussed – the gold, silver, bronze, and iron kingdoms – had the region we now know as Turkey in their empires. Scripture might be telling us the Antichrist's throne will come from Turkey.[1] Of course, the center of the former Turkish-Ottoman Empire was in Turkey.

Now we come to the interesting part of the beast: its heads, crowns, and horns. Look at the table below to compare the dragon of chapter 12 to the beast of chapter 13.

	The Dragon Satan Chapter 12	The Beast from the Sea The Final World Empire/Antichrist Chapter 13
Heads	7 Heads	7 Heads
Horns	10 Horns	10 Horns
Crowns	7 Crowns on Heads	10 Crowns on Horns

Both the dragon and the beast have seven heads. What are these heads according Revelation 17:9?

238

Here is the mind which has wisdom. The seven heads are
seven mountains on which the woman sits.

Revelation 17:9

This scripture makes me giggle because it is basically saying you have to be real smart to figure this one out! Who said God doesn't have a sense of humor? Anyone seen a giraffe? But I digress. Let's get back to our riddle. We will meet the woman referenced above when we study Revelation 17. For now, let's try to define the heads of the beast. This passage tells us that the seven heads are seven mountains. Mountains in scripture can refer to kingdoms.

Now it will come about that in the last days the mountain
of the house of the Lord will be established as the chief of
the mountains, and will be raised above the hills; and all
the nations will stream to it.

Isaiah 2:2

Is this passage talking about God's mountain or God's kingdom? Of course, it is referring to God's kingdom. Does this interpretation fit with Revelation? The beast we see in Revelation 13 is a kingdom, because it has attributes of the first three kingdoms in Daniel chapter seven. We also have discussed a fourth beastly kingdom which will come up after the three and be the most terrifying of all that have come before (Daniel 7:7). Out of this kingdom will emerge a final world system with the Antichrist at the helm (Daniel 7:8). This again matches Revelation because the beast is referred to as a "him."

The heads of the beast and Satan aren't literal mountains; they are kingdoms. Now, lets see if we can name each of the seven heads.

You already know three identities for sure: Babylon, Medo-Persia, and Greece. We also know there were two other kingdoms that came after Greece. No matter if the "mystery kingdom" of Daniel is Rome or the Turkish Ottoman, they were still kingdoms that conquered Israel. So now we have five.

So far we have in the order of conquest: Babylon, Medo-Persia, Greece, Rome, and the Turkish Ottoman. Was there an empire that conquered Israel before Babylon?

Until the Lord removed Israel from His sight, as He spoke through all His servants the prophets. So Israel was carried away into exile from their own land to Assyria until this day.

2 Kings 17:23

When Babylon conquered the remaining tribes of Israel in the southern kingdom of Judah, the northern kingdom of Israel had already been conquered by Assyria. Now, we have only one kingdom we haven't identified. It was the enemy of Israel at the time of Moses – Egypt.

In summary, seven kingdoms have controlled the Holy Land, from the time of Abraham, until now, exactly matching the seven heads we see in Revelation.

The Heads	Dates Ruled	Specific To Israel
1 Egypt	3100 BC – 1070 BC	Israel left Egypt in 1446 BC – The Exodus
2 Assyria	1800 BC – 609 BC	Northern Kingdom of Israel falls in 722 BC and is exiled (never to return)
3 Babylon	1764 BC – 689 BC	Judah (southern Israel) falls in 586 and is exiled to Babylon
4 Medo-Persia	550 BC – 330 BC	Medo-Persia starts letting Jews from Babylon return home in 538 BC
5 Greece	350 BC – 64 BC	A rebellion occurs in Israel that becomes celebrated as Hanukah
6 Roman	27 BC – 1453 AD	Jerusalem falls in 70 AD – Jews scattered
7 Islamic (Turkish-Ottoman)	637 AD – 1924 AD	Subjects the land for 1300 years

"Dates Ruled" taken from *God's War on Terror: Islam, Prophecy and the Bible* by Walid Shoebat with Joel Richardson, published in 2008 by Top Executive Media. "Specific to Israel" taken from the Zondervan NASB Bible copyright 1999.

I know this is a lot for today, but let's look at one more scripture to see if we can discover who our "mystery kingdom" is in Daniel. Will Rome or the Turkish-Ottoman Empire be the final beast of Revelation 13? John lived until about 100AD. The Roman

Empire was the kingdom in power when John saw the revelation of our Savior. John was under the rule of Rome.

Now, look at this verse.

> *The beast that you saw was...*
>
> Revelation 17:8a

If we think of the beast's heads as kingdoms, which kingdoms "were?" We have already established that Rome is now ruling. So, we need to ask, which kingdoms came before Rome? Those would be Egypt, Assyria, Babylon, Medo-Persia, and Greece.

Now, look at the next part of Revelation 17:8.

> *The beast that you saw was, and is not...*
>
> Revelation 17:8a

The kingdom that **IS** is not the beast! Rome is not the beast. Now, take a look at the rest of this verse.

> *The beast that you saw was [EGYPT, ASSYRIA, BABYLON, MEDO-PERSA, GREECE] and is not [ROME], and is about to come up out of the abyss and go to destruction. And those who dwell on the earth, whose name has not been written in the book of life from the foundation of the world, will wonder when they see the beast, that he was and is not and will come.*
>
> Revelation 17:8, explanation added

Rome is not the beast. It did not come from the Middle East. It was a western kingdom. It is not included in Daniel's statue because the statue was showing us what would come to pass in the territory of the Middle East – the territory near the Euphrates River (Revelation 9:14).

But the beast in Revelation is showing us every kingdom that subjected Israel, so Rome is included. It would not make much sense to John if the kingdom he was subject to was not shown in the vision.

Rome is not the beast. But we do know a kingdom arose after Rome that crushed everything that came before it. Daniel calls it "terrifying" (Daniel 7:7). It was the Turkish-Ottoman Empire.

What is this kingdom (the Middle East) doing now?

The beast is already among us, faithful friends, and the church as a whole does not even realize it.

More to come tomorrow.

Thought for the day:
The beast of Revelation is already alive. It is not materialized into the final political system yet, but it is here. We need to have our eyes wide open if we are to recognize its deception. Watch the news. Watch for signs. The final system is about to rise. Find out more about the beast tomorrow.

1 Shoebat, Walid, written with Joel Richardson. *God's War on Terror* (Top Executive Media, 2008), starting on page 421

Do you feel like you have been on a roller coaster? It is going to get a little more exciting today – if you can believe it. So fasten your seatbelts. We are in for a wild ride.

We left off yesterday with the seven heads of the beast which correspond to seven kingdoms that have ruled Israel: Egypt, Assyria, Babylon, Medo-Persia, Greece, Rome, and the Turkish-Ottoman Empire. There has been vast research on these kingdoms, with far more detail than I can give here. The following paragraph is taken from *God's War on Terror* by Walid Shoebat with Joel Richardson.[1]

The Egyptian Empire ruled all of Egypt and Israel, as well. The Assyrian Empire defeated the Egyptian Empire and likewise ruled over a vast portion of the Middle East, including Israel. After this, the Babylonian Empire defeated the Assyrian Empire and became even larger than its predecessor, again, ruling over Israel. Such is the pattern with each successive empire: The Medo-Persian Empire succeeded the Babylonian Empire only to be succeeded by the Greek Empire. The Greek Empire was in turn succeeded by the Roman Empire . . . Likewise it was the Islamic Caliphate of Umar Ibn al-Khattab that took Jerusalem in 637. Thus we see that it was the Islamic Empire – culminating with the Ottoman Empire – that succeeded the Roman Empire and ruled over the entire Middle East beginning with Jerusalem, for over thirteen hundred years and continued right up until 1924.

Although Rome isn't seen in Daniel's statue because it didn't emerge from the Middle East, it is included in the heads of Revelation because it did conquer Israel and subject it to foreign rule. Some of the Roman Empire's territory could quite possibly be encompassed by the final system as well. Today, there is a great Muslim influence in Europe. It is not a stretch to think that some of the Roman Empire's landmass may quite possibly fall to the Antichrist.

Now we know about the beast's heads in Revelation. What about the beast's horns? We know from Daniel there will be a final world system that will correspond to the ten horns.

After this I kept looking in the night visions, and behold, a fourth beast, dreadful and terrifying and extremely strong; and it had large iron teeth. It devoured and crushed and trampled down the remainder with its feet; and it was different from all the beasts that were before it, and it had ten horns . . . As for the ten horns, out of this kingdom ten kings will arise; and another will arise after them, and he will be different from the previous ones and will subdue three kings.

Daniel 7:7, 24

This passage is talking about the "mystery beast" that corresponds to the fourth kingdom in Daniel. This is the iron kingdom, the one that crushes and devours all the other kingdoms. From this kingdom ten horns will emerge. We know as we return to Revelation that it is the fourth kingdom that "grows" the horns. We know from our study that the fourth kingdom, the "terrifying" kingdom, is the Turkish-Ottoman Empire, because Revelation 17:8 clearly states that Rome is not the beast.

This "emergence" of ten is also seen in the statue we have been studying. Let's take another look

Then there will be fourth kingdom as strong as iron; inasmuch as iron crushes and shatters all things, so, like iron that breaks in pieces, it will crush and break all these in pieces. In that you saw the feet and toes, partly of potter's clay and partly of iron, it will be a divided kingdom; but it will have in it the toughness of iron, inasmuch as you saw the iron mixed with common clay. As the toes of the feet were partly of iron and partly of pottery, so some of the kingdom will be strong and part of it will be brittle. And in that you saw the iron mixed with common clay, they will combine with one another in the seed of men; but they will not adhere to one another, even as iron does not combine with pottery.

Daniel 2:40-43

We even see the 10 "horns" depicted in the statue, but this time, they are ten "toes." These toes are growing out of the iron in the statue, and they are different because they are formed by iron and clay. What we need to understand now is that the ten horns of Revelation 13 are the same as the ten toes in Daniel chapter two.

When this beast explodes on the world stage some system/cabinet/or kingship of ten will rule over it. This will be the kingdom we need to watch for. This will be the Antichrist's empire and the greatest persecutor of Jews and Christians since the beginning of time. We will study the horns with more detail in a later chapter, but to further clarify, the seven heads are now past, the ten horns will emerge from the last "head," the Islamic or Turkish-Ottoman territories in the future. In other words, the ten horns will be the same "kingdom" but will emerge in a completely different time period. We will study this further in chapter seventeen.

Now we come to the difference between the dragon and the beast. In Revelation 12:3 Satan is wearing seven crowns on his heads. If we remember the heads correspond to kingdoms, this makes sense. Satan is the power that has been over the seven empires that have taken over the Holy Land (recall Satan is watching the political system emerge in Revelation 13:1). Satan has been active throughout the centuries in helping bring to life the enemies of the Jews: Egypt, Assyria, Babylon, Medo-Persia, Greece, Rome, and the Islamic Empire. His primary purpose is to crush the woman, Israel (Revelation 12:13-17). Satan hates everything about the Jews. He wants to annihilate all of them because they brought forth the Messiah and they are God's chosen people. He will do everything to see the prophecies declaring the Jewish rescue and final redemption to fail. Satan, then, is crowned on all seven of his political heads (kingdoms) he helped bring to life.

The beast, however, is different. It does not have seven crowns, but ten. It is not wearing the crowns on its heads, but on its horns. The beast has ten crowns on his horns and these horns are emerging out of ONE kingdom – the fourth mystery kingdom.

The beast out of the sea, or the final political system that will arise, and the king over that system, the Antichrist, will only have power over that final empire. The final system, and the Antichrist, never had and never will have authority over the other kingdoms that have come before. He was not in existence at the time of Egypt, Assyria, Babylon, Medo-Persia, Greece, Rome, and the Islamic Empire of the past, so his heads aren't crowned. The final beast's authority, his crowns, will only be over the final political union in the end times.

In summary, Satan is the power, the originator, of the seven kingdoms that have fallen in the past. The final political system (the beast of chapter 13) will only have authority over the system that will emerge – the ten horns. The ten horns are a group of nations, regions and/or kings that will lead the beast (the political system) with the Antichrist for a short period of time.

Is anyone else just astounded by this revelation? God is so awesome! For John to pen something like this centuries ago is just amazing.

³I saw one of his heads as if it had been slain, and his fatal wound was healed. And the whole earth was amazed and followed after the beast; ⁴they worshiped the dragon because he gave his authority to the beast; and they worshiped the beast, saying, "Who is like the beast, and who is able to wage war with him?"

Revelation 13:3-4

Here we see another piece of the puzzle starting to emerge. One of the heads has been slain but its fatal wound is healed. We have learned that the seven heads represent kingdoms. The final kingdom to emerge was the Turkish-Ottoman Islamic Empire. We know Revelation is pointing to the final kingdom because in Daniel the ten horns emerge from the iron kingdom – the one that crushes everything that came before it. This system was slain, or dismantled, in 1924. Today we see the Islamic world talking about reuniting under a Caliphate. The Caliphate is a system of government that governs with Sharia law and has a leader, or a Caliph above it, similar to our president today. The Islamic system is rising again, and when it does, it will have ten prominent horns (or kings) governing it. In other words, the seventh head was slain in 1924, but it will be united again as a new kingdom.

Some scholars believe that the slain head is actually the Antichrist being killed and then magically resurrected. I tend not to hold to this view because it is very clear to me the heads represent kingdoms, and the final kingdom has already been "slain," yet I feel the need to mention it here because of its popularity. Just be aware that the slain head has already occurred. If the Antichrist dies and is resurrected it would be a double fulfillment.

246

The whole world will follow after this beast, and when they follow, they will worship the dragon because he is over this system, and they will worship the ideology of the beast itself (Islam). Some people have gone so far to say that those who follow Islam worship the same god that Christians do. This is a false and dangerous claim. Islam worships a god named Allah. Allah commands in the Qur'an to "kill them [DISBELIEVERS] wherever ye shall find them" (explanation added).[2] A famous tradition in the Islamic world says that the last hour will not come unless Muslims fight against the Jews and kill them.[3] What ideology does this sound like to you? Let's look again at what the dragon will do according to scripture:

And the serpent poured water like a river out of his mouth after the woman [ISRAEL], so that he might cause her to be swept away with the flood.
Revelation 12:15, explanation added

Islam also denies Jesus died on the cross and they deny that He is God's son.

Who is the liar but the one who denies that Jesus is the Christ? This is the antichrist, the one who denies the Father and the Son. Whoever denies the Son does not have the Father; the one who confesses the Son has the Father also.
1 John 2:22-23

I don't think this leaves much room for doubt: if you deny Jesus is the Christ, you deny the Father, and you are of the antichrist. If you want to learn more about Allah, please pick up *God's War on Terror*, by Walid Shoebot and *Antichrist: Islam's awaited Messiah* by Joel Richardson. I assure you, you won't be disappointed.

Let's dig deeper. The world will say, "Who is like the beast, and who is able to wage war with him?" We are already asking ourselves that question daily. How can you fight an ideology that doesn't play by the rules? They send their sons and daughters into crowded streets as human bombs, claiming as many innocents as they can. How do you fight that? The enemy can be your next-door neighbor. The enemy can be a child. The enemy can be a pregnant woman. The enemy has no definition.

And the enemy has oil. We all know that without oil, the world cannot survive. In the last days, oil will be key. Many will accept whatever demands the beast makes, just for an ounce of oil. May we rely on our heavenly Father and not the beast that will emerge from the sea.

⁵There was given to him a mouth speaking arrogant words and blasphemies, and authority to act for forty-two months was given to him. ⁶And he opened his mouth in blasphemies against God, to blaspheme His name and His tabernacle, that is, those who dwell in heaven. ⁷It was also given to him to make war with the saints and to overcome them, and authority over every tribe and people and tongue and nation was given to him. ⁸All who dwell on the earth will worship him, everyone whose name has not been written from the foundation of the world in the book of life of the Lamb who has been slain. ⁹If anyone has an ear, let him hear. ¹⁰If anyone is destined for captivity, to captivity he goes; if anyone kills with the sword, with the sword he must be killed. Here is the perseverance and the faith of the saints.

Revelation 13:5-10

The beast opens his mouth to speak blasphemies against the God of gods, but his power is limited to 42 months, or three and a half years. This is the same length of time the two witnesses of chapter eleven will prophesy (11:3). This is the same time that the woman (Israel) will be protected (12:14). This corresponds to the midpoint of the final seven-year period when the Antichrist will take his seat in the temple of God and display himself as god (2 Thessalonians 2:4). Although God will allow the beast's mouth to spew blasphemies, He will not allow it to continue indefinitely. There will be an answer to the beast's ravings. The answer will come on a white horse with consuming fire (Revelation 19:11, Zephaniah 1:18). Oh, wait for the day!

In Revelation 13:6 it tells us the beast blasphemes God and His name, His dwelling place (His tabernacle), and the saints in heaven. This is important. The beast (the political system), led by the dragon and the Antichrist, will try to do everything it can to tear down faith in the living God. It will try to take our hope in Jesus' return and the glory that awaits us when He does. Heaven has been trashed for centuries. True saints of God have dreaded death

248

because they fail to grasp heaven and the wonder that awaits us. By and large, we are unexcited about Christ's return. We like our home here and we feel we will miss our life once we are in heaven. Many of us fail to realize heaven is earth. As in, we come back to earth to live forever; we do not remain in the place we now call "heaven." We live on earth for eternity. We are not floating on a cloud, wearing a halo, and playing a harp. That is a lie from the enemy and we need to rebuke it. We are diving into clear blue water and playing with the dolphins. We are running with the wind as a herd of horses barrels past us. We are building houses and inhabiting them. We are feasting with joy and thanksgiving. We are living! Ah, but I digress. Just know heaven is not what you may think; it is Eden reborn. Imagine the day! Someone needs to shout, "Hallelujah!"

Satan will do everything He can to steal your joy. He will try to rob you of hope, and he will persecute you. This section of Revelation defines the Antichrist's persecution that will start at the midpoint. When he can't reach the woman (Israel), he will turn his face to God's saints. Every nation will feel his wrath. The epicenter will be the Middle East, but Satan's wrath will reach the entire world in some form or fashion. As scripture says, "Here is the perseverance and the faith of the saints." May we hold fast to our faith. If we go back to the churches in chapters two and three, we learned only two were faithful witnesses to God's truth: Smyrna suffered intense persecution; Philadelphia was protected from the hour of testing. So shall it be in the end times: some churches will be persecuted, others will be protected. The beast's influence will reach everywhere. We need to be prepared to die for our Savior if the Antichrist demands we fall to our knees and worship him. Remember, there is no compromise with the truth.

Scripture says everyone besides the faithful will worship the beast. With the way the world is today, none of us can imagine this. Everyone turning to one system? Everyone worshiping one man? But think of the horseman and what they will bring: the rise of the Antichrist, terror, severe famine, the rationing of food, and death due to the sword, famine and sickness. The world will be desperate for a savior. Even if they do not believe in the Antichrist's ideology, they will follow if they believe one man holds the answers. If the beast system tells them to fall on their knees for a loaf of bread, not many will resist. But there will be an exception. Those who dwell on the earth whose names have been written in the book of life will refuse to acknowledge the false savior. The true followers of Jesus would rather be slain than to bow to the Antichrist for a loaf of bread. They know, "It is written, 'Man shall not live on bread alone, but on every word that proceeds out of the mouth of God'" (Matthew 4:4). They also know God can provide. "Look at the birds of the air, that they do not sow, nor reap nor gather into barns, and yet your heavenly Father feeds them. Are you not worth much more than they" (Luke 6:26)? God can provide manna from heaven if need be (Exodus 16) and He can multiply oil and flour (1 Kings 17). God can work miracles and He will for His saints (Micah 7:15). Notice again Revelation 13:9:

"If anyone has an ear, let him hear."
Revelation 13:9

This was stated at the end of each and every letter to the churches. This statement is once again addressing the churches. The churches need to understand persecution is coming. That is why Jesus was so adamant that His bride be pure, that she look to Him and not the pagan system surrounding her, that she overcome! There is a time fast approaching where she will be called to bow to another. If she does, she will lose her salvation. "If anyone has an ear, let him hear!" Jesus says. You will be taken captive and you will be killed. At the midpoint of the tribulation, the beast's mask will be off. He will persecute Israel, and he will persecute the saints.

We already see the beginning of this world system, and we already see it cannot be fought. Jews and Christians are killed frequently by terrorists and governments that do not approve of our religious beliefs. They believe we deserve death. Allah commands them, and so will the Antichrist.

"Here is the perseverance and the faith of the saints." We learned in chapter three the word perseverance means patient enduring. We must ask ourselves patient enduring for what? For Christ's return! The saints will persevere because they know Christ is on His way. The birth pains are over, the hard labor has begun (Matthew 24:8-9).

Thought for the day:
The beast blasphemes God. The beast hates the one true
God. The beast wants us to do the same. It will try to sway us to
believe that it has the path of life, but it will lie, because Satan is
behind the beast and he is the father of lies. Have your eyes wide
open to its deception. Tomorrow we will meet another beast who
will help the first. He will be the greatest false prophet who has
ever lived. Know the truth and you will recognize falsehood.

1 Shoebat, Walid, written with Joel Richardson.   *God's War on Terror* (Top Executive Media, 2008), 301, 303.

2 Shoebat, Walid, written with Joel Richardson.   *God's War on Terror* (Top Executive Media, 2008), 102, Qu'ran 2:191. *The Koran* (New York, New York: Bantam Dell, 2004).

3 Shoebat, Walid, written with Joel Richardson.   *God's War on Terror* (Top Executive Media, 2008)., 31.   Joel Richardson's *Antichrist Islam's Awaited Messiah* published in 2006 by Pleasant Word in Enumclaw, WA, 46.

¹¹Then I saw another beast coming up out of the earth; and he had two horns like a lamb and he spoke as a dragon. ¹²He exercises all the authority of the first beast in his presence. And he makes the earth and those who dwell in it to worship the first beast, whose fatal wound was healed. ¹³He performs great signs, so that he even makes fire come down out of heaven to the earth in the presence of men. ¹⁴And he deceives those who dwell on the earth because of the signs which it was given him to perform in the presence of the beast, telling those who dwell on the earth to make an image to the beast who had the wound of the sword and has come to life. ¹⁵And it was given to him to give breath to the image of the beast, so that the image of the beast would even speak and cause as many as do not worship the image of the beast to be killed.

Revelation 13:11-15

We've covered a lot of ground in the past few days, Christian soldiers. I am proud that you are sticking with this study. Today won't be as labor intensive as yesterday, but your head will still be hurting when we get done. Hang with me!

Blessed is he who reads and those who hear the words of the prophecy, and heed the things which are written in it; for the time is near.

Revelation 1:3

You will be blessed, my faithful friends, because you will know what is about to come upon the earth.

Now we meet a third beast. This one is coming out of the earth. Because the sea represents the Gentile world, the earth could quite possibly represent the Jewish world, so some scholars believe this person will be a Jew. Another possibility is that the earth represents stability. This figure is described as a lamb, which contrasts with our Lord and Savior as the Lamb of God. Some scholars believe that because this figure is seen as a lamb, he is a religious figure. Whether or not this is a religious figure, a Jew, or both, this man helps the Antichrist. Revelation 19 tells us just what this person will represent.

And the beast was seized, and with him the false prophet who performed the signs in his presence, by which he deceived those who had received the mark of the beast and those who worshiped his image; these two were thrown alive into the lake of fire which burns with brimstone.

Revelation 19:20

This beast is known as the false prophet. He has two horns, representing strength (Deuteronomy 33:17), and appears as a lamb, but speaks like a dragon. We know the dragon is Satan, and the dragon always lies (John 8:44).

This is a false prophet because he will do just that – lie. Notice Revelation 13:14 says that he will deceive the whole world.

This man will be powerful (horns) and many will think him good (lamb) but he will be a dragon (liar). He will deceive the world. If this man is a religious figure, he will be batting on the wrong team. Some scholars have suggested the pope for this beast, because he has the ears of the world, and appears like the lamb, but if he is for the wrong side, he could sway many to follow. However, this person does not have to be a religious figure, he just has to be a prominent leader masquerading as someone who offers hope but who inwardly wants destruction. Whoever this beast is, he will appear harmless, and will cause many to follow the Antichrist. The Antichrist will allow this man to have great power, which will be used to further the Antichrist's empire.

This is the third persona we now see over this final end time system: Satan, the Antichrist, and the false prophet. This is a counterfeit trinity. Satan wants everything God has in order to fool the world. He knows he has to use what the Commander in Chief has already designed. Satan knows the world hungers for a Father, a Savior, and a Spirit. He will try to give them his own version for a short time. It will cause many to leave the faith (Matthew 24:10).

The false prophet will cause fire to rain down from heaven and he performs other signs that deceive the people of the earth. This is a hard prophecy. In one sense, you can take this man's power as the antithesis to the two witnesses' power. Scripture says fire will proceed from the two witnesses' mouths. We said the fire in their mouths represents God's Word being like fire to the unrepentant. Yet, the false prophet causes fire to come from heaven, a very different notion. Let's look at scripture.

The Lord said to Satan, "Have you considered My servant Job? For there is no one like him on the earth, a blameless and upright man, fearing God and turning away from evil." Then Satan answered the Lord, "Does Job fear God for nothing? Have You not made a hedge about him and his house and all that he has, on every side? You have blessed the work of his hands, and his possessions have increased in the land. But put forth Your hand now and touch all that he has; he will surely curse You to Your face." Then the Lord said to Satan, "Behold, all that he has is in your power, only do not put forth your hand on him." So Satan departed from the presence of the Lord. Now on the day when his sons and his daughters were eating and drinking wine in their oldest brother's house, a messenger came to Job and said, "The oxen were plowing and the donkeys feeding beside them, and the Sabeans attacked and took them. They also slew the servants with the edge of the sword, and I alone have escaped to tell you." While he was still speaking, another also came and said, "The fire of God fell from heaven and burned up the sheep and the servants and consumed them, and I alone have escaped to tell you." While he was still speaking, another also came and said, "The Chaldeans formed three bands and made a raid on the camels and took them and slew the servants with the edge of the sword, and I alone have escaped to tell you." While he was still speaking, another also came and said, "Your sons and your daughters were eating and drinking wine in their oldest brother's house, and behold, a great wind came from across the wilderness and struck the four corners of the house, and it fell on the young people and they died, and I alone have escaped to tell you."

Job 1:8-19

In this passage fire came down from heaven and consumed the sheep and the servants. Even though the messenger announced "God" had rained down the fire, we know from verse twelve God did no such thing. Satan rained down the fire. We find this again in Revelation 13:13. This scripture could really mean the false prophet (who is following the dragon) is able to rain down fire from heaven.

There is another slight variation we can also consider, but I do want to emphasize that Satan has been allowed to rain down fire in the past. In chapter 11 we discussed how Moses and Elijah were God's instruments of warning. Although Moses lifted his staff, God brought the plagues upon Egypt (Exodus 7-12). Although Elijah called down fire from heaven, God sent the fire in the presence of the prophets of Baal (1 Kings 18:36-40). I believe the two witnesses will do just that. "Repent or the next plague will come!" They will be harbingers to the trumpets. Will the false prophet claim that power as well? If he does, he could cause many to suspect he is the one in control of the trumpets – not the two witnesses – and not God. This is a viable possibility. He is just that, a false prophet. Could those remaining try to explain away God's wrath as the power of the false prophet? Perhaps.

What we do know is that the false prophet will deceive those on the earth and cause many to worship the Antichrist. Jesus warned this was coming when He said, "For false christs and false prophets will arise and will show great signs and wonders, so as to mislead, if possible, even the elect" (Matthew 24:24).

The false prophet also makes an image of the beast and causes people to worship the image. Satan wants obvious worship. He wants people to bow to their knees right in front of him, and you can bet your left arm that he will inhabit the Antichrist, just like he did Judas (Luke 22:3). He wants to be on display; he wants a show. Scripture says Satan wants to make himself like the Most High (Isaiah 14:12-14). The false prophet will point to the Antichrist and demand the world to fall on their knees.

He will cause the image of the Antichrist to speak. Some scholars think this refers to television or computers. John was seeing this vision approximately sixty years after Christ was crucified. To see an image on a screen speak would have been quite amazing.

On the flip side, this could actually be a statue the false prophet causes to speak. A friend of mine has been to the Middle East. She says statues of leaders and religious symbols are on every street corner. Erecting a statue to the Antichrist will be one of the first things the final political empire does if it is centered in the Middle East. In today's world, a talking statue is no miracle. In fact, a few months back I was walking through the airport and there was a flat screen in the shape of a woman. It was a computer, but the image moved – her head, her lips, her hands. Because I was aware of scripture, this talking image made my skin crawl. No matter what this image is, here is the lesson: if the inhabitants of the world do not bow down to the image, they will be killed. Choose God or the Antichrist. There will be no exceptions.

[16]And he causes all, the small and the great, and the rich and the poor, and the free men and the slaves, to be given a mark on their right hand or on their forehead, [17]and he provides that no one will be able to buy or to sell, except the one who has the mark, either the name of the beast or the number of his name. [18]Here is wisdom. Let him who has understanding calculate the number of the beast, for the number is that of a man; and his number is six hundred and sixty-six.

Revelation 13:16-18

Here we are introduced to the mark of the beast. This is probably part of the reason "beast" is referred to in seal number four. Seal number four is the midpoint of the tribulation where the Antichrist is truly revealed and the mark of the beast is introduced. In the fourth seal, a quarter of the earth's population will be killed. And in the fifth seal, if you do not take the mark, you are martyred. It is that simple. Jesus said, "Then they will deliver you to tribulation, and will kill you and you will be hated by all nations because of My name" (Matthew 24:9). Why? Because true believers in Christ will never take the mark of the beast. It will be anti-Christ and anti-God. This mark will not be something that you can accidentally take. It will mark you as loyal to the beast and his empire.

In yesterday's lesson, we studied how the seven heads of the dragon and the beast correspond to the seven kingdoms throughout history that have conquered the Holy Land. The final head was the Turkish Ottoman Empire. This head was seen "slain" but will be reformed as the ten-horned end time system. We now hear the Middle East wants to form a Caliphate, or a system of government, with one leader ruling the entire region with Sharia law government.

Scripture says the number of the beast is the number of a man. Most Bibles translate this number as six hundred and sixty-six; however some manuscripts of Revelation say six hundred and sixteen.[1] Obviously, when translating this "number" there was difficulty. What does it mean? Many have interpreted this as an

256

imperfect trinity. Because seven represents perfection and completion, the number seven hundred seventy-seven could stand for God the Father, God the Son, and God the Holy Spirit. If that is the case, then six hundred and sixty-six could mean the unholy trinity of Satan, the Antichrist, and the false prophet. I'm not satisfied yet, are you? Let's dig deeper.

Others have tried to use something called "gematria." Many cultures assign their alphabet to numerical values. So, for instance, if I wanted to say 1, 2, and 3 using gematria I would say A, B, and C. So many have tried to add up people's names in order to equate six hundred and sixty-six to an actual person. I'm still not satisfied yet, are you? Let's give this one more shot.

If you pick up Walid Shoebat's *God's War on Terror*, you might find something very interesting. He went back to the earliest manuscript available and looked at the Greek word that was translated "six hundred and sixty-six." Here is what he found:

I needed to examine the text as far back as I could go. I expected to find an Islamic declaration of some sort. As soon as I began to examine the Codex Vaticanus (AD 350) Greek text of the Book of Revelation, I immediately noticed that the supposed Greek letters (Chi Xi Stigma) that are used to translate to the number 666 very much resemble the most common creed of Islam Bismillah (or Basmalah), written in Arabic. Bismillah literally means "In the Name of Allah," and is followed by the symbol of crossed swords, which is used universally throughout the Muslim world to signify Islam . . . In light of this, is it possible that the Apostle John, while receiving his divine revelation, did not see Greek letters, but instead was supernaturally shown Arabic words and an Islamic symbol, which he then faithfully recorded? Could it be that years after John recorded these images; scribes commissioned to copy the text were unable to recognize the foreign words and symbols and thus thought them to be Greek letters? Might this be why some texts record them differently?[2]

This matches our theory so far: the final beast system from the Middle East will emerge. Its religion will spread throughout the world and a mark will be given. Could this mark be "In the Name of Allah, and the crossed swords of Jihad?" I daresay, this makes absolute and complete sense.

The Middle East is rising up and demanding their religion be "tolerated." Our first amendment allows mosques to be built in our nation even though many promote terrorism. We are allowing officials of leading "peaceful" Islamic organizations to have a say in our government. We are sending aid to terrorist ridden Middle Eastern nations. Some of us are even claiming "Allah" is the same god as our God.

We need to open our eyes. The beast is already among us, and we are letting it take control. May Daddy God, the consuming fire, be with all of us.

Thought for the day:
If the mark of the beast is "in the name of Allah" with the crossed swords of jihad, you can see where the world is already being deceived. We are trying to have peaceful relations with Middle Eastern nations, but do they really want peace with us? Their end time theology tells them Islam will become dominant across the globe. Their ideology is slowly creeping in, and we are being tolerant.

1 *English Standard Version Study Bible* (Wheaton, Illinois: Crossway, 2008), 2482.

2 Shoebat, Walid, written with Joel Richardson. *God's War on Terror* (Top Executive Media, 2008) 369, 371.

¹Then I looked, and behold, the Lamb was standing on Mount Zion, and with Him one hundred and forty-four thousand, having His name and the name of His Father written on their foreheads. ²And I heard a voice from heaven, like the sound of many waters and like the sound of loud thunder, and the voice which I heard was like the sound of harpists playing on their harps. ³And they sang a new song before the throne and before the four living creatures and the elders; and no one could learn the song except the one hundred and forty-four thousand who had been purchased from the earth. ⁴These are the ones who have not been defiled with women, for they have kept themselves chaste. These are the ones who follow the Lamb wherever He goes. These have been purchased from among men as first fruits to God and to the Lamb. ⁵And no lie was found in their mouth; they are blameless.

Revelation 14:1-5

The seventh trumpet sounded at the end of chapter eleven, but its aftermath has yet to be described. Christ's reign has been foreseen, yet He has yet to descend. We have just left chapters twelve and thirteen where we saw Satan's original fall and end time persecution of Israel. These chapters brought us right up to the midpoint of the final seven years. Chapter fourteen continues from the midpoint, where chapter thirteen left off, and brings us back to the seventh trumpet. Jesus has a few more things to show John before His faithful disciple sees the return of the King.

We meet 144,000 on Mount Zion with Jesus. This number immediately reminds us of the 144,000 we already met in chapter seven. Let's compare and contrast these two groups.

	Chapter 7	Chapter 14
# of Multitude	144,000	144,000
Where are they?	On earth	In heaven
Marked with:	Seal of Living God	Jesus' and the Father's name
Nationality	Jews	Unspecified
Doing what?	Unspecified	Singing new song
Identified as	Jews	First fruits

The phrase "first fruits" in the New Testament is used two different ways. First, it is used to denote the first converts in an area such as in Romans 16:5. First fruits is also used to denote the first to rise from the dead.

But now Christ has been raised from the dead, the first fruits of those who are asleep.

1 Corinthians 15:20

Remember, we are still describing events that lead us to the seventh trumpet, or the bowl judgments, which ushers in the return of the King. This group of people could be interpreted a few different ways.

First, many scholars say these are the same group of Jews that we met in chapter seven. Let's pursue this theory for a moment. When the group is seen in chapter seven they are on earth because they were uninvolved in the rapture (seal six). In fact, they probably converted to Christ because of the rapture. So in chapter seven they come to faith, but they remain on earth for the wrath of God. In chapter fourteen, we are looking at a scene in heaven, meaning, if these are the same 144,000 of chapter seven, every one of them has been killed for their faith and are now with Jesus. Of course, this is a viable possibility. The persecution of the dragon and the beast out of the sea will know no bounds.

However, God placed such an emphasis on the group in chapter seven being Jews from the nation of Israel, I find it hard to believe this is the same group; nothing is said about a Jewish heritage in chapter fourteen. Another possibility is that this is not the same group. Just as God names 144,000 Jews as His first converts (Revelation 7:4), so He will name 144,000 Gentiles as His first fruits. At the end of chapter thirteen, we were introduced to the mark of the beast. Here we see a group of people in heaven. Perhaps the people in this group are the first to be martyred for their faith. Because they have chosen death rather than bow to the Antichrist, they are given a special mark and learn a new song that no one else knows. Look again at Revelation 14:3:

And they sang a new song before the throne and before the four living creatures and the elders; and no one could learn the song except the one hundred and forty-four

260

thousand who had been purchased from the earth.
Revelation 14:3

The 144,000 are said to have been "purchased" from the earth. Some translations, such as the NIV, translate the Greek word "agorazo" as "redeemed." If reading one of the translations using the word "redeemed" I wouldn't have given the word a second thought. But other translations such as the NASB translate "agorazo" as "purchased." Isn't that an interesting way to put it? These 144,000 in chapter fourteen were "purchased" from the earth. Still other translations such as MSG translate "agorazo" as "bought." They have been "bought" from the earth. Isn't that an odd description? Maybe I am reading too much into this, but I find it extremely unusual. Would you describe your admittance into heaven as God "buying" you? It wouldn't be wrong, because Jesus' blood did buy us, but let's dig deeper, shall we?

Let's start by looking back at Revelation 13:17.

And he provides that no one will be able to buy or to sell, except the one who has the mark, either the name of the beast or the number of his name.
Revelation 13:17

If the 144,000 are in heaven they did not take the mark of the beast. If they didn't take the mark of the beast, that means they were unable to buy or to sell.

The Greek word "agorazo" used in Revelation 14:3 is the same Greek word used for "buy" in 13:17. In fact, we meet this group of 144,000 faithful followers two verses after we read about the mark of the beast! Without the mark of the beast, you cannot "buy" or "purchase" anything. These saints in Revelation 14 have been "bought" and "purchased" from the earth. Someone needs to shout, "Glory!" God could be saying, "Because you refused to buy with the mark that blasphemes my Son, I will buy you so you will no longer have to worry about anything!" Jesus is standing with this multitude, welcoming them to heaven because of their faithfulness. I truly believe these are the first fruits or the first faithful martyrs from the earth after the mark of the beast is initiated. Could these 144,000 still be the 144,000 of chapter seven? Possibly, but because nothing about their Jewish heritage is mentioned, I tend to believe the 144,000 in chapter fourteen are Gentiles, or at least include some Gentiles that are standing firm in their faith. Also, if the 144,000 in chapter fourteen are first fruits, they would be the first martyrs of seal five. The 144,000 in chapter seven do not convert to Christ until after seal six.

Again, remember we are leading up to the seventh trumpet in these chapters. This chapter is describing things that happen after the mark of the beast is introduced at the midpoint of the final seven years. There is not a pause in the original text until Revelation 14:6, meaning this passage of scripture is a continuation of Revelation 13. So let's go back and look at a few other passages that come before the passage in question.

It was also given to him to make war with the saints and to overcome them, and authority over every tribe and people and tongue and nation was given to him.

Revelation 13:7

And they overcame him because of the blood of the Lamb and because of the word of their testimony, and they did not love their life even when faced with death.

Revelation 12:11

"Be faithful until death, and I will give you the crown of life . . . He who overcomes will not be hurt by the second death."

Revelation 2:10b-11a

The beast is overcoming the saints, but not all of them. Scripture shows 144,000 standing firm in their faith. In fact, they are killed for it.

A voice is heard from heaven, like the sound of many waters. This is consistent with what we saw in the first chapter of Revelation: Jesus' voice sounds like rushing waters. God's voice is power. He commands and it is done (Genesis 1). Ezekiel 43:2 says, "And behold, the glory of the God of Israel was coming from the way of the east. And His voice was like the sound of many waters; and the earth shone with His glory." Here Ezekiel is talking about the millennial temple, and God's glory coming to fill it. Jesus Christ's return! And His voice is like the sound of many waters, strong, powerful, yet purifying.

Oh, can you imagine the day!

The 144,000 sing a new song before the throne and no one could learn the song except those saints who had been purchased from the earth. This is a unique relationship to the throne of grace. These saints sing a song no one else can learn. It is their special praise to the God who is now physically with them.

Scripture makes it clear that these saints haven't defiled themselves with "women." At first glance it seems like this is saying they are unmarried and have chosen to live a celibate life. Yet, does God really desire for us to live a celibate life? Is this somehow "holy?" Let's dig deeper.

In the Garden of Eden, there was Adam and there was God, yet what did God say?

Then the Lord God said, "It is not good for the man to be alone; I will make him a helper suitable for him."
Genesis 2:18

After God declared it wasn't good for man to be alone, He created Eve and said, "Be fruitful and multiply, and fill the earth, and subdue it" (Genesis 2:28b). It sounds like God intended man to marry. He designed us to have the spousal relationship. The marriage union was supposed to be an illustration of how Christ loves the church (Ephesians 5:32-33). It was to be unbroken, cherished, and even longed for. Man is incomplete without woman; God said so in Genesis chapter two.

So why does scripture say the 144,000 on Mount Zion haven't defiled themselves with women? A woman in scripture can also represent a religious ideology or a follower of a particular religious theory. A good woman is represented as a virgin (Matthew 25:1-13) and a pagan woman is represented as a harlot (Hosea 4:15). Israel is represented as a woman in Revelation 12 because she worships the one true God. In Revelation 17 we will meet another woman – a harlot – and she is the false religion that will be present in the last days (Islam).

I believe chapter 14 is saying the 144,000 have never defiled themselves with a harlot (a false religion) and have been loyal to the Lamb wherever He goes.

Thought for the day:
The martyrs were faithful until death. If given the choice, will you be?

DAY FORTY-ONE
REVELATION 14:6-13
THE THREE ANGELS

[6]And I saw another angel flying in midheaven, having an eternal gospel to preach to those who live on the earth, and to every nation and tribe and tongue and people; [7]and he said with a loud voice, "Fear God, and give Him glory, because the hour of His judgment has come; worship Him who made the heaven and the earth and sea and springs of waters." [8]And another angel, a second one, followed, saying "Fallen, fallen is Babylon the great, she who has made all the nations drink of the wine of the passion of her immorality." [9]Then another angel, a third one, followed them, saying with a loud voice, "If anyone worships the beast and his image, and receives a mark on his forehead or on his hand, [10]he also will drink of the wine of the wrath of God, which is mixed in full strength in the cup of His anger; and he will be tormented with fire and brimstone in the presence of the holy angels and in the presence of the Lamb. [11]And the smoke of their torment goes up forever and ever; they have no rest day and night, those who worship the beast and his image, and whoever receives the mark of his name." [12]Here is the perseverance of the saints who keep the commandments of God and their faith in Jesus. [13]And I heard a voice from heaven, saying, "Write, 'Blessed are the dead who die in the Lord from now on!'" "Yes," says the Spirit, "so that they may rest from their labors, for their deeds follow with them."

Revelation 14:6-13

This begins a series of proclamations by three angels. The first flies in mid-heaven declaring that everyone will hear the gospel message. What did Jesus say would happen before the end would come?

"This gospel of the kingdom shall be preached in the whole world as a testimony to all the nations, and then the end will come."

Matthew 24:14

The first angel is God's way of assuring us the gospel will be preached to all nations before the final judgment of the earth. The nations will hear about a Savior and they will have a choice.

The seventh trumpet has sounded, and Christ's reign has been foreseen. The first bowl judgment has yet to fall, and when that happens, everyone will have heard the gospel and made their choice. Remember, back in Revelation 9:20 after the sixth trumpet, no one else repents. Then after this announcement is made in Revelation nine, the seventh trumpet sounds in Revelation 11:15. Just like the seventh seal ushered in the seven trumpets, the seventh trumpet ushers in the seven bowls.

God is telling us everyone who will repent has repented. This statement of "they did not repent" will be made three additional times in the bowl judgments of chapter sixteen. God wants to assure us He has given those remaining every opportunity. Before the seventh trumpet sounds and the bowl judgments fall, everyone has chosen a side. The inhabitants of the earth are either for God and Christ or the dragon and the Antichrist. It is done. The time has come. Jesus will return and when He does you will not alter your allegiance. You have made your final decision.

Is there a literal angel flying around the world? Or is scripture telling us the spirit of the gospel, through God's servants, is heard throughout the world? I tend to believe it is the latter, and the saints of God will have done their duty proclaiming the gospel message, along with the 144,000 Jews and the two witnesses. Remember, this is John seeing a vision. It would be very hard for Jesus to show him the entire world hearing the message, but an angel flying around the world proclaiming the message is an illustration John can visualize and understand.

In either case, the nations will hear. And they will choose. Many will choose unwisely.

The angel declares, "Fear God, and give Him glory, because the hour of His judgment has come; worship Him who made the heaven and the earth and sea and springs of waters." Everything the angel mentions here has been affected by God's wrath. The luminaries have been struck in the heavens, the earth has been burned, and the sea and springs of water have turned to blood and have become undrinkable. People will do as they do today: discount things around them as coming from something other than God. They will try to explain away God's wrath as environmental catastrophes due to natural phenomena. They will declare they have the solution. They will not. The angel is telling the people of the earth: "God made all things; God is in control of all things; acknowledge Him!"

But they do not. They have made their choice. They do not repent (Revelation 9:21).

Then a second angel gives another warning. Babylon is fallen. Remember this angel is after the seventh trumpet sounds, and with the sounding of the seventh trumpet, the bowls are unleashed. We have not seen the bowls described yet, but you can rest assured, Babylon is fallen. With the sounding of the seventh trumpet, it is over for the Antichrist's empire. It will fall never to rise again. This angel is announcing what we have not yet seen. This is another reason I believe the bowl judgments cannot last for a long period of time. In fact this is a strong argument that they can last no longer than a day. If the bowls lasted longer than a day, the angel's announcement would be premature. It is not. When the bowls fall, it is done.

This angel says the nations have drunk the wine of Babylon's immorality. Wine in scripture can refer to teaching.

"And no one puts new wine [NEW IDEAS] into old wineskins [RIGID THINKING]; otherwise the new wine will burst the skins and it will be spilled out, and the skins will be ruined."
Luke 5:37, explanation added

The nations have accepted Babylon's false system. They have taken the mark. They have rejected the true Savior who can save them.

This angel is warning the earth after the first angel's gospel message reaches the nations: if you choose to ignore God and side with the dragon, your empire is already fallen. Christ's victory is assured.

The nations rumble on like the rumbling of many waters, but He will rebuke them and they will flee far away, and be chased like chaff in the mountains before the wind, or like whirling dust before a gale. At evening time, behold, there is terror! Before morning they are no more.
Isaiah 17:13-14a

They are no more. Babylon will be no more. It will be like chaff in the whirling gale of Christ's anger.

But the world will not listen. They will have made their choice. They do not repent (Revelation 9:21).

Next we meet a third angel who again warns the earth. The inhabitants of the world have heard the gospel, they have been warned the false system will fall, and now they have heard that those who take the mark will be damned. This is sobering. I have heard comments from Christians, "If my child is starving, surely God would understand if I take the mark to buy bread for my child."

Think again.

When you take the mark you will "drink the wine of the wrath of God." This is not a game. This mark is a declaration of faith. If you take it, you are accepting the wine of Babylon and the false doctrine she proclaims. If you drink that wine, you can rest assured you will drink God's. Wine in scripture also refers to God's response to idolatry such as in Jeremiah 25:15:

For thus the Lord, the God of Israel, says to me, "Take this cup of the wine of wrath from My hand and cause all the nations to whom I send you to drink it."
Jeremiah 25:15

Jeremiah 25 describes the nations that will be judged. Do you know the nations that are mentioned in this chapter? They are all Middle Eastern: Egypt (Egypt), Philistines (Gaza where Hamas resides), Gaza (Gaza), Ekron and Ashdod (cities in Gaza), Edom (Jordan, Yemen, Saudi Arabia), Moab (Jordon), Ammon (Jordan), Tyre (Lebanon where Hezbollah resides), Dedan and Tema and Buz (cities in Saudi Arabia and Yemen), Arabia (Saudi Arabia), Elam and Media (Iran). What is the wine they are drinking? That Allah (the dragon) is god and the Antichrist will be their savior. The nations toward which the wrath of God is directed in Jeremiah were the enemies of the Jews in Jeremiah's day; the enemies of the Jews today are still those same nations and their ideology has spread throughout the world. At the time of the end, God will cause all nations to drink His wrath if they do not acknowledge His Son as King.

Let me make something very clear before we move forward: Muslims aren't the enemy. They are God's children just like us. They need a Savior and they need salvation. Fundamental Islam, however, is the enemy. It glorifies death in jihad, hates Jews and Christians, and declares emphatically Jesus isn't God's Son.

Let me end this section by Jesus' response to Babylon in Jeremiah 25:

The Lord will roar from on high and utter His voice from His holy habitation; He will roar mightily against His fold. He will shout like those who tread the grapes, against all the inhabitants of the earth . . . Those slain by the Lord on that day will be from one end of the earth to the other. They will not be lamented, gathered or buried; they will be like dung on the face of the ground.

Jeremiah 25:30b, 33

The true King of kings will return, and if you have taken the Antichrist's mark, you will not be lamented. Notice the grape harvest imagery in this scripture. In many scriptures God is treading the wine press when He returns, smashing the grapes that have drunk the wine of the false system. Let's look at a few of these.

Then another angel, the one who has power over fire, came out from the altar; and he called with a loud voice to him who had the sharp sickle, saying, "Put in your sharp sickle and gather the clusters from the vine of the earth, because her grapes are ripe."

Revelation 14:18

Put in the sickle, for the harvest is ripe. Come, tread, for the wine press is full; the vats overflow, for their wickedness is great.

Joel 3:13

For a cup is in the hand of the Lord, and the wine foams; it is well mixed, and He pours out of this; surely all the wicked of the earth must drain and drink down its dregs.

Psalm 75:8

God will have a sickle in His hand, and He will reap. Those ripe with the wine of Babylon will be harvested in death. The imagery of the grape harvest and the cup of God's wrath indicate the end time harvest. When did the grape harvest occur? In the fall! The second coming of Christ will occur on Yom Kippur, in the fall, when the remnant of Israel will be saved (Isaiah 10:20-22).

If you drink the wine of Babylon (take the mark of the beast) Revelation 14:10 makes it crystal clear – you will be tormented with fire and brimstone.

If you choose to drink Babylon's wine and incur the wrath of God, you will be thrown into the lake of fire (Revelation 20:14). This is not a place you will be able to socialize with friends because friendship is a gift of God. This is not a place you will be able to build houses because everything you use to build a house is a gift of God. This is not a place you can see the sky above or the grass under your feet because the sky and the grass are gifts from God. If you reject God, you also reject everything He has made, because everything good is a gift from God. As scripture says, the smoke of their torment will go up forever and ever.

Revelation 14:13 says that the saints must have perseverance. To do this, what must we do? We must keep His commandments and have faith in the Son (Revelation 14:13).

Persevere in your faith, my faithful friends. Persevere for His name. Scripture is telling us those on earth who haven't taken the mark are noticed. The saints who endure the persecution of the Antichrist are blessed. God will reward them for their devotion.

Thought for the day:

The angels announce the fall of Babylon. This is not only the Babylon of the end times, but also all the false systems that have come before. The rock from Daniel chapter two has shattered the nations and declared a new age. There will be no more falsehood in Christ's reign. Celebrate that fact today. More on the end tomorrow.

¹⁴Then I looked, and behold, a white cloud, and sitting on the cloud was one like a son of man, having a golden crown on His head and a sharp sickle in His hand. ¹⁵And another angel came out of the temple, crying out with a loud voice to Him who sat on the cloud, "Put in your sickle and reap, for the hour to reap has come, because the harvest of the earth is ripe." ¹⁶Then He who sat on the cloud swung His sickle over the earth, and the earth was reaped. ¹⁷And another angel came out of the temple which is in heaven, and he also had a sharp sickle. ¹⁸Then another angel, the one who has power over fire, came out from the altar; and he called with a loud voice to him who had the sharp sickle, saying, "Put in your sharp sickle and gather the clusters from the vine of the earth, because her grapes are ripe." ¹⁹So the angel swung his sickle to the earth and gathered the clusters from the vine of the earth, and threw them into the great wine press of the wrath of God. ²⁰And the wine press was trodden outside the city, and blood came out from the wine press, up to the horses' bridles, for a distance of two hundred miles.

Revelation 14:14-20

Now we see the scene of the harvesters. Remember, the seventh trumpet sounded back in chapter eleven. Chapters twelve and thirteen gave us the history of Satan and his persecution of the woman from the beginning of time right up to the midpoint and the mark of the beast. Then in chapter fourteen we are taken even further all the way through the trumpet judgments, but we have yet to see the aftermath of the final trumpet. Chapter fourteen is all about assuring us that God has given the inhabitants of the earth every opportunity to repent. We are met with 144,000 people who have faithfully been martyred for their faith because of their refusal to take the mark. This scene reminds us how cruel the world has become to the faithful. Then the three angels announced the preaching of the gospel, doom for Babylon, and doom for the worshipers of the beast. This is assuring us that everything has been done to reconcile the world to the true God. But they "did not repent" (Revelation 9:21). Now we see the harvest is ripe. After we are assured the world has heard the gospel, we are met with a scene that tells us the end is here because of what the seventh trumpet will unleash. Now the bowls will begin to fall and during the course of their descent, the earth will be harvested and Jesus will take His rightful throne. This is the bowl judgments (the seventh trumpet) summed up in one scene.

We see a man sitting on a cloud having a golden crown on His head and a sharp sickle in His hands. This is our Savior. He has been crowned King in the heavenlies, and He is about to descend and harvest the earth.

And I saw heaven opened, and behold, a white horse, and He who sat on it is called Faithful and True, and in righteousness He judges and wages war. His eyes are a flame of fire, and on His head are many diadems.
Revelation 19:11-12a

We learned earlier that the national Day of Atonement is on Yom Kippur, the second Jewish feast that has yet to be fulfilled. This is when all the Jews remaining will look to their Savior and recognize Jesus for who He is: their promised Messiah who came first as a humble servant and is now retuning in the power they expected. The exact moment they come to faith is the exact moment Jesus will return and save them.

Shout for joy, O daughter of Zion! Shout in triumph, O Israel! Rejoice and exult with all your heart, O daughter of Jerusalem! The Lord has taken away His judgment against you, He has cleared away your enemies, The King of Israel, the Lord, is in your midst; you will fear disaster no more. In that day it will be said to Jerusalem; do not be afraid, O Zion; do not let your hands fall limp. The Lord your God is in your midst, a victorious warrior. He will exult over you with joy, He will be quiet in His love, He will rejoice over you with shouts of joy.
Zephaniah 3:14-17

Jesus is on a cloud. This is reminiscent of how He ascended into heaven. I know we have looked at this before, but let's take another quick look.

And after He had said these things, He was lifted up while they were looking on, and a cloud received Him out of their sight . . . "Men of Galilee, why do you stand looking into the sky? This Jesus, who has been taken up from you into heaven, will come in just the same way as you have watched Him go into heaven."

Acts 1:9, 11

Now I want you to see something exciting. Let's compare Psalm 18 to Revelation 16 and see if we see any similarities.

Then the earth shook and quaked; and the foundations of the mountains were trembling and were shaken, because He was angry. Smoke went up out of His nostrils, and fire from His mouth devoured; coals were kindled by it. He bowed the heavens also, and came down with thick darkness under His feet. He road upon a cherub and flew; and He sped upon the wings of the wind. He made darkness His hiding place, His canopy around Him, darkness of waters, thick clouds of the skies. From the brightness before Him passed His thick clouds, hailstones and coals of fire. The Lord also thundered in the heavens, and the Most High uttered His voice, hailstones and coals of fire. He sent out His arrows, and scattered them, and lightning flashes in abundance, and routed them.

Psalm 18:7-14

And there were flashes of lightning and sounds and peals of thunder; and there was a great earthquake, such as there had not been since man came to be upon the earth, so great an earthquake was it, and so mighty . . . And huge hailstones, about one hundred pounds each, came down from heaven upon men; and men blasphemed God because of the plague of the hail, because its plague was extremely severe.

Revelation 16:18, 21

Oh, my faithful friends, Psalm 18 is a second coming Psalm! He is coming with the clouds, with fire, lightning, and hailstones. Woe to the man who opposes Him.

The Son puts His sickle on the earth and reaps because the hour has come. What hour? The hour of the day of the Lord! A day in scripture can mean a number of things. In Genesis chapter one a day is a literal twenty-four hour period. "God called the light day, and the darkness He called night. And there was evening and there was morning, one day." When God says He made the earth in six days, He meant six literal days. Just so we wouldn't misunderstand God says, "there was evening and there was morning." He didn't say "evenings and mornings." To further clarify, he adds, "one day" (for more information on our beginning see my study entitled *The Beginning in Black and White*).

There are other times in scripture that "day" can refer to a period of time. For instance, in Revelation 6:17 it says, "the great day of their wrath has come, and who is able to stand!" The day referred to here is when the judgments are about to fall – the trumpets and the bowls. It is a period of time the world will be under God's wrath. We know trumpet number five will last five months (Revelation 9:5), so the "great day" referred to here isn't twenty-four hours but a period of time. We know from other scripture God's wrath will fall for at least a year.

For the Lord has a day of vengeance, a year of recompense for the cause of Zion.

Isaiah 34:8

Although the day of the Lord, God's wrath, will last for a little over a year (the trumpets – days of Noah) there will be a single day at the end when Jesus will return and save the remnant and destroy the remaining ungodly (the bowls – the day of Lot).

And the light of Israel will become a fire and his Holy One a flame, and it will burn and devour his thorns and his briars in a single day.

Isaiah 10:17

There will be a single day (the bowls) when Jesus will return, and that day will be a consuming fire. But the day of the Lord (period of time) begins with the trumpets. What initiates the trumpets? You got it, the rapture, because we are not destined for His wrath.

Sinners in Zion are terrified; trembling has seized the godless. "Who among us can live with the consuming fire? Who among us can live with continual burning?" He who walks righteously and speaks with sincerity, he who rejects unjust gain and shakes his hands so that they hold no bribe; he who stops his ears from hearing about bloodshed and shuts his eyes from looking upon evil; he will dwell on the heights, his refuge will be the impregnable rock; his bread will be given him, his water will be sure. Your eyes will see the King in His beauty.

Isaiah 33:14-17a

Remember our discussion about arising? Here is when Jesus arises with fire and the people are dwelling on the "heights" and their refuge will be an "impregnable rock."

Does this sound like Petra to you? Glory! God will be a consuming fire and rescue the Jews in Petra.

Jesus puts His sickle on the earth. The hour has come for the harvest – the bowl judgments are here. The hour of His return is now. This is the literal day of the Lord when Jesus descends to earth. An angel comes out of the temple. This is symbolic of a verdict being rendered by the one who lives there. The Father has made His final call – He tells the angel to tell Jesus to reap. Jesus places His sickle on the earth and reaps.

Then another angel comes out of temple with another sickle. Again, this is telling us a verdict has been rendered by the One who lives in the temple. A third angel, the one who has power over fire, comes from the altar and declares to the angel with the sickle that the harvest is ripe. Fire is symbolic of God's judgment and His final wrath. Remember, 2 Peter 3:10 declares God will judge the world with fire, and Jesus will be like a consuming fire when He returns. There isn't another soul on earth who is going to repent. They have made their decision to drink the wine of Babylon. They have chosen the Antichrist and not the Savior of the world. It says this angel gathers the grapes that Jesus has harvested and throws them into "the great wine press of the wrath of God."

Note that Jesus does not gather; He reaps. Jesus sticks in His sickle and cuts down the grapes of the earth (with the bowl judgments), then the angel puts in its sickle and gathers those grapes, throwing them into the great wine press of God. This scene is telling us the bowls are God's sickle and when they are beginning to be poured out, Jesus is descending and gathering His elect. It is over. Your chance is over. Oh can you imagine the day!

The gathering angel throws those who have drunk the Antichrist's wine into the great wine press of the wrath of God. "And the wine press was trodden outside the city, and blood came out from the wine press, up to the horses' bridles for a distance of

274

two hundred miles." We read scripture yesterday stating the fallen on that day will be "like dung on the face of the ground" (Jeremiah 25:33). This next scripture is an image of Jesus' treading the wine press.

"I have trodden the wine trough alone, and from the peoples there was no man with Me, I also trod them in My anger and trampled them in My wrath; and their lifeblood is sprinkled on My garments, and I stained all My raiment. For the day of vengeance was in My heart, and My year of redemption has come."

Isaiah 63:3-4

This scripture also gives us both the "year of redemption" and the "day of vengeance." And based on what we know, this makes sense. There will be a year (the trumpets) where those on earth can come to faith in our Lord and Savior, but ultimately, there will come a single day when He will return and claim the earth. It will be a day of vengeance and fire (the bowls).

It says the blood will come up to the horses' bridles for a distance of about two hundred miles. This is the approximate area of the Holy Land from north to south. This is a massacre. It could mean a river of blood, but it more significantly means judgment and destruction. Nothing will escape Jesus' wrath when He returns. God remembers His saints prayers (Revelation 8:4) and He will repay. "'Vengeance is mine, I will repay,' says the Lord" (Rom. 12:19b).

This scene is telling us the bowls will be the final reckoning.

Thought for the day:
If the wrongs done to you on this earth have not been righted on this earth, Jesus will right them in the end. His sickle is sharp. The wicked will be judged and the righteous will be rewarded. Rest assured, everything will be righted in the end. Tomorrow you will see another sign in heaven. It will be great and marvelous.

[1]Then I saw another sign in heaven, great and marvelous, seven angels who had seven plagues, which are the last, because in them the wrath of God is finished. [2]And I saw something like a sea of glass mixed with fire, and those who had been victorious over the beast and his image and the number of his name, standing on the sea of glass, holding harps of God. [3]And they sang the song of Moses, the bond-servant of God, and the song of the Lamb, saying, "Great and marvelous are Your works, O Lord God, the Almighty; righteous and true are Your ways, King of the nations! [4]Who will not fear, O Lord, and glorify Your name? For you alone are holy; for all the nations will come and worship before You, for Your righteous acts have been revealed." [5]After these things I looked, and the temple of the tabernacle of testimony in heaven was opened, [6]and the seven angels who had the seven plagues came out of the temple, clothed in linen, clean and bright, and girded around their chests with golden sashes. [7]Then one of the four living creatures gave to the seven angels seven golden bowls full of the wrath of God, who lives forever and ever. [8]And the temple was filled with smoke from the glory of God and from His power; and no one was able to enter the temple until the seven plagues of the seven angels were finished.

Revelation 15:1-8

Just like the end of chapter fourteen was a scene on earth telling us the bowls are coming and judgment is here, this is a scene in heaven telling us the same thing. This is the moment of truth. The sickle is sharp and the grapes are ripe.

Remember, man placed chapter breaks in scripture, not God. Chapter fifteen really belongs with the end of chapter fourteen. It is the same message being proclaimed in a different location.

This scene is announced as another sign. The first sign, defined as "the great sign," was the woman, Israel, of chapter twelve. Then John saw "another" sign in heaven, which was the red dragon, or Satan. In chapter fifteen, a third sign is announced and it is defined as "great and marvelous." Then John sees the seven angels with the seven bowls of wrath.

At first glance, this doesn't sound very "marvelous" to the reader. The world is about to be destroyed with fire. Let's see why God would announce the bowls as "marvelous."

A fire consumes before them and behind them a flame burns. The land is like the garden of Eden before them but a desolate wilderness behind them, and nothing at all escapes them.

Joel 2:3

This is a second coming scripture. Fire goes before God's warriors and flame follows after them. But what is happening before them? The land is becoming like the garden of Eden. Now why would fire be necessary to turn the land into Eden? The world has been ravaged by sin.

But who can endure the day of His coming? And who can stand when He appears? For He is like a refiner's fire and like fullers' soap. He will sit as a smelter and purifier of silver, and He will purify the sons of Levi and refine them like gold and silver, so that they may present to the Lord offerings in righteousness.

Malachi 3:2-3

The seven bowls of wrath are "marvelous" because their fire will help regenerate the earth to Eden (Joel 2:3) and help purify the land (Malachi 3:2).

The "marvelous" scene in heaven is announcing God's final judgment of the earth, but this judgment will usher in the Millennial Kingdom of Christ. The believer's heaven is about to become a reality. God will now make everything right. Yes, this is a marvelous sign, the greatest sign – the return of the King!

Even though the seventh trumpet was blown at the end of chapter eleven, John has been shown more details transpiring to get us right back up to the seventh trumpet. However, the reader needs to recognize, this is the next second of real time. Chapter twelve through fourteen were things John needed to understand before he saw the bowl judgments become a reality.

The wrath of God was announced at the end of the sixth seal in chapter six, where we saw people cowering in the rocks; here scripture tells us with the bowls, the wrath of God is finished. Again, this is telling us the bowls will be quick (one day – like the days of Lot). They will come with Jesus, and with their coming, the final judgment of the earth is assured.

The sea of glass is seen, this time with fire. This is symbolic of the judgments that are about to take place on the earth. The fire seen here could also stand for one more thing: those who have undergone the fiery ordeal at the hand of Satan and the Antichrist are present, holding harps and praising God. God has those who have experienced the horrific persecution of the beast front and center. This could also be the reason why we see fire depicted in this scene. God will look on those who have been persecuted because of the truth and you can just imagine God's fire blazing hotter. God will judge! The time is at hand.

The saints sing a song of Moses and the song of the Lamb. In Exodus 15, Moses sang a song after God delivered them from Pharaoh. It is a song of victory, a song of praise to the One who alone gave the victory. God worked His wonders in Egypt. The people didn't lift a finger for their deliverance. God did it all. He brought the plagues and spared the Jewish nation. It was God and God alone who fought the battle and won. It will be the same here. There is nothing the people can do. It is God and God alone who can judge the world and demand justice. That is why it is a song of Moses: it is a song of deliverance that only God can give.

It is also the song of the Lamb. God will deliver, but only through the blood of Jesus. Those who believe in the Lamb, who accept His sacrifice and overcome through their love for Him, will come through the fire unscathed. God's ways are great and marvelous and righteous and true. Although this is judgment, God is reminding us it is also righteous and true. This is the only response a Holy God can make. If you reject His salvation, if you reject the Lamb, you are condemned. The King is about to reign and every nation will glorify His name. The veil will be taken off the eyes of the peoples of the earth, and when Jesus returns, they will see their unrighteous acts and understand their condemnation.

Then we see the temple of the tabernacle of the testimony is opened. This is no longer the Holy Place the priests entered to light the altar of incense, this is the Holy of Holies, the resting place of the ark of the covenant, the dwelling place of God. There is only one day when the Holy of Holies is opened – Yom Kippur! Someone needs to shout, "Glory!" Jesus will descend on Yom Kippur, on the Day of Atonement, when the nation of Israel's sins will be washed clean. Remember, the time between chapter eleven and chapter fifteen is seconds in real time. Israel was at the threshold of belief in chapter eleven, when the Ark of the Covenant was seen; they were walking through "the Way" and realizing "the Truth" of their Messiah. They see the ark as they walk to the Holy of Holies. The veil is torn – their Messiah has come. The chamber is now opened to them. They have made their commitment and obtained "the Life." At this moment they are shouting, "Blessed is He who comes in the name of the Lord!"

They have come to faith. Israel is walking into salvation.

Now in that day the remnant of Israel, and those of the house of Jacob who have escaped, will never again rely on the one who struck them, but will truly rely on the Lord, the Holy One of Israel. A remnant will return, the remnant of Jacob, to the mighty God.

Isaiah 10:20-21

When the Antichrist strikes Israel, they will return to the God of Jacob. And as soon as they cry out, Jesus returns to save them. This next scripture is one we have looked at before. Jesus is coming from Bozrah which is south of Israel but north of Petra (Sela).

Who is this who comes from Edom, with garments of glowing colors from Bozrah, this One who is majestic in His apparel, marching in the greatness of His strength? "It is I who speak in righteousness, mighty to save." Why is Your apparel red, and Your garments like the one who treads in the wine press? "I have trodden the wine trough alone, and from the peoples there was no man with Me. I also trod them in My anger and trampled them in My wrath; and their lifeblood is sprinkled on My garments, and I stained all My raiment, for the day of vengeance was in My heart, and My year of redemption has come."

Isaiah 63:1-4

He saves them on Yom Kippur, fulfilling the feast. Remember, Yom Kippur is also known as the "great trump" and we see a trumpet call in Zechariah.

Then the Lord will appear over them, and His arrow will go forth like lightning; and the Lord God will blow the trumpet, and will march in the storm winds of the south . . . and the Lord their God will save them in that day.

Zechariah 9:14, 16a

Now look at this scripture.

The Mighty One, God, the Lord, has spoken, and summoned the earth from the rising of the sun to its setting, out of Zion, the perfection of beauty, God has shone forth. May our God come and not keep silence; fire devours before Him, and it is very tempestuous around Him. He summons the heavens above, and the earth, to judge His people; "Gather My godly ones to Me, those who have made a covenant with Me by sacrifice." And the heavens declare His righteousness, for God Himself is judge. Selah.

Psalm 50:1-6

The Mighty One is coming with a consuming fire. He is gathering together His saints and the Jewish remnant who have made a covenant to Him by sacrifice. And the Mighty One is marching to Sela. Glory Hallelujah!

It is Yom Kippur and the seven angels who have the seven plagues come out of the temple. They are dressed in white with golden sashes, the same garments Jesus wore in chapter one. The High Priest of the Jewish people wore white on Yom Kippur when he entered the Holy of Holies because it was the day Israel was cleansed from their sins and made "white." This is all a picture of the ultimate fulfillment of the Day of Atonement and the remnant of Israel's salvation.

Then one of the four living creatures gives the angels the bowls full of wrath. Why bowls full of wrath? God's judgment in scripture is associated with getting "drunk" on strong wine. Look at the following verses.

I trod down the peoples in My anger and made them drunk in My wrath, and I poured out their lifeblood on the earth.

Isaiah 63:6

God has a cup in his hand, a bowl of wine, full to the brim. He draws from it and pours; it's drained to the

280

dregs. Earth's wicked ones drink it all, drink it down to the last bitter drop!

Psalm 75:8, The Message

Awake, awake, stand up, O Jerusalem, that hast drunk at the hand of Jehovah the cup of his wrath; thou hast drunken the bowl of the cup of staggering, and drained it.

Isaiah 51:17, ASV

There may be another reason we see the final wrath of God being poured out from bowls. Let's look at some verses.

When He had taken the book, the four living creatures and the twenty-four elders fell down before the Lamb, each one holding a harp and golden bowls full of incense, which are the prayers of the saints.

Revelation 5:8

And they cried out with a loud voice, saying, "How long, O Lord, holy and true, will You refrain from judging and avenging our blood on those who dwell on the earth?"

Revelation 6:10

And I heard the angel of the waters saying, "Righteous are You, who are and who were, O Holy One, because You judged these things; for they poured out the blood of saints and prophets, and You have given them blood to drink. They deserve it."

Revelation 16:5-6

The final judgments of the earth are partially in response to the saints' prayers. God is responding to these prayers with force, and the people on earth deserve God's response.

Also, if you remember, what are the people of the world drinking? Although we have not studied chapter seventeen yet, we have mentioned a scripture that tells us the world is drinking the "wine" of the beast. They are buying into the false religious system. They have "committed acts of immorality, and those who dwell on the earth were made drunk with the wine of her immorality" (Revelation 17:2b). The nations of the earth are drinking the wine of the beast, but God will answer with His wine – His wrath.

Let's get back to chapter fifteen. Verse seven clarifies that God lives forever and ever. He was the beginning, and He will be the end. It is His creation, and He is the ultimate and final judge.

Then the temple fills with smoke from the glory of God and from His power. God is a consuming fire, and His fire has kindled. We have seen smoke associated with God's presence before.

Now Mount Sinai was all in smoke because the Lord descended upon it in fire; and its smoke ascended like the smoke of a furnace and the whole mountain quaked violently.

Exodus 19:18

This is consistent with how Jesus will appear at His second coming (Psalm 18:7-15). The smoke should also remind us of the smoke in Revelation 8:3; it came from the incense and the prayers of the saints. It went up like an offering to God. The bowls are God's final answer to those prayers.

No one is able to enter the temple until the seven plagues are finished. This is powerful. It could mean that God doesn't want to be disturbed while the final judgments are happening on earth, but I think there is more to it than that.

At the beginning of chapter nine we saw the horns of the altar; the horns told us God's mercy was still being extended to those on earth. At the end of chapter nine, scripture told us those on earth "did not repent." In chapter fourteen, the eternal gospel was preached to all the nations. We saw warnings going across the globe about the beast and his mark. Everything has been done to save the earth, every mercy extended. The inhabitants still remaining on earth have made their decision. From here on out, no one else repents. God is in His temple because when the bowl judgments start, there is no more mercy. Once Jesus returns, you have made your choice. You are either for Him or against Him. God's mercy is no longer extended. The horns of the altar have been cut off (Amos 3:14).

It is judgment day.

Thought for the day:
Once God enters the temple, there is no more choice. Everyone has made their final decision. Don't let the sun set today without praying for those in your life that haven't chosen Him. Right now, it is not too late.

282

We have come a long way, have we not? I am proud of you for sticking with this study. It can be overwhelming at times, especially because it seems to us like Revelation is not in "order." We like things neat, with bullet points and explanations. We don't like jumping here and there to piece everything together. But we need to remember, God gave Jesus the Revelation to reveal to us what will "soon take place" (Revelation 1:1). He in no way intends to confuse you. The order of events in Revelation is truly the order they need to be in for us to best understand the return of the King.

So today I want to pause and slow down and try to sort it all out. It really isn't as confusing as it seems – I promise.

Revelation 1-10 is in what we would consider "chronological order." Let's take this slow, step-by-step.

In Revelation 1:19, John is told to write the things which he saw and the things which are and the things that must take place after these things.

John had just seen Jesus in His glory, so Revelation chapter one describes the things he *saw*.

Revelation chapters two and three are the churches. These churches existed in John's day and the environments of these churches still exist today. These chapters represent the things which *are*. Revelation 4-22 are the things that take place *after these things*.

So far, so good!

In Revelation chapter four John is taken to heaven. If you remember, there is an "open door" in order to give John the revelation. Nothing has happened on earth yet, but John is seeing the preparations for the return of Christ. In Revelation chapter five John sees Jesus taking the scroll from the Father's hand. We know from our study, this scroll is the title deed to the earth.

Let me pause here to say this:

CHAPTERS ONE THROUGH FIVE ARE NOT ON OUR SEVEN-YEAR TIMELINE. THE TIMELINE STARTS WITH CHAPTER SIX. THE FIRST FIVE CHAPTERS OF REVELATION ARE SETTING THE STAGE FOR THE START OF THE FINAL SEVEN YEARS.

So at the beginning of chapter six, at the breaking of the first seal, the earth is affected – the final seven years have begun. Chapter six takes us through each seal, describing the aftermath.

Seal One brings the Antichrist.
Seal Two brings the sword.
Seal Three brings famine.
Seal Four brings death/the midpoint/the mark of the beast.
Seal Five brings not only death, but also martyrdom.

Up to this point the rapture has not occurred. We also have not seen any thing indicating that God's wrath has begun. Let me say that another way: if the pre-wrath version of the rapture is correct, we are here for the rise of the Antichrist, terror, famine, pestilence and martyrdom. Prepare your faith, my faithful friends, prepare your faith.

Seal Six brings a dark sun and a blood red moon.

There is a critical scripture associated with this seal. It is one we need to revisit.

*The sun will be turned into darkness and the moon into blood **BEFORE** the great and awesome day of the Lord comes.*
Joel 2:31, emphasis added

If that is the case, the first six seals are before the day of the Lord, or the wrath of God, begins (Revelation 6:12).
The wrath of God is announced at the end of seal six.

And they said to the mountains and to the rocks, "Fall on us and hide us from the presence of Him who sits on the throne, and from the wrath of the Lamb."
Revelation 6:16

Jesus says the time of the end will be like the days of Noah and the days of Lot (Luke 17:26, 28). Both Noah and Lot were rescued the same day the wrath fell.

Right after the sun is darkened and the moon turns to blood the wrath of God is announced (but before it falls) we see 144,000 Jews come to faith and a great multitude (the raptured saints) in heaven.

Then the seventh seal is broken at the beginning of chapter eight and the scroll is unrolled (the wrath of God or the day of the Lord begins). Then starting in Revelation chapter eight we are taken through the trumpet judgments of the earth.

Why do the trumpets have to fall?

The Lord is not slow about His promise, as some count slowness, but is patient toward you, not wishing for any to perish but for all to come to repentance.

2 Peter 3:9

He wants those remaining to repent. But by the end of the sixth trumpet the people of the world have made their choice. They do not repent (Revelation 9:21).

God wants everyone who will repent to repent. By the sixth trumpet, none are willing. As soon as everyone who will come to repentance has come to repentance, the seventh trumpet is blown, but we do not see that here. Why? Because there is something else happening before the end of the sixth trumpet. So we have a pause in the forward action.

Revelation 10 is that pause. The angel tells John to "prophesy again" (Revelation 10:11) and this is telling us what follows is not in chronological order. Are we sure about this? Yes, we are. If you recall, in chapter eight there are angels announcing the "three woes." The first woe was past at the end of the fifth trumpet (Revelation 9:12). The second woe is past only at the end of chapter 11 (Revelation 11:14). It correlates to the two witnesses deaths. So Revelation 11 takes us back in time but ends at the second woe – or the sixth trumpet. Let me say that another way – chapter 11 does not progress any further than the sixth trumpet.

The third woe is not introduced by name at all, because just like the last seal equaled the trumpet judgments, the last trumpet will equal the bowls. The seventh trumpet is blown in Revelation 11:15

Now we are back on track. But again there is a pause here because what comes immediately after the blowing of the seventh trumpet is the bowl judgments – Revelation 16. So Revelation chapters 12-15 are giving you more details and more clarification to what is happening during the final seven-year period. Why are they inserted here? I believe it is because God wants you to understand why the seventh trumpet (the bowl judgments) – the destruction of the ungodly of the earth – must take place.

Revelation 12 tells you the history of Satan right up until the midpoint of the final seven years. How do we know this? Let's read Revelation 12:14 to see what time frame is depicted.

> *But the two wings of the great eagle were given to the woman, so that she could fly into the wilderness to her place, where she was nourished for a time and times and half a time, from the presence of the serpent.*
>
> *Revelation 12:14*

This is the midpoint, when the Antichrist is unmasked and the persecution of Christians begins.

Which leads us into WHO Satan is using to persecute the Christians – the beast and the ruler over the beast – the Antichrist – and the false prophet who institutes the mark of the beast – Revelation 13.

The beginning of Revelation 14 really belongs with the end of Revelation 13. We see faithful martyrs in heaven because they did not take the mark of the beast. Then come the three angels telling us that the world has heard the gospel message, the world is warned that Babylon is fallen, and the world has been warned not to take the mark. Now, the world is harvested. We see reapers coming at the end of Revelation 15 and the joy in heaven that the end is now here.

Which leads us to chapter 16 – the details of the same harvest we just saw in chapter 14 and 15.

Clear as mud huh? One of the things that clouds our understanding of this book are the chapter breaks. We want each chapter fitting into a certain space, but again, man made chapter breaks, not God.

I have written a detailed "order" of Revelation if you want to read it through as best you can in chronological order. It is on the next page.

Stick with it and try not to be frustrated if it is still a little cloudy. The important thing is to remember . . . the King is coming . . . and He shines!

A Chronological Summary of Revelation

Rev. 12:1-5 – History of the age-old conflict between Satan and Israel.

Rev. 1-5 – Introduction to the final seven years.

Rev. 13:1-4, 17:1-14 6:1-8– Description of the beast and the prostitute – who take control in the final seven years.

Seal 1 - Rise of the Antichrist – who leads the beast. The prostitute rules over this beast.
Seal 2 - Terror. Right after the Antichrist rises – there is terror by the sword.
Seal 3 - Famine
Seal 4 - Death due to sword (seal 2), famine (seal 3), and the beasts (seal 1). Mark of the beast introduced.

Rev. 11:1-6, 12:6-17, 13:5-18- Two witnesses, persecution, Antichrist is declaring himself God at the midpoint.

Rev. 6:9-17, 7:9-17 – The GREAT TRIBULATION.

Seal 5 – Martyrs due to the mark of the beast
Seal 6 – Sun goes dark/moon to blood/earthquake and RAPTURE (We are here through the 6th seal!) We see the rapture represented by the "great multitude." WRATH of God ANNOUNCED.

Rev. 7:1-8 – Jews begin to convert to Christ.

Rev. 8-9 – Seal 7 is broken = trumpet judgments = The WRATH of God. This lasts ONE YEAR.

Trumpet 1 - Hail and fire mixed with blood.
Trumpet 2 – Great mountain thrown in sea. 1/3 sea to blood, 1/3 marine life die, 1/3 ships gone
Trumpet 3 – Star called Wormwood makes 1/3 of rivers/springs bitter. Many die.
Trumpet 4 – Sun/Moon/Stars struck to darkness
Trumpet 5 – Star falls/Abyss opened/smoke and locusts out. Deluded armies of Antichrist. FIRST WOE.
Trumpet 6 – Four bound angels released/armies of 200 million march. Armies of world. SECOND WOE.

Rev. 11:7-14, Rev. 14:1-13 – the end of the sixth trumpet = the death of the two witnesses, scenes in heaven where God is assuring us that everything has been done for the earth.

Rev. 10, 11:15-19, 14:14-15:8 – Trumpet 7 = the bowl judgments – THE DAY OF THE LORD is announced and begun. This is a 24-hour period where Jesus walks the earth.

Rev. 16:1-11 – The Bowls. THE DAY OF THE LORD.

Bowl 1 – Sores on those who have the mark of the beast.
Bowl 2 – Sea to blood. All marine life die. This is worldwide!
Bowl 3 – Rivers/Springs to blood. Worldwide. There is no more water.
Bowl 4 – Sun scorches men with fire.
Bowl 5 – Kingdom of the beast becomes dark. This is when Jesus is seen in the sky.

Rev. 19:1-16 – The King of kings and His armies descend.

Rev. 16:12-21, 19:17-21 – The armies try to fight, but the King crushes them.

Bowl 6 – Euphrates River dries up. Armies pour into Jerusalem to fight the King of kings (really stupid!).
Bowl 7 – Earthquake, hail 100 pounds each, islands flee, mountains are not found. Earth is leveled.

Rev. 18 – The lament for Babylon

Rev. 20:1-6 – Weeding out sheep from goats. Resurrection of believers who were not raptured. The 1,000 year reign of Christ.

Rev 20:7-10 – Satan freed at the end of 1,000 years. Satan thrown into lake of fire.

Rev 20:11-15 – Judgment of unbelievers where they are thrown into the lake of fire.

Rev. 21-22 – Eternity

*** Rev 17:15-18 is not included in the above summary because we do not know if this occurs closer to the midpoint or much later in the final seven years.

Thought for the day:
Tomorrow we will look at the final bowls of wrath. The people who have taken the mark will now look like the evil mark they have taken. If you are with Christ, you are sealed with the living God. Think about this: when Christ looks down on you, don't you think you shine? He is the light of the world. If you are with Him, those in the heavens should see your shimmer.

¹Then I heard a loud voice from the temple, saying to the seven angels, "Go and pour out on the earth the seven bowls of the wrath of God." ²So the first angel went and poured out his bowl on the earth; and it became a loathsome and malignant sore on the people who had the mark of the beast and who worshiped his image. ³The second angel poured out his bowl into the sea, and it became blood like that of a dead man; and every living thing in the sea died. ⁴Then the third angel poured out his bowl into the rivers and the springs of waters; and they became blood. ⁵And I heard the angel of the waters saying, "Righteous are You, who are and who were, O Holy One, because You judged these things; ⁶for they poured out the blood of saints and prophets, and You have given them blood to drink. They deserve it." ⁷And I heard the altar saying, "Yes, O Lord God, the Almighty, true and righteous are Your judgments." ⁸The fourth angel poured out his bowl upon the sun, and it was given to it to scorch men with fire. ⁹Men were scorched with fierce heat; and they blasphemed the name of God who has the power over these plagues, and they did not repent so as to give Him glory. ¹⁰Then the fifth angel poured out his bowl on the throne of the beast, and his kingdom became darkened; and they gnawed their tongues because of pain, ¹¹and they blasphemed the God of heaven because of their pains and their sores; and they did not repent of their deeds.

Revelation 16:1-11

A loud voice comes from the temple, commanding the seven angels to release the bowls of wrath. If you remember, at the end of chapter 15, God is seen alone in the temple. This voice is our Father and it is on His command that the bowls are poured out. It is done. Everyone on earth has made their choice. It is time for Jesus to return and judge mankind.

When the first angel pours out his bowl on the earth, loathsome and malignant sores appear on those who have the mark of the beast. Just like some of the plagues in Egypt, this bowl is selective and only targets those who are in the enemy's camp (Exodus 8:22, 9:4, 9:26, 10:23). In the midst of the chaos, God is showing the true nature of the people under the mark. They are ugly, repulsive, and vile. They have chosen lies over truth and a tormentor over the Savior. The world now sees their true colors.

Next we see the seas and the rivers turning to blood. We have seen a smaller scale of the second and third bowl judgments before. This was one of Moses' plagues (Exodus 7:14-25) and it was the second trumpet judgment. In the Exodus it was confined to the waters of Egypt (Exodus 7:19). In the second trumpet it was confined to a third of the earth (Revelation 8:8-9). Now it is global. The results are the same as in the second trumpet judgment – sea life is destroyed. The entirety of the earth has bloody seas, bloody rivers, and dead foul-smelling aquatic life. This is why the bowl judgments cannot last long. A man can't survive more than about four days without water. What about storage containers, you might ask? Well, lets see what happened in Egypt:

Then the Lord said to Moses, "Say to Aaron, 'Take your staff and stretch out your hand over the waters of Egypt, over their rivers, over their streams, and over their pools, and over all their reservoirs of water, that they may become blood; and there will be blood throughout all the land of Egypt, both in vessels of wood and in vessels of stone.'"

Exodus 7:19

There was no more water, not even in the vessels on your kitchen counter – if you even have a kitchen counter left! Then an angel declares, "Righteous are You, who are and who were, O Holy One, because You judged these things; for they poured out the blood of saints and prophets, and you have given them blood to drink. They deserve it." Wow. This is God's response to the persecution of His saints by the hand of the dragon and the Antichrist. When someone takes the life of God's servants they will get blood to drink. God has had enough of man's rebellion. His patience is at an end.

The angel also reminds us of Who we are dealing with. This is God the Almighty, the first and the last. He is the creator of all things and He has the right to declare whether they are good or bad. The unrighteous are violating His rules and His laws. "For the wrath of God is revealed from heaven against all ungodliness and unrighteousness of men who suppress the truth in unrighteousness" (Romans 1:18). You are either for Him or against Him (Matthew 12:30). God has had enough.

Another voice came from the altar. The voice is unidentified, but because it comes from the altar, I believe it is supposed to remind us of all the sacrifices that have been made on account of sin and the ultimate sacrifice of our Savior. The unrepentant on the earth have rejected that sacrifice and are condemned to drink blood. Because of that rejection, the bowl judgments are righteous.

When the fourth angel pours out his bowl, the sun scorches men with fire. In trumpet six we saw a statement that ushered in the bowl judgments, "and they did not repent of their murders nor of their sorceries nor of their immorality nor of their thefts." Here we see the same thing. All water has turned to blood and now the sun scorches men with fire. They are thirsty, yet there is nothing to quench their thirst. The heat is unbearable. Yet, what do they do?

They blasphemed the name of God who has the power over these plagues, and they did not repent so as to give Him glory.

Revelation 16:9b

God is again telling us, everyone has made their choice. Even if He delays His wrath indefinitely, no one else will repent.

Scorching men with the sun's fire isn't as far fetched as you might think. Solar flares are short, intense bursts of radioactive energy that can make their way to earth. On a normal day, this can disrupt power grids and communication. But bad days are ahead. Studies have shown that the earth's magnetic field is weakening.[1] The magnetic field is what protects the earth from the more damaging effects of solar flares. If a solar flare was released at a point where the magnetic field is weak or down, it could be catastrophic. It would burn the earth and the inhabitants of the earth.

I am sure the people of the earth will try to explain away this judgment as being caused by "global warming," not God. Those on earth will fail to realize God made the sun for this day and hour. God allowed the earth's magnetic field to weaken for this day and hour. God is in control. Yet, they will refuse to give Him glory.

After the sun's display in bowl four, God plunges the Antichrist's kingdom into darkness in bowl five. Still they "blasphemed the God of heaven because of their pains and their sores, and they did not repent of their deeds." Again, God is telling us the people on earth have made their decision. They will not repent.

After the heat of the sun scorches men with fire, you would tend to think the darkness would bring relief. This should seem odd to us. Why would God command the sun to heat up and then send relief to those disloyal to the Lamb by sending the darkness? What is God doing?

God knows exactly what He is doing. This darkness will bring no relief at all. Let's look at scripture.

> *Arise, shine; for your light has come, and the glory of the Lord has risen upon you. For behold, darkness will cover the earth and deep darkness the peoples; but the Lord will rise upon you and His glory will appear upon you.*
>
> *Isaiah 60:1-2*

There is darkness, and then there is Jesus. Our Savior's first coming was cloaked with humility and meekness. Our Savior's second coming will be an awesome display of power. Why is the Antichrist's kingdom plunged into darkness? Because God wants them to see the full power of His Son descending upon them. Revelation 19:11-14 tells us Jesus is mounted on a horse and descending to the earth along with His saints. In Matthew 24:31 Jesus says He also returns with angels. What does Jesus do?

> *Then the Lord will go forth and fight against those nations, as when He fights on a day of battle. In that day His feet will stand on the Mount of Olives . . . Then the Lord, my God, will come, and all the holy ones with Him! In that day there will be no light; the luminaries will dwindle. For it will be a unique day which is known to the Lord, neither day nor night, but it will come about that at evening time there will be light.*
>
> *Zechariah 14:3-4a, 5b-7*

Here again, we see the dwindling of light, and the Light of the world coming. Let's look at another verse.

> *Before them the earth quakes, the heavens tremble, the sun and the moon grow dark and the stars lose their brightness. The Lord utters His voice before His army; surely His camp is very great, for strong is he who carries out His word. The day of the Lord is indeed great and*

very awesome, and who can endure it?

Joel 2:10-11

The Lord and His army are coming. They are descending on the earth during the fifth bowl to fight on the day of the Lord. The kingdom goes dark and then we see a light. And that light will fight the wicked and annihilate the unrepentant.

In indignation You marched through the earth; in anger You trampled the nations. You went forth for the salvation of Your people, for the salvation of Your anointed. You struck the head of the house of the evil to lay him open from thigh to neck. Selah.

Habakkuk 3:12-13

The consuming fire is coming to consume the ungodly. This is judgment day. The darkness ushers in the light, our Savior, and Armageddon. That is exactly what we see when the next bowl, the sixth bowl, is released.

[12]The sixth angel poured out his bowl on the great river, the Euphrates; and its water was dried up, so that the way would be prepared for the kings from the east. [13]And I saw coming out of the mouth of the dragon and out of the mouth of the beast and out of the mouth of the false prophet, three unclean spirits like frogs; [14]for they are spirits of demons, performing signs, which go out to the kings of the whole world, to gather them together for the war of the great day of God, the Almighty. [15]("Behold, I am coming like a thief. Blessed is the one who stays awake and keeps his clothes, so that he will not walk about naked and men will not see his shame.") [16]And they gathered them together to the place which in Hebrew is called Har-Magedon.

Revelation 16:12-16

The Euphrates river is over 1,500 miles long; it starts in Turkey and continues through Syria and Iraq where it joins the Tigris river in southern Iraq.[2] This is a huge river system and all of the empires spoken of in Daniel were centered around the Euphrates river. This bowl dries up the Euphrates River so the armies of the kings of the east are able to invade the Holy Land.

Who are the kings from the east? Well, all we have to do is look at a map. If we concentrate on the area directly east of the Euphrates River, we see Iran, Georgia, Armenia, Azerbaijan, Kazakhstan, Turkmenistan, Uzbekistan, Tajikistan, Kyrgyzstan, Afghanistan, and Pakistan. If you go farther east, you get to China and India and Russia.

Revelation goes on to say spirits come out of the mouth of the dragon, the beast, and the false prophet, calling for the kings of the world to unite for the battle of Armageddon.

Remember, the trumpets have laid the earth waste, and we saw in the fifth and sixth trumpet armies marching for control of the oil rich lands of the Middle East. Whoever gets the land with the most resources has the best chance of survival. The Antichrist's empire has already taken over the Holy Land, yet other nations want that land too. This is a world war, all centered around Israel. As the world is reeling like a drunkard, the kings of the world will come to fight for control of the Middle East. There is a high probability they will be battling each other when Jesus begins His descent. At the sixth bowl, the dragon, the Antichrist, and the false prophet will swallow their pride and call on the armies surrounding them to join forces and battle God Himself (Revelation 16:13-14).

As the kings from the east ride to Israel, the Euphrates dries up and their armies pour in for battle. This will set the stage for the final battle – Armageddon. This is the great day of God, the Almighty. Jesus in all His radiant glory is descending, the ungodly armies are gathering, and the King will start His threshing.

At that time God will thresh from the River Euphrates to the Brook of Egypt, and you, people of Israel, will be selected grain by grain. At that same time a great trumpet will be blown, calling home the exiles from Assyria. Welcoming home the refugees from Egypt to come and worship God on the holy mountain, Jerusalem.
Isaiah 27:12-13 MSG

According to Isaiah 27:12-13 Jesus will start threshing at the Euphrates, the same river mentioned in the sixth bowl. On that day a great trumpet will be blown and the Lord will be worshiped.

In that day, the Lord will weed out the ungodly from the harvest of believers. He will save His people Israel. He will blow the great trumpet on Yom Kippur (known as the "great trump") and gather those who have come to faith in Him (Matthew 24:31).

Scripture puts a note in the sixth bowl.

"Behold, I am coming like a thief. Blessed is the one who stays awake and keeps his clothes, so that he will not walk about naked and men will not see his shame."

Revelation 16:15

What does this mean? And why is it placed here?

We know Jesus is coming like a thief only to those who are asleep (1 Thessalonians 5:4), but why use the imagery of "keeping your clothes." This same language was used in the letter to the church of Laodicea in chapter three. "I advise you to buy from me . . . white garments so that you may clothe yourself, and that the shame of your nakedness will not be revealed" (Revelation 3:18a). This was the lukewarm church, the church Jesus wanted to spit out of His mouth. If you remember, the high priest of the Jewish people was known to come out of the temple at night and heap burning coals on any guard he caught sleeping. If the burning coals were thrown on you, your clothes would catch fire and you would have to strip and run naked through the streets.

This warning in Revelation 16 is to the sleeping church, to those who are lukewarm, who go through the motions claiming themselves Christian but having no fire and bearing no fruit. It is placed here as a final warning to those who are hiding behind the "once saved always saved" notion. It is put here because this is the final bowl before God's ultimate answer. It is put here to tell us some in the church of Laodicea still exist, right up until Armageddon. They may take the mark to spare their life, but they are sentenced to death (Revelation 19:20). Some will be fooled into thinking they are still saved, and it is to them Jesus will come like a thief.

Tomorrow we see Jesus' answer to the gathering of troops and the arrogance of the false system which has deceived the nations into thinking they could defeat the Savior of the world.

Thought for the day:
Can you believe the arrogance of the armies of the world? They see Jesus in the clouds, yet they still think they can defeat Him. In the darkness, they look to see the light, and they think they can annihilate Him. But isn't that what most of the world does today? We still think we can win our battles against God. We need to realize who God is, and who we are compared to Him. Obviously, the armies of the world don't stand a chance, and neither do we if we want to oppose Him for His will in our lives. The seventh bowl is poured out tomorrow.

1 National Geographic News, September 9, 2004. *Earth's Magnetic Field Is Fading*, Roach, John.

2 Deluxe Then and Now Bible Maps (Torrance, California: Rose Publishing, 2008).
Butler, Trent C. et al.,eds. *Holman Illustrated Bible Dictionary* (Nashville, Tennessee: Holman Bible Publishers, 2003),*1402*.

[17]Then the seventh angel poured out his bowl upon the air, and a loud voice came out of the temple from the throne, saying, "It is done." [18]And there were flashes of lightning and sounds and peals of thunder; and there was a great earthquake, such as there had not been since man came to be upon the earth, so great an earthquake was it, and so mighty. [19]The great city was split into three parts, and the cities of the nations fell. Babylon the great was remembered before God, to give her the cup of the wine of His fierce wrath. [20]And every island fled away, and the mountains were not found. [21]And huge hailstones, about one hundred pounds each, came down from heaven upon men; and men blasphemed God because of the plague of the hail, because its plague was extremely severe.

Revelation 16:17-21

Here it is Christian soldiers – the end. This is the last and final bowl that will fall upon the earth. With this bowl "the kingdom of the world has become the kingdom of our Lord and of His Christ" (Revelation 11:15b). This scripture was quoted in chapter eleven but does not come to its final fulfillment until chapter sixteen. Again, the bowls fall in a span of one day. We will study this today.

The seventh angel poured out his bowl and a loud voice came from the temple. If you recall, at the end of chapter fifteen it says, "And the temple was filled with smoke from the glory of God and from His power; and no one was able to enter the temple until the seven plagues of the seven angels were finished" (Revelation 15:8).

God is the only one in the temple. At the pouring out of the seventh bowl, He declares, "It is done."

Glory, glory, hallelujah! Glory in the highest! It is done.

Again, we see flashes of lightning and sounds and peals of thunder, referring to God's power and wrath. There is a great earthquake, the biggest yet. Recall in chapter six, at the breaking of the sixth seal, we saw a mighty earthquake that moved every mountain and island from its place. This isn't hard to visualize after the earthquake and following tsunami ripped through Japan in 2011, causing it to move from its place and shifting the earth on its axis. There is another earthquake with the breaking of the seventh seal.

Still another earthquake occurs at the second woe, or sixth trumpet judgment where a tenth of the city (Jerusalem) fell and seven thousand people were killed. Then there is another earthquake, which begins with a hailstorm at the seventh trumpet but does not end until the seventh bowl. It is greatest earthquake of them all. Nothing like it has ever happened. "The great city was split into three parts, and the cities of the nations fell, Babylon the great was remembered before God, to give her the cup of the wine of His fierce wrath. And every island fled away and the mountains were not found."

The earth is leveled. The great city of Babylon falls and the cities of the nations fall. Everything is bowing to the King of kings and Lord of lords – cities included.

Now I want you to notice here that even though this is the destruction of the beast – the political empire that has oppressed the Jews and Christians – scripture calls this beast the "great city." Yet, understand that the beast, and the "great city" of Babylon described in this chapter are the totality of the empire collapsing. The end of the bowls equals the end of Babylon.

Every island flees away and the mountains disappear. This is quite possibly a duel reference. Taken at a literal level, the islands will probably be covered with water after the massive earthquake described. They will literally flee away, be gone, washed with the wrath of the Lamb. The mountains are also not found. They will crumble and the earth itself will be flattened. However, mountains in scripture also refer to kingdoms, and this verse comes right after the verse referring to the cities of the nations falling. This scripture is also saying the kingdoms will be destroyed, deferring to the only true leader of the earth, just like it is portrayed in Daniel.

Then the iron, the clay, the bronze, the silver and the gold were crushed all at the same time and became like chaff from the summer threshing floors; and the wind carried them away so that not a trace of them was found. But the stone that struck the statue became a great mountain and filled the whole earth . . . In the days of those kings the God of heaven will set up a kingdom which will never be destroyed, and that kingdom will not be left for another people; it will crush and put an end to all these kingdoms, but it will itself endure forever. Inasmuch as you saw that a stone was cut out of the mountain without hands and that it crushed the iron, the bronze, the clay, the silver and

the gold, the great God has made known to the king what
will take place in the future; so the dream is true and its
interpretation is trustworthy.

Daniel 2:35, 44-45

Remember, Jesus is destroying an area of influence – an area that the iron, bronze, silver, and gold empires occupied. We are destroying an ideology that the iron, bronze, silver, and gold kingdoms personify. The stone, Jesus, destroys them all.

One hundred pound hailstones also descend upon the earth. Remember after the sixth trumpet it was announced they did not repent?

At the seventh bowl, the final judgment, they still blasphemed the name of God. They did not repent. Their punishment is just. We looked at this in an earlier lesson, but let's revisit the seventh trumpet – which announces the bowls – and the seventh bowl.

The Seventh Trumpet
And there were flashes of lightning and sounds and peals
of thunder and an earthquake and a great hailstorm.

Revelation 11:19b

The Seventh Bowl
And there were flashes of lightning and sounds and peals
of thunder; and there was a great earthquake, such as
there had not been since man came to be upon the earth,
so great an earthquake was it, and so mighty . . .and huge
hailstones, about one hundred pounds each, came down
from heaven upon men.

Revelation 16:18, 21a

What starts at the seventh trumpet, ends with the seventh bowl. It is over in one day.

According to Luke 17:26-28, the coming of the Son of Man will be like the days of Noah and the days of Lot. We have already studied that Noah was on the boat for a year and ten days – the exact time frame between one year's Rosh Hashanah and the next year's Yom Kippur. Lot was taken out the same day the wrath fell down. Hum, can we equate the two to our timeline?

Yes, think about it like this. The trumpets are the "year" – the "call to repentance" and the and bowls are the "day" – or the answer to the peoples "unrepentance." Let's look at this on our detailed three and a half year timeline.

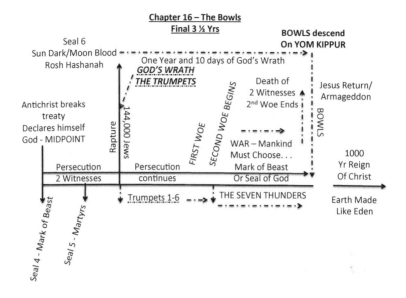

[1]Then one of the seven angels who had the seven bowls came and spoke with me, saying, "Come here, I will show you the judgment of the great harlot who sits on many waters, [2]with whom the kings of the earth committed acts of immorality, and those who dwell on the earth were made drunk with the wine of her immorality." [3]And he carried me away in the Spirit into a wilderness; and I saw a woman sitting on a scarlet beast, full of blasphemous names, having seven heads and ten horns. [4]The woman was clothed in purple and scarlet, and adorned with gold and precious stones and pearls, having in her hand a gold cup full of abominations and of the unclean things of her immorality, [5]and on her forehead a name was written, a mystery, "Babylon the Great, the Mother of Harlots and of the Abominations of the Earth."

Revelation 17:1-5

The Babylon we just saw destroyed in the seventh bowl judgment of chapter sixteen is now explicitly defined in chapters seventeen and eighteen. "The great city was split into three parts, and the cities of the nations fell. Babylon the great was remembered before God, to give her the cup of the wine of His fierce wrath" (Revelation 16:19). We glanced at this chapter briefly when we were defining the heads of the beast in chapter thirteen.

First we see one of the seven angels who had the seven bowls come and speak to John. The translation is important here because of the obvious question: does the angel still have the bowl and its contents? Or is the angel coming to John after the bowl has been poured out on the earth? Remember, after the trumpet judgments there was a pause as an angel told John to "prophesy again." The chapters that followed clarified things transpiring during both the seal and the trumpet judgments. But what we really need to understand is that this "interlude" is not really an interlude at all.

Let's say you taste my killer chocolate chip cookies. You love them and ask for the recipe. What do I do? Do I say, "you take a cup of butter and cream it, then you add a cup of sugar and cream it, then a cup of brown sugar and cream it. . . " No, I would not. First I would give you the ingredients: a cup of butter, a cup of sugar, a cup of brown sugar, two eggs . . . After I gave you the ingredients or basic structure, then I would give you the specific details or directions. This is exactly what is happening in Revelation, both with the details after the trumpets, and with the details after the bowls. Jesus gives John a quick "bullet point" of the seals and trumpets (chapter 6-9), then He goes back and clarifies other details transpiring during those judgments (chapter 11-15). This is exactly what we see happening in chapter seventeen: a clarification of additional events occurring during the seals, trumpets, and bowls.

So, when does the angel approach John?

According to the Jewish Bible translated by David H. Stern,[1] the interpretation of the Greek text is: "Then came one of the angels with the seven bowls; and he said to me, 'Come, I will show you the judgment of the great whore who is sitting by many waters.'" This says "with" the seven bowls, indicating this angel still had his bowl with him. Could this mean the judgment of this harlot transpired before the bowl judgments are poured out? That is exactly what it sounds like and we will see this illustrated at the end of chapter seventeen.

So, the bowl is still in the angel's hands, yet to be poured out. Why then, is this chapter placed here and not earlier in Revelation?

This chapter has to be placed after the initial "list of ingredients" of the bowls because of one very important reason: Babylon is not only a city, it is also an empire, it is not only an empire, but also an ideology. Yes, a city will be destroyed, but the totality of what Babylon represents and the entire region of Babylon will not be destroyed until Jesus returns. Both the empire and the ideology will ultimately be destroyed at the end of the bowls during the battle of Armageddon. However, as we will learn in this chapter, part of the religious system will be destroyed sometime earlier in the final seven years, yet its ultimate demise will culminate with the final battle. This will become clearer as we move further into our study. For now, let's meet the harlot.

She contrasts with the woman we met in chapter twelve. The woman in chapter twelve represented Israel and the one true religion. As stated when we studied chapter fourteen, when you read about a harlot in scripture, she is either a real prostitute or represents a people who worship false gods. In other words, a harlot is a false system of worship or idolatry.

> *For you shall not worship any other god, for the Lord, whose name is Jealous, is a jealous God – otherwise you might make a covenant with the inhabitants of the land and they would play the harlot with their gods and sacrifice to their gods, and someone might invite you to eat of his sacrifice, and you might take some of his daughters for your sons, and his daughters might play the harlot with their gods and cause your sons also to play the harlot with their gods.*
>
> *Exodus 34:14-16*

Thus the harlot represents false religion and idolatry. She is sitting on a beast. This woman is seen riding the beast from the sea, or the final political system that will arise in the last days (Revelation 13). We know this because the beast is described as having blasphemous names, the same description bestowed on the beast from the sea in chapter thirteen. This woman is controlling the beast because she is riding it. If we are right in our assumption that the beast is the Turkish Ottoman empire revived, she would be Islam. Islam is controlling the political empire that is rising out of the sea. This makes complete sense when we study the Middle East. Many of the leaders there do not believe in the separation of church and state. Their religion is not divorceable from the political climate. The harlot is the Islamic political climate. Laws are made based on the Qur'an and other Islamic holy books.

This harlot sits on "many waters." We have learned in our study that water in scripture represents the Gentile nations where the beast will emerge. She sits on many of them. In fact she sits on the beast himself. The kings of the earth have committed acts of immorality with her and have drunk the wine of her immorality. What does this beast, this woman, have that other nations covet? Oil! The nations of the world would do anything for her oil, even buy into her ideology. They will appease her, mollify her, in order to obtain her oil. And they are drunk with it.

Notice John is taken to the wilderness in order to see the woman on the beast. The word "wilderness" can also be translated "desert." And what do we think of when we think of the Middle East: barren desert land. If you are one that still clings to the Roman/European beast theory, you have to ask yourself why the final setting is described as a wilderness or desert in chapter seventeen. Rome doesn't fit the equation. The Middle East does.

Listen to this scripture:

> *And Babylon, the beauty of the kingdoms, the glory of the Chaldeans' pride, will be as when God overthrew Sodom and Gomorrah. It will never be inhabited or lived in from generation to generation; nor will the Arab pitch his tent there, nor will shepherds make their flocks lie down there. But desert creatures will lie down there, and their houses will be full of owls; ostriches also will live there and shaggy goats will frolic there. Hyenas will howl in their fortified towers and jackals in their luxurious palaces. Her fateful time also will soon come and her days will not be prolonged.*
> *Isaiah 13:19-22*

This scripture describes a sudden destruction of Babylon and has never been fulfilled. Historically, the city of Babylon continued to be an important city even after its conquest. It has since gradually deteriorated due to the forces of nature.[2] Babylon's sudden destruction will be fulfilled when Jesus returns and crushes the Babylon of the future, the harlot's Babylon. We will study more about the harlot tomorrow.

Thought for the day:
Today, you met the harlot. She cannot be divorced from the political system she rides. Tomorrow, you will see the world has been seduced by her. They have accepted her. They have compromised for her. They have brushed her wickedness under the rug. Do you see this happening today? Where have you almost accepted her?

1 Stern, David H. Complete Jewish Bible (Clarksville, Maryland: Jewish New Testament Publications, Inc., 1998).

2 Walvoord, John F. *Every Prophecy of the Bible* (Colorado Springs, Colorado: Chariot Victor Publishing, 1999), 99.

[4]The woman was clothed in purple and scarlet, and adorned with gold and precious stones and pearls, having in her hand a gold cup full of abominations and of the unclean things of her immorality, [5]and on her forehead a name was written, a mystery, "Babylon the Great, the Mother of Harlots and of the abominations of the earth." [6]And I saw the woman drunk with the blood of the saints, and with the blood of the witnesses of Jesus. When I saw her, I wondered greatly. [7]And the angel said to me, "Why do you wonder? I will tell you the mystery of the woman and of the beast that carries her, which has the seven heads and the ten horns. [8]The beast that you saw was, and is not, and is about to come up out of the abyss and go to destruction. And those who dwell on the earth, whose name has not been written in the book of life from the foundation of the world, will wonder when they see the beast, that he was and is not and will come. [9]Here is the mind which has wisdom. The seven heads are seven mountains on which the woman sits, [10]and they are seven kings; five have fallen, one is, the other has not yet come; and when he comes, he must remain a little while. [11]The beast which was and is not, is himself also an eighth and is one of the seven, and he goes to destruction.

Revelation 17:4-11

Yesterday we learned that the harlot (or the false religion) was riding the beast (or the final political empire). Let's dig deeper.

The woman is clothed in purple and scarlet, and adorned with gold and precious stones and pearls, symbolic of not only religious attire, but also beauty. Yet, she is an adulteress, a deceiver, and is an abomination to God. She has in her hand a golden cup, which should remind us of the cup our Lord used at the last supper. As Jesus offers the cup of the covenant (Matthew 26:28) to those who believe in His name, this woman offers her cup of abominations and tells the world to drink her ideology. She claims to have an answer and a way to God, but she lies. If you drink her cup, you will be condemned. If you buy into her false beauty, you will miss the true Messiah when He returns.

Here is an end time prophecy that describes Jesus gathering all the nations for judgment (Revelation 19:19):

"I will gather all the nations and bring them down to the valley of Jehoshaphat. Then I will enter into judgment with them there on behalf of My people and My inheritance, Israel, whom they have scattered among the nations; and they have divided up My land. They have also cast lots for My people, traded a boy for a harlot and sold a girl for wine that they may drink."

Joel 3:2-3

He judges them on how they treated the nation of Israel. He judges them for dividing up His land. What are we trying to do today? Give Israeli land to the Palestinians for peace. Dividing Israel is contrary to the will of the Lord. This is serious, faithful friends. The way we treat Israel matters to our Lord. In Joel, the people are trading their souls, their children, so that they may drink. Drink what? Her oil, and at the same time, her ideology. In order to "buy or sell" you have to claim the mark (13:17); so in order to buy or sell the nations are bowing to the beast and the harlot's ideology, idolatry, and lies.

On her forehead was a name: Babylon the Great, the Mother of Harlots and of the abominations of the earth. Recall, the beast also has blasphemous names. This woman's name is central to understanding the blasphemy of the beast.

We know a harlot in scripture represents false religions and the worship of false gods. This woman is the mother of harlots. This doesn't mean she has birthed every false religious system, but in fact she is the mother load of them all! This will be the most expansive and the most abusive system of all time. And she is clothed in mystery. I believe this means many will be unable to recognize her deception. They will look at her and wonder what all the fuss is about. They will accept her as a true religion when she is the anti-Christ religion the prophets warned us about thousands of years ago. The world will be deceived.

Think about prevailing Christian thought today. Most believe the world will be dominated by one religion in the future – one in which will bring about the mark of the beast. But most believe it will be something new. Not so. The beast has been around for over a thousand years. It is coming into our countries. It is trying to take over our courts. It is instilling doubts and fears in our young people. We are unprepared. We have bought into false thinking. We are blind.

In Revelation 9:2, we saw locusts coming up out of the pit, bringing with them a smoke that darkens the day.

God will send upon them a deluding influence so that they will believe what is false.

2 Thessalonians 2:11

The harlot is a big part of that deception. She is also identified as Babylon. In scripture, Babylon is associated with everything evil. Babylon was not only a city; it was also an empire, stretching thousands of miles. Babylon was not only a religion; it was also a way of life. Babylon represents everything apart from God. This woman riding the beast is "Mystery Babylon," and because she is a mystery, scripture is stating that the exact location of this Babylon may not be clear. Let's dig deeper.

The woman whom you saw is the great city, which reigns over the kings of the earth.

Revelation 17:18

The woman is not only a religion, she is also a city. We know Babylon will be destroyed at the time of the end, but we also know that Babylon was not only a city, but also an empire, an ideology, and a religion. So is this "city" the ancient city of Babylon that was built on the Euphrates River in modern day Iraq? Many scholars think so. It is interesting to note that Saddam Hussein was restoring the ancient city of Babylon before he was captured in 2003.

Yet, scripture calls her a mystery. Because scripture calls this city a "mystery" I tend to believe that this is probably not the ancient city of Babylon, but a city in current times that will be the beacon of the harlot in the future. There will be a religious hub and a political hub and the two do not necessarily have to be the same place. If the woman is religious Islam riding the Islamic empire, the city associated with her could be Mecca, in Saudi Arabia. Mecca is the city Muslims face five times a day to offer their daily prayers. Let's explore this possibility a little further.

Now when Daniel knew that the document was signed, he entered his house (now in his roof chamber he had windows open toward Jerusalem); and he continued kneeling on his knees three times a day, praying and

giving thanks before his God, as he had been doing
previously.

Satan wants to counterfeit every thing God does. When the Jews went into exile, they faced Jerusalem to pray. Islam counterfeits that reverence by commanding its followers to face Mecca. Could the city of the harlot be Mecca? Perhaps.

There is also a final possibility we must consider. The religion of Islam could try to dominate the world by combining their religion with others. This would answer the world's "cry" for global unity. Then the "city" the scriptures describe could be any city chosen by world leaders to lead the religious charge. It could be ancient Babylon, Mecca, Rome, or any other prominent city.

But let me reiterate, Babylon was the head of gold in the statue depicted in Daniel chapter two. Babylon started a reign in the Holy Land of complete pagan control. Since Babylon, Israel only claimed independence between 167BC and 63 BC,[1] and did not become what we know today until 1948. Israel will not gain true independence from foreign tyranny until Jesus returns to claim her. The harlot is a false religion (Islam) that resides in this same area (the Middle East). Although the harlot has never been killed, the political system was slain in 1924. Now the political system (Turkish-Ottoman Empire) is reviving; the harlot is about to mount the beast, dominate the Middle East and strive for global control.

This woman was drunk with the blood of the saints. We know after the midpoint of the final seven years, when the Antichrist will take his seat in the temple and declare himself God, there will be a mass persecution of Christians and Jews. Let's have a recap of this, shall we?

When the Lamb broke the fifth seal, I saw underneath the
altar the souls of those who had been slain because of the
word of God, and because of the testimony which they had
maintained.

And the serpent poured water like a river out of his mouth
after the woman [ISRAEL], so that he might cause her to
be swept away with the flood. But the earth helped the
woman, and the earth opened its mouth and drank up the
river which the dragon poured out of his mouth. So the

309

dragon was enraged with the woman, and went off to make war with the rest of her children, who keep the commandments of God and hold to the testimony of Jesus.

Revelation 12:15-17, explanation added

And he [FALSE PROPHET] provides that no one will be able to buy or to sell, except the one who has the mark, either the name of the beast or the number of his name.

Revelation 13:17, explanation added

If anyone is destined for captivity, to captivity he goes; if anyone kills with the sword, with the sword he must be killed. Here is the perseverance and the faith of the saints.

Revelation 13:10

When John saw the woman riding the beast, he wondered greatly, but the angel attending him asked why he wondered at all. To the angel, this was a simple vision, one which John should be able to understand, one which we should be able to understand. The angel then starts to explain the vision.

We have already used some of the angel's explanation in our study of chapter thirteen. Let's go deeper.

We learned the seven heads of the beast represent the seven kingdoms that have taken over Israel: Egypt, Assyria, Babylon, Medo-Persia, Greece, Rome, and the Turkish Ottoman Empire. We said Rome, although one of the heads, was not represented in Daniel's statue because it did not take over the entire Middle East. It did not encompass the system that would emerge in the last days.

We have already looked at this in chapter thirteen, but it is critical to understanding the beast. So let's look at it again.

The beast that you saw was, and is not, and is about to come up out of the abyss and go to destruction. And those who dwell on the earth, whose name has not been written in the book of life from the foundation of the world, will wonder when they see the beast, that he was and is not and will come.

Revelation 17:8

The beast John sees "was." This is understandable when you realize the beast and its heads represent kingdoms. The beast is past

310

tense. It has been alive for centuries. Five of the heads previously "were" the beast: Egypt, Assyria, Babylon, Medo-Persia and Greece. The area of their kingdoms will once again unite in the last days to persecute the Jews. Then the angel tells John, the beast "is not." The Roman Empire, the empire alive in John's day, is not the beast of Revelation 13. Why? It didn't encompass the land area of the other five empires that had come before. Although it is a "head" or "kingdom" that conquered Israel, Rome is in no way the final governmental system of the Antichrist. Rome even established Christianity as a state religion. Amazing. Let's go further.

The angel then tells John the beast is about to come up. What came up after the Roman Empire? The Turkish-Ottoman Empire. The beast (as the seventh head) is about to come up and go to destruction because this is the empire Jesus, our Lord and Savior, will annihilate. It will be the final system that goes to its destruction. Glory Hallelujah!

The angel emphasizes this again when he says, "And those who dwell on the earth, whose name has not been written in the book of life from the foundation of the world, will wonder when they see the beast, that he was and is not and will come." Again, the beast is past (Egypt, Assyria, Babylon, Medo-Persia, Greece) and is not (Rome) and will come (Turkish Ottoman Empire). Those whose names have not been written in the book of life will wonder when they see the beast. Like we have discussed before, many believe there are two books of life: one book in which names are written at the time of birth; the other in which names are written when they come to faith. This scripture tells me there is only one book, and some people have not been written in it. Only those under the covenant (Jews and professed Christians) are written therein. And yes, you can be blotted out when you break the covenant (Jews who do not come to faith in their Messiah and Christians who turn from Him, see Revelation 3:5).

The next few verses we discussed in chapter thirteen. This is where the heads are defined as mountains or kingdoms. It also says the mountains are seven kings, emphasizing that the mountains are in fact kingdoms.

To clarify, the five that have fallen are Egypt, Assyria, Babylon, Medo-Persia, and Greece. Rome is the kingdom that existed in John's day, or the "is" of Revelation 17:8. The one who has not yet come is the Turkish Ottoman Empire. This Islamic empire remains for a little while because it will be "slain" or abolished before rising again (Revelation 13:3).

The beast which was and is not, is himself also an eighth and is one of the seven, and he goes to destruction.

Revelation 17:11

This scripture tells us that there will be a total of eight kingdoms that form the beast's heads, but the eighth kingdom is of the seven. In other words, the eighth is a different kingdom, yet the same kingdom as one of the seven. How can this be?

I saw one of the heads as if it had been slain and his fatal wound was healed.

Revelation 13:3a

One of the heads was slain. This is the head that will rise again according to Revelation 17:11. According to Revelation 17:8 it is the last kingdom, or the seventh head, that will "go to destruction." We have learned from our study that the last kingdom to rule the Holy Land was the Turkish-Ottoman Empire. It was slain in 1924 but it will rise again. Also, the ten horns of Daniel rise from the iron kingdom which corresponds to the Turkish-Ottoman Empire and Revelation 13.

Tomorrow we will look at the horns in greater detail. Good work today. We have come a long way together. I hope your journey so far has been blessed (Revelation 1:3).

Thought for the day:
On the next page you will see the beast depicted by a seven-headed beast. You will see one of those heads slain, but the eighth is rising out of the seven – this is the revived empire of the end. From this head grows the ten horns. This beast is coming for every single person that is alive today. It wants your faith. Don't let the beast take it.

1 Butler, Trent C. et al.,eds. *Holman Illustrated Bible Dictionary* (Nashville, Tennessee: Holman Bible Publishers, 2003), 850.

[12]The ten horns which you saw are ten kings who have not yet received a kingdom, but they receive authority as kings with the beast for one hour. [13]These have one purpose, and they give their power and authority to the beast. [14]These will wage war against the Lamb, and the Lamb will overcome them, because He is Lord of lords and King of kings, and those who are with Him are the called and chosen and faithful. [15]And he said to me, "The waters which you saw where the harlot sits, are peoples and multitudes and nations and tongues. [16]And the ten horns which you saw, and the beast, these will hate the harlot and will make her desolate and naked, and will eat her flesh and will burn her up with fire. [17]For God has put it in their hearts to execute His purpose by having a common purpose, and by giving their kingdom to the beast, until the words of God will be fulfilled. [18]The woman whom you saw is the great city, which reigns over the kings of the earth.

Revelation 17:12-18

Yesterday we went over the beast with greater detail. Today we are going to talk about the horns of the beast. The angel tells John the ten horns are ten kings who have not yet received a kingdom. This is due to the fact the ten horns correspond to the end time political leadership in Revelation, the eighth kingdom, or the resurrected seventh head (Turkish Ottoman Empire). Are we confused yet? Another way to say it is this: those ten horns will arise when the final kingdom is reborn in the end times. The ten horns will be ten kings or a cabinet of ten rulers that preside over the final political system. Remember, the Turkish Ottoman Empire was disbanded in 1924 (appeared to be slain) but is now reorganizing and will be completely revived before Jesus returns. What about the Antichrist, you ask? Good question. Scripture goes on to say that the ten horns will receive authority with the beast, or the Antichrist leading the beast, for one hour.

So, the Antichrist is not one of the ten, he is over the ten, leading the beast. Do we see this clarified in scripture? Yes, we do.

After this I kept looking in the night visions, and behold, a fourth beast, dreadful and terrifying and extremely

314

strong; and it had large iron teeth. It devoured and crushed and trampled down the remainder with its feet; and it was different from all the beasts that were before it, and it had ten horns. While I was contemplating the horns, behold, another horn, a little one, came up among them and three of the first horns were pulled out by the roots before it; and behold, this horn possessed eyes like the eyes of a man and a mouth uttering great boasts.

Daniel 7:7-8

This scripture is talking about the "mystery kingdom" of Daniel and our beast of Revelation. The beast has ten horns at first, but then an eleventh grows up after them and three of the first horns are "pulled out." The eleventh horn, or the "little horn" is extremely arrogant. Let's study the horns even further.

Then I desired to know the exact meaning of the fourth beast, which was different from all the others, exceedingly dreadful, with its teeth of iron and its claws of bronze, and which devoured, crushed and trampled down the remainder with its feet, and the meaning of the ten horns that were on its head and the other horn which came up, and before which three of them fell, namely, that horn which had eyes and a mouth uttering great boasts and which was larger in appearance than its associates. I kept looking, and that horn was waging war with the saints and overpowering them until the Ancient of Days came and judgment was passed in favor of the saints of the Highest One, and the time arrived when the saints took possession of the kingdom. Thus he said: "The fourth beast will be a fourth kingdom on the earth, which will be different from all the other kingdoms and will devour the whole earth and tread it down and crush it. As for the ten horns, out of this kingdom ten kings will arise; and another will arise after them, and he will be different from the previous ones and will subdue three kings. He will speak out against the Most High and wear down the saints of the Highest One, and he will intend to make alterations in times and in law; and they will be given into his hand for a time, times, and half a time.

Daniel 7:19-25

315

So, the ten kings will come first, forming the beast, and then another horn, who will be the Antichrist, will come and subdue three of the ten. This is the horn that will wage war with the saints and persecute them. He will blaspheme God and try to change the times and the law (Daniel 7:25). Authority will be given him for three and one half years (a time, a times, and half a time). This persecution will logically start at the midpoint of our seven-year timeline when the Antichrist "takes his seat in the temple of God, displaying himself as being God" (2 Thessalonians 2:4). But the Ancient of Days will come, our Savior, and destroy the beast and the horns.

Let me pause here and mention the above prophecy that states he will "intend to make alterations in times and in law." Does this fit with the Islam theory? What are they doing in our courts today? Arguing that they need to be tried by Sharia Law. Great Britain already has Sharia law for civil cases. And note, Islam doesn't go by the Gregorian calendar like most of the world; they have their own set calendar. Does this fit the equation? Well, you decide.

What three horns will the little horn, or the Antichrist, subdue? This is not clear although the following verse might give us a clue.

> *He will also enter the Beautiful Land, and many countries will fall; but these will be rescued out of his hand: Edom, Moab and the foremost of the sons of Ammon. Then he will stretch out his hand against other countries, and the land of Egypt will not escape. But he will gain control over the hidden treasures of gold and silver and over all the precious things of Egypt; and Libyans and Ethiopians will follow at his heels.*
>
> *Daniel 11:41-43*

As we discussed earlier, Edom, Moab and the foremost sons of Ammon is referring to Jordon, and this is exactly where Petra is located, where most scholars believe the Jews will flee. Remember, in Revelation chapter 12 it says that the woman, Israel, will escape the dragon, and the dragon will go in search of the rest of her offspring (Christians). Jordan will evade the Antichrist's dominion because God will be protecting the Jewish remnant. But Egypt, Libya and Ethiopia (modern day Sudan) will follow at his heels. Perhaps these are the three horns the Antichrist will subdue? Only time will tell.

Scripture goes on to say that the horns give their power to the beast (the political kingdom with the Antichrist, or little horn, leading them). This is their sole purpose, to give their power to the beast. Scripture says they will give their power to the beast "for one hour." Is this a literal hour or does it mean a short period of time? To understand this, we must look at other places in the New Testament where the word "hour" is used.

The Greek word "hora" translated "hour" here can literally mean an hour or a certain set moment such as in Revelation 9:15 or Matthew 8:13. Now, look at the following verses that use the word "hora" and see how it is translated.

He was the lamp that was burning and was shining and you were willing to rejoice for a while (hora) in his light.
John 5:35

For though I caused you sorrow by my letter, I do not regret it; though I did regret it – for I see that that letter caused you sorrow, though only for a while (hora).
2 Corinthians 7:8

So, the "one hour" reference can also mean a short period of time or a while, and I believe this is the better translation of the scripture. Scripture goes on to say that the horns give their power to the beast (the political kingdom with the Antichrist, or little horn, leading them). This is their sole purpose, to give their power to the beast. The ten horns and the Antichrist will be given authority to rule for a certain time – set by God. They will not be allowed to continue indefinitely. Jesus, the Messiah, will make sure of that. God has forewarned us of their rule, but their time is set. The horns will wage war with the Lamb, but we all know the outcome. Jesus will be victorious.

Scripture then describes what the "many waters" mean in which the harlot sits: peoples and multitudes and nations and tongues. This is consistent with the "Gentile" system she will emerge from.

Next we see a twist in the story, and it may seem contradictory.

And the ten horns which you saw, and the beast, these will hate the harlot and will make her desolate and naked, and will eat her flesh and will burn her up with fire.
Revelation 17:16

317

What?

Didn't we just say that the harlot is the religious system driving the beastly political system? If this is, in fact, Islam, is scripture saying that the political system will destroy the religion of Islam? That doesn't make too much sense does it? Let's dig deeper.

If we look in verse 18, scripture tells us "the woman whom you saw is the great city, which reigns over the kings of the earth." We looked at this yesterday. The woman is both a religion (Revelation 17:4) and a city (Revelation 17:18). Just like you cannot divorce Judaism from Jerusalem, you cannot divorce the harlot from her city.

At the end of the trumpets we saw two armies. The first, we said, was the army of the Antichrist. The second was the armies of the world. These armies are marching to Israel. Scripture has told us that God will gather the armies of the world together in Israel. First, he will bring out the armies of the Antichrist.

> *I will turn you about and put hooks into your jaws, and I will bring you out, and all your army, horses and horsemen, all of them splendidly attired, a great company with buckler and shield, all of them wielding swords.*
> *Ezekiel 38:4*

Then we see the rest of the world gathering.

> *His [JESUS] breath is like an overflowing torrent, which reaches to the neck, to shake the nations back and forth in a sieve, and to put in the jaws of the peoples the bridle which leads to ruin.*
> *Isaiah 30:28, explanation added*

Why is Jesus putting a bridle in the nations' jaws? Why is He putting hooks in their jaws? To lead them to Armageddon for judgment! He is drawing them out, hooking them, and reeling them in. Hallelujah!

> *I will gather all the nations and bring them down to the valley of Jehoshaphat. Then I will enter into judgment with them there on behalf of My people and My inheritance, Israel, whom they have scattered among the nations; and they have divided up my land.*
> *Joel 3:2*

The city the harlot represents could be destroyed during the gathering of armies, when the world is battling for control of the Middle Eastern oil reserves. This would mean that she would be destroyed during the fifth or sixth trumpet judgment. If the harlot's city is Mecca, the trumpet judgments and gathering of the armies seem like a likely place for her destruction. Some might question why even consider destroying an Islamic city if the heart of the harlot is in fact Islam. We must remember, Saudi Arabia has always been "friendly" to the west and the rest of the Middle East does not care for her "loyalties."

Walid Shoebat, who believes Mecca could be the harlot's city says this:

"Yet when it comes to Mecca, plenty of Muslims have attacked the city before . . . And as recently as 2003, three al-Qaeda militants blew themselves up during an attack in Mecca. The idea of Muslims attacking Mecca or Saudi Arabia is far from impossible."[1]

There are extreme tensions in the Middle East between Sunni and Shiite sects. They disagree and wage war continuously. No matter how much they cooperate, they go together like oil and water. Let's remind ourselves of how this final empire holds together. Remember scripture is telling us the seventh head is revived, meaning it will be the "same" kingdom but because it exists in a different point in time, it becomes the eighth head, the ten horns, and the ten toes of Daniel.

It will be a divided kingdom . . . They will not adhere to one another.
Daniel 2:41, 43 exerts

However, let's consider the second possibility. What if the city of the harlot isn't Mecca, but another city entirely? If the Antichrist and his followers "compromised" their religion in any way and "merged" it with other popular religions in order to become a dominate force, then at the midpoint, when the Antichrist takes his seat in the temple, the harlot will be hated. Why? Because they will want fundamental Islam, not a watered down version. When the Antichrist takes his seat in the temple of God, displaying himself as god, his mask is off (2 Thessalonians 2:4). They will burn the city of the harlot and strive for global dominion. In other words, the religious center of the harlot could be destroyed as early as the midpoint of the final seven years, when peace is no longer a pretense and global dominion is the name of the day.

In either case, the religious center of the harlot will fall. Because of the expansive control of the Antichrist (due to his control of the oil-rich Middle East) he has the entire world at his mercy. The revolt will be of global proportions, never before seen. The armies of the world will come together in a final conflict – yet instead of battling each other, they will see the Lord of lords descending with the clouds. More on this in chapter nineteen. For now, realize, the armies will unite, the harlot will fall, and the world will be holding its breath to see who will gain control.

Little do they know no man will claim the victory. The Lion of the tribe of Judah will roar and when He roars the world will fall to its knees. Amen and amen, come quickly, Lord Jesus!

Thought for the day:
Sharia law is already in England. It has also been used in America's courts for certain cases. Do you think it will be long until our courts accept it? The beast is already among us, and we are doing little about it. Babylon is judged tomorrow.

1 Shoebat, Walid, written with Joel Richardson. *God's War on Terror* (Top Executive Media, 2008), 407.

DAY FORTY-NINE
REVELATION 18:1-24
BABYLON IS FALLEN

[1]After these things I saw another angel coming down from heaven, having great authority, and the earth was illuminated with his glory. [2]And he cried out with a mighty voice, saying, "Fallen, fallen is Babylon the great! She has become a dwelling place of demons and a prison of every unclean spirit, and a prison of every unclean and hateful bird. [3]For all the nations have drunk of the wine of the passion of her immorality, and the kings of the earth have committed acts of immorality with her, and the merchants of the earth have become rich by the wealth of her sensuality." [4]I heard another voice from heaven, saying, "Come out of her, my people, so that you will not participate in her sins and receive of her plagues; [5]for her sins have piled up as high as heaven, and God has remembered her iniquities. [6]Pay her back even as she has paid, and give back to her double according to her deeds; in the cup which she has mixed, mix twice as much for her. [7]To the degree that she glorified herself and lived sensuously, to the same degree give her torment and mourning; for she says in her heart, 'I sit as a queen and I am not a widow, and will never see mourning.' [8]For this reason in one day her plagues will come, pestilence and mourning and famine, and she will be burned up with fire; for the Lord God who judges her is strong."

Revelation 18:1-8

We march onward today with the last of Babylon. First, we see an angel coming down from heaven announcing Babylon's fall. This angel is described as "another angel" because it is not one of the angels who have the bowls.

Chapter 17 just announced that the city the harlot represents will fall. In chapter 18 we realize the city's destruction will ultimately be the beginning of the end of the political empire as well. And when Babylon falls, when the harlot is cast from her seat, the earth will mourn. Because the nations have drunk her wine, they are allowing her religion to go unchecked. They are accepting her ideology in order to charm her into a relationship, but in actuality she is the one seducing the nations into complacency.

Babylon is described as being a dwelling place of demons, a prison of every unclean spirit, and every unclean and hateful bird.

321

Babylon is filled with the filth of the Antichrist's political and religious ideology. Those in Babylon who have bought the ideology are unclean. This is consistent with what will happen to Babylon based on biblical prophecy.

"I will also make it a possession for the hedgehog and swamps of water, and I will sweep it with the broom of destruction," declares the Lord of hosts.

Isaiah 14:23

It will never be inhabited or lived in from generation to generation; nor will the Arab pitch his tent there, nor will shepherds make their flocks lie down there. But desert creatures will lie down there, and their houses will be full of owls; ostriches also will live there, and shaggy goats will frolic there. Hyenas will howl in their fortified towers and jackals in their luxurious palaces. Her fateful time also will soon come and her days will not be prolonged.

Isaiah 13:20-24

The owl and the ostrich are unclean animals to the Jew (Leviticus 11:16) and the shaggy goat is associated with demons in Leviticus 17:7. The Babylonian system is totally and completely unclean. Why? Because the Babylonian territory of Revelation will encompass the Babylonian territory of the past. The Arab will never again pitch his tent there.

It is emphasized again that the nations have drunk her wine (religion) and the kings of the earth have courted her because of her wealth (oil). They are getting drunk from her both because they are allowing her ideology to infiltrate their nations and because they are dependent on her oil.

A voice from heaven calls God's people from Babylon (remember we are in a review period; some of God's people are still on earth and others might repent and turn to Him). This is another reason her destruction has to begin sooner than Armageddon. God is calling out His people, urging them to flee. This cry is mirrored in Jeremiah.

Flee from the midst of Babylon, and each of you save his life! Do not be destroyed in her punishment, for this is the Lord's time of vengeance; He is going to render recompense to her. Babylon has been a golden cup in the hand of the Lord, intoxicating all the earth. The nations have drunk of her wine; therefore the nations are going mad.

Jeremiah 51:6-7

God says, "Flee! Judgment will be swift!" God has seen her sins and has remembered her iniquities. Remember, the beginning of Babylon's destruction starts at the beginning of God's wrath (the trumpets) and continues until Jesus returns at Armageddon (the bowls). This scripture tells us that judgment will be swift – its final destruction will come about in one day. This passage is about the bowl judgments. God is calling the redeemable from Babylon before the bowls fall so His people can escape its destruction. Just like Babylon, the earth's destruction begins with the trumpets and ends with the final descent of Christ in the bowls. Israel, however, will not meet a complete destruction.

"For I am with you and will save you," says the Lord. "I will completely destroy the nations where I have scattered you, but I will not completely destroy you. I will discipline you, but with justice; I cannot let you go unpunished."

Jeremiah 30:11

Babylon's sins are piled up as high as heaven. This reminds us of the first Babylon, the tower of Babel, and the attempt to build the tower to the heavens (Genesis 11). This time, Babylon has succeeded, but it isn't a physical structure they have built. It is their iniquity that has reached heaven. She has repeatedly denied God and blasphemed His holy name (Revelation 17:3).

The voice continues to say, "Pay her back even as she has paid, and give back to her double according to her deeds; in the cup which she has mixed, mix twice as much for her. To the degree that she glorified herself and lived sensuously, to the same degree give her torment and mourning." Again, God is saying, "Vengeance is mine, I will repay, says the Lord" (Romans 12:19). There is nothing that has gone unnoticed by God. The Babylon (or evil) that has wronged God's people will get its just due. God is a loving God. That means He is also a just God (Psalm 89:14). He cannot allow evil to go unchecked.

The scripture about Babylon tells us she will be repaid double for her deeds. This is a comforting scripture. Sometimes the wrongs done to us are irreparable. You cannot compensate someone for the death of a loved one, or the rape of a child, or the abuse of a friend. But God says He will pay Babylon back double. Praise the Lord! Babylon thinks she sits as queen and will never see mourning. Think again, Babylon. A similar prophecy is found in Isaiah 47.

> *"Come down and sit in the dust, O virgin daughter of Babylon; sit on the ground without a throne, O daughter of the Chaldeans! For you shall no longer be called tender and delicate . . . Your nakedness will be uncovered, your shame also will be exposed; I will take vengeance and will not spare a man." Our Redeemer, the Lord of hosts is His name, The Holy One of Israel. "Sit silently, and go into darkness, O daughter of the Chaldeans, for you will no longer be called the queen of kingdoms . . . Now, then, hear this, you sensual one, who dwells securely, who says in your heart, 'I am, and there is no one besides me. I will not sit as a widow, nor know loss of children.' But these two things will come on you suddenly in one day; loss of children and widowhood. They will come on you in full measure in spite of your many sorceries, in spite of the great power of your spells."*
>
> *Isaiah 47:1, 3-5, 8-9*

This scripture says, "in one day" and mirrors the "in one day" in Revelation 18:8. Remember, Babylon is both a city and a territory, a religion and an ideology. Its hub is the Euphrates River, yet it spans the entire Middle East. You could even argue her influence has reached the entire world. We have just witnessed the harlot's fate (as a city) in chapter 17 and in chapter 18 we see the lamentation for that city, but Babylon is far more than a city – it is an entire political and social system. When Jesus returns during the bowls, this is the fate of the entire Babylonian sphere of influence.

Babylon will be burned suddenly, in one day, and there will be a lament across the world.

[9]"And the kings of the earth, who committed acts of immorality and lived sensuously with her, will weep and lament over her when they see the smoke of her burning, [10]standing at a distance because of the fear of her torment, saying, 'Woe, woe, the great

city, Babylon, the strong city! For in one hour your judgment has come.' [11]And the merchants of the earth weep and mourn over her, because no one buys their cargoes any more – [12]cargoes of gold and silver and precious stones and pearls and fine linen and purple and silk and scarlet, and every kind of citron wood and every article of ivory and every article made from very costly wood and bronze and iron and marble, [13]and cinnamon and spice and incense and perfume and frankincense and wine and olive oil and fine flour and wheat and cattle and sheep, and cargoes of horses and chariots and slaves and human lives. [14]The fruit you long for has gone from you, and all things that were luxurious and splendid have passed away from you and men will no longer find them. [15]The merchants of these things, who became rich from her, will stand at a distance because of the fear of her torment, weeping and mourning, [16]saying, 'Woe, woe, the great city, she who was clothed in fine linen and purple and scarlet, and adorned with gold and precious stones and pearls; [17]for in one hour such great wealth has been laid waste!' And every shipmaster and every passenger and sailor, and as many as make their living by the sea, stood at a distance, [18]and were crying out as they saw the smoke of her burning, saying, 'What city is like the great city?' [19]And they threw dust on their heads and were crying out, weeping and mourning, saying, 'Woe, woe, the great city, in which all who had ships at sea became rich by her wealth, for in one hour she has been laid waste!' [20]Rejoice over her, O heaven, and you saints and apostles and prophets, because God has pronounced judgment for you against her." [21]Then a strong angel took up a stone like a great millstone and threw it into the sea, saying, "So will Babylon, the great city, be thrown down with violence, and will not be found any longer. [22]And the sound of harpists and musicians and flute players and trumpeters will not be heard in you any longer; and no craftsman of any craft will be found in you any longer; and the sound of a mill will not be heard in you any longer; [23]and the light of a lamp will not shine in you any longer; and the voice of the bridegroom and bride will not be heard in you any longer; for your merchants were the great men of the earth, because all the nations were deceived by your sorcery. [24]And in her was found the blood of prophets and of saints and of all who have been slain on the earth."

Revelation 18:9-24

As Babylon burns, the kings of the earth will mourn. They will stand at a distance and weep. Now get this, they will also "fear" her torment.

Why?

Because they fear living without her. Remember even though we are lamenting Babylon as a whole, this is also a lamentation for the harlot's (the city's) destruction. Whether the harlot's city is ancient Babylon, Mecca, Rome or another great city – it will be just that – a great city. The kings of the earth will lose one of the biggest importers the world has ever known. They will cry, "Woe, woe, the great city, Babylon, the strong city! For in one hour your judgment has come."

Then it says the merchants of the earth will weep over her because no one buys their cargoes. Scripture names what this "Babylon" buys: "gold and silver and precious stones and pearls and fine linen and purple and silk and scarlet, and every kind of citron wood and every article of ivory and every article made from very costly wood and bronze and iron and marble, and cinnamon and spice and incense and perfume and frankincense and wine and olive oil and fine flour and wheat and cattle and sheep, and cargoes of horses and chariots and slaves and human lives."

That is quite a list! Does this fit with any of the cities we discussed as potential cities for the harlot? Below is an exert from *"God's War on Terror."*

Remarkably, these are the very imports of Saudi Arabia today. The items may be divided into three categories – but they are all things that she cannot produce herself. The three categories are luxury items, food items – both livestock and produce – and human slaves. Saudi Arabia imports humans for various reasons; some may be legitimate, but others clearly are not . . . While most would like to imagine that slavery is a thing of the past, slavery thrives in various forms in many parts of the world today. Mystery Babylon imports men, women, and children, no doubt to maintain and bolster her excessively luxurious and sinful lifestyle. Saudi Arabia has been repeatedly condemned by numerous human-rights watch groups for its horrific treatment of its vast foreign labor force. They have been repeatedly reported to have a serious problem with importing young women and children as sex-slaves. [1]

We need to remember, the beginning of "Mystery Babylon's" destruction comes from the "horns" of the beast (Revelation 13:16). A city is destroyed. The area is devastated. Is there something else that can place this description within the Middle East area? Let's see where the people are mourning.

And every shipmaster and every passenger and sailor, and as many as make their living by the sea, stood at a distance and were crying out as they saw the smoke of her burning saying, "What city is like the great city?"
Revelation 18:17b-18

The sailors are mourning, and they can see her burning from where they are making their living – by the sea. But what sea are we talking about? In scripture, when it says "the sea" in other locations it is talking about the sea beside Israel – the Mediterranean. [2] In Joshua 16:8 and Acts 10:6 the Mediterranean is referred to as "the" sea.

There is another sea referred to a lot in scripture but instead of labeling it "the sea" it is usually described as "the reed sea" (Exodus 15:4, Deuteronomy 1:40). Some translations have gone ahead and translated "reed," which is the true meaning of the Hebrew word, to name the actual sea being referred to – the Red Sea.

It seems more likely that the Mediterranean is intended in Revelation 18:17 because in scripture the Mediterranean is called "the sea," and we also know that an actual sea is intended because this is where they can see "the smoke of her burning." If you look at a map of that area, there are many possibilities for where the harlot's city might be located. Mecca is near the coast of the Red Sea, Rome is near the coast of the Mediterranean, and ancient Babylon is inland but her smoke just might be visible from both seas. Now listen to this scripture.

The earth has quaked at the noise of their downfall. There is an outcry! The noise of it has been heard at the Red Sea.
Jeremiah 49:21

We know this scripture is discussing the end times because both before and after this scripture we see prophesies of Jesus' return.

For who is like Me, and who will summon Me into court? And who then is the shepherd who can stand against Me?". . . Behold He will mount up and swoop like an eagle and spread out His wings against Bozrah; and the hearts of the mighty men of Edom in that day will be like the heart of a woman in labor.

Jeremiah 49:19b, 22

This is discussing the second coming of Christ! It seems more likely that this will be Mecca, the city near the Red Sea who is already a "harlot" in her own right. But I do not want to completely focus on her when the "peace" movement of the final seven years might very well combine some of the world's religions under an Islamic shadow. The harlot's city might very well transform into something the Antichrist and the horns will love to burn.

Then there is a command in heaven: Rejoice over her destruction! There will be no more cause for rejoicing in her, there will be no more celebration in her. She will be no more. Why? Because "in her was found the blood of the prophets and of saints and of all who have been slain on the earth."

The horns and the Antichrist begin "Babylon's" destruction by the destruction of the religious city she represents. Scripture says, "For God has put it in their hearts to execute His purpose" (Revelation 17:17a). But the end of Babylon will only occur when Jesus returns and claims the earth. He will "tread the wine press of the fierce wrath of God" (Revelation 19:15b). And Babylon will be no more. Let me say that another way: because Babylon the religion will continue until the end, both of these chapters had to be placed after the bowls. Only with the outpouring of the bowls will the entirety of the city, the empire, and the ideology be destroyed. Amen!

Thought for the day:
Babylon has fallen! Evil is crushed! The system of greed we have today will be no more. Can you imagine living without the fear of thieves, or liars, or killers? Can you imagine living under a government you actually trust? Can you imagine going to bed at night and not worrying about locking your door or setting your alarm? Guns? They won't be necessary. Insurance? No need. Can you imagine living truly FREE? Tomorrow we will discover the ruler who can make it all right. Tomorrow we will be walking into true freedom.

1 Shoebat, Walid, written with Joel Richardson. *God's War on Terror* (Top Executive Media, 2008), 413-414.

2 Butler, Trent C. et al.,eds. *Holman Illustrated Bible Dictionary* (Nashville, Tennessee: Holman Bible Publishers, 2003), p1097.

[1]After these things I heard something like a loud voice of a great multitude in heaven, saying, "Hallelujah! Salvation and glory and power belong to our God; [2]because His judgments are true and righteous; for He has judged the great harlot who was corrupting the earth with her immorality, and He has avenged the blood of His bond-servants on her." [3]And a second time they said, "Hallelujah! Her smoke rises up forever and ever." [4]And the twenty-four elders and the four living creatures fell down and worshiped God who sits on the throne saying, "Amen, Hallelujah!" [5]And a voice came from the throne, saying, "Give praise to our God, all you His bond-servants, you who fear Him, the small and the great." [6]Then I heard something like the voice of a great multitude and like the sound of many waters and like the sound of mighty peals of thunder, saying, "Hallelujah! For the Lord our God, the Almighty, reigns."

Revelation 19:1-6

Ah! Now there is the sound of a great multitude in heaven. Could this be the same great multitude we saw in chapter seven? Yes! The saints in heaven sing! We lift up our voices and shout, "Hallelujah! Salvation and glory and power belong to our God; because His judgments are true and righteous; for He has judged the great harlot who was corrupting the earth with her immorality, and He has avenged the blood of his bond-servants on her."

Now wait, wasn't it the ten horns back in chapter seventeen that destroyed the harlot (or the city)? Yes! However, the harlot, who also represents Babylon, is far more than a city. Yes, the city was destroyed, but no, Babylon as a whole is not destroyed completely until the bowl judgments descend and our Lord and Savior returns to thresh her. So, again, we need to be aware the religious center of Babylon is destroyed sometime after the midpoint of the final seven years, but the totality of Babylon, the region, the restored empire of Daniel, and the religious ideology that controls it, is not destroyed until God himself does so during the final bowl judgment. That is why chapter seventeen and eighteen are sandwiched between the description of the harlot and the return of the King. Chapter 18 is a duel fulfillment of both the city's destruction and Babylon as a whole burning to the ground when Jesus returns to the earth.

So, the harlot as a city is burned in chapter eighteen, but Babylon's harlotries as a whole will be burned when Jesus returns.

In verse two the crowd announces the judgment of God is just and righteous because God has avenged the blood of the bond-servants. Remember back in chapter six when we saw the martyrs under the altar?

"How long, O Lord, holy and true, will You refrain from judging and avenging our blood on those who dwell on the earth?"

Revelation 6:10b

The answer to that question appears at the end of Revelation 10:6: "There will be no more delay."

Chapter 10 came after the sixth trumpet, just before the seventh trumpet blew and the bowl judgments descended. Even though we have studied many things since chapter twelve, the bowl judgments came right after the angel declared, "There will be no more delay." The bowl judgments were the answer, the vengeance of God on the Babylon that has shed the blood of His saints.

For the second time the multitude speaks, "Hallelujah! Her smoke rises up forever and ever." This is prophesied in Isaiah.

Its streams will be turned into pitch, and its loose earth into brimstone, and its land will become burning pitch. It will not be quenched night or day; its smoke will go up forever. From generation to generation it will be desolate; none will pass through it forever and ever.

Isaiah 34:9-10

Here we see the imagery of the day of vengeance (Jesus' return, the bowls) and the year of recompense (wrath of God, the trumpets), which encompass the "day of the Lord." Here we also see Babylon's smoke going up forever and ever. And what will it be turned into? Pitch! What is pitch? Oil! And who has the oil? The Middle East! When Babylon is destroyed, she could easily be turned into pitch. And the smoke from her burning, well, you understand.

Isn't the Bible the most interesting book you have ever read? The Word of the Lord! "Great and marvelous are Your works, O

Lord God, the Almighty; righteous and true are Your ways, King of the nations!" Hallelujah!

Then we see the twenty-four elders and the four living creatures falling down before the throne in worship and all they say is "Amen. Hallelujah!" They are responding to the shouts of the multitude. The word "amen" means truth. When Jesus says, "Truly, truly, I say to you, if anyone keeps My word he will never see death." The Hebrew word for "truly" is "amen." So when we say, "Amen!" in response to a preaching or teaching, we are pronouncing it "true." So the twenty-four elders and four creatures, after the praise of the multitude shout, "Amen!" They concur with the multitude's praise.

God then speaks, because it is a voice from the throne, and He says, "Give praise to our God, all you His bondservants, you who fear Him, the small and the great." This seems slightly odd that God would command His bondservants to praise God until you realize that the second member of the trinity is about to claim the earth. He is ordering the bondservants returning with Christ, the great multitude, to praise Him!

The great multitude gives their response and it is like the sound of many waters and like the sound of mighty peals of thunder. The multitude's voice now matches the awesome power of Jesus' voice in chapter one. We are now with Him, the King of kings, we know Him, our Savior, and our united voices sounds like His own. We say, "Hallelujah! For the Lord our God, the Almighty, reigns."

Jesus is about to claim the earth.

[7]"Let us rejoice and be glad and give the glory to Him, for the marriage of the Lamb has come and His bride has made herself ready." [8]It was given to her to clothe herself in fine linen, bright and clean; for the fine linen is the righteous acts of the saints. [9]Then he said to me, "Write, 'Blessed are those who are invited to the marriage supper of the Lamb.'" And he said to me, "These are the true words of God." [10]Then I fell at his feet to worship him. But he said to me, "Do not do that; I am a fellow servant of yours and your brethren who hold the testimony of Jesus; worship God. For the testimony of Jesus is the spirit of prophecy."

Revelation 19:7-10

The multitude continues to praise God by announcing the marriage of the Lamb. The bride has now made herself ready. Now wait, isn't the church the bride and isn't the church in heaven? Why on earth are we announcing now, at the end of the book of Revelation, that the bride is just now ready?

Yes, the church is the bride (Ephesians 5) but she is only part of the bride.

> *But if some of the branches were broken off, and you, being a wild olive, were grafted in among them and became partaker with them of the rich root of the olive tree, do not be arrogant toward the branches; but if you are arrogant, remember that it is not you who supports the root, but the root supports you. You will say then, "Branches were broken off so that I might be grafted in." Quite right, they were broken off for their unbelief, but you stand by your faith. Do not be conceited, but fear; for if God did not spare the natural branches, He will not spare you, either . . . For I do not want you, brethren, to be uninformed of this mystery – so that you will not be wise in your own estimation – that a partial hardening has happened to Israel until the fullness of the Gentiles has come in; and so all Israel will be saved; just as it is written, "The deliverer will come from Zion, He will remove ungodliness from Jacob. This is my covenant with them, when I take away their sins."*
>
> *Romans 11:17-21, 25-27*

Remember back in chapter 15 we saw the Holy of Holies, which is only opened on Yom Kippur. We also learned that Yom Kippur is Israel's national Day of Atonement. It is when Israel is cleansed from their sins. It is when Israel will come to faith in their Messiah.

Why is the multitude declaring the bride has made herself ready? Because Israel had come to faith! Once that happens, Jesus will mount His horse and ride to save them. The Old Testament is full of verses that declare God the husband of Israel.

> *For your husband is your Maker, whose name is the Lord of hosts; and your Redeemer is the Holy One of Israel, who is called the God of all the earth.*
>
> *Isaiah 54:5[1]*

Yes, we are part of the bride of Christ, but Israel is the other part. We will be joined as one in the millennial reign of Christ! Hallelujah!

Then Christ will say:

> *I will betroth you to Me forever; yes, I will betroth you to Me in righteousness and in justice, in lovingkindness and in compassion, and I will betroth you to Me in faithfulness. Then you will know the Lord.*
>
> *Hosea 2:19-20*

Israel has been devastated in the past and they will be devastated again during the final seven-year period. At the point of faith, that is no longer the case. Jesus will return and save them.

> *It will no longer be said to you, "Forsaken," nor to your land will it any longer be said, "Desolate": but you will be called, "My delight is in her," and your land, "Married"; For the Lord delights in you, and to Him your land will be married. For as a young man marries a virgin, so your sons will marry you; and as the bridegroom rejoices over the bride, so your God will rejoice over you.*
>
> *Isaiah 62:4-5*

God will rejoice over Israel and the people in her, and the saints returning with God, the church, will be forever joined with Him.

Remember, although we are in chapter nineteen, this chapter occurs during the bowl judgments of chapter sixteen. Just like the seals and trumpets gave us an overview of the rise of the Antichrist and the aftermath of his deception, the chapters following the seals and trumpets (chapter 10-15) revealed more things transpiring during that time. Likewise, as chapter 16 gave us an overview of the bowls, the next chapters (17-19) are giving the details of what is happening during the bowls. Chapter 19 is a description of Jesus' second coming – but His visible return is during the fifth bowl judgment: "Then the fifth angel poured out his bowl on the throne of the beast, and his kingdom became darkened" (Revelation 16:10a). As you recall, Jesus returns during this darkness.

*Then the Lord, my God, will come, and all the holy ones
with Him! In that day there will be no light; the
luminaries will dwindle. For it will be a unique day
which is known to the Lord, neither day nor night, but it
will come about that at evening time there will be light.*

Zechariah 14:5b-7

Let's look at a famous scripture even though we have looked at
it before.

*In the beginning was the Word, and the Word was with
God, and the Word was God. He was in the beginning
with God. All things came into being through Him, and
apart from Him nothing came into being that has come
into being. In Him was life, and the life was the Light of
men. The Light shines in the darkness, and the darkness
did not comprehend it.*

John 1:1-5

Jesus is the light, and when He comes He will shine, and the
darkness will not be able to defeat Him. The darkness will also not
know Him, and as we saw in chapter sixteen, the darkness will fight
Him. We will see the outcome of that fight in this chapter.

It was given to the bride fine linen, bright and clean. This is
bridal attire. Just as today, a bride wears white, a symbol of purity,
so will the cleansed saints wear white, symbolizing their purity, due
to the bridegroom who has taken away all their sin. Yom Kippur is
the day all Jews will wear white – representing their atonement
from sin. This is a picture in heaven of Yom Kippur, the day Israel
will be cleansed of sin and made right with her Savior. This is the
day Jesus will descend to the earth and lay claim to it. Amen!

Then the angel speaking with John tells John to write, "Blessed
are those who are invited to the marriage supper of the Lamb."
Those invited are the ones who have accepted Jesus as "husband."
They are the Old Testament saints, the church, and the remnant of
Israel that has come to faith. Remember, a person individually is
not the bride; God's people as a whole are the bride.

*And I saw the holy city, new Jerusalem, coming down out
of heaven from God, made ready as a bride adorned for
her husband.*

Revelation 21:2

The New Jerusalem is described as a bride because the entirety of the bride will live there. Again, individually we are not the bride. The bride of Christ is the redeemed as a whole. This is why the New Jerusalem is announced as the bride because it will hold the people of God: the church universal and the saved of Israel. Together, we make up the bride.

The angel adds, "These are the true words of God." This is a declaration of truth, a definitive answer to the evil in this world. The saints from all time can be comforted by this and know the bridegroom will return. The day will come. No matter what we go through in this life, no matter if we are in the grave or struggling through the end times, the bride will make herself ready, and our bridegroom will return and establish His kingdom. Amen!

John is so overcome by this vision he falls down at the angel's feet and worships. The angel admonishes him, telling him to worship God alone. John knows not to worship an angel, but I believe he is so overwhelmed by the vision of Christ's return he just automatically falls to his knees. I am quite positive tears of joy were dripping from his chin. And then what does the angel say when John tried to worship?

"Do not do that; I am a fellow servant of yours and your brethren who hold the testimony of Jesus; worship God. For the testimony of Jesus is the spirit of prophecy."
Revelation 19:10b

First, what is the testimony of Jesus? We said in the beginning, Revelation is a revelation of Christ. Everything in this book is about the return of the King. Everything from the Garden of Eden until the final bowl judgment is about the return of the King. Jesus is the reason, not only for the season, but also for everything. His testimony, His witness, His very existence is why we are here. The definition of testimony according to Google is "evidence or proof provided by the existence or appearance of something." Someone needs to shout, "Glory!" First off, Jesus is the proof of salvation. He is the way, the truth, and the life. He appeared the first time to offer us that proof, and He will appear the second time to assure us of that proof.

"Testimony" is also a word used for the Torah (the first five books of the Bible (see Exodus 25:16). When we say "the testimony" we could also be referring to the Ten Commandments

336

engraved on the stone tablets. Again, Jesus embodied those commandments. "Do not think that I came to abolish the Law or the Prophets; I did not come to abolish but to fulfill" (Matthew 5:17). Jesus was the answer to that law. We also saw the word "testimony" used in chapter fifteen to refer to the Holy of Holies, the place the stone tablets (or testimony) were kept. Jesus is the way into the tabernacle, the truth you need to enter the Holy Place and the life when you accept Him as your Savior. In other words, Jesus is the Holy of Holies. Only through Him do we gain eternal life.

Jesus' testimony is the spirit of prophecy because His first coming and resurrection assure us of His ultimate return.

Someone needs to say, "Amen!"

Thought for the day:
The earth now belongs to the King. The earth now belongs to us, because we will be with Him. We will be in the heavenlies while the bowls are poured out. Then we return to claim the land that rightfully belongs to our Savior. Earth is ours, not only now, but also for eternity. We return to the earth; we do not stay in heaven. We will see our ride to earth tomorrow. It will be a sight to behold!

1 See also Isaiah 61:10-62:5, Jeremiah 2:32, Hosea 2:16-20, and Ezekiel 16:32.

DAY FIFTY-ONE
REVELATION 19:11-16
THE RETURN OF THE KING

¹¹And I saw heaven opened, and behold, a white horse, and He who sat on it is called Faithful and True, and in righteousness He judges and wages war. ¹²His eyes are a flame of fire, and on His head are many diadems; and He has a name written on Him which no one knows except Himself. ¹³He is clothed with a robe dipped in blood, and His name is called The Word of God. ¹⁴And the armies which are in heaven, clothed in fine linen, white and clean, were following Him on white horses. ¹⁵From His mouth comes a sharp sword, so that with it He may strike down the nations, and He will rule them with a rod of iron; and He treads the wine press of the fierce wrath of God, the Almighty. ¹⁶And on His robe and on His thigh He has a name written, "King of kings, and Lord of lords."

Revelation 19:11-16

I love this section of Revelation because it shows the return of the King! We have looked at some of these verses throughout our study, so we are going to go over this fairly quickly. However, before we begin, someone needs to shout: "Hallelujah! For the Lord God Almighty reigns!"

Heaven is opened and the King of kings is sitting on a white horse. The last time we saw Jesus mounted on an animal was when He rode into Jerusalem on a donkey (Luke 19:35) in fulfillment of prophecy (Zechariah 9:9). The donkey was a symbol of peace in ancient times. When you saw a king riding a donkey, he came in peace. A horse, however, was different. If you saw a king riding in on a horse, he was coming for war.[1] This is exactly what we see here. Jesus is returning to fight: He "wages war."

Scripture reminds us in verse 11 that Jesus is Faithful and True, and that He judges and wages war in righteousness.

Does that sound like a contradiction? No, faithful friends, it is not. Jesus is faithful and true, and because He is faithful and true He has to judge and wage war. He is a righteous judge, but He is a judge, and judgment day has come. We see this reiterated in Isaiah 11:4:

But with righteousness He will judge the poor, and decide with fairness for the afflicted of the earth; and He will

338

strike the earth with the rod of His mouth, and with the
breath of His lips He will slay the wicked.

Isaiah 11:4

We saw at the beginning of Revelation our Savior's eyes as a
flame of fire (Revelation 1:14) and that is exactly what we see here.
He is coming as King and as judge. He is not seeing the world
through eyes of mercy anymore, for mercy was extended in the
trumpet judgments (Revelation 9:13), yet it was adamantly rejected
by the inhabitants of the earth (Revelation 9:21, 16:9, 16:11, 16:21).
He is now seeing the world through eyes of judgment:

For a complete destruction, one that is decreed, the Lord
God of hosts will execute in the midst of the whole land.

Isaiah 10:23

Jesus is wearing many crowns. In ancient times kings wore
multiple crowns to show that they ruled over more than one nation.[2]
The important thing to note about this scripture is that He is not
coming back as a suffering servant but as the reigning King of all
the earth. He also has ultimate authority. The Greek word used for
"many" is "polus" which can also be translated as "great." This is a
"great" crown. No one will be able to take His authority away.

"For from the rising of the sun even to its setting, My
name will be great among the nations, and in every place
incense is going to be offered to My name, and a grain
offering that is pure; for My name will be great among the
nations," says the Lord of hosts.

Malachi 1:11

He has a name written on Him which no one knows except
Himself. This is an interesting scripture. Back in chapter two Jesus
said He would give those who overcome a new name written on a
white stone (2:17). In Isaiah 65:15 it says God's servants will be
called by another name. Because the Father gives Jesus a new
name, Jesus in turn gives us a new name. Jesus said, "Just as the
Father has loved Me, I have loved you" (John 4:9). I believe this
shows the intimacy between the Father and the Son. Although both
are God, they also have a unique relationship. Jesus wants that kind
of relationship with us, which is why He gives us a new name
"which no one knows but he who receives it" (Revelation 2:17).

Ever had a pet name? It makes you feel special, loved, and cherished. So it will be with our new name. It is a special name, given by God, as a gift to us, reminding us of how precious we are to the King.

He is clothed with a robe dipped in blood. At the end of chapter 15 we saw the Holy of Holies opened on Yom Kippur, or the Day of Atonement. This is the only day the high priest could enter the Holy of Holies and sprinkle the blood of the sacrifice on the ark to atone for the nation of Israel. It was Israel's national day of repentance. This is the day the Jews would look on their high priest and see his white garments stained red. This is the day the Jews will look on Jesus and see His garments stained red.

On the day the Jewish remnant comes to faith, the earth will be plunged into darkness (bowl five) and a light will appear in the sky. It will be Jesus, their High Priest, coming with garments stained red, to save them. The blood on His robe is a reminder of the repentance symbolized on Yom Kippur. It is also symbolic of war.

Why is your apparel red, and your garments like the one who treads in the wine press? "I have trodden the wine trough alone, and from the peoples there was no man with Me. I also trod them in My anger and trampled them in My wrath; and their lifeblood is sprinkled on My garments, and I stained all My raiment."

Isaiah 63:2-3

Jesus' apparel is red because Israel has come to believe in the Savior's blood that was shed for them. His garments are red because His wrath started with the trumpets. He has already been trampling the unrepentant in His wrath even though His feet have yet to touch the earth's soil. As He rides down from the heavens, more blood will be shed by those following the dragon and the Antichrist.

The gospel of John tells us that Jesus is the Word of God. "In the beginning was the Word, and the Word was with God, and the Word was God. He was in the beginning with God. All things came into being through Him and apart from Him nothing came into being that has come into being" (John 1:1-3). Everything in scripture leads us to Christ. Creation came into being (John 1:3), the fall led us to Christ (Genesis 3:15), the tabernacle and the sacrificial system pointed us to Christ (Exodus 12), and the prophets prophesied about Christ (Isaiah 53). He is the Word!

The armies that are in heaven are following Him on white horses. Some scholars believe these armies are angels. However we just learned in verse eight white linen stands for the righteous acts of the saints. That is not to say the angels aren't with Jesus as well. Other scriptures indicate the angels are also present when Jesus reclaims the earth (Matthew 24:31). But in Revelation 19 scripture is talking about the redeemed, and they are coming back with their commander in chief. They are coming to lay claim to the earth. Let's look at these armies in other sections of scripture.

I have commanded My consecrated ones, I have even called My mighty warriors, My proudly exulting ones, to execute My anger. A sound of tumult on the mountains, like that of many people! A sound of the uproar of kingdoms, of nations gathered together! The Lord of hosts is mustering the army for battle. They are coming from a far country, from the farthest horizons, the Lord and His instruments of indignation, to destroy the whole land.

Isaiah 13:3-5

The word used for "consecrated ones" or "sanctified ones" in the Hebrew is "qadash" and means "to be set apart" to be "holy." "Farthest horizons" in some translations of the above scripture is literally translated "end of heaven." This army is coming from the end of heaven, and Jesus is summoning them. Let's look at Revelation 19:14 again.

And the armies which are in heaven, clothed in fine linen, white and clean, were following Him on white horses.
Revelation 19:14

Does this sound like the "end of heaven" to you?

Can you imagine riding to earth behind the Savior? Can you imagine His hand lifted high as He commands us to move forward? What a day that will be!

We also see this army represented in Joel:

As the dawn is spread over the mountains, so there is a great and mighty people; there has never been anything like it, nor will there be again after it to the years of many generations. A fire consumes before them and behind

341

them a flame burns. The land is like the garden of Eden before them but a desolate wilderness behind them, and nothing at all escapes them.

Joel 2:2b-3

Jesus doesn't need any help cleansing the earth, but He allows us to do what He engrained deep within our souls: the need to fight for justice. He will include us in His plans for the end time cleansing just as He involves us in spreading His message now. And Joel says we are walking into Eden. Listen to Jesus' own words:

"Truly I say to you, that you who have followed Me, in the regeneration when the Son of Man will sit on His glorious throne, you also shall sit upon twelve thrones, judging the twelve tribes of Israel."

Matthew 19:28

Jesus tells the disciples they will have the privilege of judging the twelve tribes of Israel when He sits on His throne. When will He sit on His throne? After the final seven years on earth when He returns from heaven with His army. What does He say will happen during this time? The earth will be regenerated. This is quite exciting for us. Regeneration means "new birth, renewal, recreation, and a restoration of a thing to its pristine state." Glory! After so much destruction and chaos, Jesus is going to remake the world into Eden – to His original design and creation!

Indeed, the Lord will comfort Zion; He will comfort all her waste places. And her wilderness He will make like Eden, and her desert like the garden of the Lord; joy and gladness will be found in her, thanksgiving and sound of a melody.

Isaiah 51:3

Can you imagine walking into God's original creation? If the earth will be regenerated don't you think those extinct species we always wanted to see will return? If that is true, we will see dinosaurs! I so want to slide down a brachiosaurus tail into a pristine pool of water. I want to meet a tyrannosaurus. I want to see a stegosaurus. Can you imagine the day!

342

Now wait, you say. Dinosaurs? You can't be serious! Oh, yes I am. Did you know the word "dinosaur" wasn't created until 1841?[3] Before that, a "dinosaur" was known as a dragon. The Bible even talks about them. They walked with Job. Want to look? Of course you do!

> *Behold now, Behemoth, which I made as well as you; He eats grass like an ox. Behold now, his strength in his loins and his power in the muscles of his belly. He bends his tail like a cedar; the sinews of his thighs are knit together. His bones are tubes of bronze; his limbs are like bars of iron.*
>
> *Job 40:15-18*

Some scholars try to say the above creature is an elephant. Really? Have you seen an elephant's tail? I don't think so. This sounds like a brachiosaurus. Let's look at another strange beast.

> *Can you draw out Leviathan with a fishhook? Or press down his tongue with a cord? . . . His sneezes flash forth light, and his eyes are like the eyelids of the morning. Out of his mouth go burning torches; sparks of fire leap forth. Out of his nostrils smoke goes forth as from a boiling pot and burning rushes. His breath kindles coals, and a flame goes forth from his mouth.*
>
> *Job 41:1, 18-21*

You can't tell me this isn't a fire-breathing dragon! Glory! I have already asked God to give me one. I want to get on a dragon's back and take to the sky! If they don't have wings, I will ask if He wouldn't mind commanding one to grow them. I do believe He will humor me (Matthew 7:7).

Hallelujah! Who said heaven was boring? Satan may have put that thought in your mind before (Revelation 13:6), but don't let him do so again. Now you know better. Jesus is exciting. So is Daddy God. We are going to have a lot of things to do in the Millennium and even more in eternity. But I digress.

The earth will be regenerated, and that regeneration starts when we return with the King.

A sharp sword comes from Jesus' mouth. We saw this imagery in chapter one. Again, this is the other sword referred to throughout scripture – the word of God (Hebrews 4:12). And

343

remember, Jesus is the Word of God (John 1:1). All He has to do is speak and it is done (Isaiah 11:4).

Jesus will strike down the nations with His words. "Behold, the day of the Lord is coming, cruel, with fury and burning anger, to make the land a desolation; and he will exterminate its sinners from it" (Isaiah 13:9-10). He will tread them down like a wine press. The fury of the Lord is many times associated with the wine harvest which occurs during the fall feasts. This is consistent with the theory that He does, indeed, return during those feasts.

> *Put in the sickle, for the harvest is ripe. Come, tread, for the wine press is full; the vats overflow, for their wickedness is great. Multitudes, multitudes in the valley of decision! For the day of the Lord is near in the valley of decision.*
>
> *Joel 3:13-14*

What is the valley of decision? It is the valley where the final conflict occurs. It is where the nations' armies fight Christ. Many scholars have claimed the "valley of decision" is the valley of Megiddo (referred to as Armageddon in Revelation 16:16) which is about 75 miles north of Jerusalem. However, Revelation says the armies will gather at Armageddon. It does not say the valley of Megiddo will be the actual place of the battle. The more likely place for the final showdown is the Kidron Valley, which runs along the eastern side of the temple mount in Jerusalem and separates the temple mount from the Mount of Olives. And where is Jesus touching down?

> *In that day His feet will stand on the Mount of Olives, which is in front of Jerusalem on the east.*
>
> *Zechariah 14:4a*

And how does He enter the temple?

> *Then He brought me back by the way of the outer gate of the sanctuary, which faces the east . . . As for the prince, he shall sit in it as prince to eat bread before the Lord; he shall enter by way of the porch of the gate.*
>
> *Ezekiel 44:1a, 3a*

Jesus will enter on the east side of the tabernacle, the side facing the Mount of Olives. And what lies in the middle? The Kidron Valley! Jesus will do some threshing in the Kidron Valley.

Now this will be the plague with which the Lord will strike all the peoples who have gone to war against Jerusalem; their flesh will rot while they stand on their feet, and their eyes will rot in their sockets, and their tongue will rot in their mouth.

Zechariah 14:12

Please, faithful friends, be part of the Lord's army when He returns, not among those in the Kidron Valley.

But this brings up another question, does it not? How and where will Jesus come? Will He come directly to the Mount of Olives? Didn't we look at some scriptures stating that He would be coming from Bozrah, which is south of Jerusalem? Yes, we did. We will try to map out His path tomorrow. Good work today, Christian soldiers! Soon we will be marching to war.

Thought for the day:

Can you imagine following Jesus down from heaven in order to cleanse the world of evil? We will be part of this cleansing, because Revelation 19 calls us His "armies." It will be very easy to identify the people of the beast – God has marked them with "loathsome and malignant" sores in the first bowl. We will know them. They will know us. We will do some threshing. More on our march tomorrow.

1 *The Gospel of John Volume Two* by William Barclay, published in 2001 by Westminster John Knox Press in Louisville, Kentucky, 137.

2 Kassian, Mary. *Knowing God By Name, A Personal Encounter* (Nashville, TN: Lifeway Press, 2012), 89.

3 Nelson, Vance. Dire Dragons: *Untold Secrets of Planet Earth* (Alberta, Canada: Untold Secrets of Planet Earth Publishing Company, 2011), 14.

Yesterday we were left with the question: Where will Jesus go first? We know His feet will touch on the Mount of Olives (Zechariah 14:4), but we also know He is coming from Bozrah, which is south of Jerusalem and north of Petra (Isaiah 63:1). We have learned He will rescue the Jewish remnant in Petra. But where does He go first? Scripture does not give us a play-by-play march of our Savior, but we just might be able to piece it together.

In order to do so, we must first go back in time.

Abraham was called by God to be the father of many nations. When Abraham was first called he journeyed from the land of Ur to the Promised Land (Genesis 11:31, 12:1-5). Right after he arrived in the Promised Land, something went wrong.

Now there was a famine in the land; so Abram went down to Egypt to sojourn there, for the famine was severe in the land.

Genesis 12:10

Now that's odd. God told Abraham to leave his homeland (Genesis 12:1), but as soon as Abraham gets to his destination he has to turn around and go to Egypt because of a famine. Interesting. We know years later, Moses brought the Israelites out of Egypt in the Exodus. But Abraham, the father of Israel, came out of Egypt hundreds of years earlier. Let's look at another scripture that should be very familiar to us.

When Israel was a youth I loved him, and out of Egypt I called My son.

Hosea 11:1

Now, the direct reference here is Israel and the fulfillment of this scripture was when Moses brought the Israelites out of Egypt, but in the Hosea reference it calls Israel God's "son." Do you recall what happened after the birth of Jesus when the wise men left Him?

Now when they had gone, behold, an angel of the Lord appeared to Joseph in a dream and said, "Get up! Take the Child and His mother and flee to Egypt, and remain

there until I tell you; for Herod is going to search for the
Child to destroy Him.

Matthew 2:13

God sent them to Egypt. So the Hosea scripture referenced
previously also applies to Jesus. "Out of Egypt I called My son"
(Hosea 11:1b). Matthew even references Hosea 11:1 two verses
after we see Joseph fleeing to Egypt with Mary and Jesus (Matthew
2:15). After the death of Herod, God appeared to Joseph in another
dream and tells him to return to the land of Israel (Matthew 2:20-
21).

So, Abraham was called out of Egypt, Israel was called out of
Egypt, and Jesus was called out of Egypt. Now let's look at another
scripture.

The oracle concerning Egypt. Behold, the Lord is riding
on a swift cloud and is about to come to Egypt; the idols
of Egypt will tremble at His presence, and the heart of the
Egyptians will melt within them.

Isaiah 19:1

Do you remember how Jesus is said to return?

And after He had said these things, He was lifted up while
they were looking on, and a cloud received Him out of
their sight . . . "Men of Galilee, why do you stand looking
into the sky? This Jesus, who has been taken up from you
into heaven, will come in just the same way as you have
watched Him go into heaven."

Acts 1:9, 11

Acts says He will return with the clouds and in Isaiah 19:1 we
see Him "riding on a swift cloud" to Egypt. Add this to the Hosea
passage, "Out of Egypt I called My son," and we might have a clue
where Jesus appears first. I believe Jesus will first be seen over
Egypt, and what will happen?

And the Lord will utterly destroy the tongue of the Sea of
Egypt; and He will wave His hand over the River with His
scorching wind; and He will strike it into seven streams
and make men walk over dry-shod. And there will be a
highway from Assyria for the remnant of His people who

will be left, just as there was for Israel in the day that they
came up out of the land of Egypt.

Isaiah 11:15

The Lord will wave His hand over them, and there will be a highway from Assyria. Jesus is clearing a path! This allusion is most likely referring to the King's Highway, an ancient road that connected the two major powers of the day: Assyria and Egypt. Many scholars place the King's Highway running from Egypt to the gulf of Aqaba then turning north and running through Petra and Bozrah and on up the east side of Israel into Damascus and the heart of Assyria. Others show the King's Highway only on the east side of the Jordan, from Damascus, through Bozrah and ending in the Gulf of Aqaba. If the King's Highway itself didn't travel to Egypt, an offshoot did (known as the Trans-Sinai Highway) still connecting Egypt to Assyria. However, I have seen still other maps that chart the King's Highway taking a slightly more northern route, going through a region south of Judah known as Teman and almost intersecting Bozrah in Edom. In fact, we know from Scripture Moses sent word to the king of Edom from Kadesh.

"Now behold, we are at Kadesh, a town on the edge of your territory. Please let us pass through your land. We will not pass through field or through vineyard; we will not even drink water from a well. We will go along the king's highway, not turning to the right or left, until we pass through your territory." Edom, however, said to him, "You shall not pass through us, or I will come out with the sword against you."

Numbers 20:16b-18

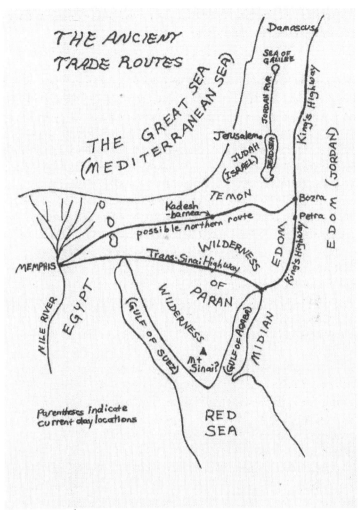

The Ancient Trade Routes

Parentheses indicate current day locations

Bible Maps[1] places Kadesh south of Israel at the boarder of Edom. If this is the case, the King's Highway, or an offshoot of the King's Highway, ran through here to Bozrah. Let's look at another scripture.

God comes from Teman, and the Holy One from Mount Paran. Selah. His splendor covers the heavens, and the earth is full of His praise. His radiance is like the sunlight; He has rays flashing from His hand, and there is the hiding of His power. Before Him goes pestilence, and plague comes after Him. He stood and surveyed the earth; He looked and startled the nations. Yes, the

349

perpetual mountains were shattered, the ancient hills
collapsed. His ways are everlasting.

Habakkuk 3:3-6

Jesus is coming back with splendor, and His radiance will be
like the sun. Remember, darkness is covering the Antichrist's
empire (bowl five) and Jesus will appear over him with glory.
Teman means "southland" according to the NASB Study
Bible, and this refers to the land south of Judah. Mount Paran is
"northwest of the Gulf of Aquaba and south of Kadesh-barnea."[2]
So, could Jesus be coming from Egypt on the northern route of the
King's Highway, through the southland of Teman – to Bozrah? I
believe that is exactly what He will do. The King of kings will
march down the King's Highway where Israel was denied to travel
before. He will retrace that exodus route, and this time, the people
of the land will be unable to refuse His passage. Then what will He
do? He will tread the winepress and rescue the Jewish remnant in
Petra.

Who is this who comes from Edom, with garments of
glowing colors from Bozrah, this One who is majestic in
His apparel, marching in the greatness of His strength?
"It is I who speak in righteousness, mighty to save." Why
is your apparel red, and Your garments like the one who
treads in the wine press? "I have trodden the wine trough
alone, and from the peoples there was no man with Me."
I also trod them in My anger and trampled them in My
wrath; and their lifeblood is sprinkled on My garments,
and I stained all My raiment. For the day of vengeance
was in My heart, and My year of redemption has come."

Isaiah 63:1-4

He is walking on the earth here. The day of vengeance (the
bowls) have come after the year of wrath being poured out (the
trumpets). The King of king's is marching down the King's
Highway, from Bozrah, with the blood of the unrepentant on His
garments. Those in Petra will be rescued.

I will surely assemble all of you, Jacob, I will surely
gather the remnant of Israel. I will put them together like
sheep in the fold; like a flock in the midst of its pasture
they will be noisy with men. The breaker goes up before

350

them; they break out, pass through the gate and go out by it. So their king goes on before them, and the Lord at their head.

Micah 2:12-13

He will gather His faithful remnant in Petra and lead them up the King's Highway to Israel. There, Jesus' feet will stand on the Mount of Olives and He will annihilate the enemy in the Kidron Valley.

After Jesus treads the wine press, exterminating the sinner from the earth, what will He do?

From His mouth comes a sharp sword, so that with it He may strike down the nations, and He will rule them with a rod of iron; and He treads the wine press of the fierce wrath of God, the Almighty.

Revelation 19:15

Once all the sinners are gone, why does He have to rule with a rod of iron? It sounds like the rod used for discipline: "Foolishness is bound up in the heart of a child; the rod of discipline will remove it far from him" (Proverbs 22:15). Yet, Jesus is ruling with a rod of iron. We will see the reason for this in the next chapter.

Jesus will be wearing a robe that says, "King of kings, and Lord of lords." In case you didn't know the rider of the white horse, wearing many crowns, with eyes of flaming fire, is the true King of the earth – all you have to do is look at His robe. Up His thigh, He dons His title. Make no mistake: He is the true ruler of the world.

In those days and at that time I will cause a righteous Branch of David to spring forth; and He shall execute justice and righteousness on the earth. In those days Judah will be saved and Jerusalem will dwell in safety; and this is the name by which she will be called: the Lord is our righteousness.

Jeremiah 33:15-16

So how will Jesus come? My best guess is this: He will come from Egypt (Isaiah 19:1) and pass through the land south of Israel (Habakkuk 3:3-6), marching through Bozrah (Isaiah 63:1-4), and continuing south until He arrives in Petra to rescue the Jews who have fled the Antichrist's persecution. Then He will lead His remnant up the King's Highway to the Kidron Valley where He will sit in judgment (Joel 3:2).

I can't tell you for sure this is Jesus' path, but from examining the scriptures, this is what I believe. Please dig in deep and let me know if you find another clue. I would love to hear from you, Christian soldiers!

Thought for the day:

Unlike the exodus, no one will deny the King and His people upon His return. No one will be able to stop Him. Tomorrow we will see the final scene of the war. Pause here to consider the true arrogance of the beast and his followers. They will see the King, with eyes of flaming fire, and they will still fight Him; they will still deny Him. Their punishment will be swift.

1 *Deluxe Then and Now Bible Map* (Torrance, CA: Rose Publishing), 2008.

2 *New American Standard Bible* (Grand Rapids, Michigan: Zondervan, 1999).

[17]Then I saw an angel standing in the sun, and he cried out with a loud voice, saying to all the birds which fly in midheaven, "Come, assemble for the great supper of God, [18]so that you may eat the flesh of kings and the flesh of commanders and the flesh of mighty men and the flesh of horses and of those who sit on them and the flesh of all men, both free men and slaves, and small and great." [19]And I saw the beast and the kings of the earth and their armies assembled to make war against Him who sat on the horse and against His army. [20]And the beast was seized and with him the false prophet who performed the signs in his presence, by which he deceived those who had received the mark of the beast and those who worshiped his image; these two were thrown alive into the lake of fire which burns with brimstone. [21]And the rest were killed with the sword which came from the mouth of Him who sat on the horse, and all the birds were filled with their flesh.

Revelation 19:17-21

John sees an angel standing in the sun. If you remember from chapter sixteen, when Jesus returns, the sun is dark. Jesus himself becomes the light as He descends to earth. The word for "sun" in verse 17 is the same word used to describe Jesus' face in chapter one. It is also the literal "sun" in chapter 21. Which is meant here? I don't know. But I like to think of Jesus' glory shining so brilliantly as He returns that this angel looks like he is standing before the literal sun, when in fact he is eclipsed with the glory of the Son!

The angel speaks to the birds of the sky and tells them, "Come, assemble for the great supper of God." This is referring to the final battle in the Kidron Valley. This is consistent with scripture.

"You will fall on the mountains of Israel, you and all your troops and the peoples who are with you. I will give you as food to every kind of predatory bird and beast of the field.

Ezekiel 39:4

353

The armies of the Antichrist will be littered on the ground and the birds of the air will be able to feed on the flesh of commanders, mighty men and horses.

The announcement is made, the birds are gathering, and the beast and the kings of the earth and their armies assemble themselves against the One riding a white horse and descending from the heavens. Can you imagine the arrogance! But we know from scripture, the Antichrist will be arrogant.

> *Then the king will do as he pleases, and he will exalt and magnify himself above every god and will speak monstrous things against the God of gods.*
>
> *Daniel 11:36a*

But he will come to an end. "The court will sit for judgment, and his dominion will be taken away, annihilated and destroyed forever" (Daniel 7:26).

Let me clarify. Although the bowls were seen back in chapter 16, this chapter occurs during bowl number five – the darkness. Chapter 19 is just giving you a better image of the return of the King.

> *And I saw coming out of the mouth of the dragon and out of the mouth of the beast and out of the mouth of the false prophet, three unclean spirits like frogs; for they are spirits of demons, performing signs, which go out to the kings of the whole world, to gather them together for the war of the great day of God, the Almighty.*
>
> *Revelation 16:13-14*

> *And I saw the beast and the kings of the earth and their armies assembled to make war against Him who sat on the horse and against His army.*
>
> *Revelation 19:19*

So, back in the bowl judgments, we saw the armies trying to assemble. In Revelation 19 they are assembled. So what is the outcome?

> *And the beast was seized, and with him the false prophet who performed the signs in his presence, by which he deceived those who had received the mark of the beast*

354

and those who worshiped his image; these two were thrown alive into the lake of fire which burns with brimstone. And the rest were killed with the sword which came from the mouth of Him who sat on the horse, and all the birds were filled with their flesh.

Revelation 19:20-21

There wasn't much of a fight was there? The beast is seized, and with him the false prophet. They are both thrown alive into the lake of fire. We know from Revelation 20:14 that the lake of fire is the second death. The rest were also killed. Who are the rest? The rest are those who have taken the mark of the beast – the unrepentant still remaining on the earth. Let's look at Isaiah 13:9 to see what the day of the Lord will do.

Behold, the day of the Lord is coming, cruel, with fury and burning anger, to make the land a desolation; and He will exterminate its sinners from it.

Isaiah 13:9

Remember, we saw in chapter 16 that no one else repented. Everyone on earth has made their decision before Jesus descends in judgment. Now it is just a matter of sifting.

Did you notice something strange? There were three beasts in Revelation, but the above scripture says nothing about the beast behind it all – the dragon.

Where, oh where, is Satan? We find that out in the next passage.

[1]Then I saw an angel coming down from heaven, holding the key of the abyss and a great chain in his hand. [2]And he laid hold of the dragon, the serpent of old, who is the devil and Satan, and bound him for a thousand years; [3]and he threw him into the abyss, and shut it and sealed it over him, so that he would not deceive the nations any longer, until the thousand years were completed; after these things he must be released for a short time. [4]Then I saw thrones, and they sat on them, and judgment was given to them. And I saw the souls of those who had been beheaded because of their testimony of Jesus and because of the word of God, and those who had not worshiped

the beast or his image, and had not received the mark on their forehead and on their hand; and they came to life and reigned with Christ for a thousand years. [5]The rest of the dead did not come to life until the thousand years were completed. This is the first resurrection. [6]Blessed and holy is the one who has a part in the first resurrection; over these the second death has no power, but they will be priests of God and of Christ and will reign with Him for a thousand years.

Revelation 20:1-6

An angel comes down holding a great chain. He takes Satan and throws him in the abyss for a thousand years.

Is anyone thinking what I am thinking? A thousand years? Why not forever and ever? Anyone?

Odd isn't it? But let's not dwell on this too long. Let's push on until we see Satan rearing his ugly head once more.

So Satan is bound and thrown into the abyss while the beast and the false prophet are thrown alive into the lake of fire. What is the difference between the abyss and the lake of fire? There are four different distinct words used in scripture to denote a place we call "hell." But they are not the same place. Let's dig deeper.

Hell or hades is the Greek word used to translate the Hebrew word "sheol." It is also translated grave or place of the dead. We hear of this place when we read Jesus' parable of the rich man and Lazarus.

> "Now the poor man died and was carried away by the angels to Abraham's bosom; and the rich man also died and was buried. In Hades he lifted up his eyes, being in torment, and saw Abraham far away and Lazarus in his bosom. And he cried out and said, 'Father Abraham, have mercy on me, and send Lazarus so that he may dip the tip of his finger in water and cool off my tongue, for I am in agony in this flame.' But Abraham said, 'Child, remember that during your life you received your good things, and likewise Lazarus bad things; but now he is being comforted here, and you are in agony. And besides all this, between us and you there is a great chasm fixed, so that those who wish to come over from here to you will not be able, and that none may cross over from there to us.'"

Luke 16:22-26

356

We know the rich man was in hades (or sheol) and Lazarus was in "Abraham's bosom." Is this the same place with a chasm separating them? We do not know for sure, but we do know that the good guys go to the good place (Abraham's bosom) and the bad guys go to the bad place: hades, or the place of the dead.

There are other references in scripture to a place called the abyss. This is the place referred to in Revelation that holds Satan for a thousand years. This is a distinct place. Let's see where else we see the word Abyss in scripture. Luke 8:26 describes the story when Jesus heals the man possessed by "Legion" or many demons. The demons implore Jesus not to send them to the abyss, but to send them into a herd of pigs. Jesus grants their wish but the pigs go so mad they rush into the lake and drowned (Luke 8:26-33). The abyss is also referred to in trumpet number five. It is where the smoke from the pit ascends.

There is also a place referred to as "tartarus" in the Greek and translated as "hell" in 2 Peter 2:4. This is where angels were cast after they sinned. Some believe the abyss and tartarus are one and the same and I tend to agree. Based on what we have just learned, it seems like the abyss is reserved for angels, while hades or sheol is reserved for humans. This could be the same "place" yet different sections, or it could be an entirely different place altogether. On that, scripture is unclear. What we need to know is that the abyss is for angels and hades is for humans. I find it interesting the word abyss means "pit" or "chasm." Could the chasm separating the good place and the bad place actually be the abyss? Fascinating, but we may not know the answer in this lifetime. To summarize, hades and the abyss are for humans and angels respectively that have rejected God.

The lake of fire is "Gehenna" in Greek. It is named for a place outside of Jerusalem called the Valley of Hinnom. This was a place used as a garbage dump.[1] When Jesus mentioned "gehenna" the Jews would have an immediate visual of the "torment" to which He referred. In gehenna carcasses were thrown and trash burned continuously. There the worm never went hungry and the fire never died (Mark 9:46). It was a disgusting visual and one which Jesus mentioned often. The lake of fire is the second death. At the end of the Millennium, those in hades will be resurrected and thrown into the lake of fire. I tend to believe the abyss is a more intense level of Hades that is reserved for the angels who rebelled against God. If that is the case, these angels will also be thrown into the lake of fire. Hades will be no more.

After Satan is bound in the abyss, John sees thrones. He states, "they sat on them, and judgment was given to them." Who is he referring to?

> "Truly I say to you, that you who have followed Me, in the regeneration when the Son of Man will sit on His glorious throne, you also shall sit upon twelve thrones, judging the twelve tribes of Israel. And everyone who has left houses or brothers or sisters or father or mother or children or farms for My name's sake, will receive many times as much, and will inherit eternal life."
>
> *Matthew 19:28-29*

We know from Joel 2:3 the regeneration Jesus refers to is the earth reverting back to its pristine state – Eden! This is what we see in Revelation 20. The disciples will receive their reward by sitting on their thrones in the Millennial Kingdom of Christ.

Jesus then resurrects those who have died in Him since the rapture, those who have been beheaded by the beast and his followers. These people are those who have lived through the wrath of God but have come to faith in Him during that final year on earth. Remember, part of the reason the wrath of God falls is to entreat people to come to faith. Although they missed the rapture, they have found Him and they will be resurrected by the King and enjoy His reign for a thousand years. Those who were previously raptured are already with Jesus; they were the armies following Christ. Those who have died since then have yet to receive their new bodies. They do so here and enter into the Millennial Kingdom of Christ. That is not to say they are not "with us" in heaven, but because they missed the rapture, their bodies are not made new until Jesus returns to the earth. This contrasts with the Revelation 20:5.

> The rest of the dead did not come to life until the thousand years were completed.
>
> *Revelation 20:5*

Scripture names those who are resurrected when Jesus returns to earth the "first resurrection." So what is the first resurrection? Let's take a closer look.

But now Christ has been raised from the dead, the first fruits of those who are asleep.

1 Corinthians 15:20

The tombs were opened, and many bodies of the saints who had fallen asleep were raised; and coming out of the tombs after His resurrection they entered the holy city and appeared to many.

Matthew 27:52-53

After these things I looked, and behold, a great multitude which no one could count, from every nation and all tribes and peoples and tongues, standing before the throne and before the Lamb, clothed in white robes, and palm branches were in their hands.

Revelation 7:9

Then I saw thrones, and they sat on them, and judgment was given to them. And I saw the souls of those who had been beheaded because of their testimony of Jesus and because of the word of God, and those who had not worshiped the beast or his image, and had not received the mark on their forehead and on their hand; and they came to life and reigned with Christ for a thousand years.

Revelation 20:4

The first resurrection is the believer's resurrection, even though it comes in different phases. Jesus came first (1 Corinthians 15:20), then some Old Testament saints after Jesus' resurrection (Matthew 27:52-53), then came the rapture at the sixth seal, and finally those who came to faith and died after the rapture – they are resurrected at Jesus return. Every one of these has taken part in the "first resurrection."

Scripture calls those involved in the first resurrection "blessed and holy." Why? Because they are all believers who will reign with Christ in the Millennial Kingdom. Scripture says the second death, or the lake of fire, will have no power over them (Revelation 20:14). Why? Because the lake of fire is only reserved for the unrepentant.

So, at the start of the Millennial Kingdom, only believers inhabit the earth. Scripture teaches at His second coming, Jesus will exterminate all unbelievers from the earth (Isaiah 13:9) by His judgment of fire (Isaiah 66:16). If anyone escapes the fire, they will not escape judgment.

But when the Son of Man comes in His glory, and all the angels with Him, then He will sit on His glorious throne. All the nations will be gathered before Him; and He will separate them from one another, as the shepherd separates the sheep from the goats; and He will put the sheep on His right, and the goats on the left. Then the King will say to those on His right, "Come, you who are blessed of My Father, inherit the kingdom prepared for you from the foundation of the world". . . Then He will also say to those on His left, "Depart from Me, accursed ones, into the eternal fire which has been prepared for the devil and his angels . . ."

Matthew 25:31-34,41

When Jesus returns, all believers will be united, and those who are still alive will be judged and sifted when Jesus sits on His glorious throne in Jerusalem.

So, according to these scriptures, at the beginning of the Millennium, there will be no unbelievers present.

Scripture is clear: if you are an unbeliever and are able to survive the trumpet and bowl judgments you will still be unable to enter into the Millennial Kingdom of Christ. You will be sifted in the judgment of the sheep and the goats. Only those of faith are allowed into Christ's Kingdom.

But eventually, there will be unbelievers there. How do we know this? Why else would Satan be re-released?

More to come tomorrow. Who said God's Word wasn't exciting?

Thought for the day:
Why did God bind Satan for a thousand years? Why not just destroy him like the beast and the false prophet? Have you figured it out yet? Because Satan's job is not yet complete. He has one more task to do. We will see this task tomorrow.

1 New American Standard Bible (Grand Rapids, Michigan: Zondervan, 1999).

[7]When the thousand years are completed, Satan will be released from his prison, [8]and will come out to deceive the nations which are in the four corners of the earth, God and Magog, to gather them together for the war; the number of them is like the sand of the seashore. [9]And they came up on the broad plan of the earth and surrounded the camp of the saints and the beloved city, and fire came down from heaven and devoured them. [10]And the devil who deceived them was thrown into the lake of fire and brimstone, where the beast and the false prophet are also; and they will be tormented day and night forever and ever.

Revelation 20:7-10

When I first read Revelation as a young girl, this confused me to no end. Why on earth would God release Satan? I thought we had "been there done that" so to speak. But I hadn't walked through my life and seen the injustice done to God's children. Tragedy hadn't happened in my life. There was nothing that God needed to "make right." Then life happened and tragedy struck. I was on my knees asking God about heaven. He gave me 1 Peter 5:10:

And after you suffer for a short time, God, who gives all grace, will make everything right. He will make you strong and support you and keep you from falling. He called you to share in His glory in Christ, a glory that will continue forever.

1 Peter 5:10 (NCV)

God promises He will make it right. Then I started studying verses on the Millennium. I had always been a little confused as to why there would be a thousand years reserved at the end of history. I knew only believers would inhabit the Millennium, so why not get on with eternity?

The Millennial Kingdom is special to us. It is God's gift to us. In the Kingdom He will make things right. My tragedy will be turned on its head and I will get to live my life the way God intended me to live it. Your tragedies will be righted, and you will be made whole. The Millennial Kingdom will be Eden. Jesus will be on the throne. The tragedy in our lives can affect us here, but it cannot have the victory. God promises us that. This life is a choice – a choice to choose the only true God. If we choose rightly, we have the Millennium. God gives us this gift because He loves us. Let's see what scripture says about the Millennial Kingdom. One of the best scriptures to look at is Isaiah 65:21-25.

"No longer will there be in it an infant who lives but a few days,
Or an old man who does not live out his days
For the youth will die at the age of one hundred
And the one who does not reach the age of one hundred
Will be thought accursed.
They will build houses and inhabit them;
They will also plant vineyards and eat their fruit.
They will not build and another inhabit,
They will not plant and another eat;
For as the lifetime of a tree,
So will be the days of My people,
And My chosen ones will wear out the work of their hands.
They will not labor in vain,
Or bear children for calamity;
For they are the offspring of those blessed by the Lord,
And their descendants with them.
It will also come to pass that before they call, I will answer;
And while they are still speaking, I will hear.
The wolf and the lamb will graze together, and the lion will eat
straw like the ox;
And dust will be the serpent's food.
They will do no evil or harm in all My holy mountain," says the
Lord.

This scripture says very explicitly that children will be born during the millennial reign. It also says people will be dying. Does that surprise you? Yes, there is death in the millennial reign of Christ. Let's look at another strange scripture found in Ezekiel 40-48, which gives us a description of what will be happening in the millennial temple.

And you shall provide a lamb a year old without blemish
for a burnt offering to the Lord daily; morning by
morning you shall provide it.
Ezekiel 46:13

Now, why on earth would we need animal sacrifices in the Millennial Kingdom of Christ? Well, if babies are still being born, then God will give them a choice. If God gives them a choice, not everyone will choose rightly.

Animal sacrifices will continue as a reminder of the sacrifice that Jesus made for them. These children will see Jesus, they will hear the stories of their parents, and they will live in complete peace, yet many will reject the King. How do we know this? Isaiah 65:20 says, "For the youth will die at the age of one hundred." The NASB translates the next part of Isaiah 65 as a separate declaration: "and the one who does not reach the age of one-hundred will be thought accursed." Many other translations of scripture, including the NIV translates this latter part of Isaiah 65 in a similar way by saying anyone who "fails to reach one hundred is accursed," but this is not how the original Hebrew reads. The original Hebrew implies that if you die, you will be considered accursed. And if you die at one hundred, you will be thought of as a mere youth! Look at the New Living Translation of the Isaiah 65:20 passage.

No longer will people be considered old at one-hundred!
Only the cursed will die that young.
                                        Isaiah 65:20b (NLT)

This is the better translation for that section of scripture. Yes, there will be death in the Millennial Kingdom of Christ, but those who die will be the sinner who has not accepted Jesus as reigning King. Those who are born in the Millennium and accept Him as Lord will continue to live. Long life spans will be back. If you remember, after the fall, Adam lived to 930 years of age (Genesis 5:5). Jesus will be on the throne in the Millennium. The earth will be regenerated. There is no reason to think those who accept Him will die. Many scholars believe (and scripture seems to indicate) that at the age of one hundred, if you have not accepted the King of kings as your Savior, you will die and descend to hades to await the second resurrection (the unbelievers' resurrection).

Remember Revelation 19:15 says Jesus will rule with a rod of iron when He returns to cleanse the earth. Psalm 23 says, "I fear no evil for You are with me; Your rod and your staff, they comfort me." The rod here is used for guidance and protection. In Proverbs 22:15 it talks about the rod of discipline. In the Millennium Jesus' rod will offer guidance and protection, but He will also discipline those who rebel. It is iron in order to convey strength and authority because there will still be sin in the millennial reign. At the beginning of the millennial reign, only believers will inhabit, but as the years pass, and children grow, some of those born will make unwise choices and Jesus will have to rule with justice. He will have to use the rod of discipline.

Now we know why Satan is released after the Millennium: there will be those still remaining who have not yet made their final choice. Satan will shed light on man's inner rebellion and many will follow the deceiver. Once eternity begins, there can be no more rebellion and no more fall. God cannot allow sin to enter the human heart again. Satan is released so those remaining on earth will make their decision quickly. Look again at the description of Satan's army:

> *And will come out to deceive the nations which are in the four corners of the earth, God and Magog, to gather them together for the war; the number of them is like the sand of the seashore.*
>
> *Revelation 20:8*

The sad reality is that when Satan is released at the end of the thousand years, he amasses a large army "like the sand of the seashore." You could look at this two ways: first, Satan deceives the majority of those who have been born; second, there is such a population explosion on earth any army Satan amasses is large. I believe it is the latter. God's children are so blessed in the Millennium the population cannot be fathomed.

Many scholars will insist only the tribulation saints, those who are still alive at Christ's return, will have the privilege of repopulating the earth. Their logic goes something like this: "Because those who have died in Christ will receive perfected bodies at the rapture they won't be capable of bearing children."

Scripture is unclear when these tribulation saints (both Jew and Gentile) will receive their perfected bodies, but I can't imagine those who have gone through the final years on earth, who were faithful to Jesus through the worst of times, would grow old and die during the Millennium. I believe they will receive the same "new" body those in the rapture have received when Jesus sits on His throne and weeds out the "sheep" from the "goats."

Look again at the sheep and the goats passage we have looked at previously.

364

"But when the Son of Man comes in His glory, and all the angels with Him, then He will sit on His glorious throne. All the nations will be gathered before Him; and He will separate them from one another, as the shepherd separates the sheep from the goats; and He will put the sheep on His right, and the goats on the left. Then the King will say to those on His right, 'Come, you who are blessed of My Father, inherit the kingdom prepared for you from the foundation of the world'"

Matthew 25:31-34

Just as the raptured saints are rewarded when they meet Jesus in the heavenlies (Luke 14:14), so should the sheep (those remaining faithful on the earth) be rewarded when they meet Jesus at His second coming. They will be rewarded with their perfected, glorified bodies just like those taken at the rapture and those resurrected from the dead. Why? They have made their choice. They have chosen the King. I truly believe everyone who enters the Millennial Kingdom will have their "glorified body."

So, if everyone receives their "glorified body" at the beginning of the Millennial Kingdom, who will repopulate the earth?

Scholars insist glorified bodies cannot give birth. I disagree. Let's go back to Adam and Eve. God made everything right in the beginning. The Garden of Eden was paradise. Adam and Eve walked with God and had fellowship with Him (Genesis 3:8). There was no death, no tears, no crying, and no pain in Eden. God didn't create Adam and Eve to decay; He created them to live forever. God gave them a directive before the end of the sixth day, while everything was still "good." This means God's command came before the fall, before sin, and before the curse of death. What was God's directive? What did God commanded Adam and Eve to do?

God blessed them; and God said to them "Be fruitful and multiply, and fill the earth, and subdue it; and rule over the fish of the sea and over the birds of the sky and over every living thing that moves on the earth."

Genesis 1:28

Adam and Eve were supposed to fill the earth with children while their bodies were "perfect," without sin or death. Eve was meant to give birth and Adam was equipped to help her out a bit. God told Adam and Eve, who had bodies that could live forever, to bear children! What does Isaiah 65 say? "They will not labor in vain, or bear children for calamity; for they are the offspring of those blessed by the Lord, and their descendants with them" (23). Why are they blessed by the Lord? Because in Revelation 20:6 it says those who are part of the first resurrection (all believers) are "blessed and holy."

Perfected bodies were meant to give birth. It was God's plan in the beginning. It will be God's plan in the end. He hasn't lost sight of that goal; He hasn't lost sight of Eden; He hasn't lost sight of the directive, "Be fruitful and multiply and fill the earth, and subdue it." What else will we be doing in the Millennium?

Isaiah 65 says we will build houses and inhabit them (21), we will plant vineyards and enjoy the produce (21), we will enjoy the work of our hands (22), see the animal kingdom living in perfect peace (25), and we will have instant access to our King (24). And there is more.

The eyes of the blind will be opened and the ears of the deaf will be unstopped. Then the lame will leap like a deer, and the tongue of the mute will shout for joy. For waters will break forth in the wilderness and streams in the Arabah.

Isaiah 35:5-6

Sickness and disease will be eradicated. We will be living in Eden-like conditions.

A fire consumes before them and behind them a flame burns. The land is like the garden of Eden before them but a desolate wilderness behind them.

Joel 2:3

Indeed, the Lord will comfort Zion; He will comfort all her waste places. And her wilderness He will make like Eden, and her desert like the garden of the Lord; joy and gladness will be found in her, thanksgiving and sound of a melody.

Isaiah 51:3

We are walking into Eden. The destruction of the trumpets and the bowls will be turned into Eden.

Does that sound like what you've always wanted? Look again at the scripture I quoted at the beginning of this chapter.

And after you suffer for a short time, God, who gives all grace, will make everything right. He will make you strong and support you and keep you from falling. He called you to share in His glory in Christ, a glory that will continue forever.

1 Peter 5:10 (NCV)

If the Millennial Kingdom is what we have just said, this scripture makes sense does it not? God will make everything right. What will God make right for you? What has happened in your life?

Let's consider miscarriages. Has God forgotten those children? Of course not! God knit them together in the womb (Psalm 139:13); He knows all the hairs on their head (Luke 12:7). He hasn't forgotten them or their parents. I believe parents who have miscarried will be able to raise that child and that child will be able to live in the Millennial Kingdom.

What about abortions? Has God forgotten those innocent children? Of course not! How can He make it right for those children? Well, don't you think they will have a chance at life in the Millennial Kingdom? They will have a chance to choose the perfect King who rules them. They too will grow in the Millennial Kingdom and they will have a choice. Why do I believe this? Because God said He would make everything right. There are arguments across the board on whether or not babies automatically go to heaven when they die.

But now he has died; why should I fast? Can I bring him back again? I will go to him, but he will not return to me.

2 Samuel 12:23

Behold, I was brought forth in iniquity, and in sin my mother conceived me.

Psalm 51:5

In the first passage, David's son had just died, but David knew that when he died he would be reunited with his son. However, the second passage sounds like we are sinful at birth. If we are sinful at birth, the argument goes, how then could a newborn child get to heaven?

I'm sure most of you doing this study do believe children will be in heaven, but let's look at a few more scriptures to see if there is further clarification on the matter.

> *But Jesus said, "Let the children alone, and do not hinder them from coming to Me; for the kingdom of heaven belongs to such as these."*
>
> *Matthew 19:14*

In the truest sense, the "kingdom of heaven" is the Millennium. Now look at another scripture.

> *"Moreover, your little ones who you said would become a prey, and your sons, who this day have no knowledge of good or evil, shall enter there, and I will give it to them and they shall possess it."*
>
> *Deuteronomy 1:39*

This scripture is a verdict God rendered when the spies gave an unfavorable report after scouting out the Promised Land. God told the Israelites to go and possess it, and the spies came back and told the Israelites the people of the Land would be too strong for them. After the Israelites believed the spies unfavorable report, God told them because of their unbelief their children would be the ones to possess the Promised Land. Why? Because they "have no knowledge of good or evil."

I truly believe this scripture can also be used to argue a spiritual truth. God rendered a verdict in the wilderness (this life) that those who do not have the knowledge of good and evil (certain children) will enter the promised land (heaven). The Promised Land is Israel, but it is also "thy kingdom come." This verse tells me there is an age when children are accountable to God. There is an age when they have "the tree of knowledge of good and evil" experience. What is this age? I believe it is probably different for each and every child. Only God can judge the heart (1 Samuel 16:7). What Deuteronomy 1:39 conveys to me is that children aborted, miscarried, and those who have died young without

368

"knowledge of good and evil" will be in the Millennial Kingdom. But this admittance does not give them a "free pass" into eternity. They will still have to make a choice, just like we do here.

Now, what I do not want you to take away from this study is that everyone will have a second chance. That is not biblical. We have just been over hades and how multitudes are there awaiting judgment. They do not have a second chance. We have looked at the devastation of the trumpets and the bowl judgments and how angels declared them "righteous" judgments for those remaining on earth. Even though God gave the earth ample warning they "did not repent." God's judgments are righteous and true. The only people in question here are children too young to make a choice, but that is the exception, not the rule. In this life we have a choice. We can either choose the tree of life or the tree of knowledge of good and evil. But God is a fair God. He will make it right. Children who were denied a choice here will have that choice in the Millennium. That is what the Millennial Kingdom is all about. God will make everything right.

What did Jesus say? "For whoever wishes to save his life will lose it; but whoever loses his life for My sake will find it." Why? Because we have the Millennial Kingdom of Christ.

Isn't God fabulous? The believer's life doesn't end here; it continues in the Millennium. The wrongs that have happened to us will be righted, and Jesus will reign for a thousand years.

If you aren't shouting, "Glory!" we need to have a serious discussion over some coffee, and I mean a serious discussion.

More on the Millennium tomorrow.

Until then, may your days be filled with hope.

Thought for the day:
Eden. We will see it reborn. We will see animals living in peace. We will see people living in peace. We will not worry, because Jesus is on the throne. The wrongs in this life will be righted. If you are crippled, you will dance; if you are mute, you will sing; if you are blind, you will see; if you are insecure, you will be free. What will your life look like? It will be better than you have ever dreamed. And Satan? He will get what he deserves. You will see his fate tomorrow.

[7]When the thousand years are completed, Satan will be released from his prison, [8]and will come out to deceive the nations which are in the four corners of the earth, God and Magog, to gather them together for the war; the number of them is like the sand of the seashore. [9]And they came up on the broad plan of the earth and surrounded the camp of the saints and the beloved city, and fire came down from heaven and devoured them. [10]And the devil who deceived them was thrown into the lake of fire and brimstone, where the beast and the false prophet are also; and they will be tormented day and night forever and ever.

Revelation 20:7-10

When Satan is rereleased at the end of the thousand years, scripture says he gathers people from the four corners of the earth (as in this is a world wide rebellion). It then mentions Gog and Magog as if this too describes the four corners of the earth. Let's dig deeper.

The reference to Gog and Magog is in Ezekiel 38 and 39. Gog, who is from the land of Magog, leads a coalition of nations to attack Jerusalem. Many people place this war at the beginning of the final seven years. Upon closer examination, however, this war sounds suspiciously like the final battle we call Armageddon (that will take place in the Kidron Valley). Let's look at scripture.

> *"After many days you will be summoned; in the latter years you will come into the land that is restored from the sword, whose inhabitants have been gathered from many nations to the mountains of Israel which had been a continual waste; but its people were brought out from the nations, and they are living securely, all of them."*
>
> *Ezekiel 38:8*

> *"I will magnify Myself, sanctify Myself, and make Myself known in the sight of many nations; and they will know that I am the Lord."*
>
> *Ezekiel 38:23*

"My holy name I will make known in the midst of My people Israel; and I will not let My holy name be profaned anymore. And the nations will know that I am the Lord, the Holy One in Israel."

Ezekiel 39:7

"With pestilence and with blood I will enter into judgment with him; and I will rain on him and on his troops, and on the many peoples who are with him, a torrential rain, with hailstones, fire and brimstone."

Ezekiel 38:22

"You will fall on the mountains of Israel, you and all your troops and the peoples who are with you; I will give you as food to every kind of predatory bird and beast of the field."

Ezekiel 39:4

"Behold, it is coming and it shall be done," declares the Lord God. "That is the day of which I have spoken."

Ezekiel 39:8

Ezekiel 38 and 39 says Gog attacks Israel when it is restored from the sword and living securely (Ezekiel 38:8). Israel is not living securely until the beginning of the final seven years, so how could Gog attack them before the peace treaty is signed? This sounds like the war would start at or after the midpoint of the final seven years, when the peace treaty is broken.

Jesus says He will make Himself known when He destroys Gog (Ezekiel 38:23) and He will not allow His name to be profaned anymore (Ezekiel 39:7). Throughout Revelation we see the people of the earth "blaspheming" God. God's name will no longer be profaned at the end of the seven years, but until then His name will be denigrated.

When Jesus responds to Gog, He will turn every man's sword against His brother (Ezekiel 38:21), He will rain down hail, fire and brimstone (Ezekiel 38:22) and Gog's army will be eaten by the birds of the sky and beasts of the field (Ezekiel 39:4, 17). This sounds like the final battle that we call Armageddon. When describing Jesus' battle with the Antichrist and his armies, scripture says every hand will be against another (Zechariah 14:13), that hail comes down on the enemy (Revelation 16:21), and birds will eat the enemy's flesh (Revelation 19:17).

It is the "day of which I have spoken" (Ezekiel 39:8). What is the day the Lord speaks about throughout scripture? The day of the Lord – the return of the King – the second coming of Christ at the end of the seven-year period!

If Gog of Magog is really the Antichrist's persecution of Israel and the church at the midpoint, or the gathering of armies during the fifth and sixth trumpet, the outcome of that war is Jesus' return at the battle of Armageddon. Why then is Gog mentioned again in Revelation 20? I believe it is because, when Jesus returns, every nation is gathered together to fight.

I will gather all the nations and bring them down to the valley of Jehoshaphat. Then I will enter into judgment with them there on behalf of My people and My inheritance Israel.

Joel 3:2a

The reference to Gog in Revelation 20 is telling us, once again, that Satan amasses an army from the entire world – just like he did at the battle of Armageddon. Again, this is a worldwide conflict. Once again, they come down to Jerusalem and surround it. But this time, unlike the last time, there is even less of a fight. Fire comes down from heaven and devours them. Resistance is crushed before it could ever begin. Hallelujah!

The devil is then thrown into the lake of fire, where the beast and the false prophet already reside. Satan can never deceive the people of the earth again. He is gone forever. Yet, he's not destroyed, just like the false prophet, the Antichrist, and the unrepentant who will soon join them. God didn't create us to die. He created us to live forever. It's our choice to be with Him or against Him. May God put a holy fear in our souls of His majesty.

[11]Then I saw a great white throne and Him who sat upon it, from whose presence earth and heaven fled away, and no place was found for them. [12]And I saw the dead, the great and the small, standing before the throne, and books were opened; and another book was opened, which is the book of life; and the dead were judged from the things which were written in the books, according to their deeds. [13]And the sea gave up the dead

which were in it, and death and Hades gave up the dead which were in them; and they were judged, every one of them according to their deeds. [14]Then death and Hades were thrown into the lake of fire. This is the second death, the lake of fire. [15]And if anyone's name was not found written in the book of life, he was thrown into the lake of fire.

Revelation 20:11-15

When we see the great white thrown, every believer will have already been judged. Those of us who are raptured receive judgment at the judgment seat of Christ in the heavenlies (Luke 14:14). Those who become believers during the final years on earth after the rapture will receive their rewards when Jesus sits on His throne at the beginning of the Millennium (Revelation 20:4). Those who are born in the Millennium and choose Christ will be deemed worthy when they don't enter the rebellion of Satan at the end of the thousand years.

Now, it is the unbeliever's time for judgment. Only unbelievers will stand before the great white throne.

Jesus is sitting on the great white throne. This matches scripture.

For not even the Father judges anyone, but He has given all judgment to the Son, so that all will honor the Son even as they honor the Father. He who does not honor the Son does not honor the Father who sent Him.

John 5:22-23

All judgment is left to the Son. Jesus will sit and judge those who rejected Him. Woe to the man! "It is a terrifying thing to fall into the hands of the living God" (Hebrews 10:31). Look closely at this next verse.

And I saw the dead, the great and the small, standing before the throne, and books were opened; and another book was opened, which is the book of life; and the dead were judged from the things which were written in the books, according to their deeds.

Revelation 20:12

I find it highly significant that those resurrected at the great white throne are referred to as "the dead." They will be forever

373

"dead" to the believer, yet forever alive in torment. Oh, how dreadful it sounds! Yet, those judged at the great white throne have rejected a perfectly loving God and the Savior who sacrificed everything to save them. To reject God is to reject everything God has made. It is to reject light and goodness. It is to reject fellowship and friendship. They are doomed to the second death, or the lake of fire.

Our image of hell or the "lake of fire" has been warped by the deceiver. We imagine hell as a big party, with lots of friends, food, and drinking. If there are flames, they are a fair distance from the dinner table and seem to have little affect on those present. I beg to differ. Everything good comes from God. None of those things will be present in the lake of fire. Those thrown in the lake of fire will have a solitary existence. The rich man who called for Lazarus in Luke 16 wasn't with anyone else. He wasn't talking to the man next to him. He was suffering independently. The lake of fire is rejecting everything God is and if you reject those things God gave us, you don't get to enjoy them in eternity. The lake of fire is real. It should scare the living daylights out of us. We need to beg our friends who haven't accepted Christ to flee from there and choose the Savior. Heaven is a free gift, yet many will reject it. Woe, woe, woe to them!

The books were opened. "Books" is in the plural, meaning there is more than one book, and a third book is identified: the book of life.

The first book we read about in scripture is the book of the law (Galatians 3:10).

For whoever keeps the whole law and yet stumbles in one point, he has become guilty of all."

James 2:10

No one can be found innocent if judged by the law. We know no one except Jesus has perfectly kept the law. "For all have sinned and fall short of the glory of God" (Romans 3:23). If anyone is judged on the law, he will be found guilty.

The second book, based on Revelation 20, is the book of deeds. Those who haven't been saved by grace are judged based on their deeds according to the law. That's why both books have to be opened. Jesus will look at a person's deeds and compare that to the law. Of course, all will be found guilty. Then the book of life is mentioned. Because they are found guilty, Jesus opens up the book of life and searches for the person's name in the hopes his name is found written there.

We studied the book of life when we looked at chapter two. It is the book where the names of those who "overcome" and continue to hold fast to their faith are written. If you profess a faith in the living God, you are written in the book of life. This book is also identified as the Lamb's book of life in certain scriptures, but they are one in the same book. If you have "life" you have the "Lamb." Only through Him can you have life!

Once you are written in the book of life, scripture teaches you can be blotted out (Revelation 3:5). We know this scripture refers to believers because Jesus is addressing His church. David even says about his enemies: "May they be blotted out of the book of life" (Psalm 69:28). Who was David talking about? How were his enemies even in the book of life if they were his enemies? Well, in this particular Psalm, David is talking about those close to him, those who were his brothers (8) and those who sit in the gate (12), meaning the city gate of Jerusalem. They were Jews! David says "blot them out of your book." This indicates that the Jews, who were in a covenant relationship with God, could be blotted out. They could break the covenant! This is no different from the church today. We are in a covenant relationship with God, but we can choose to walk away and break the covenant. Then and only then can our name be blotted out.

The dead who are judged have either never been in the book of life (unbelievers) or are those who broke the covenant and turned from God (their names were blotted out).

Once the dead are judged according to their deeds and based on the law, this is the final check. When their names are not found in the book of life they are thrown into the lake of fire.

Death and hades are also thrown into the lake of fire (14). Death is not abolished until after the millennial reign of Christ. As we have already studied, there is still death in the Millennial Kingdom. Hades, or the place of the dead, is also thrown into the lake of fire. This is significant. Judgment is final. Because there is no more death, there will be no one else entering Hades. The Judge has sat and the verdict has been rendered. The lake of fire has acquired its maximum number of inhabitants. Death and hades are no more.

Revelation 20:11 says that once Jesus sat on the throne "earth and heaven fled away, and no place was found for them." Another way to translate "fled" is "shun." The cosmos faded in comparison to our Lord and Savior. He is on the throne of judgment and those who have rejected Him will see nothing but Him. Everything else fades in comparison to the King of kings.

Jesus' face is like the sun (Revelation 1:16). When His majesty is rendering judgment it is a sight to behold. Those involved in this judgment will cower in terror. Those of us looking on will be somber. The entire universe fades to nothing at the glory of God and His righteous judgment. Those facing the King have rejected goodness and light. They have rejected their Savior. The cosmos stands still as judgment is rendered.

And it is final.

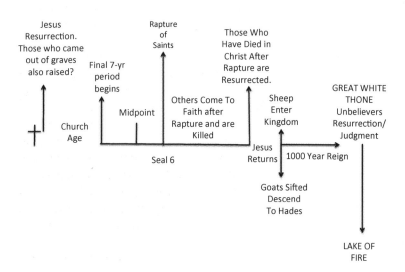

Resurrection of Dead

Thought for the day:

Satan is gone. He will never be able to deceive the world again. Can you imagine living without the threat of the devil? Can you imagine living for a thousand years under Christ's rule and seeing the final rebellion? We have warned those born about the devil; yet, many will take his side. This proves how rebellious the human heart can be. Even with perfect peace, some will still choose evil. It is mind-boggling. But if they do, they will be unable to enter eternity and see the New Jerusalem. More on this tomorrow.

[1]Then I saw a new heaven and a new earth; for the first heaven and the first earth passed away, and there is no longer any sea. [2]And I saw the holy city, new Jerusalem, coming down out of heaven from God, made ready as a bride adorned for her husband. [3]And I heard a loud voice from the throne, saying, "Behold, the tabernacle of God is among men, and He will dwell among them, and they shall be His people, and God Himself will be among them, [4]and He will wipe away every tear from their eyes; and there will no longer be any death; there will no longer be any mourning, or crying, or pain; the first things have passed away. [5]And He who sits on the throne said, "Behold, I am making all things new." And He said, "Write, for these words are faithful and true." [6]Then He said to me, "It is done. I am the Alpha and the Omega, the beginning and the end. I will give to the one who thirsts from the spring of the water of life without cost. [7]He who overcomes will inherit these things, and I will be his God and he will be My son. [8]But for the cowardly and unbelieving and abominable and murderers and immoral persons and sorcerers and idolaters and all liars, their part will be in the lake that burns with fire and brimstone, which is the second death." [9]Then one of the seven angels who had the seven bowls full of the seven last plagues came and spoke with me, saying, "Come here, I will show you the bride, the wife of the Lamb."

Revelation 21:1-9

In yesterday's lesson, we saw the cosmos fading to a distant memory as Jesus takes His seat on the great white throne. Here we see the announcement of a new heaven and a new earth. Does this mean the old earth is completely destroyed?

There are multiple scriptures that seem to support this understanding. Let's look at a few of these.

Of old You founded the earth, and the heavens are the work of Your hands. Even they will perish, but You endure; and all of them will wear out like a garment; like clothing You will change them and they will be changed.
Psalm 102:25-26

377

"Heaven and earth will pass away, but My words will not pass away."

Matthew 24:35

But the day of the Lord will come like a thief, in which the heavens will pass away with a roar and the elements will be destroyed with intense heat, and the earth and its works will be burned up.

2 Peter 3:10

On the flip side, there are other Bible verses that say the earth will remain forever.

A generation goes and a generation comes, but the earth remains forever.

Ecclesiastes 1:4

And He built His sanctuary like the heights, like the earth which He has founded forever.

Psalm 78:69

"So you shall keep His statutes and His commandments which I am giving you today, that it may go well with you and with your children after you, and that you may live long on the land which the Lord your God is giving you for all time."

Deuteronomy 4:40

So, which one is it? Is God going to destroy the earth or let it continue forever? Scripture can't be wrong, so it must be both. Let's dig deeper.

In Psalm 102 (quoted previously) it says heaven and earth will perish, yet it also says God will change them. It sounds like He will transform them. Yes, the world as we know it, the decaying, sinful world will perish, but a new, glorious earth will be reborn.

Our bodies are perishing, each and every day. As we sit here, we are dying. Not a comforting thought, but it is truth. God told Adam and Eve they would die if they ate from the tree of knowledge of good and evil, but they didn't die right away. Adam lived nine hundred and thirty years (Genesis 5:5). Their bodies slowly started to perish – they started to decay the instant they ate the fruit. The same thing is happening to the earth.

378

For the anxious longing of the creation waits eagerly for the revealing of the sons of God. For the creation was subjected to futility, not willingly, but because of Him who subjected it, in hope that the creation itself also will be set free from its slavery to corruption into the freedom of the glory of the children of God. For we know that the whole creation groans and suffers the pains of childbirth together until now.

Romans 8:19-22

What does "the pains of childbirth" mean in this passage? Luke 21:25-26 says:

There will be signs in sun and moon and stars, and on the earth dismay among nations, in perplexity at the roaring of the sea and the waves, men fainting from fear and the expectation of the things which are coming upon the world; for the powers of the heavens will be shaken.

Luke 21:25-26

The entire world is under the curse of sin just like our bodies, and it is perishing just like our bodies, but both our bodies and the earth will be made new. God is not going to get new dust to make our heavenly bodies. He is going to reconstruct the old. The old will be made new and we will be a "new" creation.

Behold, I tell you a mystery; we will not all sleep, but we will all be changed, in a moment, in the twinkling of an eye, at the last trumpet; for the trumpet will sound, and the dead will be raised imperishable, and we will be changed.

1 Corinthians 15:51

Are our skin and bones going to disappear before we get "new" skin? No! God is making our old bodies new. He will make the earth new as well. Let's see how scripture describes the earth after the flood.

Whereby the world that then was, being overflowed with water, perished. But the heavens and the earth, which are now, by the same word are kept in store, reserved until

379

fire against the day of judgment and perdition of ungodly men.

2 Peter 3:6-7 (KJV)

The earth perished, but it wasn't completely destroyed. It was a surface destruction. The old earth was laid bare and then renewed – purified through water. This is what will happen when Jesus returns. Remember, He is like refiner's fire and a fullers' soap (Malachi 3:2). He is cleansing the surface of the earth with fire, purifying it if you will. The earth will once again become Eden (Joel 2:3). I do believe the "new heaven" and "new earth" will be the same situation. In the Millennium, there will still be sin (hence the rebellion Satan amasses). The earth has to be purified again at the end of the Millennium. God won't destroy the earth completely because if He did, Satan would win. God declared the heavens and the earth "good" in Genesis 1:31. There is no reason to destroy something good.

We also need to understand that when scripture speaks of "heaven" it is not necessarily the entire cosmos. The atmosphere surrounding the earth is deemed "heaven" as well.

Then God said, "Let the waters teem with swarms of living creatures, and let birds fly above the earth in the open expanse of the heavens."

Genesis 1:20

Birds don't fly in space; they fly above the earth, in our atmosphere. So, when Jesus says, "heaven and earth will pass away," He could be referring to the atmosphere surrounding the earth itself, not necessarily four galaxies over. Paul said in 2 Corinthians 12:2 that he was caught up into the third heaven, or God's throne. Is this 'heaven' destroyed? We know from studying the trumpets and the bowls cosmic things will happen to the earth. The atmosphere surrounding the earth is going to be damaged just like the earth itself. These scriptures do not indicate either way if we are discussing the entirety of heaven (our atmosphere, distant space, and God's throne) or if it is referring to the heaven that we see surrounding us. We will have to leave that mystery to God.

Scripture also says there will no longer be any sea in the new earth (Revelation 21:1). I have attended Bible studies with individuals who cringe at this. The earth without any sea is something most of us don't want to contemplate. We like sitting on the beach and watching the waves roll in while we dig our toes in the sand. We don't want to give that up.

However, the "sea" we see today (no pun intended) represents judgment and separation. For the Lord to tell us there won't be any "sea" is actually a beautiful statement. Before the flood, the huge bodies of water we now have weren't the dominant feature of the planet. After Noah's flood, the earth was a very different place. In Noah's flood God said, "the fountains of the great deep burst open" (Genesis 7:11). Scholars say this was the water inside the earth's crust; it burst forth, along with the "floodgates of the sky" and covered every mountain on the face of the earth. When the waters receded, much of the water remained, creating what we now call seas and oceans.

We know from the creation story God made large bodies of water He called "seas" in the beginning (Genesis 1:10). There is no reason to think there won't be large beaches that will be similar to our oceans today, just like in the creation story. Those bodies of water, however, will not be enough to separate us from our fellow man. God is telling us there will no longer be any separation or isolation. We will be a family in eternity and nothing at all will interfere with that.

John then sees the New Jerusalem coming down out of heaven. He equates this city to a bride adorned for her husband. As we have said before, the city, by itself, is not the bride of Christ, but the people who will dwell there are the bride!

Isaiah 62:2-5 is a passage talking about Israel. It speaks of the land being married to the Lord.

The nations will see your righteousness, and all the kings your glory; and you will be called by a new name which the mouth of the Lord will designate. You will also be a crown of beauty in the hand of the Lord, and a royal diadem in the hand of your God. It will no longer be said to you, "Forsaken," nor to your land will it any longer be said, "Desolate"; But you will be called, "My delight is in her," and your land, "Married"; for the Lord delights in you; and to Him your land will be married. For as a young man marries a virgin, so your sons will marry you; and as the bridegroom rejoices over the bride, so your God will rejoice over you.

Isaiah 62:2-5

The land will be married to the Savior, meaning, the people as a whole in the land will be married to the Savior. This is exactly what is being stated in Revelation 21 about the New Jerusalem. The city will be the Lords. Glory!

Then John hears a loud voice from the throne.

The throne we have just seen is the great white throne and the Savior is sitting there. Jesus announces the "tabernacle of God is among men, and He will dwell among them, and they shall be His people, and God Himself will be among them."

Jesus is already with us. Now God the Father is coming down with the New Jerusalem. So in essence, heaven comes to earth!

Oh, I need to say that again. Heaven comes to earth!

God's home is descending to the earth and God Himself will be among us for eternity.

Now we come to the really good news.

And He will wipe away every tear from their eyes; and there will no longer be any death; there will no longer be any mourning, or crying, or pain; the first things have passed away.

Revelation 21:4

Jesus says all tears will be wiped away, all mourning will be gone, all crying and pain will be extinguished, and death will be a distant memory. Do you remember at the end of chapter twenty death itself was thrown into the lake of fire? "The last enemy that will be abolished is death" (1 Corinthians 15:26). During the Millennial Kingdom, animals will still be sacrificed and some people will die when they reject Jesus as King (Isaiah 65:20). In eternity, there is no more death. Scripture doesn't state this, but it is logical to assume that there is no more childbirth. Only believers will occupy eternity and if anyone should be born, God would logically allow them the choice He gave to us – to accept or reject Him. In eternity, there cannot be another fall, hence, it seems reasonable to conclude no more children are being born. Scripture does somewhat corroborate this theory in verse four. It says that the "first things" have passed away.

In Isaiah 65 the "former things" will not be remembered, but the word "things" is not in the original Hebrew. The "former" in Isaiah 65 is referring to "earth." We will not remember our life of sin. Here, in Revelation 21, the "the old order of things have passed away" (NIV). The order we have on earth, both now and in the

382

Millennial Kingdom, is made new in eternity. Why? There can be no more sin in eternity, no more fall. Does this mean no special relationships with our friends or our spouse? Scripture is unclear; however, I believe the special relationships we have in the Millennial Kingdom will continue to grow and flourish. God made us to be relational. He in no way intends for those relationships to disappear in any way. The Millennial Kingdom will actually increase those relationships in such a way we cannot really fathom the depth and wonder of them. We have to trust our Creator and know that whatever the new order is, we won't miss the old.

Jesus then announces He is making all things new. This is announced right after we are told the old order will pass away. Jesus is creating the new order. He is renewing all things. And it will be glorious. He then tells John to write His words down because they are faithful and true. Jesus was called Faithful and True in Revelation 19:11 when He first came down to claim the earth.

Jesus is reminding us here that He is the same Jesus that came to rule for a thousand years. He is the same One who gave us the gift of the thousand years. He won't deviate from His faithfulness in eternity. We need not worry about the new order. It will be exactly what we want.

He says, "It is done." He is the Alpha and the Omega. He is the beginning and the end. He was there in the beginning and the world was created through Him (John 1:3). He will also be at the ending, a faithful and true King, creating a new order. He declares He can give the water of life without cost. This is a statement for those reading Revelation. "Choose Me," He is saying. "By grace you are saved. There is no cost for my gift. I laid down my life freely for you. Take it and be saved." It is the same offer He gave the woman at the well, "Whoever drinks of the water that I will give him shall never thirst; but the water that I will give him will become in him a well of water springing up to eternal life" (John 4:14).

Believe and have eternal life.

We will stop here for today. Tomorrow we will dig a little deeper into Revelation 21. Well done Christian soldiers. You have made it to the home stretch. Only a few more days and we will say goodbye. Even if we don't meet in this life, we will meet in the place where there are no more tears.

Hallelujah!

Thought for the day:

His words are faithful and true. He is Faithful and True. His promises will come to pass. The book of Revelation tells how those promises will come to pass. When He says He "will make everything right," you can be assured He will – because He is Faithful. When He says you can have "eternal life" you can be assured you will – because His words are True. Faithful friends, He is faithful; He is true. Believe this book. Believe His promises. They will soon come to pass.

[10]And he carried me away in the Spirit to a great and high mountain, and showed me the holy city, Jerusalem, coming down out of heaven from God, [11]having the glory of God. Her brilliance was like a very costly stone, as a stone of crystal-clear jasper. [12]It had a great and high wall, with twelve gates, and at the gates twelve angels; and names were written on them, which are the names of the twelve tribes of the sons of Israel. [13]There were three gates on the east and three gates on the north and three gates on the south and three gates on the west. [14]And the wall of the city had twelve foundation stones, and on them were the twelve names of the twelve apostles of the Lamb. [15]The one who spoke with me had a gold measuring rod to measure the city, and its gates and its wall. [16]The city is laid out as a square, and its length is as great as the width; and he measured the city with the rod, fifteen hundred miles; its length and width and height are equal. [17]And he measured its wall, seventy-two yards, according to human measurements, which are also angelic measurements. [18]The material of the wall was jasper; and the city was pure gold, like clear glass. [19]The foundation stones of the city wall were adorned with every king of precious stone. The first foundation stone was jasper; the second, sapphire; the third, chalcedony; the fourth, emerald; [20]the fifth, sardonyx; the sixth, sardius; the seventh, chrysolite; the eighth, beryl; the ninth, topaz; the tenth, chrysoprase; the eleventh, jacinth; the twelfth, amethyst. [21]And the twelve gates were twelve pearls; each one of the gates was a single pearl. And the street of the city was pure gold, like transparent glass. [22]I saw no temple in it, for the Lord God the Almighty and the Lamb are its temple. [23]And the city has no need of the sun or of the moon to shine on it, for the glory of God has illumined it, and its lamp is the Lamb. [24]The nations will walk by its light, and the kings of the earth will bring their glory into it. [25]In the daytime (for there will be no night there) its gates will never be closed; [26]and they will bring the glory and the honor of the nations into it; [27]and nothing unclean, and no one who practices abomination and lying, shall ever come into it, but only those whose names are written in the Lamb's book of life.

Revelation 21:10-27

We are near the end of the road, faithful friends. Can you believe it? I hope there has been a lot of learning and growing. I hope there is a renewed excitement in you about the return of the King. Today we will go a little deeper and use a little bit of our imaginations. It will be a fun day. Before we read the next section of scripture, I want to look back at a statement we became very familiar with in the letters to the churches in chapters two and three.

He who overcomes will inherit these things, and I will be his God and he will be My son.

Revelation 21:7

These things I have spoken to you, so that in Me you may have peace. In the world you have tribulation, but take courage; I have overcome the world.

John 16:33

You have to do more than profess belief to be saved, you have to overcome and continue to choose Jesus and His living water. You have to live with a victorious faith. We have to overcome complacency (Ephesus), tribulation (Smyrna), idolatry (Pergamum), false-teaching (Thyatira), dead faith (Sardis), weariness (Philadelphia), and lukewarmness (Laodicea).

Don't be tricked into believing just because you are a member of a church that you are a true follower of Christ. Search your heart and see if you have the living water Jesus offers.

We have looked at "overcoming" before, but it is important enough to revisit here. It is a tall task to overcome the world. You can't do it. Let me repeat that again: you can't do it. Only one man was able to conquer the world, and His name was Jesus. So, in order for us to conquer the world, what do we need to do?

"I am the vine, you are the branches; he who abides in Me and I in him, he bears much fruit, for apart from Me you can do nothing. If anyone does not abide in Me, he is thrown away as a branch and dries up; and they gather them, and cast them into the fire and they are burned. If you abide in Me, and My words abide in you, ask whatever you wish, and it will be done for you."

John 15:5-7

We must remain in Him. If we remain in Him, we will be overcomers. How are we to be sure we remain in Him? One way to remain in Him is to remain in the Word – because Jesus is the Word. That is what Ephesus, Pergamum, Thyatira, Sardis, and Laodicea did not do. They drifted away from Him. If you remain in Christ, you will not be fooled by false teachers, you will not be led away by the world, and you will shun lukewarmness. You will overcome.

Then Jesus makes another announcement to assure the believer and warn the unrepentant: no evil will touch the New Jerusalem: no coward, no unbeliever, no abomination, no murderer, no immoral person, no sorcerers, no idolaters, and no liars. They will remain in the lake of fire.

The city is glowing with the glory of God as she descends to the earth. Her brilliance is described like a very costly stone, like crystal clear jasper. Many scholars believe this is referring to the gem we now know as the diamond. There is nothing more brilliant than a diamond shimmering in the light. The New Jerusalem will have that brilliance, and much more. She will almost be blinding.

The city has a great and high wall with twelve gates named for the twelve tribes of Israel. We studied the twelve tribes of Israel when we looked at Revelation chapter seven. If you recall, when the tribes were listed, Dan was missing and Levi (the priestly tribe who normally was not counted in the twelve) was included. Also, Joseph's name appeared instead of his youngest son Ephraim. However, in Ezekiel 48 when it is talking about the land division in the Millennium, the original twelve tribes are listed. As in, Dan is included and so is Ephraim. Will the gates read the original twelve tribes (excluding Levi as the priestly tribe) or could they possibly be the tribes listed in Revelation chapter seven. It will be interesting to walk under those gates and see just who is named.

Angels station themselves at the gates, guarding those who enter the city.

At first glance it seems the walls and the angels stationed at the gates are there to keep people out, but I believe this is a constant reminder for those who enter the city and live there: God is a constant hedge of protection around them. After the horrors of this life, there will never be any reason to fear. The angels remind us of that every time we pass through the gates. The walls assure us that we are protected every time we circle their perimeter. We are chosen and protected by God.

In Revelation 21:18 it says the walls are made of jasper and in verse 11 it says the brilliance of the city was like a crystal-clear jasper. If the walls are clear, we can look through them! Think about that for a minute. I think the walls are clear because when we are inside the city we will feel protected but we will also feel free because we can look out! These walls aren't confining, it is as if God is encircling the city with a huge hug.

The twelve gates are evenly distributed around the city, providing easy access to God, and they will never be closed. We are His children; we are never without access to His throne. Scripture says the gates are made of twelve pearls and the streets are made of gold. Everything is glorious in heaven. There is no more asphalt or concrete. We will be walking on gold and surrounded by jewels.

The wall of the city has twelve foundation stones, each named for one of the apostles of the Lamb. I believe these stones will form a glorious rainbow underneath the New Jerusalem, and as we climb up those foundation stones and up that rainbow we will be reminded of God's mercy – just like in the days of Noah. Only this time, the rainbow means He will never destroy the earth again. His wrath has passed. Now, all that remains is mercy and grace.

Now you might be thinking, who are the twelve apostles of the Lamb? We know Judas betrayed Jesus, and based on scripture it sounds like he never fully repented.

"The Son of Man is to go, just as it is written of Him; but woe to that man by whom the Son of Man is betrayed! It would have been good for that man if he had not been born. "

Matthew 26:24

Even though Judas felt remorse and threw the money he received back into the temple (Matthew 27:1-10), that in itself doesn't prove he accepted Jesus as his Savior (see Acts 1:25).

So, if Judas didn't repent, whose name will be written on the foundation of the New Jerusalem? In Acts 2:15-26 Peter gets up and speaks to the disciples and tells them that because Judas betrayed Jesus and has since perished, they need to choose another disciple. Two men are mentioned: Barsabbas and Matthias. The lots cast fell on Matthias.

Have you read anything else about Matthias? Didn't think so. Do you have any other person in mind that might have fulfilled this twelfth position?

"But it happened that as I was on my way, approaching Damascus about noontime, a very bright light suddenly flashed from heaven all around me, and I fell to the ground and heard a voice saying to me, 'Saul, Saul, why are you persecuting Me?' And I answered, 'Who are you, Lord?' And He said to me, 'I am Jesus the Nazarene, whom you are persecuting'. . . And I said, 'What shall I do, Lord?' And the Lord said to me, 'Get up and go on into Damascus, and there you will be told of all that has been appointed for you to do.'"

Acts 22:6-8, 10

Jesus himself chose Saul, or Paul, to be His disciple.

You can make up your own mind exactly who will be the twelfth name on the foundation of the New Jerusalem, but I think Paul is a much more likely candidate than Judas or Matthias.

It is hard to pinpoint exactly what colors these foundation stones will be. Different versions of scripture translate the names of the stones differently, and each stone can have a variety of colors. Just imagine a rainbow and I believe you will get a very accurate picture of the stones. If you want my best guess on the foundations stones, they might be as follows: jasper (clear crystal in appearance), sapphire (deep blue), chalcedony (sky blue), emerald (deep green), sardonyx (light red), sardius (deep red), chrysolite (light apple green), beryl (orange gold), topaz (yellow), chrysoprase (metallic green), jacinth (deep purple), amethyst (light purple). Can you imagine the beauty of this city? Glory!

John then measures the city, which is laid out like a square. The city is 1,500 miles wide, long, and tall. Some people interpret the New Jerusalem as a pyramid, because a pyramid can be described with the same dimensions as a cube. However, I tend to believe it is a cube, based on one very important fact.

Then he prepared an inner sanctuary within the house in order to place there the ark of the covenant of the Lord. The inner sanctuary was twenty cubits in length, twenty cubits in width, and twenty cubits in height, and he

*overlaid it with pure gold. He also overlaid the altar with
cedar.*

1 Kings 6:19-20

*"There I will meet with you: and from above the mercy
seat, from between the two cherubim which are upon the
ark of the testimony, I will speak to you about all that I
will give you in commandments for the sons of Israel."*

Exodus 26:22

The Holy of Holies, the inner sanctuary of the temple, God's
dwelling place, was a cube. And God met with His people there.

This city is a 1,500 mile cube. For perspective, if you placed
this city on the United States it would stretch from Canada to the
Gulf of Mexico and from Atlantic Ocean to Denver, Colorado. And
it is as high as it is wide!

That is one big city.

If someone tells you there is no way all the redeemed could
live in the New Jerusalem, you may want to remind them of its size.

If you place this city on the earth as it is now, it might appear
quite humorous. The earth would look completely lopsided. That is
why I believe the new earth (really the renewed and reborn earth)
might possibly be larger than the earth we have now. It needs to
accommodate the size of the New Jerusalem!

You see, God knows the exact size of the city needed to hold
all of His faithful servants. And in order for the earth to
accommodate that city, it will be made new.

I just love God's Word!

So far, we have a rainbow foundation, pearly gates, crystal
clear walls, and streets of gold. Can you imagine anything so
beautiful?

There is no temple in the city because the Father and the Son
are the temple. We have complete and total access to our Creator.
Look again at Revelation 21:23.

*And the city has no need of the sun or of the moon to shine
on it, for the glory of God has illumined it, and its lamp is
the Lamb.*

Revelation 21:23

We have looked at the verse that says, "there is no longer any
sea." As I said then, imagining the earth without the sea makes

people uncomfortable. Revelation 21:23 indicates there is no sun or moon, but notice scripture doesn't say the sun and the moon no longer exist. What it does say is that there is no need of a sun or a moon in the city. In Genesis God declared everything very good. I believe the sun will still be in existence, but in the city, God's glory is so brilliant you will be unable to see the sun or the moon. If you travel across the earth, you will probably be able to marvel at the stars in the sky and the sun rising. But there is no need of those things in the city. Jesus is so brilliant, why would you?

Glory!

The nations will walk by the city's light, the Lamb's light. In verse 24 it mentions kings. The new order of eternity still has rulers and governance in it. I tend to believe we will explore all of God's creation in eternity. Why not? God created the universe. So far, we have been confined, for the most part, to earth. Don't you think God wants us to see Saturn? Even distant galaxies? Can you imagine the day!

At the end of this chapter, scripture once again makes it clear who has access to the New Jerusalem. Only those whose names are written in the Lamb's book of life are allowed to enter the gates and walk the golden street and approach the throne.

Thought for the day:
Can you imagine a city almost as big as the United States – and almost as tall? Where do you think your house will be? Jesus said He was going to prepare a place for you (John 14:3). Do you know why you are never fully satisfied with your house now? Because Jesus hasn't made it. Only He knows what will make you truly happy. Long for your room. Long for the One who builds it. We celebrate a feast tomorrow.

Yesterday we looked at the New Jerusalem and its amazing beauty, but we left out a very important element that we need to look at today – the Feast of Tabernacles or the Feast of Booths. This is the final Jewish feast that has yet to be fulfilled. The Feat of Tabernacles begins five days after Yom Kippur and lasts for seven days (perfection and completion).

The Feast of Tabernacles is the most joyous of all the Jewish feasts and is mentioned more often in scripture than any other feast.[1] On this feast the Jews gather in Jerusalem and build temporary shelters or booths to celebrate the final ingathering of crops. It is simply referred to as "the holiday." It was on the Feast of Tabernacles that Solomon dedicated the first temple to God (2 Chronicles 5:3).

Although we are now studying eternity, let's go back to the Millennial Kingdom for a brief period. We have already seen there will be animal sacrifices in the Millennium. Will we celebrate the feasts as well?

> *"They shall also keep My laws and My statutes in all My appointed feasts and sanctify My Sabbaths."*
>
> *Ezekiel 44:24b*

God tells us the feasts are to be observed; however, if you read further into Ezekiel you will discover God's command of observance does not include four of the seven feasts. The ones that are missing are the Feast of First Fruits, the Feast of Weeks (Pentecost), Rosh Hashanah, and Yom Kippur. The Passover with the Feast of Unleavened Bread and the Feast of Booths are specifically mentioned (Ezekiel 45:21-25). Let's look at these one at a time.

The Feast of First Fruits commemorated the first to rise from the dead. This was fulfilled at Christ's resurrection. Pentecost has also been fulfilled with the outpouring of the Holy Spirit. The rapture fulfilled Rosh Hashanah and Jesus' second coming fulfilled Yom Kippur.

What about the Passover, you might ask? Yes, the Passover and the Feast of Unleavened Bread (which immediately follows the Passover) were fulfilled at the death of Christ, but in the

Millennium, babies are being born that need to understand the sacrifice of their Savior. The Passover and the Feast of Unleavened Bread need to be observed so that those who have not accepted Christ have every chance to understand His sacrifice.

Now we come to the Feast of Booths. We looked at this scripture previously, but let's look at it again.

> *If the family of Egypt does not go up or enter, then no rain will fall on them; it will be the plague with which the Lord smites the nations who do not go up to celebrate the Feasts of Booths. This will be the punishment of Egypt and the punishment of all the nations who do not go up to celebrate the Feast of Booths.*
>
> *Zechariah 14:18-19*

Now isn't that strange. This is the only feast that initiates the plague of no rain. Why? Why would Jesus send a plague at this particular feast and not at the Passover?

Scripture is unclear, but we might be able to infer the reason. The Feast of Tabernacles (or Booths) celebrates God residing with us. This feast will be partially fulfilled when Jesus returns and sets up His kingdom, but the final fulfillment will be God the Father descending with the New Jerusalem.

> *"Behold, the tabernacle of God is among men, and He will dwell among them, and they shall be His people, and God Himself will be among them."*
>
> *Revelation 21:3b*

The Feast of Tabernacles will not be completely fulfilled until heaven comes to earth and the New Jerusalem descends to dwell with us forever. God's desire is to dwell among His people. It was His desire in the beginning:

> *They heard the sound of the Lord God walking in the garden in the cool of the day . . .*
>
> *Genesis 3:8a*

He wanted to dwell with them even after they sinned, even though it had to be "at a distance."

Let them construct a sanctuary for Me, that I may dwell among them.

Exodus 25:8-10

And in the end He will.

"Behold, the tabernacle of God is among men . . . "

Revelation 21:3

This is amazing. The God of the Universe, Abba our Father, will live with us on earth for eternity. Can you imagine the day!

So to recap, why is Jesus so adamant that everyone attends the Feast of Tabernacles in the Millennial Kingdom? To honor His Father who has yet to descend!

Amen and amen! Come quickly, Lord Jesus!

Thought for the day:

God the Father wants to dwell among us – an earth! That is an amazing sentence and one we really need to wrap our minds around. Just like He walked with us in Eden, He will again walk with us in eternity. What questions do you have? You have an eternity to ask Him. What is the first thing you will say? What is the first thing you will do? Do you want to see the Tree of Life? You will – tomorrow.

1 *Feasts of the Lord.* Kevin Howard and Marvin Rosenthal. Published in Nashville, Tennessee by Thomas Nelson, Inc., 1997, p135.

DAY FIFTY-NINE
REVELATION 22:1-9
THE TREE OF LIFE

[1]Then he showed me a river of the water of life, clear as crystal, coming from the throne of God and of the Lamb, [2]in the middle of its street. On either side of the river was the tree of life, bearing twelve kinds of fruit, yielding its fruit every month; and the leaves of the tree were for the healing of the nations. [3]There will no longer be any curse; and the throne of God and of the Lamb will be in it, and His bond-servants will serve Him; [4]they will see His face, and His name will be on their foreheads. [5]And there will no longer be any night; and they will not have need of the light of a lamp nor the light of the sun, because the Lord God will illumine them; and they will reign forever and ever. [6]And he said to me, "These words are faithful and true"; and the Lord, the God of the spirits of the prophets, sent His angel to show to His bond-servants the things which must soon take place. [7]"And behold, I am coming quickly. Blessed is he who heeds the words of the prophecy of this book." [8]I, John, am the one who heard and saw these things. And when I heard and saw, I fell down to worship at the feet of the angel who showed me these things. [9]But he said to me, "Do not do that. I am a fellow servant of yours and of your brethren the prophets and of those who heed the words of this book. Worship God."

Revelation 22:1-9

We have come to the last chapter of one of the most exciting books of the Bible. Does anyone want to start over? I sure do. I just love Revelation! I can't get enough of it. But let's focus our attention and turn to one of the most mysterious things of scripture: the tree of life.

Then He said to me, "It is done. I am the Alpha and the Omega, the beginning and the end. I will give to the one who thirsts from the spring of the water of life without cost."

Revelation 21:6

The water Jesus refers to in chapter 21 is now seen here as a river coming out of the throne of God and of the Lamb. It flows down the middle of the street and on either side of the river the tree of life appears. We have not seen the tree of life since Genesis chapter three when Adam and Eve were driven out of the Garden of Eden. Let's go back to the first book of the Bible and learn what we can about the tree of life.

Out of the ground the Lord God caused to grow every tree that is pleasing to the sight and good for food; the tree of life also in the midst of the garden, and the tree of the knowledge of good and evil.

Genesis 2:9

The Lord God commanded the man, saying, "From any tree of the garden you may eat freely; but from the tree of the knowledge of good and evil you shall not eat, for in the day that you eat from it, you will surely die."

Genesis 2:16-17

The tree of life was in the midst of the garden, just like the tree of the knowledge of good and evil, yet God does not talk to the man about the tree of life, only the tree of knowledge. Interesting.

Then the Lord God said, "Behold, the man has become like one of Us, knowing good and evil; and now, he might stretch out his hand, and take also from the tree of life, and eat, and live forever" . . . So He drove the man out; and at the east of the garden of Eden He stationed the cherubim and the flaming sword which turned every direction to guard the way to the tree of life.

Genesis 3:22, 24

If Adam and Eve had stayed in the garden and eaten from the tree of life, they would be forever in a fallen state.

We do not know if Adam and Eve even knew about the tree of life. Let's think about this for a minute.

Did one bite from the tree of life cause them to live forever? Or did they have to continuously eat from the tree of life to have immortality?

Scripture is unclear. However, when we turn to Revelation 22 the tree of life once again enters the scene. It is beside the river of life and we can literally say this tree's roots drink from God's throne. It is right on the banks of the river, drinking from the water of life that comes directly from God.   Now turn your focus to Revelation 22:2.

In the middle of its street. On either side of the river was the tree of life, bearing twelve kinds of fruit, yielding its fruit every month; and the leaves of the tree were for the healing of the nations.

Revelation 22:2

It bears twelve kinds of fruit, one fruit for each month, and its leaves are for healing the nations. The word "healing" can also be translated "health." This tree is for the health of the nations.

Now, after these passages has your opinion of the tree of life changed? Did Adam and Eve have to eat once or continuously?

There is no clear answer to this question, but if we could eat the fruit just once and live forever I don't believe God would have painted such a dramatic picture of the tree of life. It is right before God's throne, drinking the water coming from the throne.

Water in scripture also represents God's Word (Ephesians 5:26).

But whoever drinks of the water that I will give him shall never thirst; but the water that I will give him will become in him a well of water springing up to eternal life.

John 4:14

If you drink God's water you will never be thirsty again. It springs up to eternal life. And in Revelation 22:1 the water is coming from the throne and the Word is coming from the One sitting on the throne. Once you feed on God's Word, it is like the water of life. Just so, in eternity, you will need constant fellowship with God. You will want to approach the throne, listen to His wisdom and truth, drink in His life, and bask in His glory.

This is not to say the tree of life is symbolic. On the contrary, it is quite literal. Its fruit is food to our bodies; its roots provide the fruit with water drink directly from the throne of God. We will come to the tree of life in eternity to replenish our bodies and when we do, we will fellowship with God. This is a beautiful way of saying everyone will long for fellowship with God! They will long to drink from the river, hear His Word, and take the fruit that symbolizes eternity with our Creator.

Now I want you to turn to a passage in Ezekiel that is describing the Millennial Kingdom.

By the river on its bank, on one side and on the other, will grow all kinds of trees for food. Their leaves will not wither and their fruit will not fail. They will bear every month because their water flows from the sanctuary, and their fruit will be for food and their leaves for healing.

Ezekiel 47:12

Although this passage does not say these trees are the "tree of life" they sound curiously similar don't they? These trees in the Millennial Kingdom do the exact same thing as the "tree of life" in eternity.

What's up with that?

Are these trees the same trees as the trees in eternity? Well, if we could eat from the tree of life once and live forever, it just doesn't quite fit the scenario, but if we have to eat continuously from the fruit, then perhaps. Let's read a passage we looked at in yesterday's lesson about the Millennial Kingdom.

If the family of Egypt does not go up or enter, then no rain will fall on them; it will be the plague with which the Lord smites the nations who do not go up to celebrate the Feasts of Booths. This will be the punishment of Egypt and the punishment of all the nations who do not go up to celebrate the Feast of Booths.

Zechariah 14:18-19

Remember, in the Millennial Kingdom there is still sin. If people don't want to worship Jesus, they will not go to Jerusalem. If they don't go to Jerusalem, they would be unable to eat from the trees of healing. If they don't eat from the trees of healing will they decay just like Adam and Eve?

No longer will there be in it an infant who lives but a few days, or an old man who does not live out his days; for the youth will die at the age of one hundred and the one who does not reach the age of one hundred will be thought accursed.

Isaiah 65:20

There is no answer to this question, but I find it fascinating to think about. I can't wait to sit at Jesus' feet and hear His explanation.

In the Garden of Eden, one sinful choice separated us from God, hence Adam and Eve were cast out, separated from the One who created them. Currently we have access to God's throne because of Jesus' sacrifice. His blood washes us clean and we are able to stand in front of a Holy God without fear of death (separation). Did you wonder why God the Father wasn't seen in the Millennial Kingdom? Because there will still be rebellion there. In the Millennium death and evil will not be completely obliterated. There is still a separation from the Father due to the trace amounts of sin that are still present in the thousand-year reign. Those being born will have their "tree of the knowledge of good and evil" experience. Will they choose wisely? Or will they ultimately take part in the rebellion?

Once the final rebellion is crushed and death is thrown into the lake of fire, the Father is able to descend to earth. Now we have complete physical access to God's throne; we can crawl into His lap. Someone needs to shout, "Glory!"

We also have access to the tree of life. Can you imagine a world not under the curse of sin? No weeds, no thorns, no strained human relationships. We will love each other and we will love the Lord. We will live in peace and fellowship with one another. We will serve our loving God and see His face. Isaiah 59:2 says: "But your iniquities have made a separation between you and your God, and your sins have hidden His face from you so that He does not hear." No more in eternity. We will see His face.

Scripture also says His name will be written on our foreheads. We have seen this in our study of Revelation. Those who reject God will take the mark of the beast. The 144,000 Jews who accept Him after the rapture will be sealed with the seal of the living God. Another group of 144,000 Gentiles will be sealed with His name and the name of His Father. The seal of the believer indicates they have accepted Jesus as their Savior. The seal of the beast means they will be forever doomed. These two opposing groups clash throughout the book of Revelation. The seal we see in the last chapter of Revelation reminds us that we are sealed for eternity. There is no more rebellion and death. We are marked by the living God. We have unlimited fellowship and access to the throne of grace. Will this be a visible seal? It quite possibly could be. It is also possible scripture is telling us that by Jesus' blood we are covered for all eternity. We are His and we are holy.

And there will no longer be any night; and they will not have need of the light of a lamp nor the light of the sun, because the Lord God will illumine them; and they will reign forever and ever.

Revelation 22:5

This matches Revelation 21:23 which indicates the sun and moon aren't needed in the New Jerusalem. God's glory fills the place with such light the luminaries aren't necessary. Every rock crevice, every foundation stone, every pearly gate, will glow with the glory of God.

Again, Jesus says to us, "These words are faithful and true." The sentiment of this is echoed in Matthew 24:35.

"Heaven and earth will pass away, but My words will not pass away."

Matthew 24:35

Nothing can be done to hinder the things written in this book from coming to pass. God is faithful and true – He will bring His promises to fruition.

John then explains that the Lord sent this word to His bondservants to show them what must soon take place. The message is pertinent to every generation. Do you know why the early church was on fire? They expected Jesus to return at any moment. Our Lord wants us to look up and long for Him as a pure bride awaiting her groom. Wouldn't a groom be disappointed if his bride wasn't looking longingly for his return? How does Jesus feel when He looks at you? Are you Philadelphia? Or Laodicea?

Just like in chapter one, we see a blessing on those who read and heed this book. To be clear, you not only have to read, but also heed the messages in Revelation. If you do, you will understand what is coming and you will be prepared. Read and heed this book!

I dread tomorrow because it is our last day. I always hate closing the book of Revelation.

Thought for the day:
You are His bride. Are you longing for His return? Are you excited? Get ready. Look up! He is coming!

[10]And he said to me, "Do not seal up the words of the prophecy of this book, for the time is near. [11]Let the one who does wrong, still do wrong; and the one who is filthy, still be filthy; and let the one who is righteous, still practice righteousness; and the one who is holy, still keep himself holy." [12]"Behold, I am coming quickly, and My reward is with Me, to render to every man according to what he has done. [13]I am the Alpha and the Omega, the first and the last, the beginning and the end." [14]Blessed are those who wash their robes, so that they may have the right to the tree of life, and may enter by the gates into the city. [15]Outside are the dogs and the sorcerers and the immoral persons and the murderers and the idolaters, and everyone who loves and practices lying. [16]I, Jesus, have sent My angel to testify to you these things for the churches. I am the root and the descendant of David, the bright morning star." [17]The Spirit and the bride say, "Come." And let the one who hears say, "Come." And let the one who is thirsty come; let the one who wishes take the water of life without cost. [18]I testify to everyone who hears the words of the prophecy of this book: if anyone adds to them, God will add to him the plagues which are written in this book; [19]and if anyone takes away from the words of the book of this prophecy, God will take away his part from the tree of life and from the holy city, which are written in this book. [20]He who testifies to these things says, "Yes, I am coming quickly." Amen. Come, Lord Jesus. [21]The grace of the Lord Jesus be with all. Amen.

Revelation 22:10-21

Let me offer a word from Daniel. "Go your way, Daniel, for these words are concealed and sealed up until the end time" (12:9). The words of Daniel were sealed until the time of the end. For hundreds, if not thousands of years there have been theories on what the book of Daniel means, but until recently there hasn't been a full understanding of the final end time system. Many have set their sights on Europe becoming the revived Roman Empire that tries to take over the world, but upon closer scrutiny of Daniel, that is just not the case. As we focus our attention on the Middle East, biblical prophecy is slowly coming into sharper focus – as is Revelation.

The angel tells John not to seal up the words of this book for the time is near. Remember, during the course of our study, it has become clear that although Jesus' words are appropriate for all times, they are particularly appropriate for the final generation that will witness the end time prophecies coming to pass. The letters to the churches are so pertinent to the churches in the end times they become almost painful to read. Revelation and Daniel are books that cannot be interpreted without each other. To unlock Revelation, you have to first unlock Daniel. Once Daniel is unlocked, Revelation comes into clear focus, and the generation Revelation is most applicable to will suddenly have the keys to understand the beast, the Antichrist, the false prophet, and the harlot.

Next we see what would appear to be an odd addition to Revelation.

Let the one who does wrong, still do wrong; and the one who is filthy, still be filthy; and let the one who is righteous, still practice righteousness; and the one who is holy, still keep himself holy.

Revelation 22:11

This verse has always puzzled me. Why doesn't this verse call for the repentance of the wrongdoer? Why doesn't this verse shout out a warning to those who have yet to repent?

We have to remember, this is the final chapter of Revelation. Judgment has already been given. This is a somber warning. Once you have made your decision, there is no going back. You are either a wrongdoer or righteous, filthy or holy. Once you have made your decision, God will honor that decision.

Behold, I am coming quickly, and My reward is with Me, to render to every man according to what he has done. I am the Alpha and the Omega, the first and the last, the beginning and the end.

Revelation 22:12-13

Jesus is telling us He is the final word, and although we are saved by grace (Ephesians 2:8), our deeds matter to our Savior. We are rewarded based on our faithful service to the King (1 Corinthians 9:24-25, 1 Thessalonians 2:19-20, James 1:12, Revelation 2:8-11, 2 Timothy 4:8, 1 Peter 5:1-4). Our life is the final opportunity to earn those rewards. May we be faithful to our Lord.

The tree of life is mentioned again, right after Jesus mentions our rewards. The tree of life is one of those rewards. The righteous who have washed their robes in the blood of the Savior have access to the tree of life. They can enter the gates of the New Jerusalem and approach the throne for eternity. In contrast, Revelation 22:15 lists those who aren't included with the righteous. This is reminding us the final sentence has been reached and the judge has made His decision. Once you make your choice, it is for eternity.

Jesus then reminds us of who He is. He is the descendant of David, the fulfillment of all the Old Testament prophesies about the coming King. He is the root of David (Revelation 5:5).

Again Isaiah says, "There shall come the root of Jesse, and He who arises to rule over the Gentiles, in Him shall the Gentiles hope"

Romans 15:12

Jesus is the root from which all branches spring. Although Jesus came "after" Jesse and David, He also was before. Jesus tells the Pharisees about this prophesy in Matthew 22:

"What do you think about the Christ, whose son is He?" They said to Him, "The son of David." He said to them, "Then how does David in the Spirit call Him 'Lord,' saying, 'The Lord said to My Lord, sit at My right hand, until I put your enemies beneath your feet?' If David then calls Him 'Lord,' how is He his son?"

Matthew 22:42-45

Don't you just love Jesus! No one could trap Him! David called the future Messiah his "Lord" yet Jesus was supposed to be David's son. The only way this could happen is if the Messiah was God Himself.

The Spirit and the bride say, "Come." And let the one who hears say, "Come." And let the one who is thirsty come; let the one who wishes take the water of life without cost.

Revelation 22:17

404

This is a beautiful statement. The Spirit stirs the bride of Christ to be excited about the reunion. Once the bride understands His Revelation, "she" should hunger for the bridegroom to return. The bride will know the future awaiting her and hunger for it like rain in the desert.

Just before the final pen stroke of Revelation, there is a solemn warning.

> *I testify to everyone who hears the words of the prophecy of this book: if anyone adds to them, God will add to him the plagues which are written in this book; and if anyone takes away from the words of the book of this prophecy, God will take away his part from the tree of life and from the holy city, which are written in this book.*
>
> *Revelation 22:18-19*

Sounds harsh doesn't it? Why is God so adamant that nothing be taken away or added to this book? Let's remind ourselves of a few things:

> *The Revelation of Jesus Christ . . .*
>
> *Revelation 1:1*

> *For the testimony of Jesus is the spirit of prophecy . . .*
>
> *Revelation 19:10*

Jesus' testimony is this prophecy. Jesus is the revelation. If you add to or take away from Him, you are adding to or taking away from God. You cannot compromise with truth. You cannot compromise God.

If you add to the Revelation, you will inherit the plagues of this book. What is this saying? You will suffer the wrath of God! Why? Because you have compromised Jesus.

If you take away from the Revelation, you will not have access to the tree of life. What is this saying? You will not be ushered into an eternity with Jesus. You will descend to the lake of fire. Why? Because you have compromised Him.

This is in stark contrast to the blessing you will receive if you heed the Revelation (Jesus).

He is coming quickly (Revelation 22:20).

Christian soldiers, He is coming quickly. Someone needs to shout, "Amen!" He is coming quickly. I hope you have a newfound fire in your veins for His return. I hope you are looking forward to the sound of the trumpet and not dreading it. I hope you can't wait to see His light shining in the darkness.

If this study has helped you at all, please feel free to e-mail me at nic@nicsrevations.com. I would love to hear from you Christian soldier!

"The Spirit and the bride say, "Come. . . The grace of the Lord Jesus be with all."

Amen and amen, come quickly Lord Jesus!

Final Thought:

I hope this study has given you a vision of heaven. When my husband was killed in action in 2006 that is exactly what I prayed for, on my knees, day in and day out, until God poured into me the book that is now in your hands. I hope the words and visions of Revelation have fueled your faith with newfound excitement and filled your heart with incredible longing for the joy awaiting us. I know after God gave me the vision, my life has never been the same.

Remember, blessed are those who heed THE REVELATION.

Until the shofar sounds,

Nic

Anti Christ
Islams Awaited
Messeah

Joel Richardson

72634892R00223

Made in the USA
Columbia, SC
22 June 2017